The Bakken Goes Boom

Oil and the Changing Geographies of Western North Dakota

THE BAKKEN GOES
BOOM
OIL AND THE CHANGING
GEOGRAPHIES OF WESTERN
NORTH DAKOTA

Edited by William Caraher and Kyle Conway

The Digital Press @
The University of North Dakota
Grand Forks

2016 The Digital Press @ The University of North Dakota

Book Design: William Caraher
Cover Design: Kyle Cassidy

Library of Congress Control Number: 2016933953
The Digital Press at the University of North Dakota, Grand Forks, North
Dakota

ISBN-13: 978-0692643686 (The Digital Press at The University of North
Dakota)

ISBN-10: 0692643680

Table of Contents

vi

Acknowledgements

This book would not have been possible without the support of our contributors who were prompt in their submissions, responses to our queries, and last minute revisions. Special thanks goes to the artists who granted permission for their work to appear in this volume. Kyle Conway's graduate seminar on Communication and the Rural Community in Spring 2014 at the University of North Dakota helped frame many of the debates engaged by this work.

The book benefited immeasurable from the keen editorial eye of Amanda Osgood Jonientz and spot checks from Susan Caraher and Danielle Skjelver. The publication of this book was supported by a Arts and Humanities Research and Creative Activities Grant from the College of Arts and Sciences. Kyle Cassidy designed the book cover. We adapted the drilling rig that appears at the start of each chapter from a photograph by Beverly Conway.

INTRODUCTION

THE CHANGING GEOGRAPHIES OF WESTERN NORTH DAKOTA

Kyle Conway and William Caraher

This book is about the human side of the oil boom in the Bakken formation in western North Dakota. We began work on it in 2013, when a barrel of crude oil sold for a little more than $90. At that time, economic optimism was the order of the day. People were asking, would the boom last twenty, forty, or sixty years? Harold Hamm, the billionaire CEO of Continental Resources, went so far as to tell the Williston Basin Petroleum Conference, "I still think we will reach 2 million barrels a day [by 2020]. I don't think that's over the top, folks" (quoted in Burnes 2014).

Now, as we write this introduction at the end of 2015, that same barrel sells for less than $40. What we did not know—what we could not know—when we began was that the Organization of the Petroleum Exporting Countries (OPEC) would refuse to cut production in the face of dropping oil prices, in an apparent attempt to make oil production from shale, such as in the Bakken, too expensive to continue (Murtagh 2015; Olson and Ailworth 2015). In retrospect, the estimates of a forty- or sixty-year boom seem naive: by all appearances, we were at the boom's peak. In December 2014, there were 174 rigs drilling in the oil patch; a year later, there are 65. There are also five thousand fewer jobs, and monthly in-state income on oil royalties has dropped from $128 million to $69 million (Donovan 2015). Inadvertently, it seems, we captured an important moment, when the bust people dreaded (but thought would never happen) was just on the horizon.

Our purpose in putting this book together was to give voice to as wide a range of people as we could. We were both professors at the University of North Dakota, so we sought out other scholars. We researched the boom, so we sought out our collaborators. We taught about the Bakken, so we sought out students. But we also read the news, went to art galleries, and read poetry, so we also sought out journalists, artists and museum curators, and poets. The boom was one of the most interesting things we had ever seen, and there were more ways to know it than through the cold rationality we privileged in our scholarship. Journalists, artists, and poets could reveal things we would not otherwise see, experiences or emotions that academic prose could not capture, but art or poetry could. As much as drilling for oil in the Bakken produced an economic and demographic boom, it also was an intellectual and cultural moment for North Dakota, and our book tries to capture that.

Our approach was propitious, if the controversies around hydraulic fracturing (or simply "fracking") are any indication. In the time since we began soliciting submissions, a wide range of books have been published, each more polemical than the last. In one, an environmentalist asks what happens when she inherits mineral rights in North Dakota and has to choose between her ideals and financial security (Peters 2014). In another, a conservative media darling calls out environmentalists for what he sees as their duplicity and willful ignorance of the human rights abuses inflicted by governments of oil-rich countries on their own citizens (Levant 2014). In yet another, an investigative reporter tells the story of an Alberta woman's fight for justice from the oil industry (and her own government) after fracking poisons her water supply (Nikiforuk 2015).

In this back-and-forth, it is clear that the pro- and anti-fracking groups are talking past each other. This is where our book does something different. By and large, contributors sidestep the controversies about fracking and focus instead on the social impact of the boom. There is much to learn here: whether we support or oppose fracking, it has had a significant impact on people's lives. For people living in the Bakken region, life has changed, and we want to understand how. What impact did the boom have on longtime residents? On newcomers? On women? On Native Americans? How did it reshape the healthcare infrastructure? Housing? The media? These are the questions we asked our contributors to answer.

Scholars and journalists shared insight that they gained from their particular perch. But artists and poets did something more: as they talked about how the boom has reshaped North Dakotans' sense of self—how North Dakotans see themselves and imagine their future—they evoked something akin to emotional truth. For that reason, we have devoted considerable space in this book to their work. Because art has the potential to affect viewers at a gut level, we included, among other things, a catalogue from an exhibit about the Bakken at the Plains Art Museum in Fargo. We also included comments left by members of the public.

We also decided to open this book with a prologue in the form of a prose poem. Language is an imperfect tool. It serves us relatively well when we describe technical aspects of a situation, but in other cases it falls short. We know this most acutely when we experience powerful emotions such as joy or grief and words fail us. In the Bakken, for instance, it is relatively easy to describe the monetary or environmental costs of an oil boom, but it is much harder to find words for the ache we feel when our home no longer looks the same. But in poetry, language comes closest to breaking free of its bounds. When poet Heidi Czerwiec writes, "Given enough time, a sea can become a desert; given enough time, even a desert has value," she presents us with an image not unlike the art in the catalogue. In the dried up sea, we see our own fall from plenitude to emptiness. But the loss is paradoxical, in that it brings a new type of value. Her image brings the contradictions that undergird our experience into view. Even if we cannot put them into words, we can see them and feel them.

So what do we learn from all of this? What do scholars, journalists, artists, and poets reveal about the human side of North Dakota's oil boom? Resources are stretched thin, and to compensate, people have had to rethink the social and physical networks that link them to others. As a result, the geographies of western North Dakota—the ways people understand their relationship to space and place—have changed. Part of this change is material, such as the demographic shift from the eastern part of the state to the western part. A decade ago, nearly a third of the state's residents, those in Grand Forks and Fargo, lived in the narrow strip between Interstate 29 and the Red River. In other words, almost one out of three people lived within five miles of Minnesota. No longer is that the case, as towns such as Williston, Watford City, and Dickinson have doubled or tripled in size, creating unmet needs in social services, law enforcement, healthcare, housing, and other forms of infrastructure.

Part of this change is psychological, too. The stories people tell to make sense of their place in their community or the world have changed. They understand their relationships with their neighbors differently. Some longtime residents and newcomers view each other with a suspicion that grows out of a disparity in wealth and access to resources. Others look for what they share in common.

One result of these changing physical and mental geographies is that many people have had to make do with less, especially those who were already in vulnerable positions. Rents have gone up, but the stock of quality housing has gone down. Travel takes longer and is more dangerous, and unfamiliar people congregate in once familiar places. Even as the boom has subsided, social networks remain stretched for longtime residents, who face new disparities of wealth and ongoing political challenges, and for newcomers, who have left families in faraway homes in search of work. In short, there are more cracks to slip through.

But there is also resilience and creativity. Longtime residents have found ways to extend hospitality to newcomers. Artists have found ways to reimagine their place—which is to say, our place—in a landscape punctuated by oil rigs and tanker trucks. We cannot understand the challenges posed by the boom without considering the creativity it has brought about, nor the creativity without the challenges. One tugs constantly on the other.

To close, let us consider an interesting potential symmetry. In 2013, the bust was on the horizon, but we could not yet make it out. We must not forget that booms and busts are cyclical. Perhaps the next boom is on the horizon now, but as with the bust, we will see it most clearly in retrospect. As Karin Becker writes in her chapter, change has reached a plateau. North Dakota in 2015 is not the same as North Dakota in 2005. People talk of a "new normal." The state has reversed its longstanding trend of outmigration, and the population is up almost 20 percent compared to a decade ago. The median age is younger, and jobs pay better: even Wal-Mart has to pay $17 an hour to its employees in Williston, where the average annual salary is still more than $75,000 (Donovan 2015).

The changes North Dakota has undergone are real, and we owe it to ourselves to ask how they have shaped us. We would do well to listen to everyone—citizens, public figures, artists, poets, and even scholars. This book is not the final word on the Bakken oil boom, but we hope readers will find in it something useful, a starting point for understanding how the boom has affected us and who it is we have come to be.

References

Burnes, Jerry. 2014. "Hamm: Bakken Will Double Production by 2020." *Williston Herald*, May 23. bit.ly/1JDpCHv.

Donovan, Lauren. 2015. "Oil Patch Slides Toward a New Normal." *Bismark Tribune*, December 25. bit.ly/1Sk2ULN.

Levant, Ezra. 2014. *Groundswell: The Case for Fracking*. Toronto: McLelland & Stewart.

Murtagh, Dan. 2015. "Shale's Running Out of Survival Tricks as OPEC Ramps Up Pressure." *Bloomberg Business*, December 27. www.bloomberg.com/news/articles/2015-12-28/shale-s-running-out-of-survival-tricks-as-opec-ramps-up-pressure.

Nikiforuk, Andrew. 2015. *Slick Water: Fracking and One Insider's Stand Against the World's Most Powerful Industry*. Berkeley, CA: Greystone Books.

Olson, Bradley, and Erin Ailworth. 2015. "Low Crude Prices Catch Up with the U.S. Oil Patch." *Wall Street Journal* November 20. www.wsj.com/articles/ low-crude-prices-catch-up-with-the-u-s-oil-patch-1448066561.
Peters, Lisa Westberg. 2014. *Fractured Land: The Price of Inheriting Oil.* Minneapolis: Minnesota Historical Society Press.

PROLOGUE

EXCERPTS FROM:

SWEET/CRUDE: A BAKKEN BOOM CYCLE*

Heidi Czerwiec

I.

From Teddy Roosevelt's cabin in western North Dakota, as far as the eye could see was sea: the Cannonball Sea, last of the North American interior, brimming with paleobiology, swimming with lithe dinosaurs. Later, Lake Agassiz (the *–siz* sounds like *sea*), named for the Swiss geologist who read books of stone in the old epic mode, who posited the immense glacial lake, greater than all Great Lakes collected, fed by the end of the last Ice Age. Later still, geologists tell us all that life went underground: carbon-rich shale trapped beneath aquifer-rich sandstone trapped beneath nutrient-rich soil. And buffalo grass: a species whose fine roots lace to dense sod seven feet deep.

What lies beneath you?

(This is all connected.)

Labeled the Great American Desert on old maps of hostile horizons, the Plains become a place that settlers bypass on their way out West seeking the auguries of timbers, pilgrims bristling with hoop-iron and axles. Until a blacksmith named John Deere invents steel plow blades that can break through sod to soil beneath. Until the Homestead Act claims "rain follows the plow." Until settlers staking their claims realize the previous claim is buffalo shit, but learn to tap the aquifers, to siphon off for farming. Until Henry Bakken, a farmer in western North Dakota, taps oil until no more seeps out. Until a U.S. Geological Survey estimates the shale holds 7.4 billion barrels. Until they learn to frack.

Given enough time, a sea can become a desert; given enough time, even a desert has value.

---

* Excerpted from Heidi Czerwiec, *Sweet/Crude: A Bakken Boom Cyle*. Fairfax, VA: Gazing Grain Press. 2016.

8

II.

Given enough time, an inland sea can become a desert; given enough
time, even a desert has value. The Fertile Crescent has been called the
cradle of civilization, of incunabular vocabulary, inventing the alphabet
so I can tell you these things. Inventing the wheel, literally. Inventing
agriculture by irrigation, diverting two rivers to preserve a land alluvially
lush. Lavish: a king deviates the Euphrates to water cascading terraces
of fruited trees for the pleasure of a favored concubine longing for the
meadows of her Persian mountains. Crescent, the sweet kisses she
lavishes on his brow.

Today, the gardens are legendary. Today, less than a tenth of the
crescent's fertility remains, almost completely dried up, scrub marking
the ancient shore, its gardens gone underground, its only liquid sweet
crude. Double-edged sword that continues to support and yet thwart
civilization, its foreign hungers and wars. Its land increasing in demand,
increasingly wasted, unstable – some in ways we've been implicated,
participated. I fill my car even as I listen to NPR, my fool deity, my
black idolatry. Men's covenants are brittle.

Don't blame us, the oil companies say. It's the Taliban's fault, they claim,
as people in the streets raise signs that read *No Blood for Oil*.

III.

No blood for oil implies distance, implies foreign. But this is here, this
is North Dakota (trademark: Legendary!), one of the worst states for
workplace safety. Blame the Wild West culture of risk. Blame an influx
of green employees with no industry experience, disordered recruits
afoul outcountry. Blame fatigue from long shifts – 12-hour days for 2
weeks straight, mud effigies jagged with blood among the dull clank,
the blackened pools of grease – work that goes on regardless of weather.
(Don't blame us, the oil companies say, it's the contractors' fault. Don't
mention drug use: word is, they skimp on testing to fill out their crews.)
Nearly all state fatalities investigated by OSHA occur in the Bakken:
two-thirds are pulled into pumpjacks or set afire. (An employee was
changing valves when a tank ruptured, soaking the employee in oil; he
burst into flame and died as a result of his injuries.) One-third killed
in falls or "struck by" hazards. (An employee was hit by a set of power
tongs on a rig and died as a result of his injuries.) The death rate in
North Dakota is 18 times higher industry-wide. (Word is, it's bad
luck to wear another man's hardhat; word is, you have better odds of
winning the lottery than getting a visit from a regulatory industry; word
is, the payoff is up to $300,000.) None of this includes the near-daily
occurrence of truckers sliding off slick highways glassy and treacherous,
the force of 40-ton tankers colliding with cars on the back roads of
North Dakota: flyover, but not foreign.

IV.

North Dakota is a foreign country. Alien. A flyover state, even from
space. When we show our foreign friend a photo of a satellite flyover,
he's astonished. At nightfall, light clusters on the frozen prairie, phantom
city emerged from among the ghost towns. A blooming midnight
meridian. Stars in a lake of blackness, a constellation of ignited eyes.
The natural gas that emerges alongside the oil costs more to capture
than flare. The foreign companies that drill here burn money, a billion
a year in flames and fines. A Little Kuwait on the Prairie whose dread
watchfires smelter under the dark more brightly than Minneapolis.
More broadly than Chicago. In winter, truckers cluster for warmth
beneath the flares, which fling their flapping rags of fire six yards into
space, toward the stars and satellites and passing planes.

Foreigner, flyover passenger, when you peer out your window, what do
you see? What lies beneath you?

PART 1

BOOM TOWN
PHENOMENA

Chapter 1

The Paradox of Plenty: Blessings and Curses in the Oil Patch

Karin L. Becker

The press has descended on the oil patch, centering on Williston as the new ground zero for America's energy renaissance. Whether it be by sound, like NPR audio podcasts, by sight, like the countless documentaries circulating on Youtube, or by print, as national, regional, and local media outlets cover North Dakota's oil boom, the Bakken boom is receiving lavish attention. Just within the last year, writers from *Harper's*, *National Geographic*, *The Atlantic*, *New York Times*, *Washington Post*, and *Huffington Post* have devoted boots-on-the ground journalists and lengthy spreads to cover the oil boom. The oil boom has garnered national and international publicity and put North Dakota in the limelight. With the spotlight cast on the oil patch, the question that journalists are trying to answer is whether the oil boom is a blessing or a curse.

Much publicity has been given to the economic benefit of the oil boom. Equally, time, energy, and resources have been dedicated to documenting the social, health, and environmental impacts the oil boom has caused on this frontier region and the rural communities. While reporters and policy makers are busy making their T-bar lists and tallying the positive outcomes against the negative ones, what is missing from this conversation is the long-casting vision. While an oil boom is not unique to North Dakota, nor unprecedented (this is the third one to occur in six decades), media accounts neglect to talk about similar communities that have endured boom and bust cycles. Therefore, there is critical need to look at how boomtown communities are impacted both positively and negatively over time. Many current conversations attend to documenting the pressing problems stemming from the frantic race of oil companies to get there first and start drilling and are exacerbated by the needs caused by the influx of people. However, more efforts need to be made to better understand the phenomena of boom and bust communities.

14

To help explore the question of whether the oil boom is a blessing or a curse, this chapter will review the research compiled from communities that have experienced similar booms and then apply those findings to circumstances in western North Dakota. While these historic case studies provide insight into the current oil boom phenomena, much remains unknown in terms of final outcomes. While oil industry experts and geologists estimate there is enough oil to sustain the oil boom anywhere between three to seven decades to come, the answer may not be apparent until after the boom. Determining outcomes of the boom is important, both for economic and community impacts, but the evidence needed to answer the question is not yet available. In the meantime, while the oil boom continues to play out, a revised question is needed—one that accounts for the concept of time. For when the question is asked, pre-boom, peak-boom or post-boom, may determine its answer.

Boomtown Phenomena

North Dakota is situated atop the Bakken Formation, the largest contiguous oil deposit in the lower forty-eight states, with the U.S. Geological Survey estimating there are 7.4 billion barrels of recoverable oil resting below its surface (Rucker and Volcovici 2013). Oil produced in North Dakota helped the U.S. become the world's leading oil producer and has ushered in a geopolitical shift and economic prosperity in North Dakota (Krogstad 2014). Yet this is not North Dakota's first oil boom. As a result of new fracking technology that has changed the ways in which oil is extracted, this oil boom has made the largest footprint and is predicted to last the longest.

Longtime residents of western North Dakota are familiar with the boom and bust oil cycles, but this one feels distinctly unique. The first major exploration in the Bakken occurred in Tioga, N.D. in 1951 when Amerada Corporation struck oil in a farmer's field (MacPherson 2008). According to Debbie Iverson, wife of Clarence Iverson on whose farm oil was first discovered over sixty years ago, this current oil boom has had a greater impact on the community. "I've seen boom and bust times, but this boom is the biggest and longest and has the most infrastructure" (personal communication, October 1, 2012).

Reviewing the literature with an eye for themes emerging from boomtown communities reveals pervasive concerns surrounding rapid expansion and decline, and heavy demands on community services and infrastructure (Camasso and Wilkinson 1990). Specifically, three themes emerge concerning community impacts: social disruption due to rapid population influx, loss of identity, and uncertainty and anxiety. These themes will be explored and then applied to the oil boom in western North Dakota.

Looking at oil boom community impacts in midwestern states, Little (1977) claims the most distinguishable characteristic of boomtowns is an accelerated population growth. Stemming from community impact studies conducted in the late 1970s and early 1980s on governmental regulated extraction projects carried out in rural areas of the western United States, a "boomtown model" was developed to measure social impacts (Gramling and Brabant 1986). Gramling and Brabant (1986) recognized common characteristics when large, complex extraction projects were constructed near small, rural, isolated, homogenous, agricultural-based economies. Specifically, the type and lifespan of the projects necessitated certain labor demands that the local community could not supply. The shortage of workers led to a large in-migration of workers, followed by an out-migration once the project was completed. The rapid population growth and ensuing decline were responsible for both the positive and negative economic, infrastructural, fiscal, and sociocultural impacts on the local community (Gramling and Brabant 1986).

When a community is suddenly faced with a swelling population, economic problems associated with the influx are readily apparent. "There is very little delay between the onset of the new population and the economic costs of providing community services for these new residents" (Little 1977, 404). Small, rural communities are particularly ill-prepared to absorb population growth. There are many ways to define rural according to population density (having less than one hundred persons per square mile) and location (having fewer than 2,500 inhabitants and being located outside of an urban area) (U.S. Census Bureau, n.d.). According to the Health Resources and Services Administration, all five counties within the oil patch region of North Dakota (Dunn, McKenzie, Mountrail, Stark and Williams) are listed as rural counties.

According to Little (1977), rapid population growth leads to a breakdown in municipal services, planning lags behind need, and control of the community rests with forces outside the immediate environment. Communities can usually absorb a population growth rate of 5 percent with a breaking point threshold at 15 percent. As communities approach the 10 percent growth rate, institutional malfunctioning and community fragmentation begin (Little 1977).

Social Disruption

The oil patch region of North Dakota, which consists of counties in the far northwest corner, has experienced astronomical population growth.

Williams County, where Williston is located, has witnessed a 32.1 percent population change in just three years, from 2010–13 (U.S. Census 2014). Williston is braced to expand from 12,000 to an estimated 90,000 within 15 years (Chiaramonte 2013). Similarly, neighboring McKenzie County to the south and Mountrail County to the east have experienced a 46.4 percent and 22.2 percent population change respectively in the same time period (US Census 2014). According to the Williams County Comprehensive Plan 2035 planning report, these counties are anticipating a continued population growth for the next twenty-five years.

Population growth is a new trend as North Dakota's population for the past one hundred years has remained stagnant. Fearful of the shrinking trend that has caused some small, rural towns to become ghost towns, at first residents welcomed the expansion the oil industry brought. Some communities which were close to dying are now flourishing. Schools are no longer consolidating, but growing. The demographics are changing as well. It is predominantly young, single men between 20 and 35 years of age who are moving in compared to the majority of the existing residential population who are between 45 and 59 years of age (U.S. Census 2014).

As a result of the population increase, communities are experiencing severe growing pains. Increases in traffic, accidents, dust, litter, and stress have been reported by residents living in oil-impacted counties (Becker and Hall 2012–13; Becker and Hall 2013; Hall and Becker 2012–13). A recent study examining community health need assessment data from oil patch communities reveals that the most pressing community health needs are a health care workforce shortage, excessive drinking rates, traffic safety, and a lack of affordable housing (Becker 2014). What is significant about these results is that they are expressed and prioritized by community members living in the oil patch. Community members report they no longer know their own community; it is not the same town they grew up in and they no longer feel safe to go outside for walks (personal communication, January 6, 2013).

Crime, domestic violence, prostitution, depression, isolation, and unmet mental health needs have also been reported to have increased since the oil boom (Becker 2014). Some attribute the increase to a numbers game: the more people you have in a given area, the more conflict will arise. Others point to the cramped living quarters where a family of five may be living in a single-wide trailer that is positioned six feet away from the next trailer. In the initial rush of the oil boom, some trailer parks lacked electricity and running water. Further, long hours of monotonous work are blamed for increasing substance abuse. Living as an outsider in a small town away from family members can bring feelings of isolation and marginalization which are often soothed by alcohol. While not readily noticed or addressed as economic factors, social factors are important corollaries affecting communities as a result of the population boom.

Kennedy and Mehra (1985) indicate the major social disruption resulting from rapid social change. Their research focuses on communities in western Canada that have undergone similar significant economic and social change with an oil boom. They conclude that instability in population size and composition, as well as shifting economic conditions, wreaks havoc on a community's social climate. Seydlitz and a group of researchers (1993) have studied the impacts of oil and gas extraction on communities in the gulf region, and their research has demonstrated that higher levels of rapid changes in development are associated with higher homicide and suicide rates, especially in communities that are involved in resource extraction. Moreover, their research shows increased strain on local infrastructure and increases in poverty during the height of mineral extraction (Seydlitz et al. 1995).

Demand for high paying oilfield jobs has put a squeeze on local businesses in the oil patch. Employers are experiencing turnover as employees quit their jobs or careers for more lucrative oil field employment. Hospitals are losing their custodial and administrative staff as well as certified nurse assistants. Emergency medical services are strained immensely. For hospitals serving the oil patch, call volume has increased three to four times with the recent influx. Tioga Medical Center CEO Randall Peterson states, "In 2007 we would see 600 patients in the ER per year. In 2012, we anticipate seeing over 2,000. That means in a five-year period, Tioga's emergency room visits have more than tripled" (McChesney 2012).

Recruitment efforts are stymied because of the housing shortage. Tioga Mayor Nathan Germundson says "there is literally no place to sleep" (Holeywell 2011, section 5). Residents are sleeping in churches or in their vehicles. To alleviate the housing crisis, oil companies are providing housing, in the form of mobile homes, for oilfield and construction workers. Called man camps, since they are primarily occupied by men, these camps are tightly run with rules including residents cannot drink alcohol, smoke, host guests, or have pets on the premises (Klimasinska 2013). A tour the author took in the fall of 2013 of Tioga Lodge, a man camp run by Target Logistics located on the outskirts of Tioga, revealed a sprawling compound consisting of rows and rows of trailers, each with pickup trucks parked outside, entirely enclosed by a metal fence. The camp housed approximately 1,200 people, about the same size of Tioga, and has led some to call the influx of workers a "man rush" (Krogstad 2014). During my tour, dust was kicked up on the dirt roads and my tour guide said his favorite pastime of hunting was scratched as the dust and noise pushed the wildlife out.

For the rural residents who elect to live in a small town, the growth comes with a price. "Every system you take advantage of is taxed," says Upper Missouri District Health nurse Janine Oyloe (personal communication, January 13, 2013). The systems she is referring to are roads, traffic lights, repair shops, retail items and medical services. Although new fees have been drafted for the camps to support fire and ambulance services, the increase in call activity is heavily straining the local communities, both in terms of personnel and finances. For many small towns, the oil boom has "come to embody the danger of growing too big too fast, cluttering formerly idyllic vistas, straining utilities, overburdening emergency services and aggravating relatively novel problems like traffic jams, long lines and higher crime" (Sulzberger 2011, section 2).

Identity Fragmentation

Freudenberg (1984) claims the problem of hasty social change produces two viewpoints. One view suggests that rapid social change loosens traditional systems and as a result, greater economic and social opportunities appear. Individuals experience positive effects and opportunities for growth. It is important to point out that age is an important variable; younger people are more apt to benefit from rapid social change (Freudenberg 1984).

The alternative viewpoint posits that rapid growth creates substantial disruption for local residents. This is the dominant view from the body of literature surrounding boomtowns and rapid social growth. Communities, especially small, rural ones, thrive upon creating a web of continuing relationships. This process is a slow one, developed over time where the emphasis is on coming together, sharing resources, and experiencing a sense of belonging to the community. With increasing mobility and population migration, the psychological sense of community fades. The perception of community as a stable and secure place of one's long term home becomes a source of change and fear; negative consequences ensue as individuals are less securely embedded in a family, a workplace, a neighborhood, or community (Pilisuk et al. 1996).

The hurried pace of the oil boom leaves little time for planned growth. City planners in the small rural towns of western North Dakota are overwhelmed with the population influx as the towns are growing too big, too fast, overburdening housing, utilities, and emergency services. Although city planners and local leaders across the western prairie placed an indefinite moratorium on man camp developments in 2011 and gathered at a conference to discuss regional infrastructure needs, the fact remains that the boom is booming too quickly (Donovan 2012). Even though this growth has anchored oil patch communities' viability, the population surge has happened so quickly it has strained local services and resources. With the increase of traffic and rail accidents, the dangerous nature of the work, and the demanding twelve- to fourteen-hour shifts, oil and gas industry professionals are admonishing caution. Even high profile proponents of the boom, like Robert Harms, Chairman of North Dakota's Republican party, are calling for a slower, more "moderated approach" (Breiner 2014, section 1).

Moreover, rural communities typically have antiquated or seriously strained public facilities prior to the additional stress created by the new industry. The primary method of information dissemination in small towns is word of mouth and face-to-face interactions (Solomon et al. 1981). These communication methods favor local, insider knowledge and can make communicating to newcomers difficult. A central repository of information is lacking and often websites are not updated. The lack of a viable communication network tends to make newcomers feel excluded from the community. Alternately, longtime residents may view newcomers as uninterested and detached from the local community. These perceived differences can result in weakening relationships between economic, social, environmental, and political dimensions of community involvement, agency, and political mobilization (Brown and Schafft 2011).

The combined forces of increased population, change in demographics, and economic and infrastructure development can erode a community's identity. Brown and Schafft (2011) claim one of the principle foundations of rural communities is the role of locally oriented social interaction where community members share common interests. However, differences in values and commitment to the local community vary between newcomers and longtime residents. Gramling and Freudenburg (1990) attest to the external origins of large-scale industrial projects where the magnitude of exterior boom/bust forces may be so great that they overwhelm the local community. For example, a new workforce may view the local community as only a temporary situation; therefore, motivation for community involvement may be low. The temporary trailers in the man camps situated on the outskirts of town reinforce the workforce as outsider status. The distribution of news and promotion of local events that occur casually at convenience stores and cafés keep newcomers uninformed. Consistent with Freudenberg's (1984) analysis of boomtowns in western Colorado, this lack of identity with and lack of trust in their community has a destabilizing effect on residents, leaving them with feelings of alienation and normlessness. Yet in the midst of the merge between newcomers and longtime residents, new structures of identity and community are emerging and worthy of study.

Uncertainty and Anxiety

Another major theme identified in the research on boomtowns is uncertainty (Brown and Schafft 2011). Although North Dakota has the nation's best economy, tops the country's jobless rate, and has an education system rich with dollars flowing into it, community members are quick to ask "for how long" (Bureau of Labor Statistics 2013)? While it is clear the oil boom has a strong economic impact to local, state and national economies, it is unclear how sustainable this growth is.

According to the U.S. Energy Information Administration (2014), North Dakota is now the second leading oil producing state, behind only Texas in nationwide output. Oil production has generated an economic boom in the state and a domestic energy spike for the nation. Oil output in North Dakota broke a million barrels per day for the first time in history (Petroleum Supply Monthly 2015). The Bakken oil field has close to 10,000 wells, with each one generating on average $24 million in net profit, and many more in the works as the boom transitions from the discovery phase into the production phase (O'Donoghue 2014). For every dollar the industry earns, the state takes 11.5 cents, which totaled more than $2 billion as of October 2012 and supports more than $1 trillion in total value added to the economy, or 7.3 percent of U.S. GDP (North Dakota Energy Forum 2014). However, forecasts for future oil production are marked with tremendous uncertainty. The Energy Information Administration anticipates oil production to continue to rise until about 2020 and then to plateau for a few years, before starting a gradual decline (Casselman 2014). A newfound dependence upon the mining of non-renewable resources such as oil makes communities apprehensive about sustaining the economic base and infrastructure once the extractive activity is completed. Residents that lived through previous booms are quick to point out the results of the bust cycles — the vacant buildings that remain from previous booms when growth happened too soon, too fast and was not sustained.

With North Dakotans already having two boom and bust cycles under their belts, there is an attitude of wariness that pervades. Haunted by the memories of vacant hotels and empty lots, boomtowns turning into ghost towns over night with the fall of oil prices in the 1980s, North Dakotans are careful not to repeat history by adding to the "too much, too fast" recipe (Robinson 1959). Business owners and elected officials are proceeding prudently with development, sure that the bust is imminent.

While no one can predict when the fall may happen, it is certain that a bust is inevitable. As recently as 2009, the Federal Reserve Bank reported the pulse of the Bakken boom was weak; economists were forecasting dismal oil projects, causing oil companies to continue with caution, cutting down drilling and downsizing staff. "Their anxiety is reflected in a slowdown of business and consumer spending, less demand for bank loans and falling rents for apartments" (Davies 2009, 2).

In hindsight, we know the opposite of this happened. Rents are higher in Williston than in Manhattan, indicative of the demand for housing and workers due to the boom exploding (Grandstrand 2014). Yet it is the idea of the bust being ever-present on the horizon that clouds the vision. The scathing memory of previous busts and the cyclical nature that a boom also includes a bust creates an atmosphere of apprehension. At any moment, all of the growth, the influx of people and the economic gain could come crashing to an end. Combined with the extent of social disruption experienced from the in-migration of workers and the amount of change to the rural communities, the ever-present worry of the end exacerbates residents' feelings of anxiety.

Another uncertainty expressed by community members living in the oil patch is the unknown environmental effects of the oil boom (Becker and Hall 2013). Fracking is controversial for many reasons including its spread of natural gas drilling and for the wastewater its produces (Prud'homme 2014). The chemical makeup of this briny wastewater is toxic—it's eight times saltier than seawater and is laced with carcinogenic chemicals and heavy metals that can be radioactive, kill vegetation, destroy farmland, and contaminate drinking water (Dawson 2015). A three million gallon spill of wastewater from a North Dakota pipeline near Williston that occurred in January 2015 has the capacity to wipe out aquatic life in streams and wetlands and sterilize farmland (Valentine 2015). Although the brine is supposed to be injected thousands of feet underground into disposal wells, spills by tanker trucks and ruptured pipelines are common (Kusnetz 2012; Dawson 2015), with 74 saltwater spills in 2013 alone (Valentine 2015).

In addition to wastewater spills, oil patch residents are concerned about oil spills and railroad hazards due to the increase in rail traffic (Becker & Hall, 2012-13). The Tesoro Logistics pipeline that spilled more than 20,000 barrels of crude oil in a wheat field in Tioga in the fall of 2013 highlighted the environmental threat the oil boom poses (Atkin 2014). An oil train's explosive derailment in Quebec that killed forty-seven people in June 2013 drew attention to the need for rail safety (George-Cosh 2014). In December 2013, a freight train carrying crude oil that collided with another train, shooting black fireballs up more than one hundred feet, prompted the evacuation the town of Casselton in December, and reinforced the danger of the boom and drew attention to the need for rail safety. With the Bakken pumping out more oil and relying on trains to transport it, railroads are being heavily utilized but not readily maintained. As North Dakota Representative Kevin Cramer said, "Booms happen first and then the infrastructure catches up" (Potter 2014, section 3). Of the 1.2 million gallons of oil spilled in the U.S. in 2013, all but 10,000 came from the oil fields in western North Dakota (Potter 2014). More than one thousand accidental releases of oil, drilling wastewater, or other fluids have been documented in 2011 alone, with many more lethal releases going unreported (Kusnetz 2012).

Furthermore, the process of hydraulic fracking forces the sought after crude oil to come out of the earth, but also pushes out natural gas which, if not processed, is flared or burned off (Quick and Breennan 2014). Pipelines which could capture the natural gas are at capacity, resulting in burning nearly a third of the natural gas produced in the region and consequently generating thousands of flares—enough to light up the prairie night sky (Quick and Breennan 2014). Flaring raises the atmospheric levels of carbon dioxide and has contributed to the U.S. moving from fourteenth up to fifth place on the list of gas-flaring nations (Brown 2013). Because many companies offer incentives for low injury rates, many of the environmental impacts are unreported or underreported. What remains to be determined are the environmental risks and negative health factors associated with living in an oil boom environment. The lack of reporting combined with the aggressive pace of drilling creates an atmosphere of suspicion and mistrust.

Timing is Everything

Consistent with boomtown phenomena, North Dakotans living in the oil patch are affected by social disruption due to rapid population influx, loss of identity, and uncertainty and anxiety. However, these impacts do not necessarily determine that the oil boom is a more of a curse than a blessing. Trying to measure the benefits against the detriments of the oil boom leads researchers to conclude they are a "paradox of plenty" (Karl 2004). Proponents of oil-led development highlight the augmented economic growth and job creation, increased government revenues to offset poverty, technological advancements, improvements in infrastructure, and growth of related industries. However, the experience of almost all oil-exporting countries to date illustrates few of these benefits. Overwhelmingly, the consequences of oil-led development tend to be negative, including slower than expected growth, barriers to economic diversification, poor social welfare indicators, and high levels of poverty, inequality, and unemployment (Karl 2004).

However, it is important to point out that much of this research has been conducted at the peak of extraction. What this list of consequnces does not convey is that these needs are observed during the height of the boom when communities are at the breaking point and social services are in crisis mode. While the intensity and severity of needs are not doubted, a long-term look at how past oil booms have fared may help to answer the blessing-versus-curse question, allowing communities to prioritize the most pressing concerns and better plan for the growing needs. What is needed is research collected on the extent of social disruption at five, ten, and twenty years after the boom cycle.

A longitudinal study of community change conducted by Brown (2005) using Delta, Utah, as a case study to examine pre- and post-boomtown phenomena reveals that time has the potential to heal wounds. Looking at measures of community satisfaction such as likelihood to move, willingness to borrow from neighbors, and number of friends in the community, Brown's research shows that the dimension of wellbeing was enhanced ten years after the boom. Indeed, throughout the twenty-four year history, periods reporting the lowest levels of community satisfaction and the greatest likelihood of residents moving over the twenty-four-year reporting history occurred at times of substantial population growth. This study has significant implications for oil patch communities in western North Dakota. As some experts say the oil boom is currently at its peak, it is understandable that community erosion and feelings of dissatisfaction are strong. Brown's study concludes that time can heal many of the social interactional wounds caused by the rapid growth; having a hearty attachment to one's place through "thick and thin" can help residents adjust to disruptions (Brown 2005, 19).

Smith, Krannich, and Hunter (2001) agree that social disruption occurs in several dimensions of wellbeing such as social integration of newcomers and community change, but their research contends the effects are not permanent. Among four boomtown communities studied for social disruption in western states, none continued to show declines in overall community satisfaction. In fact, where boomtown disruption was evident, it was followed by a sharp rebound in social wellbeing. Fifteen years down the road, the communities that had experienced the strongest boom effects reported greater wellbeing. Moreover, age may have a more profound impact on community satisfaction. In examining attitudinal differences between residents of a boomtown and of surrounding stable communities, no difference existed for adults although adolescents exhibited less satisfaction and greater alienation in post-boomtown communities (Freudenburg 1984). Given the aging population of most rural areas, this finding holds promise for cooperative outcomes.

Blessing or Curse

Before we can answer if the oil boom in western North Dakota is more of a blessing or a curse, we need to be patient and allow for a longitudinal perspective to unfold. The drama of the oil boom will continue to play out as time moves forward. Once the boom has subsided and in the years following its decline, the answer to the aforementioned question will become clearer. Perhaps the benefits have not yet been realized but will emerge over time. Perhaps the question needs to be reframed so that it allows for a both/and response instead of an either/or solution.

In the meantime, residents of the oil patch can help foster a capacity for flexibility where they can simultaneously remember and forget the oil boom. The cyclical nature of booms and busts necessitate that residents learn from the oil boom to avoid repeating mistakes, but there is also a need for residents to choose to let go of their fears and anxieties in order to move forward. This boom is distinctively different than past booms and experts predict it is here to stay.

Given the amount of change and displacement community members are experiencing, it is natural for a certain amount of resistance to be expected. Their small communities are becoming unrecognizable to them, and the quickly changing environs are cause for fear. Yet the propensity for patience about the social disruption experienced at the peak times and the ability to focus on long-term planning may help alleviate the feelings of uncertainty. An attitude of openness to change may help longtime residents accept the changes that are occurring. There are many positive outcomes stemming from the oil boom, although in the immediacy of the day-to-day changing environment, the inundation of new faces, the amount of change in traffic and daily routines, especially for rural communities, the positives may be hidden.

The ability to loosen one's grip on the tightly held memory of how things used to be before the boom may encourage healing and usher in an elasticity that allows for some change, some shifting in the ideation of what their community looks like, feels like, and is comprised of. Although not denying the impact of the social change, nor attributing the disruption to hype or heresy, a future vision where the shape of community is not yet drawn may be the cushion needed to rethink boundaries and priorities and allow the time needed to determine if the oil boom is a blessing or a curse. While much has been written and there is much to be learned from boomtowns across the U.S., whether they come in the form of coal mines or oil rigs, looking at boomtown phenomena on a long-term scale may help lessen the community erosion and allow for an invitation to be extended to new residents to help shape the face of the oil patch and steer the conversation to long-term planning.

References

Atkin, Emily. 2014. "'It Will Never Be the Same': North Dakota's 840,000-Gallon Oil Spill One Year Later." *Climate Progress, October 21.* thinkprogress.org/climate/2014/10/21/3582480/north-dakota-spill-one-year-later/.

Becker, Karin L. 2014. "Emerging Health Trends in North Dakota: Community Health Needs Assessments Aggregate Data Report." Grand Forks: Center for Rural Health, University of North Dakota School of Medicine and Health Sciences.

Becker, Karin L., and Ken Hall. 2013. "Community Health Needs Assessment: Mountrail County Health Center, Stanley, N.D. The North Dakota Medicare Rural Hospital Flexibility (Flex) Program." Grand Forks: University of North Dakota School of Medicine and Health Sciences.

Becker, Karin L., and Ken Hall. 2012–13. "Community Health Needs Assessment: Tioga Medical Center, Tioga, N.D. The North Dakota Medicare Rural Hospital Flexibility (Flex) Program." Grand Forks: University of North Dakota School of Medicine and Health Sciences.

Breiner, Andrew. 2014. "Unexpected Source Calls For a Slowdown in Oil-Booming North Dakota." *Climate Progress,* January 7. thinkprogress.org/climate/2014/01/07/3125191/slow-oil-boom-north-dakota/.

Brown, Ralph B. 2009. "The Boom-Bust-Recovery Cycle: Dynamics of Change in Community Satisfaction and Social Integration in Delta, Utah." Rural Sociology 70, no. 1: 28–49. doi: 10.1526/0036011053294673.

Brown, Chip. 2013. "North Dakota Went Boom." *New York Times Magazine,* January 13. www.nytimes.com/2013/02/03/magazine/north-dakota-went-boom.html.

Brown, David L., and Kai A. Schafft. 2011. *Rural People and Communities in the 21st Century: Resilience and Transformation.* Malden, MA: Polity Press.

Camasso, Michael J., and Kenneth P. Wilkinson. 1990. "Severe Child Maltreatment in Ecological Perspective: The Case of the Western Energy Boom." *Journal of Social Science Research* 13, no. 3: 1–18.

Casselman, Ben. 2014. "North Dakota's Oil Bonanza Is Unsustainable." *FiveThirtyEight Economics*, July 21.

Chiaramonte, Perry. 2013. "Christmas in the Bakken Formation: North Dakota City Sees Growth from Fracking Industry." *Fox News*, December 24.

Davey, Monica. 2008. "Oil in North Dakota Brings Job Boom and Burdens." *New York Times*, January 1. www.nytimes.com/2008/01/01/us/01dakota.html.

Davies, Phil. 2009. "After the Oil Rush." *Fedgazette* 21, no. 5: 1–6.

Dawson, Chester. 2015. "Leak of Oil-Well Wastewater Taints River in North Dakota." *The Wall Street Journal*, January 22. www.wsj.com/articles/bakken-shale-oil-well-wastewater-leak-taints-river-in-north-dakota-1421977006.

Donovan, Lauren. 2012. "Williams County Extends Man Camp Ban." *Bismarck Tribune*, March 3. bismarcktribune.com/news/state-and-regional/williams-county-extends-man-camp-ban/article_87024584-6505-11e1-8140-001871e3ce6c.html.

Freudenberg, Nicholas. 1984. "Citizen Action for Environmental Health: Report on a Survey of Community Organizations." *American Journal of Public Health* 74: 444–48. doi: 10.2105/AJPH.74.5.444.

Freudenburg, William R. 1984. "Differential Impacts of Rapid Community Growth." *American Sociological Review* 49: 697–715.

George-Cosh, David. 2014. "After Lethal Crash, Quebec's Lac-Megantic Fears Return of Oil Trains." *Wall Street Journal*, July 4. www.wsj.com/articles/after-lethal-crash-quebec-town-fears-return-of-oil-trains-1404502664.

Gramling, Robert, and Sarah Brabant. 1986. "Boomtowns and Offshore Energy Impact Assessment: The Development of a Comprehensive Model." *Sociological Perspectives* 29, no. 2: 177–201.

Gramling, Robert, and William R. Freudenburg. 1990. "A Closer Look at 'Local Control': Communities, Commodities, and the Collapse of the Coast." *Rural Sociology* 55, no. 4: 541–58. doi: 10.1111/j.1549-0831.1990.tb00696.x.

Grandstrand, Katherine. 2014. "Williston Tops List of Most Expensive Places to Rent in U.S., Dickinson Ranks Fourth." *Grand Forks Herald*, February 18.

Hall, Ken, and Karin L. Becker. 2012-2013. "Community Health Needs Assessment: Mercy Medical Center, Williston, N.D. The North Dakota Medicare Rural Hospital Flexibility (Flex) Program." Grand Forks: University of North Dakota School of Medicine and Health Sciences.

Holeywell, Ryan 2011. "North Dakota's Oil Boom Is a Blessing and a Curse." *Governing*, August. www.governing.com/topics/energy-env/north-dakotas-oil-boom-blessing-curse.html.

Health Resources and Service Administration. N.d. "U.S. Department of Health and Human Services. Rural Health Grants Eligibility Analyzer." datawarehouse.hrsa.gov/RuralAdvisor/RuralHealthAdvisor.aspx.

Karl, T.L. 2004. "Oil-Led Development: Social, Political, and Economic Consequences." In *Encyclopedia of Energy*, edited by C. J. Cleveland, 4th ed., 661–72. Oxford, UK: Elsevier Science.

Kennedy, Leslie W., and N. Mehra. 1985. "Effects of Social Change on Well-Being: Boom and Bust in a Western Canadian City." *Social Indicators Research* 17, no. 2: 101–13.

Kirsch, Mike. 2015. "The Other Side of the Oil Boom in North Dakota." CCTV America, January 25. www.cctv-america.com/2015/01/25/the-other-side-of-the-oil-boom-in-north-dakota.

Krogstad, Jens M. 2014. "How North Dakota's 'Man Rush' Compares with Past Population Booms." Pew Research Center, July 16. www.pewresearch.org/fact-tank/2014/07/16/how-north-dakotas-man-rush-compares-with-past-population-booms/.

Kusnetz, Nicholas. 2012. "North Dakota's Oil Boom Brings Damage Along With Prosperity." *ProPublica*, June 7. www.propublica.org/article/the-other-fracking-north-dakotas-oil-boom-brings-damage-along-with-prosperi.

Little, Ronald L. 1977. "Some Social Consequences of Boom Towns." *North Dakota Law Review* 53: 401–26.

McChesney, John. 2012. "Oil Boom Crunches Rural Medical Facilities." *Daily Yonder*. October 12. www.dailyyonder.com/oil-boom-crushes-rural-health-facilities/2012/10/08/4528.

MacPherson, James. 2008. "North Dakota's Millionaires Multiplied After Oil Discovered." *Houston Chronicle*, October 26. www.chron.com/news/nation-world/article/North-Dakota-s-millionaires-multiplied-after-oil-1764772.php.

Newcomb, Alyssa. 2014. "Costliest Place for Renters Has Yellowstone River Views." *ABC News*, February 17.

North Dakota Energy Forum. 2014. "North Dakota Revenue." www.ndenergyforum.com/topics/north-dakota-revenue.

O'Donoghue, Amy. 2014. "Crude Reality: North Dakota Oil Boom Has Utah Envying Its Surplus Green." *Deseret News*, January 12.

Pilisuk, Marc, JoAnn McAllister, and Jack Rothman. 1996. "Coming Together for Action: The Challenge of Contemporary Grassroots Community Organizing." *Journal of Social Issues* 52, no. 1: 15–37.

28

Potter, Kyle. 2014. "Danger on the Rails." *Grand Forks Herald*, February 2.

Prud'homme, Alex. 2014. *Hydrofracking: What Everyone Needs to Know.* New York: Oxford University Press.

Quick, Brad, and Morgan Brennan. 2014. "Fracking Boom Waste: Flares Light Prairie With Unused Natural Gas." *NBC News*, August 25. www.nbcnews.com/business/energy/fracking-boom-waste-flares-light-prairie-unused-natural-gas-n186946.

Robinson, Elwyn B. 1959. "The Themes of North Dakota History." *North Dakota History*, Winter. webapp.und.edu/dept/library/Collections/robinson/themes.php.

Rucker, Patrick, and Valerie Volcovici. 2013. "US Doubles Oil Reserve Estimates at Bakken, Three Forks Shale." *Reuters*, April 30.

Seydlitz, Ruth, Shirley Laska, Daphne Spain, Elizabeth W. Triche, and Karen L. Bishop. 1993. "Development and Social Problems: The Impact of the Offshore Oil Industry on Suicide and Homicide Rates." *Rural Sociology* 58: 93–110. doi: 10.1111/j.1549-0831.1993.tb00484.x.

Smith, Michael D, Richard S. Krannich, and Lori M. Hunter. 2001. "Growth, Decline, Stability, and Disruption: A Longitudinal Analysis of Social Well-Being in Four Western Rural Communities." *Rural Sociology* 66: 442–50. doi: 10.1111/j.1549-0831.2001.tb00075.x.

Solomon, Gary, John Hiesbergr, and Jane L. Winer. 1981. "Confidentiality Issues in Rural Community Mental Health." *Journal of Rural Community Psychology* 2, no. 1: 17–37. www.marshall.edu/jrcp/archives/Vol21/v21Solomon.htm.

Sulzberger, A.G. 2011. "Oil Rig Brings Camps of Men to the Prairie." *New York Times*, November 25. www.nytimes.com/2011/11/26/us/north-dakota-oil-boom-creates-camps-of-men.html.

U.S. Bureau of Labor Statistics. 2013. "Unemployment Rate." Last modified December. www.bls.gov.

U.S. Census Bureau. 2014. "Profile of General Population and Housing Characteristics." Last modified January 6. quickfacts.census.gov/qfd/states/38000.html.

U.S. Census Bureau. N.d. "Urban and Rural Classifications." www.census.gov/geo/reference/pdfs/GARM/Ch12GARM.pdf.

U.S. Energy Information Administration. 2014. "North Dakota and Texas Now Provide Nearly Half of U.S. Crude Oil Production." July 1. www.eia.gov/petroleum/supply/monthly/.

U.S. Energy Information Administration. 2015. "Petroleum Supply Monthly." March 30. www.eia.gov/petroleum/supply/monthly/.

Valentine, Katie. 2015. "Nearly 3 Million Gallons of Drilling Waste Spill from North Dakota Pipeline." *Climate Progress*, January 22. thinkprogress.org/climate/2015/01/22/3614226/north-dakota-brine-spill/.

"Williams County Comprehensive Plan 2035." 2012. www.williamsnd.com/usrfiles/WilliamsCountyCompPlan.pdf.

CHAPTER 2

NOTES FROM THE GLOBAL HINTERLANDS: WHAT IT FEELS LIKE TO BE GLOBAL IN NORTH DAKOTA

Kyle Conway

Since the Bakken-fueled oil boom picked up pace in about 2008, Williston's residents have taken a wild ride. They are excited because the boom brings economic vitality, but they are anxious because vitality comes at a cost. They have mixed feelings about the new people in their midst. They are open to newcomers, as long as they get to know them as individuals with families and stories not unlike their own. But they are wary of those whose stories they do not know as they bring big-city traffic to their small-town streets.

This chapter is about three things. First, it is about the ambivalence the boom has provoked. It is a map of the tug-and-pull people feel as the familiar becomes strange. It is about geography and emotion, the way people experience distance and proximity and the way their sense of identity changes. North Dakotans recognize that, with the exception of Native Americans, they all come from someplace else, and they take pride in the hard work and neighborliness that go together in remote places. Because they were once in the same position, many feel a sense of responsibility to people who are newly arrived, but they recognize the complexity of the task of making room for the newcomers.

Thus this chapter is also about hospitality and the relationships its conventions entail. The Latin roots of the word (*hos-* comes from *hostis*, meaning "guest," *-pit-* from *potis*, meaning "master") describe a relationship of reciprocity. According to linguist Émile Benveniste (1973, 77):

> A *hostis* is not a stranger in general. In contrast to the *peregrinus*, who lived outside the boundaries of the territory, *hostis* is "the stranger in so far as he is recognized as enjoying equal rights to those of Roman citizens". This recognition of rights implies a certain relation of reciprocity and supposes an agreement or compact. Not all non-Romans are called *hostis*. A bond of equality and

reciprocity is established between this particular stranger and the citizens of Rome, a fact which may lead to a precise notion of hospitality. From this point of view *hostis* will signify "he who stands in a compensatory relationship" and this is precisely the foundation of the institution of hospitality.

This idea remains current. People in Williston welcome those they get to know as individuals because individuals can reciprocate their gestures; they are anxious about those who remain distant because they cannot.

Finally, this chapter is about what it feels like to be global in North Dakota. We talk of "global companies," "global cities," "global warming," and so on. What does the adjective "global" mean? Can people embody what it describes? What is the experience of "being global" for the people of Williston? One challenge we face is that, if we want to understand experience, we can speak with assurance only about what we know as individuals. The idea of collective experience is a useful abstraction, but it relies on our inference, based on other people's words and actions, that they pass through the world in ways similar to our own. We can know their ways only indirectly. So to write about experience, we must also write about perspective. Although my family lives in Williston, I grew up elsewhere, and I now live on the other side of the state in Grand Forks.[1] I write from my office in the University of North Dakota. My sight is clear, but what I see is refracted through an identifiable prism. My focus is on long-time residents' experience of the boom because they are the people I know best.

But speaking of perspective has value precisely because it helps us make the inferences necessary for understanding collective experience, abstraction though it may be. That is my purpose here: to provide tools to understand North Dakotans' experience of the oil boom, to identify what is individual and what is shared. The idea that people share something in common can strengthen our sense of connection with them (if we think we share something, too) or our sense of alienation (if we don't). Another challenge we face is that globalization does not result from just one thing. Many forces shape how capital, people, and ideas move and the patterns they follow. Arjun Appadurai (1990) calls these patterns the "financescape" (the movement of capital), the "ethnoscape" (the movement of people), and the "ideoscape" (the movement of ideas). He asks what happens when we fall into the gaps between "scapes"—what

---

[1] Since I first wrote these words, I have moved again, this time to a university in Ottawa, Canada. And in the intervening time, conditions have changed as the price of oil has dropped. I am maintaining this chapter largely as I first wrote it to preserve the snapshot it provides of a specific historical moment.

happens when people come from a different place than capital? What happens when the ideas people bring clash with those of their new home? These questions guide me here. What patterns does capital, transformed through labor into oil, follow in and out of western North Dakota? How do people—long-time residents and those who come looking for work—move from place to place? And when ideas about the oil industry (such as the objection to hydraulic fracturing) come to North Dakota, do they resonate with the people here?

The answers to these questions help us see that people maneuver through space in literal and figurative ways: they move not only through a geographic space—western North Dakota—but also through a metaphorical space of relationships with others. We can describe these relationships along three axes. The first is proximity: where are people located in relation to western North Dakota? Are they in North Dakota, or are they somewhere else? The second is agency: do people feel they are actors, or do they feel acted upon? The third is orientation: are people turned outward toward others, or are they turned inward toward their own community? Each axis represents a continuum. Many people live in more than one place.[2] They both act and are acted upon, and they may hold contradictory ideas about the effects of the oil boom. They are not defined by easy dichotomies: the space they maneuver through is too complex.

What emerges from this analysis is the picture of a place undergoing dramatic changes. If we examine the axes of proximity, agency, and orientation, we can begin to see how wealth and power (or feelings of powerlessness) influence people's sense of belonging to a place and the communities that are situated there. There is the very real risk that North Dakotans—those of long-standing and those who have recently arrived—will yield to the anxiety that the oil boom has brought, but it is not a foregone conclusion. As I write in the conclusion, there is still room for hospitality in a region increasingly affected by conflict, if everyone—long-time residents and newcomers alike—can cultivate the mutual trust that will be necessary to engender it.

---

[2] For this reason, I will favor the term "long-time residents" over "locals" to differentiate between people who have lived in North Dakota since before the boom. Newcomers can also become "locals," in their eyes and others', but that dynamic is more than I can address in this broad account of western North Dakotans' sense of identity. (Ann Reed's chapter in this volume traces out some of the ways people negotiate the meaning of the two terms.)

The Financescape: The Global Impinges on the Local

Most of the oil in western North Dakota is in the Bakken Formation, named after Henry Bakken, the farmer on whose land oil was first found in the 1950s. The Bakken covers much of the northwestern part of the state and stretches into Montana to the west and Saskatchewan to the north. It has been at the center of two previous but relatively short booms, the first in the 1950s, when oil was discovered, and the second in the 1980s. The challenge has always been to find a way to extract oil from a narrow layer of sandstone sandwiched between two layers of carbon-rich shale. Two factors have made the current boom possible: the high price of oil since the mid-2000s and new drilling technology (hydraulic fracturing or "fracking"), which allows engineers to extend their wells horizontally through the sandstone once they have reached the right depth. Since the current boom began, the number of wells has tripled to about 9,000, and the North Dakota Department of Mineral Resources predicts it will rise to as many as 45,000 within two decades (Wirtz 2013a, 2).

The boom is taking place within the context of a global oil and gas market worth about $3.1 trillion in 2012. Of that market, crude oil is the largest segment (about 63 percent of its total volume). The Asia-Pacific region accounts for the largest part of the market, about 36 percent, while the United States, whose national market was worth $612 billion in 2012, accounts for about 20 percent (MarketLine 2013a, 2013b). In other words, the Bakken is embedded in a national and international market, subject to fluctuations in oil prices that are shaped by global geopolitics and the policies enacted by the United States in response, such as those meant to encourage domestic fuel production and "energy independence."

However, none of the biggest companies operating in North Dakota are from the state. The four biggest are based in Colorado, Oklahoma, Texas, and New York, and the fifth is from Norway, as Figure 1 shows.

Their areas of operation in the United States are largely in the west, around the Rocky Mountains, in the shape of a crescent stretching from Texas and Louisiana to Colorado to North Dakota (and then into Canada), as illustrated in Figure 2.[3] Some also operate in states bordering the Great Lakes.

---

[3] The map in Figure 2 comes from the companies' annual reports. It is only approximate because each company reports the geography of its operations

Most people date the boom's beginning to 2005, but it really took off in about 2008. Since then, oil has become the dominant industry in North Dakota, as measured by the tax revenues it generates. Before the boom, during the 2003–5 biennium, oil and gas taxes brought in about $120 million (Wirtz 2013a, 4). For the 2011–13 biennium, they brought in about $4.1 billion, more than the amount of the next two biggest taxes combined (use and sales taxes at $2.4 billion and individual income taxes at $1.1 billion) (Fong 2013, 15). For the 2013–15 biennium, economists predict they will bring in $5 billion (Wirtz 2013a, 4).

This situation has had two important economic impacts on the state, the first related to infrastructure, the second to employment. The influx of people has taken a toll on the local infrastructure and put cities, counties, and the state in a difficult situation. Oil workers drive big trucks to carry machinery into drill sites and to carry oil out, and the increased traffic is more than local highways were designed to handle. Many county highways, for example, are unpaved because before the boom they served mostly to provide farmers and ranchers access to their fields. Now they are falling into disrepair. Similarly, municipal sewage systems struggle to keep up with the increased demand. Maintenance of the infrastructure is expensive. In January 2013, the city of Williston, the region's largest city right at the center of the boom, predicted it would need $625 million in infrastructure upgrades within six years (Wirtz 2013a, 3).

School districts face similar challenges. Many that had had declining enrollments now have to find ways to accommodate hundreds of new students. For instance, the McKenzie County School District, south of Williston, had 512 students in 2008 and 868 in 2013, and it faces the prospect of 1,600 students by 2016–17 (Wirtz 2013a, 3). The state provides some help to supplement the local property taxes that fund schools, but it cannot act quickly. North Dakota's budget is biennial, but city and county governments face unforeseen expenses on a regular basis. When the state acts, it is always playing catch-up, and it is hampered by a labyrinthine process for spending tax revenue. And despite the dramatic increase in oil tax revenue, very little goes into the state's general fund. In 2011–13, only $300 million went into the fund, while another $410 million went to help local governments cover infrastructure-related costs (Wirtz 2013b).

The second economic impact has been on the expansion of the service industries that support the boom. Both wages and demand for oil workers are high. As a result, unemployment is low, and jobs in the service industry must pay a premium to attract workers, especially those who have

---

differently. Of the five biggest companies, one—Hess Corporation—did not provide a map.

Company	Headquarters	Average daily production (in thousands of barrels)	Number of wells	Total cumulative production in Bakken (in millions of barrels)
Whiting Petroleum	Denver	119.8	673	80.8
Continental Resources	Oklahoma City	109.2	769	70.6
EOG Resources	Houston	91.3	488	93.4
Hess Corporation	New York	87.5	668	65.2
Statoil	Stavanger, Norway	60.2	356	10.1

Figure 1. Five biggest oil companies operating in the Bakken, as measured by average cumulative daily production. (source: Zawadzki 2013 and company annual reports)

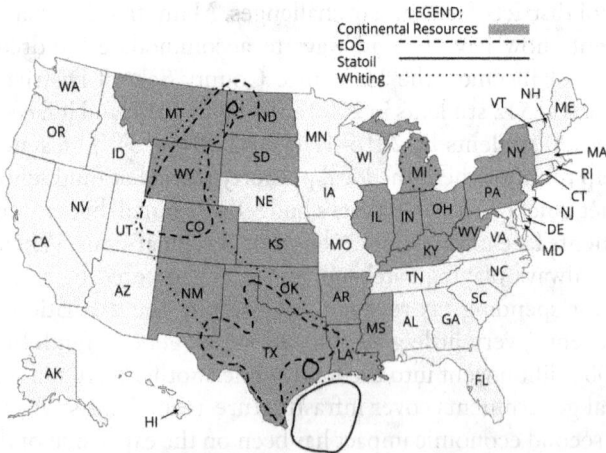

Figure 2. Areas of operation of the biggest oil companies operating in the Bakken. (source: company annual reports)

the option of working in the oil fields. In the Bakken area, unemployment has dropped to less than 2 percent, and wages have increased 140 percent since 2001. There is also a ripple effect outside the Bakken: within one hundred miles, there has been an increase in wages (although not as large as in the Bakken), and within two hundred miles there has been a decrease in unemployment (Batbold and Grunewald 2013, 14). For instance, in Minot, about two hours east of Williston, the home-improvement store Menards has had to fly in workers from its headquarters in Eau Claire, Wisconsin (MacPherson 2012).

In this way, the Bakken is embedded in a number of overlapped, criss-crossing global economic networks involving oil, technology, and the materials necessary to support the boom. Many residents feel as a result that large corporations without roots in the region now have an outsize influence over their lives. Money gives people living at a distance power over western North Dakota. But what is the nature of that power?

The Ethnoscape: Flows To and Through North Dakota

Who exactly are the residents of western North Dakota? This is no easy question. So many people have come recently that standard demographic tools are inadequate, and many oil workers split their time between North Dakota and their homes in other states. They also often stay in more or less temporary forms of housing, making any sort of census difficult (Bangsund and Hodur 2013).

To get an idea of the changes western North Dakota is undergoing, I will focus on Williston, which has been affected more than any other city in the region. In 2011, 63 percent of oil jobs were in the Williston area, 21 percent in Dickinson (about two hours south), and 14 percent in Minot (Hodur and Bangsund 2013, 9). Before the boom, Williston had about 13,000 permanent residents. In 2013, depending on the demographic model used, its total population was about 30,000, or with the surrounding townships, about 38,000. By 2017, demographers estimate the city's total population will be about 42,000, or with the surrounding townships, just under 54,000. Of those residents, about two thirds are permanent, and one third non-permanent (Hodur and Bangsund 2013, 26).[4] People have come from across the country (and world). Between

---

[4] "Permanent population is an estimate of individuals who work in the region and are established residents. Spouses and children of permanent workers living in the region also would be counted as permanent residents. Permanent population is consistent with population measured by the U.S. Census Bureau" (Hodur and Bangsund 2013, 18).

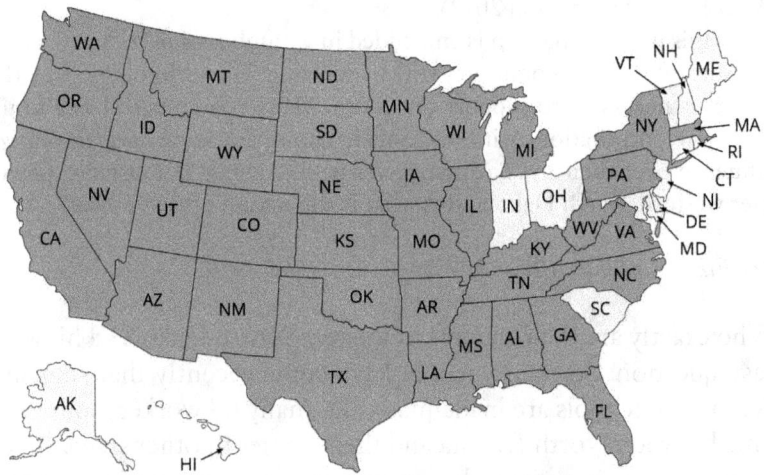

Figure 3. States of origin of students transferring into Williston Public School District #1 between 2011–12 and 2013–14 (source: the district)

the 2011–12 and 2013–14 school years, for instance, the larger of Williston's two school districts had transfer students from the states highlighted in Figure 3. It also had students from countries including Cameroon, Ghana, Indonesia, the Philippines, Honduras, Turkey, Nigeria, Taiwan, China, Russia, Mexico, Canada, and islands in the south Pacific Ocean.[5]

Although the district did not record how many students came from each state, if the district followed patterns observed elsewhere, it is likely that closer states provided more students. The North Dakota Department of Transportation, for instance, reported in 2014 that people in its directory of prequalified contractors came from twenty-eight states, with North Dakota, Minnesota, and South Dakota being the best represented (Nowatzki 2014).

Long-time residents have a range of reactions to the boom and the influx of newcomers. Surveys since the beginning of the boom have shown state-wide support for oil development, but it is not as strong among long-time residents who are most directly affected. According to one survey conducted in 2013, 83 percent of all North Dakotans (and 80 percent of those in the west) supported development of the oil industry (Dalrymple 2014). But according to another conducted in 2012, people who had lived in the region for at least six years had mixed feelings about the boom: 58 percent thought it had been good for their community, but 68 percent thought there were too many newcomers (Rundquist et al. 2012).

Long-time residents' feelings about newcomers have been shaped as much by the people themselves as by their impressions of the effects of the boom and the role played by oil companies. Core-periphery models of globalization, such as the ones explored in William Caraher's chapter in this volume, treat such companies as agents of capitalist expansion, actors who impose their will (or that of the governments they represent) upon people in the hinterlands who have natural resources but not the industry to develop them. According to these models, the people in the hinterlands develop a dependence on wealthy countries (and companies), and they are made passive: they do not act but are acted upon. At first glance, such might appear to be the case in western North Dakota. Oil companies are very powerful: they can (and do) acquire rights to drill more wells, and they have been buying apartment buildings and evicting long-time residents so their employees have a place to live.

But the core-periphery models miss how long-time residents, most of whom lack the oil companies' wealth, have found ways to resist the

[5] Special thanks to the administration of the Williston Public School District #1, in particular Superintendent Viola LaFontaine, for providing this information.

companies' efforts. Long-time residents are concerned about their identity. As one wrote in a letter to the editor in the *Williston Herald*:

> Most of us longtime Dakotans kind of liked what we had before this extreme "boom," namely the blue sky, good roads with light traffic, an agriculturally driven economy along with modest oil activity, relative safety from the afflictions of the rest of America, and the reasonable expectation that our rural, western innocence was a good thing ... Yet we are now creating a monster oil "bubble" which will inevitably bust, leaving [us] stoic "locals" with a very real mess to clean up—again (remember the last boom?). (Heiser 2012)

They also have practical concerns, as another letter-writer explains:

> I am ... a North Dakota citizen who is becoming very alarmed by what I have read, heard and seen regarding this unprecedented turn of events. Infrastructure problems, inflation, housing shortages, crime, traffic congestion, dust and safety issues, massive water and electricity consumption, environmental degradation, the list goes on. (Hermann 2010)

They are also concerned about rent hikes, which prompted some Willistonites to petition their mayor to take action (Dalrymple 2013a), and about the loss of public spaces such as the Lewis and Clark National Park (Bauer 2011).[6]

But their responses to newcomers go beyond anxiety and resistance. Although people in the 2012 survey thought there were too many newcomers, nearly half also thought the community welcomed them (Rundquist et al. 2012). Four churches, for instance, have come together to offer weekly meals open to all comers. The dinners, called Banquet West, provide a way to extend hospitality to people who are new or who are far from their families. In 2012, they served 6,300 people, with sixty to one hundred attending each Sunday (Spaulding 2013).

Thus the old core-periphery models also miss how long-time residents interact with newcomers, and they miss how newcomers and the companies they work for interact with long-time residents. In December 2013, about forty companies in oil-related businesses collected about 45,000 pounds of food for local food banks, while others contributed to

---

[6] See Weber et al. (2014) for an overview of these concerns from a social work perspective.

toy drives (Dalrymple 2013b). Such efforts were undoubtedly motivated by a desire to generate positive publicity to counter long-time residents' anxiety, but there is no reason to believe that the people who participated were not also sincere in their desire to say "thank you" to the community. People, after all, can be motivated by more than one thing.

If we rephrase this description in Appadurai's (1990) terms, we see that the financescape and ethnoscape—the patterns of movement of capital and of people—intersect in the Bakken, but they do not overlap. People come from different places than the money that finances the boom. Long-time residents and newcomers have different ideas about each other and their relationship to the region and the oil companies. Long-time residents are ambivalent about the region's new wealth, which they see as coming at a high social cost. Newcomers who don't feel the same connection to the region have different loyalties, having come to North Dakota because of the jobs made possible by the investment that makes long-time residents anxious.[7] In the gap between the financescape and ethnoscape, a space has opened up, one of contention and resistance on the one hand and negotiation, hospitality, and even mutual accommodation on the other. To understand how people maneuver through this gap, it is worthwhile to ask how ideas about the boom spread and resonate differently among different groups of people.

The Ideoscape: Pragmatism and Self-Reliance

I alluded above to the mixed feelings North Dakotans have about the oil boom. Although mixed, these feelings are structured by historical circumstances. In a narrow sense, people in Williston are concerned about the lingering effects of past oil booms, especially that of the 1980s, after which they felt abandoned by those who came to find riches and burdened by the loans the city took out to pay for infrastructure. In a broad sense, North Dakotans in general are sensitive to the state's status as a "colonial hinterland" that has worked to become more self-reliant, as described by historian Elwyn Robinson ([1958] 1996). North Dakotans know nothing will change the state's remoteness, but it need not be a colony, metaphorical or otherwise.

Williston residents remember the booms—and more importantly, the busts—of years past. As Josh Young demonstrates in his chapter in this volume, residents tell stories and develop a sense of publicly shared

---

[7] Of course, some newcomers stay and, with time, become longterm residents. These categories are only relatively stable, and as the boom continues, it will be important to ask what causes people to stay and how their self-understanding changes in the process.

42

memory as a way to work through the past trauma. They tell of crime, housing shortages, overbuilt (and underfunded) infrastructure, and abandonment. Contemporary residents act on these anxieties in the context of a pragmatic conservatism that was shaped by the state's historical circumstances and pattern of European settlement. Robinson ([1958] 1996) writes that in the nineteenth century, North Dakotans' resentment of outside interference by railway barons and others prompted them to find ways to become self-sufficient. In contrast to now, early residents reacted by becoming radicalized. They founded the socialist Nonpartisan League and created state-owned institutions such as the Bank of North Dakota and the North Dakota Mill. But today, as a result of the machinations of politics too complex to describe in detail here, these efforts find expression in conservative politics that emphasize the free market as the means to self-sufficiency. Republicans outnumber Democrats by about two to one in western North Dakota, and people overwhelmingly identify as conservative or moderate, but not liberal (Rundquist et al. 2012). People are still wary of outside interference, and they are especially wary of the federal government and of activist groups that, as they see it, do not understand local concerns.

The dominance of this pragmatic conservatism helps explain why some ideas prominent in other parts of the country, especially the opposition to fracking, have not taken root here. In New York, Pennsylvania, and other eastern states, the fracking industry has faced opposition from a coalition of environmental groups, as websites such as nofracking.com show. In North Dakota, people are concerned about the environment, but their reasons differ. In the 2012 survey cited above, more than 70 percent of long-time residents thought their community was "less environmentally sound" than it had been five years before.[8] They thought the air and soil were more polluted and there was more litter. They also thought that North Dakota needed better longterm land-use planning, and that farmland and rangeland should be protected. But a majority did not think the federal government should play a role, and they were even more strongly

---

[8] Evidence shows they are right. Fracking involves pumping water and chemicals into wells to break the sandstone that holds the oil in order to release it. This process creates a lot of waste, which must be disposed of (Kusnetz 2012). The number of oil spills has also increased. The biggest so far was near Tioga, North Dakota, in September 2013. Finally, shipping oil has proven difficult. The oil from the Bakken is carried by train, but it is more flammable than other forms of oil, leading to explosions such as the one that consumed eighteen train cars and dumped 400,000 gallons of oil near Casselton, North Dakota, in December 2013 (NTSB 2014).

opposed to interference from outside environmental groups such as the Sierra Club (Rundquist et al. 2012).[9]

In other words, North Dakotans' concerns about the environment are rooted in practical concerns about land-use rather than things that seem more abstract, such as climate change. (In the 2012 survey, only about a quarter of respondents thought global climate change was a major problem [Rundquist et al. 2012].) They want to protect their livelihoods and the identities they attach to "the blue sky, good roads with light traffic, an agriculturally driven economy along with modest oil activity, relative safety from the afflictions of the rest of America," as one person wrote in the letter to the editor quoted above. They know that booms end, and they want to handle their new wealth in ways that will lessen the impact of the bust many see as inevitable.

Of course, we should not discount the appeal of new wealth. North Dakota had more than 3,000 more millionaire households in 2013 than in 2008, a 30 percent increase in a state with only 300,000 households (Phoenix Marketing International 2014). Many of them had mineral rights they leased to oil companies. This new wealth helps smooth over the distrust some residents have of oil companies. At the same time, it creates divisions between those who benefit and those who don't. If western North Dakotans have mixed feelings about the boom, it is no surprise. The benefits are spread unevenly, and even people who *do* benefit can feel uncomfortable with the way the boom is putting their less fortunate neighbors at a disadvantage.

What Does It Feel Like To Be Global In North Dakota?

I opened this chapter with the observation that to describe experience, we can speak with assurance only about what we know as individuals. Collective experience is an abstraction we make because we think other people are like us, but we can never confirm this intuition directly. In the sections that followed, I marshaled evidence such as letters to the editor that expressed people's individual experience, as well as surveys that reflected an aggregation of individual experiences. How do we get from those expressions to something broader? What do those individual experiences tell us about what it feels like to be global in North Dakota?

As my discussion of the financescape, ethnoscape, and ideoscape showed, there are certain external factors that structure the range of choices people can make. In western North Dakota, some factors are

[9] At the same time, a majority did not think their county had a good land-use plan, either.

Orientation	Proximity	
	People/organizations at a distance (e.g., oil companies)	Local people/ organizations (e.g., long-time residents)
Actions benefit one's own group	Companies acquire rights to new drill sites, buy housing for workers, etc.	Residents resist companies' efforts to drill, to evict long-time residents, etc.
Actions benefit others	Companies give back to community through volunteer work, etc.	Long-time residents extend hospitality to newcomers.

Figure 4. Proximity and orientation in the experience of being an active agent.

political. The global politics of oil, linked inextricably to the politics of trade and security, influence U.S. policy-makers, who make decisions to encourage domestic oil production. Bismarck, like the capitals of other oil-rich states, then enacts laws and policies to govern land-use and give city governments the ability to deal with the new demands placed on their local infrastructure.

These political factors are also linked to the economy. The price of oil has remained high enough to sustain oil development in the Bakken because of the global, national, and local business communities' concern about political unrest in the Middle East. Oil development in turn shapes the options available to North Dakota and its cities, as they find ways to maintain roads and ensure access to housing. Their decisions shape the choices individuals and communities can make when maneuvering through their relationships with others and the places where they live. Individuals must find ways to act in circumstances that are not of their own making.

Thus the broad circumstances people face in western North Dakota are similar for everyone. This is not to say that two individuals facing a specific choice will necessarily act the same—they might choose different options, given their individual preferences. But we can say with confidence what their likely options will be. Our ability to describe how political and economic factors circumscribe people's range of options allows us to speculate about people's shared experience.

One thing that differs is people's access to resources, depending on where they are geographically. Distant oil companies use their capital to gain access to drill sites by buying or leasing mineral rights. Through extraction and refinement, which takes place far from North Dakota, they generate more capital, which buys them more access to resources. Long-time residents' access depends on whether they own mineral rights or whether they find jobs working for the oil companies. These are different types of access: although long-time residents can reinvest their money, they cannot do so as easily as oil companies.

In this way, proximity (or distance) influences people's access to resources, and that access puts people in a position to act or be acted upon. But it does not determine how they act. Oil companies do more than take—they also make visible efforts to give back to the community. Such efforts likely have ulterior motives such as positive publicity, but the local community still benefits. Similarly, even long-time residents who do not have the oil companies' access to resources can resist companies' actions or welcome newcomers into their community. Their lack of access does not reduce them to passivity.

46

People's access to resources influences how they orient their actions. They operate out of a complex mix of self-preservation and self-interest on the one hand and goodwill and neighborliness on the other. They are more willing to be open to people like themselves. Many long-time residents are suspicious of the oil companies, but they are sympathetic toward people living far from their families, as made clear by the Banquet West dinners. Proximity (and access to resources) shapes agency and orientation.

So what does it feel like to be global in North Dakota? Figure 4 illustrates the dimensions of proximity and orientation as they characterize North Dakotans' experience as active agents. Some actions benefit one's own group: oil companies acquire new drilling rights or buy housing for works; residents resist those efforts. Other actions benefit people from outside one's own group: companies give back to the communities they have joined; long-time residents extend hospitality. But the inverse of what it describes is also true: each action implies its opposite. Consequently, figure 4 also suggests how proximity and orientation shape the experience of being acted upon. When companies acquire housing, long-time residents lose it. When local people resist oil companies' efforts to evict long-time residents, oil companies must adapt. Similarly, when companies give back to local communities, those communities benefit, and when local people invite newcomers to community dinners, newcomers feel welcomed.

For long-time residents, the experience is one of finding ways to act, rather than be acted upon, while navigating through a space where powerful actors are often absent because they are far away. For newcomers, it is an experience of finding a literal and figurative place to occupy where they must be attentive to the sometimes contradictory needs of the companies that employ them and the community in which they live. People's horizons of choice are restricted, but they still find ways to maneuver within them.

Conclusion: Questions of Hospitality

Western North Dakota is facing dramatic changes, and people who have lived there since before the boom have seen their lives upended. The risk of conflict is real. So is the challenge of hospitality. Many long-time residents want to welcome newcomers, but they do not want to do so at the cost of their home or their sense of identity.

The evidence I've cited suggests that an openness toward strangers is not enough on its own. People also have a need for trust or, even more than trust, reciprocity. Old ideas about hospitality remain relevant: when people reach out to others, they also make themselves vulnerable, to rejection if nothing else. But on a bigger scale, the act of inviting a person into one's space requires a leap of faith that the person will not violate one's trust. People become more comfortable making those leaps when those they invite respond in kind.

The exercise of power from a distance is the opposite of reciprocity, and it is no wonder some long-time residents feel the need to resist or protest, especially when what is at stake is, in a very real way, their home. But because politicians, policy-makers, and even many long-time residents find the promise of wealth to be a compelling reason to continue developing the oil industry, companies' ability to shape western North Dakotans' lives will continue. There is no easy solution to the problems oil has caused, but there is reason for North Dakotans—new and old—to continue to seek out ways to be active in shaping their community. The health of the community depends on their willingness to engage in that search, not just now, but for as long as the boom continues.

References

Appadurai, Arjun. 1990. "Disjuncture and Difference in the Global Economy." *Theory, Culture & Society* 7: 295–310.

Bangsund, Dean A., and Nancy M. Hodur. 2013. "Williston Basin 2012: Projections of Future Employment and Population North Dakota Summary." Agribusiness and Applied Economics Report 704. Fargo: North Dakota State University, Agribusiness and Applied Economics. purl.umn.edu/142589.

Batbold, Dulguun, and Rob Grunewald. 2013. "Bakken Activity: How Wide Is the Ripple Effect?" *Federal Reserve Bank of Minneapolis Fed-Gazette*, July: 14.

Bauer, David. 2011. "Oil and Parks Don't Mix." *Williston Herald*, September 29.

Benveniste, Émile. 1973. *Indo-European Language and Society*, translated by Elizabeth Palmer. Coral Gables, FL: University of Miami Press.

Continental Resources. 2012. *Annual Report*. Oklahoma City: Continental Resources.

Dalrymple, Amy. 2013a. "Group Protests Rent Hikes in Williston, Seeks Help from City." *Grand Forks Herald*, November 10. www.grandforksherald.com/content/group-protests-rent-hikes-williston-seeks-help-city-0.

Dalrymple, Amy. 2013b. "Oil Industry Gives Back to the Bakken during the Holidays." *Oil Patch Dispatch*, December 26. oilpatchdispatch.areavoices.com/2013/12/26/ oil-industry-gives-back-to-the-bakken-during-the-holidays/.

Dalrymple, Amy. 2014. "Support Strong for Oil In N.D." *Grand Forks Herald*, January 22.

EOG Resources. 2012. *Annual Report*. Houston: EOG Resources.

Fong, Cory. 2013. *51st Biennial Report: For the Biennial Period of July 1, 2011 through June 30, 2013*. Bismarck: North Dakota Office of the State Tax Commissioner.

Heiser, John A. 2012. "Fed Up with the Oil Boom Way of Life." *Williston Herald*, January 24.

Hess Corporation. 2012. *Annual Report*. New York: Hess Corporation.

Hermann, Janell. 2010. "What's the Cost of Oil and Natural Gas Development?" *Williston Herald*, September 17.

Hodur, Nancy M., and Dean A. Bangsund. 2013. "Population Estimates for City of Williston." Agribusiness and Applied Economics Report 707. Fargo: North Dakota State University, Agribusiness and Applied Economics. purl.umn.edu/157412.

Kusnetz, Nicholas. 2012. "North Dakota's Oil Boom Brings Damage Along with Prosperity." *ProPublica*, June 7. www.propublica.org/ article/the-other-fracking-north-dakotas-oil-boom-brings-damage-along-with-prosperi.

MacPherson, James. 2012. "Menard to Fly Wisconsin Workers In to Staff ND Store." *Associated Press*, November 30. bigstory.ap.org/ article/menard-fly-wis-workers-staff-nd-store.

MarketLine. 2013a. "MarketLine Industry Profile: Global Oil and Gas." Reference code 0199-2116. EBSCOhost.

MarketLine. 2013b. "MarketLine Industry Profile: Oil and Gas in the United States." Reference code 0072-2116. EBSCOhost.

Nowatzki, Mike. 2014. "Contractors Flocking to N.D. for Work." *Grand Forks Herald*, February 23. www.grandforksherald.com/content/ contractors-flocking-nd-work.

NTSB (National Transportation Safety Board). 2014. "Preliminary Report: Railroad DCA14MR004." www.ntsb.gov/investigations/Ac-cidentReports/Reports/Casselton_ND_Preliminary.pdf.

Phoenix Marketing International. 2014. "Rankings of U.S. States by Millionaires Per Capita, 2006–2013." w3.phoenixmi.com/ wp-content/uploads/2014/01/Phoenix-GWM-U.S.-Ranking-States-By-Millioinaires-Per-Capita-2006-13.pdf.

Robinson, Elwyn B. (1958) 1996. "The Themes of North Dakota History." In *The Centennial Anthology of North Dakota History*, edited by

Janet Daley Lysengen and Ann M. Rathke, 1–15. Bismarck: State Historical Society of North Dakota.

Rundquist, Bradley C., Devon A. Hansen, Enru Wang, and Stanley D. Brunn. 2012. "Perceptions of the Recent Oil Boom Among Long-term Residents of Williston, Stanley, and Watford City, North Dakota." University of North Dakota. arts-sciences.und.edu/geography/_files/docs/oil_boom_survey_results.pdf.

Spaulding, Sara. 2013. "Churches Come Together to Provide Free Meals to Those in Need." *Williston Herald*, April 10.

Statoil. 2012. *Annual Report on Form 20-F*. Stavanger, Norway: Statoil.

Weber, Bret A., Julia Geigle, and Caranlee Barkdull. 2014. "Rural North Dakota's Oil Boom and Its Impact on Social Services." *Social Work* 59, no. 1: 62–72.

Whiting Petroleum Corporation. 2012. *Annual Report*. Denver: Whiting Petroleum Corporation.

Wirtz, Ronald A. 2013a. "Congratulations on Your Oil Boom … Now the Real Work Begins." *Federal Reserve Bank of Minneapolis FedGazette*, July: 1–8.

Wirtz, Ronald A. 2013b. "Oil Tax Spending: 'Pots for This and Pots for That.'" *Federal Reserve Bank of Minneapolis FedGazette*, July: 6–7.

Zawadzki, Sabina. 2013. "Factbox: Top Oil Producers in North Dakota's Giant Bakken Play." *Thomson Reuters*, November 21. articles.chicagotribune.com/2013-11-20/news/sns-rt-us-shalebakken-factbox-20131120_1_bakken-north-dakota-data.

Chapter 3

Unpackaging Boomtown Tropes: Insider/Outsider Dynamics in North Dakota's Oil Patch

Ann Reed

In describing the social impacts of North Dakota's oil boom, newspaper reporters often present a dichotomy between out-of-state "roughnecks" and small town farmers and ranchers. The roughnecks are painted as economic opportunists who are simply looking to get rich quick but also contribute to spikes in crime and drug use. They work for an industry that is threatening the way of life in North Dakota communities spanning the oil patch. The local North Dakotans who have farmed or ranched for several generations resent the dramatic change in their small town way of life that, paralleling John Denver's assessment of commercial tourism's impact on the Colorado Rockies: "they try to tear the mountains down to bring in a couple more, more people, more scars upon the land" (Denver and Taylor 1972). At least that is the impression that is often conveyed in media outlets about the current oil play in western North Dakota. In this chapter, I would like to present a slightly different scenario, one that includes more shades of gray in depicting the complicated nature of insider and outsider interactions in this most recent boom, dating back to 2008. Cultural constructions of who is regarded an "insider" or an "outsider" vary depending upon the context of a conversation, and this means that these dynamics cannot be boiled down to North Dakotans vs. out-of-state residents alone.

Lynn Helms, director of North Dakota's Department of Mineral Resources, estimated that in 2012 roughly 25,000 people were directly employed by 201 drilling rigs in North Dakota (McChesney 2012). Helms figures that each new rig creates 120 new direct jobs, plus an additional fifty jobs associated with laying pipes to the productive wells or building natural gas processing plants (McChesney 2011). This does not include additional supportive employment such as construction or transportation—important for hauling oil to refineries and large quantities of water

52

for hydraulic fracturing. A 2013 web article reported that North Dakota had 50,000 oil jobs and that 14,000 of these were located in and around Williston (Layne 2013). A construction industry web site emphasized the enormous demand for new housing in the Bakken, citing a hard-to-believe figure of a 50,000 percentage increase in new jobs since 2008, "with almost 99% of the oil field workers com[ing] from out of state" (SunDance Foundation 2012). Clearly, many oil workers have migrated to North Dakota from out of state, but it is actually difficult to know exactly what the ratio of in-state to out-of-state oilfield workers is, as the Bureau of Labor Statistics does not record these data, nor is it included in the North Dakota's oil and gas economy labor market information. Anecdotally, plenty of high school graduates from western North Dakota are working in the oil patch instead of attending college, and many additional North Dakotans have found lucrative short-term or longer-term employment there.

Locals' Reflections on the Changes Brought About By the Oil Boom

I ground my discussion in ethnographic fieldwork with residents of Parshall, ND, a community of approximately one thousand people situated on the eastern edge of the Bakken formation and whose residents are a mix of mostly Mandan, Hidatsa, and Arikara (MHA) people, and whites descending primarily from Norwegian and German homesteaders, as well as a growing stream of very recent economic migrants from other parts of North Dakota, other states in the United States, and Mexico. In 2013, I brought my ethnographic methods students to Parshall to carry out face-to-face interviews with community members in order to contribute to a centennial history book as well as to my own research on the impacts of the oil boom.[1] The following section illustrates how the frame of "insider/outsider" actually shifts depending upon the context of the discussion. In addition, we found that most Parshall residents were reluctant to discuss the details surrounding drug use or violent crimes happening in their area. Interviews were audio recorded and transcribed in the interviewee's exact words; however, I use pseudonyms below in order to protect their identities.

The concept of agency can be usefully applied to understanding the costs and benefits different individuals associate with the most recent oil boom. Loosely defined as "the socioculturally mediated capacity to act"

[1] Thanks to the University of North Dakota Department of Anthropology for funding a student field trip and to the Digital Working Group for loaning us equipment. Most of all, thanks to the kind people of Parshall, ND, for sharing their stories with us.

(Ahearn 2001), agency is associated with an individual's ability to reflect upon available options and take independent action. It is socioculturally mediated in that the range of alternatives is constrained by the structure of society and available meanings derived through culture. In paying attention to the words of Parshall residents, it is important to think about how advantages and disadvantages are framed, the extent to which individuals feel that they have agency in the dramatic changes that are taking place in their communities, and to reflect on how this relates back to insider/outsider cultural constructions.

Suzanne is a twenty-five-year-old whose fiancé has worked in the oil field since 2006. In this case her oil worker fiancé is not an out-of-state migrant, but a local resident. Her response to my question about how the oil boom has affected her family shifted from talking about her fiancé and daughter to the changing population brought about by the extractive industry:

> He started before I even graduated high school ... He has maintained his job and we have been planning on getting a house out in the country. My little girl has benefitted a lot [from the oil boom], 'cause we can provide everything for her. He really helped me through college with the oil boom—he paid for most of my stuff, living expenses. I am very affected by [the oil boom] ... People always try to blame [the negative parts of living here] on the oil field, and I say it is not all oil field people, because my fiancé is part of that. I had one friend who was from Wyoming and he moved up when I was still in college and he told me—he is from the area of Rock Springs, which they had a huge [coal mining] boom ... And he said, "You just wait, the drugs and the grungy people aren't even here yet. You have all the good guys right now, because they are bringing up people that have experience and know how to work. But you wait in five years," he said, "and you are going to see how gross it is and how it's not really beneficial to everybody." And I'm finally starting to see it, and it has only been four years since he said that to me.

For Suzanne, agency is related to her family's ability to generate enough income to provide well for themselves, pay for her college education, and accumulate savings towards buying a house. She and her fiancé have chosen to accumulate earnings derived from the oil industry and spend them in particular ways. In addition, Suzanne relays a conversation that suggests some of the limited benefits of extractive economies. Interpreting her words, we may recognize that her agency is constrained by her perception and fear that increasing numbers of unsavory outsiders are moving to her community to take jobs in the industry. She suggests that later economic migrants bring drugs with them, and the increase in "grungy" people and drugs becomes a threat to the local way of life.

Mike is a seventy-three-year-old who views the insider/outsider dynamic more in terms of locals who are from Parshall or other small towns in the oil patch and outsiders who may even be from North Dakota but who are taking advantage of the oil field workers:

> Well I feel sorry for the people that are here—came for work in the oil and are living in these campers. They're charging them $1100 *a month* to park their camper. They have no grass. They can almost knock on their next-door neighbor. It's ridiculous. People are out of Fargo that came up and set up the camp. But they're making a fortune on people that are ... Well if they're working to try to send money home, they are charged so much ... (emphasis in original)

Mike's statement points to the idea that oil workers are economic migrants with limited agency; this is because they have to pay such high rent to their city-based landlords who Mike views as outsiders. Further, their living conditions are restricted by the dearth of housing available: they must put up with the hardships of having no grass or privacy.

Mike and his wife Paula have a great nephew who works for the oil industry and is able to balance his work responsibilities with being a devoted husband and father. He works eight hours a day for so many days in a row (shifts are often in two weeks on, two weeks off cycles), but is a family man and helps to raise his children. Mike and Paula talked about how people in rural areas like Parshall relate to new-found wealth:

> In a small town, people are not showy. Like, our son-in-law got a new pick up and he didn't even take it out of the garage for about a month! He left it in the garage because he didn't want people talking about it ... [laughing] People would go up and ask him, "Oh, how much do you make?" [laughing] There are no barriers. But that's small town people where everybody knows everybody else's business. [laughing]

People in places like Parshall may be uncomfortable with conspicuous consumption and displaying trappings of their new-found oil wealth for all to see. Plenty of people—both insiders and outsiders—have quickly amassed considerable wealth from oil development. This situation also threatens the sense of community in places like Parshall because there is a dramatic economic gap between the locals who have become million- aires (the haves) and those who are barely scraping by to keep up with the increased costs of groceries and rent (the have-nots). This gives rise to another interpretation of insiders as those with economic capital and outsiders who inequitably bear the burdens of this oil-driven economy. Given the spike in the cost of living, these outsiders have less agency in being able to afford basic necessities, both in relation to what they could buy in the past and in relation to the range of consumables that insiders can purchase.

Steve is a sixty-nine-year-old who has gotten to know some of the oil field workers through golfing and hanging out at the local hardware store that is owned by his close friend. Overall, he has a good impression of the oil workers:

> I see quite a few of the [oil] workers coming and going and for the most part they are just like you and I. They are normal people, they visit … and they just add to the community, it's not a big deal. Maybe the bars have experienced some changes, because of more people coming in, but most of the people that I … see are here to earn money, support their families someplace else. They are not here being crazy … they work a lot of hours and maybe when they are off they do some relaxing or whatever, but I haven't seen anything crazy going on with the workers coming in. And we hear about it, certainly, in other areas especially … Williston where they have such a large influx of people and lots of man camps, and it's just a percentage thing. There is always a couple—and if there are three people that end up in the newspaper, then it's kinda like "Wow!" [causes a stir]
>
> … From what I see, then again just kinda looking from the outside in, the people who are coming here are, for the most part, just hardworking people … I am sure they get drinking once in a while and get in some trouble, but the percentage of good people far outweighs that. I was talking to a guy one day who was a retired teacher from Ohio, and fairly young—he must've retired fairly early, I would guess he was like in his 50s. But he was up here driving truck because he could make a lot of money and put it in the bank and have a retirement and take care of his family. So he said, "I'm just here trying to earn some extra money." And they're not here for a good time, they're here for work. And I think, if they come here to North Dakota thinking, "Let's just go see what's

going on in the oil patch and have fun," after the first winter, they're probably going to go back home. [laughing]

People from Parshall expressed concern for not knowing the people at the local grocery store anymore and had mixed feelings about the relationship of the oil boom to crime. Although Steve suggests that higher crime rates[2] are simply proportional to higher population rates and that the crime is really more of a problem in Williston, other residents said that they were uneasy about the potential for crime in their town. A certain amount of drug use and crime were present in the community before 2008, but drug use has increased in recent years. Some townspeople report that they do not want their kids to go out unsupervised—especially at night, that they lock their doors now, and are vigilant to check the back of their cars when entering.

Wally, a forty-seven-year-old who works closely with recovering addicts, reported that alcohol and methamphetamines had been the most widely used drugs, but since the oil boom started, there has been an unprecedented level of cocaine and heroin addiction. This uptick in drug use is not limited to recent arrivals to the community; in some cases, the newfound wealth of locals with mineral rights or oil jobs may be used to buy drugs. Abusing drugs and alcohol is connected to car accidents as well as different forms of crime.

> We need to learn how to live together. And there's good people and bad people everywhere. That criminal element that's out there, though, some of those people—they have malicious intent! They do. They're gonna come in, they're gonna push their heroin. Whether it is outright male prostitution, or they're taking some of our young women and our young boys, and selling their butt on the corner. The underground market for that—especially if you're a mom or a dad, a grandma or grandpa, those are disheartening themes.
>
> ... I think there is an apprehension there, but the more that you get to know somebody, the more ... we get to be at ease about things. And I don't want to get caught up in a complacency about

---

[2] However, if one looks closely at the percentages of each, it is clear to see that crime has spiked dramatically since 2008 in oil patch counties. Crime rates in 2013 were up nearly 8 percent for the state and are the most prevalent in counties affected by oil field development. The 2012 Attorney General's report noted that rapes and robberies witnessed decade-high increases. Figures for aggravated assaults continue to be alarmingly high (North Dakota Attorney General 2015; Scheurer 2013; Nowatzki 2014; Michael 2013).

any of that stuff … There is a seriousness about what we're doing. Drugs and alcohol—people die from this stuff! When you're talking about a thousand trucks going down the highway, people are going to get killed … I'll tell you I sit here and, the war on drugs and alcohol, we're getting our butts kicked. And now we have heroin—it used to be very few, pre-oil boom, lucky if you see one out of a hundred that had a usage history—now it's closer to 20 percent or 30 percent.

How the fear of outsiders works is that unknown people and the forces that they represent (including the potential for unprecedented drug use, violence, and crime) become solidified in the label "outsiders" and are in contrast to the folks from within the community who are known, the "insiders." These negative impacts also represent a constraining of agency for individuals and long-term residents. Dorothy, a seventy-year-old, re-layed a few incidents that have influenced her decision not to drive at night any more:

One of the truckers assaulted one of our Native women. A little bitty old thing too she was. And he had thought she cut him off, but I don't know what the situation was, but [from what I heard] he jumped out of his car and ran over there. She put the window down, not knowing and he had a bat and he reached in and hit her. You know, she had a little baby in the back seat strapped in … I don't drive at night anymore because I'm scared. I'm afraid.

[In a separate incident], my niece … her and one of her [co-workers] were out going to visit an individual … and they were hit by a semi. Killed the [co-worker] and put [my niece] in the hospital … So it's a fear of getting on the roads, it's a fear of talking to people. When you get in your car, and you immediately lock your doors. It's just changed people… Things like that happen and so you don't feel safe in your home anymore. You lock the doors, you don't want to talk to strangers, and before it was always like, "Hi, what are you doing?" and "Where are you from? Are you new here?" … Like I said before there was that dichotomy [between Native and non-Native people], but still you always recognized an outsider and you weren't mean or ugly to them. But now it's, it's different.

Dorothy's quotation illustrates perfectly how the fear of outsiders turns into insider/outsider dichotomies and even into a reported behavior change on the part of insiders (locking your doors, not talking to people).

58

Her discussion includes an example of how outsiders can become insiders: by being transformed through small-talk from unknown individuals who represent that which is threatening and uncontrollable to known people with commonalities shared with insiders. She revealed that the main insider/outsider dichotomy in her community has always been between Native Americans and whites; now with the oil boom, recent arrivals to the area are the new category of outsiders in contrast to the long-term residents of Fort Berthold Indian Reservation (both Native and non-Native), who are the insiders. The "Native woman" is not referenced by name, but she is automatically put in the category of insider because she is an American Indian from Fort Berthold, even though it is unclear whether or not Dorothy knows her personally. The old dichotomy of Native/non-Native is still there, but is overlaid by emergent contrasts of out-of-state roughnecks with permanent residents.

Reaching Out to Out-of-Staters

In May 2014, the State of North Dakota launched a campaign called "Find the Good Life in North Dakota." This initiative targets people with ties to the state, people with families, and former military personnel. Its website suggests that "the American dream" is still attainable in North Dakota where there are "25,000 job openings" and "more jobs than people to fill them" (North Dakota State Government 2014). For people from states with high unemployment rates, North Dakota is held up as a beacon of opportunity for both career and family; video testimonials underscore the great people, teachers, and business-friendly climate of the State. According to the Bureau of Labor Statistics' figures for May 2014, North Dakota has the lowest unemployment rate in the United States at 2.6 percent (Bureau of Statistics 2014b), whereas the national average is 6.3 percent (Bureau of Labor Statistics 2014a). The North Dakota Labor Market Information Center lists a 0.8 percent unemployment rate across all industries for core oil and gas producing counties for December 2013, compared to a 3.3 percent rate for non-oil and gas producing counties. In February 2014, there were a total of 20,205 job openings: 3,077 openings in core oil and gas producing counties; 4,100 openings in counties that produced less than 25 percent of the state's oil; and 13,028 openings in non-oil counties (North Dakota Labor Market Information Center 2014). Non-oil counties have the most job openings and highest unemployment rates in the state; this combination makes no sense intuitively, unless we factor in the kinds of unskilled, low paying jobs that comprise the pool of openings, coupled with the fact that core oil counties have the high paying jobs that are most in demand. So it is not that people are simply attracted to North Dakota for jobs but that they are attracted by the prospects of earning high wages.

Undeniably, job opportunities in the oil industry are the main reason why people from out-of-state are moving to North Dakota. However, it is unclear how many people are making plans to stay for the long term. There seems to be a general consensus that eventually the current boom will go bust[3]—it has happened before in North Dakota (most recently in the 1980s)—so newcomers may not want to make the personal and economic investments in establishing strong social networks with locals or buying a house, particularly with the scarcity of affordable housing. Oil field workers from Oklahoma, Texas, or Mississippi work 80–100 hours per week in two weeks on, two weeks off rotations, they send remittances back to family in their home states and visit them during their time off, and most have no intention of moving to North Dakota permanently. Hannah Wight is a twenty-two-year-old from eastern Montana who moved to Watford City with her boyfriend and helps to manage a property of trailers. They plan to stay for five years to make money before moving back to Montana to settle down. Her boss goes back to visit his family in Minneapolis every few weeks and said, "It's not that I don't like it here, but my family is back in Minnesota and my wife is not interested in moving here" (Gahagan 2014).

Jesse Moss, a filmmaker who produced a documentary about a Williston church that provided shelter for newcomers in search of oil jobs, reported that most of the individuals he filmed did not stay in the state: "It was extremely hard for them. Many of them found work. That wasn't the problem. It was the pain of separation from their families, the pain of surviving in a place without friends and a community around them, and the harshness of the climate" (Dalrymple 2014a). These very hardships of long working hours, separation from loved ones, isolation from community, and long, frigid winters also point to the limited agency that out-of-state oil workers experience. Some may choose to return home for good if they cannot cope with the weather or feel alienated, while others stick it out and try to socially integrate themselves into their new residence.

In an effort to break down social barriers between out-of-state oilfield workers and long-term residents, Williston area churches have organized Sunday "Banquet West" dinners that provide free meals and hospitality to newcomers in the area (Frykholm 2013). The oil industry has also tried to reach out to local communities in the North Dakota oil patch by helping

---

[3] The price Bakken oil fetches on the open market has dropped, as have rental rates in places like Williston (Brooks 2015; Scheyder 2015).

to sponsor events like the 2011 Williston Energy Festival and the 2014 Parshall Centennial Celebration (McChesney 2011). Parades for these events included industry trucks advertising their names to community members and drivers tossing tootsie rolls and suckers to children. In June 2014, the North Dakota Petroleum Council sponsored the "One Million Barrels—One Million Thanks" Celebration in Tioga, nearby where the state's first oil deposits were discovered in 1951 (Dalrymple 2014b). Approximately two thousand participants[4] reportedly took advantage of the free Southern barbecue, air show by the Texas Flying Legends, and oil history exhibition. Newspaper accounts of these events typically demonstrate how local residents appreciate the industry's efforts in providing jobs and lessening American dependence on foreign oil. What is often left out of the mix is the view of some long-time residents who resent the growing domination of oil wells on their prairie landscape or the concerns of some farmers and ranchers who worry that fracking threatens their ability to maintain their livelihoods over the long term. Brenda Jorgenson was reported to be the only protester present at the event. She kept quiet in spite of her concerns about fracking and the enormous Tioga oil spill in September 2013. She wrote in an email to *New York Times* staff, "I'm not that brave (or stupid) to protest among that ... I've said it before: we're outgunned, outnumbered and out-suited" (quoted in Sontag 2014). Here, Jorgenson reveals her lack of agency. Although she would like to challenge the dramatic rate of oil development, she is uneasy about publicly expressing her minority position.

The fact that Jorgenson did not feel comfortable speaking publicly about her concerns over the dramatic oil development in North Dakota relates both to local cultural sensibilities[5] and to the political economy of oil development. Community outreach initiatives sponsored by the oil industry and local officials remind us that it is never just about jobs and money, but about fostering sustainable social relationships, so that (ideally) no one is disenfranchised. First, for established residents and newbie oil workers to happily coexist, social interaction is critical. Many oil field workers find themselves living in man camps or hotels that are cordoned

---

[4] One of the reviewers of this manuscript suggested that this was a gross exaggeration reported in the press that was as much as ten times the number of people in attendance; I have been unable to locate any sources to confirm this rate.

[5] For example, "North Dakota nice" is a named phenomenon that relates to the tendency of North Dakotans to maintain friendly relations and avoid conflict when interacting face-to-face. In some cases, individuals may have strong disagreements with one another, but those may be aired to a third party, rather than directly opposing someone.

off spatially from local residents. In light of this, some workers may crave opportunities to get to know the local residents. Second, for permanent residents of the oil patch, a safe space needs to be created so that they may voice their concerns about fracking, waste disposal, and long-term health and environmental consequences of oil extraction without being labeled "outsiders" by the governor and other powerful state officials (Sontag 2014). Whenever the industry and state government have aligned interests and there is a lack of opportunity for serious democratic debate—as appears to be the case in North Dakota—we should be deeply concerned and try to create conditions that promote increasing agency for diverse individuals.

Boomtown Tropes and Long-term Hopes

Some of the people my students and I have interviewed about their experiences living in the Bakken have referred to it as "the Wild West," and this representation of life in the oil patch is in turn reinforced by media portrayals and internalized by everyday people. For example, in her online memoir about working as a stripper in Williston, Susan Elizabeth Shepard argues that the current oil boom in North Dakota and demand for strip clubs and sex follows a much longer pattern of resource extraction coupled with an informal economy of sex workers:

> California in 1849, Colorado in 1859, Montana in 1883, Texas and Oklahoma in 1912, Alaska in 1970, North Dakota in 2008—every time there's a mining boom, it plays out thusly: Someone finds a valuable resource. People hear about it and flock to the area. These people are mainly men. The newly populated area is lawless and lacks the civilizing influence of family life. Among the first women to show up are prostitutes. For a while, everyone makes money and has fun. Or some people do, some gambles pay off. Then the resource dries up or its price drops, and the gamble isn't profitable anymore, and the town eventually dries up or turns into a tourist attraction. (Sheppard 2013)

This master narrative is precisely what permanent residents of North Dakota's boomtowns are concerned about: (1) that outsiders bring crime and an unseemly way of life to their small town and (2) that once the oil boom goes bust, people will move on to greener—or oilier—pastures without any concern for the communities that are left behind.

In spite of these representations, plenty of the people who have migrated to North Dakota's oil patch in recent years do not fit this image.

Julie is a forty-two-year-old from Missoula, Montana, who followed her oil worker husband to Parshall after waiting sixteen months for affordable housing. She told me that back in Montana she was working two to three jobs, her husband was working two jobs, and they could barely make ends meet. They joke that their motto is, "If it wasn't for the Bakken, we'd be walkin'." Julie has always wanted to live in a small town because of the sense of community that residents often share; she plans to stay in Parshall permanently but says that she has had to make some adjustments. She explained that she has become used to ordering products online because there are not many nearby options for shopping. Alluding to the limited housing available in Parshall's RV Park—used by oil workers and their families—Julie suggested that most of the oil field wives cannot cope with living in a small, cramped trailer in the winter, with nowhere to shop and nothing to do for recreation.

This idea is supported in some of the scholarly literature about construction worker wives who follow their husbands working in energy boomtowns. For example, in her study of Western Colorado coal mining towns, Elizabeth Moen (1981, 104) explains, "by living in mobile homes these women are deprived of many of the activities of the traditional homemakers, especially the more creative outlets such as gardening, remodeling, decorating, and entertaining. Consequently they … are subject to depression and more severe mental illness." Since the 1970s, scholarly research has firmly established the social disruption model (also known as the "Gillette Syndrome" [Kohrs 1974] after Gillette, Wyoming, where the phenomenon was first documented) as a pattern experienced by many U.S. communities brought about by large-scale resource extraction and resulting in higher rates of crime and mental illness, higher costs of living, weakened social ties within a community, inadequate housing and recreational facilities for newcomers combined with anxiety, loneliness, and extreme work-related stress, leading to high rates of divorce, depression, alcoholism, and physical abuse (Kohrs 1974; Smith et al. 2001; Walsh and Simonelli 1986). The assumption here is that whenever resources are extracted within boom contexts (sometimes involving the large-scale relocation of people) for fueling energy, social ills will inevitably follow. While some of the broad structural patterns associated with the Gillette Syndrome (Kohrs 1974) may appear to be found any time there is an energy boom, we need to be somewhat cautious in assuming that whenever resource extraction promotes boomtown growth, the inevitable result is community disintegration. On the contrary, Rolston (2013; 2014) has argued that men and women coal workers in Wyoming's Powder River Basin have relied on kinship networks, joking relationships, and camaraderie to sustain their families and communities over multiple generations.

Such recent ethnographically-informed scholarship suggests that the social disruption model is too monolithic and causal in explaining the diversity of experiences (both positive and negative) faced by boomtown residents. Of course, one should also ask the extent to which coal, gas, and oil industries impact communities in similar ways in order to understand the potential for generalizable models.

Unlike many of the oil field families who have no other option than to live in a trailer and must negotiate a spouse's long working hours, Julie and her husband tapped into their social networks to find an affordable rental house in Parshall, and they actually get to spend *more* time together than they used to in Montana often going fishing together at nearby Lake Sakakawea. Further, Julie has made an effort at getting to know the locals. She used to work at the post office and now works at the public library and the bar just across the street from it that is frequented by long-term residents. When I observed how she interacted with locals at the library, it was obvious to me that many Parshall residents recalled her friendly face but not necessarily her name when they saw her. Julie told me she is attracted to Parshall and has already bonded with the people there. However, she noted that the locals kept their distance from her initially. Julie had a few pieces of advice for anyone intending to move to a small town in the oil patch:

> Don't come into the community and expect to be accepted right away. You have to earn your place. Even though everybody had heard of me and everything else, I wasn't just accepted with open arms. I had to learn to make friends and learn that not everybody thinks like you do and that's okay. Be open-minded. It's just a different way of life and you have to—if you can't embrace and accept the changes, then you shouldn't come here. There's the weather, the people, the shopping, everything. It's like, be prepared ... Be open minded, be prepared ... I wouldn't trade it for the world, though.

Julie's actions and words bear witness to her commitment to socially integrate herself into the community of Parshall. Certainly, not all newcomers will share her interest and enthusiasm, but the potential is there for shifting from an outsider to an insider in repositioning one's relationship to a community.

64

Conclusion

Parshall residents are concerned about their small town way of life being threatened by economic and environmental changes brought about by the rapid pace of oil development and outsiders who are drawn to the region for oil related jobs. Earlier scholarship on the social impacts of energy booms found that migrant workers were often perceived by locals to be "irresponsible people who do not share the local values for roots and a home" (Moen 1981, 103). Not surprisingly, transplanted workers resented how local residents often prejudged them before getting to know them. Even bumper stickers like "Oil Field Trash and Proud of It" seemed to reinforce the "us/them" dichotomy between oil field workers and local residents (Walsh and Simonelli 1986, 51n6).

Contemporary news reports from North Dakota's oil patch reflect these same boomtown tropes. New economic migrants are reportedly called "oilfield trash," and those from places like Texas or the South who speak a different dialect feel that they are sometimes overcharged and treated with contempt by long-term residents (Layne 2013). A newcomer from Montana told a pastor at a Banquet West supper, "I bet you wish we'd all go away, don't you?" (Frykholm 2013) Social ills including increased traffic fatalities, drug and alcohol abuse, domestic violence, sexual assault, abduction, and murder have been associated with the "growing pains" of American towns that support the fracking industry (Hotaling 2013). The mayor of Dickinson, ND, has attributed the 300 percent increase in assault and sex crimes from 2011–12 to the oil boom (Jerving 2012). Many small towns in North Dakota's Bakken region are experiencing a sense of fear of outsiders fueled by the rapid changes that go hand-in-hand with resource extraction.

While some of this fear of outsiders was evident in my interviews with Parshall's long-term residents, several individuals reported that oil workers were just ordinary people trying to make a decent living and send money back to family members. Those who had taken the time to get to know some of the oil workers shared positive comments about them. Elderly Parshall residents expressed concern that their community was in danger of becoming a ghost town before the most recent oil boom hit. Before 2008, young people were moving away for educational or employment opportunities. In addition, the local nursing home had closed prompting some older residents to move to Minot or other cities that could provide assisted living services. Now, instead of worrying about the possible death of their town, Parshall residents are excited about the possibilities in attracting new, hopefully longer-term residents. People like Julie are interested in making Parshall their lasting home. They have recognized that in order to make it work, they will have to "earn their place" and make an effort to fit in with the local way of doing things.

However, the local way of doing things is also affected by the larger structure of the oil industry and the extent to which individuals may access valued economic resources. As alluded to above, this means that boomtown economies can add a new layer to the palimpsest of what it means to be an insider or an outsider: those with high-paying oil jobs or mineral rights generating significant wealth become the insiders, and those without these resources who must carry on in a climate of inflated living costs become the outsiders. Interviews with Parshall residents revealed that some local families have been torn apart according to which individuals are receiving checks from the oil industry and which individuals have no mineral rights. This kind of economic dichotomy may be masked by the larger discourse evident in (inter-)national media outlets touting the virtues of energy independence and state-based campaigns to attract workers to the land of opportunity, where they are to be welcomed as insiders and perhaps even extended family (recall that the North Dakota initiative specifically targets individuals with ties to the state, people with families, and former military personnel).

What is "good and desirable" for North Dakota and the United States as promoted by news reports and politicians tends to drown out community-level concerns about the long-term sustainability of boomtown economies and the level of agency individuals have in living their own lives. When we think about the concept of agency, it is important to think not only of one's ability to earn a decent living. One's ability to maintain a reasonable quality of life involves more than this. Being able to pay for food and shelter is important, but so are other considerations: the ability to openly express even politically unpopular views without being called names like "outsider"; the ability to live in a place without fear or threat of physical or emotional violence; and the ability to have healthy and productive social relationships allowing for full participation in a given community. It is these latter considerations that seem to get less attention yet are at the core of what long-term residents and newcomers to North Dakota's oil patch value in building a sense of community together.

66

References

Ahearn, Laura M. 2001. "Language and Agency." *Annual Review of Anthropology* 30: 109–37.
Brooks, Jennifer. 2015. "Hard Times Could Be Ahead for North Dakota's Oil Boom Towns." *Star Tribune*. Accessed April 17, 2015. www.startribune.com/lifestyle/health/287422241.html.
Bureau of Labor Statistics. 2014a. "Unemployment Rate." Accessed June 24, 2014. data.bls.gov/timeseries/LNS14000000.
Bureau of Labor Statistics. 2014b. "Unemployment Rates for States (May 2014)." Accessed June 24, 2014. www.bls.gov/web/laus/laumstrk.htm.
Dalrymple, Amy. 2014a. "Documentary about Williston Newcomers Debuts at Sundance." *Bakken Today*, January 17. Accessed June 24, 2014. www.bakkentoday.com/event/article/id/36045/.
Dalrymple, Amy. 2014b. "Oil Industry Says Thanks to North Dakota, Celebrates Million-barrel Milestone." *Oil Patch Dispatch*, June 25. Accessed June 28, 2014. oilpatchdispatch.areavoices.com/2014/06/25/oil-industry-says-thanks-to-north-dakota-celebrates-million-barrel-milestone/.
Denver, John, and Mike Taylor. 1972. "John Denver Lyrics: Rocky Mountain High." Accessed June 24, 2014. www.azlyrics.com/lyrics/johndenver/rockymountainhigh.html.
Frykholm, Amy. 2013. "Racked by Fracking: Ministry Challenges in the Oil Boom." *The Christian Century*, June 12. Accessed June 24, 2014. www.christiancentury.org/article/2013-06/racked-fracking.
Gahagan, Kayla. 2014. "Oil Boom Jars Small-Town North Dakota." *Al Jazeera America*, May 3. Accessed June 16, 2014. america.aljazeera.com/articles/2014/5/3/oil-boom-changingthelandscapeofsmalltown-northdakota.html.
Hotaling, Angela L. 2013. "The Moral Layers of Fracking: From Basic Rights and Obligations to Human Flourishing." Master's thesis, University of Montana.
Jerving, Sara. 2012. "The Fracking Frenzy's Impact on Women." *PR Watch*, April 4. Accessed October 2, 2013. www.prwatch.org/news/2012/04/11204/fracking-frenzys-impact-women.
Kohrs, El Dean. 1974. "Social Consequences of Boom Growth in Wyoming." Paper presented at the Annual Meeting of the Rocky

Mountain American Association for the Advancement of Science, Laramie, Wyoming.

Layne, Ken. 2013. "Oilfield Trash and a Boom that Won't Last." *Gawker*, October 8. Accessed June 16, 2014. gawker.com/ oilfield-trash-and-a-boom-that-wont-last-1442085599.

McChesney, John. 2011. "Oil Boom Puts Strain on North Dakota Towns." *NPR*, December 2. Accessed June 16, 2014. www.npr.org/2011/12/02/142695152/ oil-boom-puts-strain-on-north-dakota-towns.

McChesney, John, dir. 2012. *An Unquiet Landscape: The American West's New Energy Frontier*. Accessed June 16, 2014. web.stanford.edu/ group/ruralwest/cgi-bin/projects/energyvideo/.

Michael, Jenny. 2013. "Crime up 7.9 Percent Last Year in North Dakota." *Bismarck Tribune*, July 30. Accessed March 25, 2015. bismarcktribune.com/bakken/crime-up-percent-last-year-in-north-dakota/article_f0a23ec4-f940-11e2-ad25-0019bb2963f4.html.

Moen, Elizabeth. 1981. "Women in Energy Boom Towns." *Psychology of Women Quarterly* 6, no. 1: 99–112.

North Dakota Attorney General. 2015. "Crime Homicide Reports." Accessed April 17, 2015. www.ag.nd.gov/Reports/BCIReports/ CrimeHomicide/CrimeHomicide.htm.

North Dakota Labor Market Information Center. 2014. "North Dakota's Oil and Gas Economy." Accessed June 24, 2014. www. ndworkforceintelligence.com/analyzer/default.asp.

North Dakota State Government. 2014. "Find the Good Life in North Dakota." Accessed June 16, 2014. findthegoodlifeinnorthdakota. com/.

Nowatski, Mike. 2014. "North Dakota Violent Crime, Drug Arrests Up in 2013; Attorney General to Request More Resources for Western ND." *WDAY News*. Accessed March 24, 2015. www.wday.com/ content/north-dakota-violent-crime-drug-arrests-2013-attorney-general-request-more-resources-western.

Rolston, Jessica Smith. 2013. "Specters of Syndromes and the Everyday Lives of Wyoming Energy Workers." In *Cultures of Energy: Power, Practices, Technologies*, edited by Sarah Strauss, Stephanie Rupp, and Thomas Love, 213–26. Walnut Creek, CA: Left Coast Books.

Rolston, Jessica Smith. 2014. *Mining Coal and Undermining Gender: Rhythms of Work and Family in the American West*. New Brunswick, NJ: Rutgers University Press.

Scheuer, Steph. 2013. "Attorney General Releases Crime Statistics." *KX News*. Accessed March 25, 2015. www.kxnet.com/story/22970716/attorney-general-releases-nd-crime-statistics.

Scheyder, Ernest. 2015. "Apartment Rates in North Dakota Collapse as Oil Boom Goes Bust." *Reuters*. Accessed April 17, 2015. www.rawstory.com/rs/2015/03/apartment-rates-in-north-dakota-collapse-as-oil-boom-goes-bust/.

Sheppard, Susan Elizabeth. 2013. "Wildcatting: A Stripper's Guide to the Modern American Boomtown." *BuzzFeed BuzzReads*, July 25. Accessed September 24, 2013. www.buzzfeed.com/susanelizabethshepard/wildcatting-a-strippers-guide-to-the-modern-american-boomtow.

Smith, Michael D., Richard S. Krannich, and Lori M. Hunter. 2001. "Growth, Decline, Stability, and Disruption: A Longitudinal Analysis of Social Well-Being in Four Western Rural Communities." *Rural Sociology* 66, no. 3: 425–50.

Sontag, Deborah. 2014. "Where Oil and Politics Mix." *New York Times*. Accessed April 17, 2015. www.nytimes.com/interactive/2014/11/24/us/north-dakota-oil-boom-politics.html.

SunDance Foundation. 2013. "Bakken Oil Fields." Accessed June 16, 2014. sundancefoundation.org/bakken,.

Walsh, Anna C., and Jeanne Simonelli. 1986. "Migrant Women in the Oil Field: The Functions of Social Networks." *Human Organization* 45, no. 1: 43–52.

PART 2

HISTORY
AND THE
BOOM

Chapter 4

Booms and Busts: Haunting Memories in the North Dakota Oil Boom

Joshua E. Young

North Dakota is one of the few states that has avoided devastating budget cuts under the economic downturn as oil companies tap into the Bakken formation with new fracking technologies to produce more than 113 million barrels of crude oil and huge increases in revenues and to provide the state with record-setting budget surpluses. However, North Dakota has experienced previous oil booms, each promptly followed by a bust, all of which haunt long-time community members with the debts of earlier investments.

The current boom has helped North Dakota maintain an unemployment rate of less than 3 percent and has contributed to a more than 3 percent growth each year in population (Seman 2013). Despite the increase in oil production and the economic position of the state, officials say there is still not enough human capital available within the state. In 2014, North Dakota embarked on an $800,000 campaign to attract more workers to the state, citing 25,000 positions that go unfilled (Macpherson 2014). However, drastic increases to state population create infrastructure needs that small towns of western North Dakota are not able to fulfill leaving the needs of residents and immigrants to the area unsatisfied. Along with these strains, increases in crime and bad debt coupled with stress on infrastructure and social services have created a loss of community within boomtowns. Residents and immigrants alike bemoan the loss of community and the trauma of actual as well as symbolic relocation. These traumatic losses haunt efforts of community members to perform as a public, as communal rhetorics recede in the presence of histories remembered and futures lost.

What is needed to find middle ground is some sort of understanding between longtime residents and newcomers. However, the memory of the boom-bust cycle edges out the position of compromise. Within this chapter, I wish to provide one understanding for those struggling to comprehend why more action has not been taken to invest in the community. Key to this is interrogating how memory works for community members. As stakeholders in local governance, these individuals hold power in political discourse and in the future of the community. Bringing together work by Kendall Phillips, Charles Scott, and Barbie Zelizer on the trope of synecdoche, where a part stands in for the whole, brings a more nuanced understanding of memory and how it is at work in the Bakken. I examine how the haunting of the Bakken bust memories is best considered through a subjunctive translation, a voice of contingent and compromising positions, of localized rural memories. Such a project articulates the role of memorial phantoms in the erasure of the middle voice, and considers the utterances that might have unraveled the threads of the polarizing discourses now paralyzing the community's efforts to forge a political path forward. To begin, I will first address the way memory is constituted within communities.

Memories and Remembering

Memories are inherently rhetorical devices that affect the contingencies in which communities find themselves forced to act in. Stakeholders must recognize that memories are constructed as they are recollected and distributed through discourse surrounding political and social action by themselves as well as outsiders. I do not wish to deny the physiological capacity to recall events but to emphasize the way that even this recalling is situated by the ability to constitute these conscious memories into useful public devices. What is chosen to be remembered by the community and the presentation of those memories can have a significant effect on the deliberative process and on the building of communities. Within the Bakken boom, this is especially true. In this section, I wish to address some of the basic components of memory and to provide a lens through which we might be able to read the historical and contemporary booms and busts.

First, it is essential to understand the situated nature of memory. Memories do not happen in a vacuum and when memories appear, they do so in particular places for particular reasons. Charles Scott (2004, 153) notes, "Appearing thus seems to happen with a peculiar memory; its occurrence recalls the mutability of everything that is manifest, as though appearing where a circle of temporality that wheels whatever appears by an axis of perishability, returning even the most persistent appearances to the reminders of non-appearing and the need for care." Scott's suggestion points to the fact that memories become circulated for consideration and consumption. They circulate in community cultures and are strategically chosen for appearance. "I hope to arrive at a point where we can hear the sense of saying that public memory happens in and as appearing, that public memory occurs as an appearing event" (Scott 2004, 149).

Furthermore, appearances are inherently tied to cultural locations. Community stakeholders build the cultures of locations and have power to veil and unveil certain memories. "In its broader usage, *culture* means, of course, development and transmission of practices, beliefs, and knowledges. The word also carries in its history the sense of *wheel*. It derives in part from the Greek word *kyklos* (circle, wheel)" (Scott 2009, 150). Memories are circulated within a particular group of people, making them publicly shared across time and groups of individuals. Furthermore, recurring memories that return and foreshadow similar results have a greater impact on public memory. Memories must be cared for and the more investment across cultures, the more time individuals will be more concerned about the circulation of memories. "For when we bring together culture and care, we arrive at the basic meaning that is found in the word *memory*, which connotes returning to something vital for people but something that is lost in its earlier and initiatory presence" (Scott 2009, 150).

Scott's later point brings attention to the fact that memories are themselves not real, but we tend to think of their impact as something that makes them surreal. What I mean is that the constitutive power of language in creating reality is more present in work that deals particularly with language than other kinds of work. Scott (2009, 148) says "public memory does something—acts—and one of these nouns [we, I, or memory] receives the action. And all the while the language in those statements is making 'us' and the meaning of 'public memory' public in a voice of activity that manifests a subject that is not the object of its action."

Memories, then, are constitutively conjoined fragments of circulated meanings of actual events experienced by individuals. These fragments are subsequently affected by misremembering as much as they are by remembering. "Collective or public memory is inherently nomadic because it encompasses a mnemonic landscape comprised not of stability but ongoing redistribution or, better still, *re*-membering" (Vivian 2004, 190). In fact, this act of remembering, according to Philips, is the most powerful component of memory for the early Greek rhetoricians who placed such an importance on memory. Contemporarily for us, the instability of memory serves as a way of coalescing public support around a constitutive memory of events and others opening a place for action. "While forgetting is conceived as a kind of occlusion or even erasure, the process of 'other-judging,' or here misremembering, constitutes an active process of making knowledge claims about the past that are in error" (Philips 2010, 212). Although we might read this as error, I would argue for others this becomes a way of opening a voice for memories and the promise of social action.

There are two distinct voices that I find particularly helpful for examination for our purposes. First, work has been done by Scott and Zelizer on the subjunctive or middle voice as a way of viewing possibility. Drawing upon styles of grammatical writing, Scott (2009, 154) claims, "Subjunctive phrasing indicates or betokens indeterminate contingency, possibility and mood." This suggests a way of theorizing the possibility of social action within acts of remembering, but also indicates that there might be a way of closing possibility as well.

Specifically, Barbie Zelizer has done work on the way that images indicate a way of thinking about what is going to happen or the prospect of action. Looking at the images of 9/11 jumpers, she points out that an intimate relationship is created between the viewer and the image giving a voice to the victims in the photos and to the spectator. "Taken together, voice is extended here to refer to the relationship developed between the spectator and the image—involving state of mind, attitude, temporal and sequential positioning—and to those aspects of the image that help the spectator develop the relationship" (Zelizer 2004, 162). Once this relationship is established, viewers find themselves writing the conclusions to the photos depending on their linguistic/cultural commitments to particular memories. Zelizer goes on to argue, "For the powerful presence of the subjunctive within our capacity to remember the past suggests that we often willingly engage in a kind of irrational game-playing with what we see projecting altered ends on the screens through which we see" (180). However, as suggested by Scott and Philips above, this is always contingent on the cultural commitments and circulations.

When memories are used to close off the possibility of symbolic action, middle voice or subjunctivity is closed off. This can lead to a lack of agency for actors who have high stakes in political deliberation. David Schulz and Mitchell Reyes detail the means by which as well as the consequences of shutting down a middle voice, Examining Ward Churchill's equivocation of Americans in general and victims of 9/11 specifically to the role Nazi Adolf Eichmann played in Nazi Germany, Schulz and Reyes point out that collective trauma triggers collective memory of former events. "This is especially true following collective trauma, after which societies often retreat to familiar and traditional modes of remembrance" (Schulz and Reyes 2008, 633). When Churchill drew on collective memory of the Holocaust to define the tragedy of 9/11, he triggered a particular memory of the gruesomeness and cruelty of genocide. By claiming that Americans deserved the terrorist attack, he afforded them no agency to avoid guilt associated with the troublesome foreign policy in which they were complicit. Without this agency, individuals closed all routes of engaging Churchill's or their own memories of the past and the constitutive meaning of 9/11. Ultimately, Churchill's comments led to the end of his career in academics and an inability to create possibility for symbolic action. This is because there was no possibility of agency. "Offering a sense of agency is especially important following trauma, for it allows individuals to move beyond the tragedy and into its commemoration" (Schulz and Reyes 2008, 647).

What has been outlined above is a framework for understanding memory as it has been theorized by researchers. In particular, it is important to note that memory is bound to the constitutive nature of language and that any set of memories does not necessarily go uncontested. The constitutive nature of memory also means that memory is destined to fall victim to the same issues associated with linguistic location and circulation. In other words, memories as cultural products that are passed around are marked by their flow and articulation to other cultural meanings with dominant discourse being circulated more readily. It is also important to note that memories, although subject to contestation based on real events, act upon those among whom they are passed and traded as much as those individuals act upon these memories. The constitutive nature of memory within circulations then opens up the inventional process of memory in the process of deliberation allowing individuals to use memories for political ends. It also results in the opening or closing of the possibility of symbolic action and democratic deliberation. To allow a better understanding of the consequences of memory, I will turn my attention to the implications of boom-bust culture in general before addressing North Dakota's oil history specifically.

The Boom-Bust Cycle in the United States

Boom-bust cycles have been studied extensively in academic scholarship. Experts point out some of the typical experiences of boom-bust towns that are similar to North Dakota's current situation. Some scholars note very particular differences, though. In this section, I wish to review that literature in hopes that it might add to our understanding of booms-busts in general and North Dakota specifically.

Research conducted by Smith, Krannich, and Hunter (2001) indicates that throughout the 1970s and 1980s regions of the United States experienced similar effects during oil booms. Gramling and Brabant (1986) helped to establish what has become known in the literature as the boomtown model and led to breakthroughs in other research during the height of American oil production. Specifically, Smith, Krannich, and Hunter (2001) highlight how economic expansion and demographic shifts led to strain on community member psychological well-being and community infrastructure. Scholarship from the 1980s booms showed that rapid growth was characterized by major social problems including crime and other community disruptions. However, years later in their longitudinal study of busts, Smith, Krannich, and Hunter found that a sense of social well-being did in fact return or that communities achieved higher levels of well-being compared to those prior to the booms. They state specifically, "For most indicators, the period of peak boom growth is associated with a significant decline in well-being among local residents … In short, the disruptive effects associated with boom growth apparently dissipate in the years after the boom phase has ended" (446).

Brown, Dorius, and Krannich (2005, 45) support this hypothesis noting in their research in the Utah Delta that communities often experience an "inverse association between community satisfaction and the occurrence of population growth." They note that although previous research has focused explicitly on population shifts as a site of disruption, these shifts cannot account for the significant social changes observed in their own study. Particularly interesting is their finding that long-time residents maintained the highest levels of community satisfaction as well suggesting that longterm residents in places like Williston and other towns in western North Dakota will find greater satisfaction in the long term because of the oil boom they are currently experiencing.

Early research points to the fact that individuals flooding oil booming communities have a dramatically negative effect on the social fabric of the communities they flock to. Later inquiry has brought that research into question, especially after busts. This is not to negate the fact that negative effects do come from rapid migration out of these communities; however, these effects are short-lived depending on the communities' motivation to overcome them. It is important to note, nevertheless, that much of this research has not been conducted in North Dakota, which offers a specific context that may change the meaning of the boom-bust cycle.

Oil Booms and Busts Past of North Dakota

Previous oil booms came as surprises to members of the communities in western North Dakota. The same can be said of the boom the state is experiencing now. Similarly, in the two previous booms, communities experienced many of the same infrastructure and social service issues faced in today's boom (Robinson 1966; Porter 2009). These memories linger and haunt the community members dealing with contemporary issues.

According to Robinson, the first oil boom began with the discovery of oil at the Clarence Iverson No. 1 drilling site on April 4, 1951. However, the process was some time coming. Robinson tracks the beginning of oil exploration to 1916 with unsuccessful attempts by Pioneer Oil and Gas Company, up until the 1930s with unsuccessful attempts by the Big Viking Oil Company (Robinson 1966, 458). It would be the Amerada Petroleum Corporation that would strike first oil in 1951 producing over three hundred barrels the first day of production.

> Discovery set off an exciting boom. Wildcat drilling mushroomed, and by the end of the year nearly two-thirds of the state was under lease. Crowds of strangers—oil operators and scouts, promoters, geologists, drillers, lease buyers and brokers, as well as unskilled labor—invaded the oil region. The newcomers turned granaries, sheds and garages into living and business quarters. They and their families jammed community services, crowded schools, wore out roads, and brought on a boom which meant dozens of new enterprises, ranging from lunch counters to oil-field equipment houses. (Robinson 1966, 459)

Success lasted nearly ten years, and towns like Tioga and Williston saw large increases in population. Oil flooded the North Dakota market becoming the third most important economic contributor. Porter notes, "During their first decade of production, 1951–1961, the western oil fields produced some 110,000,000 barrels of oil and with its accompanying natural gas, generated approximately $280,000,000 in revenue for investors … The drilling peak for North Dakota came in 1966 when 1,965 active wells produced 27,000,000 barrels of oil over the course of the year" (Porter 2009, 26). However, success was unevenly distributed across the patch. Robinson notes that in 1955, six out of fifty-eight attempts at new wells were prosperous. As production decreased over the years, jobs were eliminated, and individuals left the communities, leading to the first economic bust. Porter (2009, 36) notes, "Towns such as Tioga and Williston, which had once bustled with oil field activity and its ensuing calls upon housing, social services, schools, and the like, found themselves faced with an overbuilt infrastructures as the 1970s dawned."

Memories of the first oil boom have aged considerably as Liz Cantarine, a former resident of the area, notes. However, one thing seems apparent in the memories of the first oil boom. Those who flocked to North Dakota tended to stay despite the overbuilding. "While the first oil boom went on only a few years, many of those oilmen stayed and continued to build their families and fortunes and remained lifelong friends" (Cantarine 2012). Many of these individuals would shift their attention from oil to farming which would help sustain North Dakota through the bust.

Agriculture remained the top economic product of North Dakota through the first boom and helped to steer the state through the bust. Porter (2009, 36) notes, "If agriculture for the most part boomed in the early 1970s, the oil industry did not. Indeed, after an initial decade and a half oil rush, the international price of oil, as well as the expense of drilling for North Dakota's deeply seated basins, discouraged continued exploration and exploitation." However, many young people were disinclined to go into farming and would leave their communities for other opportunities. Population shifts from the oil busts and the implications of the bust, such as lack of employment opportunities, were exacerbated by a lack of enthusiasm for farming (Porter 2009).

International events surrounding OPEC's decision to cut oil sales to countries supporting Israel would lead to new incentives to drill domestically. Advances in technology and economic pay-offs would lead to a second boom. Between 20 and 25 million barrels a year were produced between 1972 and 1979. Only when production topped at 52.7 million barrels did the state begin to see a decline (Porter 2009). However, Porter notes, "Despite a lagging economy and declining prices for crude oil in much of the 1980s, production remained significant" (77). After 1985, wells began to dry up and oil became impossible to produce in a cost effective way in the Williston Basin. Again, large population centers began to find themselves with newly built infrastructure paid for on borrowed money. Diaspora would dramatically affect the revenues of communities in the oil patch. "As might have been anticipated, the largest drops in population, by county, came from the western portion of the state; the regions hardest hit by the drought and decline in oil prices" (Porter 2009, 85).

Faced once again with over-developed communities, cities like Tioga and Williston were forced to find ways to pay for investments (Porter 2009). Many ranchers and farmers would remain in the area, which helped to mitigate the effects of the bust. However, even after many oil companies left, oil and mineral exports remained important for North Dakota. "The energy industry remained a significant portion of North Dakota's economy during the latter 1990s, yet not at the level to which it rose in the latter 1980s. North Dakota ranked 9th among oil-producing states in terms of production, providing approximately two percent of the oil extracted in the United States" (Porter 2009, 102). Oil production would remain steady until summer 2005 when the third and most recent boom would hit the region.

Understanding the actual history behind the previous oil booms is essential for understanding how the memories that circulate within the current boom are understood. Furthermore, understanding them in light of North Dakota's history and boom-bust cycles in general ought to provide a nuanced reading of public texts. I now turn my attention to the current oil boom and the circulation of memories.

Ghosts in the New Boom of North Dakota

The current oil boom has forged opposing sides creating a dialectical tension between those who wish to be excessively conservative in their approach to the new boom and those who wish to be spectacularly liberal. In order to track down the voices of deliberation, I chose to analyze the *Williston Herald* searching for news and opinion pieces from 2009–14. According to Jackson Bolstad (2012), 90 percent of the oil drilling lies within seventy miles of the city of Williston. Williston has experienced major shifts from all three oil booms and is currently geographically and politically in the middle of the current oil play. Approximately 110 articles in the five-year period mention the word "boom" or "bust" specifically as related to the three oil booms. What are represented here are the most prominently circulated memories of the Bakken oil boom-busts from actual citizens of the area.

The contemporary boom is plagued by the same kinds of issues associated with population increases cited above in the boom-bust literature. Williston and surrounding communities have faced increased crime, lower quality service in the service industries, infrastructure problems in social services, and a myriad of other issues each informed by the busts that long-time community members have endured.

One theme that emerged from my research was the impact of crime. Ellis (2011a) reported that Williston Police went from having roughly 4,000 calls between 2007–09 to more than 1,000 calls in a single month. A comparison of 2012 and 2013 rates reveals that crime had risen 7.9 percent in North Dakota as a whole (and 41 percent in the region affected by the oil boom) (Burnes 2013b). Williston is searching for additional hires to the police force bringing total officers to thirty-eight for county services and forty-five for the city proper (Killelea and Burnes 2014). Citizens note the similarities to the previous oil booms; however, officials seem to downplay the impact. Williston chief-of-police Jim Lokken argues that "the inflating number of emergency calls, accidents and other issues resembles the situation in the last boom. 'We had the same thing then. It's just repeating itself on a larger scale'" (quoted in Ebersole 2013). However, community members are not confident in the ability of the city to deter crime on any level. "The boom has brought this change to our lives—whether it's a violent crime, a traffic accident, some other criminal activity or an environmental disaster, it's no longer 'if' something happens, it's 'when'" (Ventsch 2012).

Housing has become a major problem as well. Outside the region, reports come of man camps and people living in campers in the parking lots of Walmart (Ellis 2011b). The city has made efforts to spur housing development in the region, but have had mixed reception. Citizens are concerned about housing values short and long term, a similar problem faced in the previous boom. "For so many years, houses didn't have any appreciation in value, it was either a decline or they were steady, and now we've seen an increase in prices, which is something Williston hasn't seen since the early 1980s," according to Tate Cymbaluk of Basin Brokers Claims (Willey 2012). The region on a whole has seen housing appreciate 10–22 percent according to Cymbaluk (Willey 2012). Even where longtime residents were only renters, problems persist. Ebersole (2012b) documented one case where a family went from paying $350 prior to the boom and were evicted for not being able to pay the increased rent of $3,500 a month. Senior citizens have been hit especially hard as many property owners find it more lucrative to sell properties to oil companies for employee housing. This has led to increased rent across the region, and landlords justify price gouges by claiming the market is digesting the cost because of the high demand for housing (Burnes 2012).

Population increases have hit hospitals and schools the hardest. Hospitals in the area are plagued by bad debt from migrants to the area that lack insurance or other resources to pay for emergency services. According to Ebersole (2012c), "Bad debt at the hospital has doubled since before the boom four to five years ago to more than half a million dollars … the hospital sees 10–20 returned bills per week, with a post office that is overwhelmed and has no forwarding address on file for a former patient." With healthcare costs and wait times increasing due to population increases, the hospital fears that bad debt will soon affect non-emergency care as well (Ebersole 2012c). Stretching the already stressed resources of the education system in western North Dakota, schools have seen a dramatic increase as well. According to Superintendent of schools, Viola LaFontaine, Williston area schools are looking at an increase of 1,200 new students and are struggling to hire fifty-two new teachers (Mathews 2012). Furthermore, following budget issues created in part by the 1980s boom led to the closing of one school leaving the property in disrepair. To accommodate the influx of students, the school is now under renovation, but funding continues to be tight, and the district has turned to individuals and businesses to sponsor classrooms.

Service industries are currently struggling to provide quality experiences as well because of the boom. One reason is that service jobs pay significantly less than oil industry jobs and employee shortages in the service industry leaves employers limited in their resources. One anonymous community member noted that this also might be because long-time companies struggled in the past and even new companies understand what happened before. "The reality is probably more to the effect that the service industry does not buy into the longterm future of the region. They know the past as well, and just like the locals who are pessimistic about the lasting power, big business has reason to be too" ("Potential Signs" 2011).

The strains associated with the current boom create a traumatic event for longtime community members. Many articles noted that citizens felt that they had lost their home. "Most of us longtime Dakotans kind of liked what we had before this extreme 'boom,' namely the blue sky, good roads with light traffic, an agriculturally driven economy along with modest oil activity, relative safety from the afflictions of the rest of America, and the reasonable expectation that our rural, western innocence was a good thing" (Heiser 2012). Those that have lost all hope are simply moving to eastern North Dakota or even out of the state. "There is another reason people are leaving, one not mentioned. The core of our towns is being lost because locals simply don't want to live here anymore. They are leaving because the home they knew and loved is no more. They are leaving because they have lost their cherished lifestyle, their peace of mind, their safety—they have lost their western North Dakota" (Ventsch 2012). According to one survey (Rundquist et al. 2012), two-thirds of western North Dakotans hate the boom for what it has done to their communities and 60 percent of those who have lived in the area for more than six years say they are better off financially but only 17 percent claim their quality of life has improved.

This loss of home and agency to do anything about it is exacerbated by memories of loss associated with the most recent bust. Jerry Burnes (2013a) notes how service industries and housing were amongst the most visible indications of the previous bust and indicate an understanding of citizens' uneasiness. "During the last oil boom, Williston grew and grew, and so did hotels, apartments, businesses and prices. When the bottom fell out, the housing market tipped over, buildings were abandoned and the economy went back to being driven by agriculture—like it used to be" (Burnes 2013a). Furthermore, even suggestions to address housing issues are haunted by memories of the 1980s. "The temporary housing projects may be required to put up a bond against removal if they are ever abandoned, as I've heard was often the case during the 1980s boom and bust" (Mayhugh 2010). Kyle Mayhugh does not note the negative impact of the previous bust, but citizens are exposed to the memory of the previous busts as a warrant for current housing bonds. These memories serve as a warrant for rejecting development.

Even city officials legitimate the haunting memories of community members. Williston Mayor Ward Koeser stated that "in the 1980s the city put in millions of dollars' worth of infrastructure. When the oil went bust, the developers walked, leaving the city with a crippling level of debt" (Smith 2011). The bust of the 1980s left the city with $28 million in bad debt, forcing the city to allocate 75 percent of property taxes to pay off the debt and 25 percent to economic development (Ebersole 2012a). Koeser notes the ease in which many walked away from the bust. "You would hear comments that this is here forever, and it literally went away overnight. The boom was wonderful, the bust was terrible and you literally hang on from your fingernails to survive," said Koeser (quoted in Burnes 2013a). Koeser also reminded individuals of the problem of community pride during the previous boom further indicating the community's unwillingness to travel down the bust road again (Macphereson 2012).

Nearly all of the negative effects of the current boom are shaped by the busts of the pasts, but not all views are negative. Many have noted the difference between the previous cycles and note the importance of changing one's perspective. Although many articles admitted the infrastructural and service industry ailment, they argued that the alternative would be seen as worse.

First, as mayor, Koeser was seen as attempting to keep community investment going forward by drawing distinctions between the cycles of boom-bust Williston had previously experienced. "Booms go up fast, busts go down even faster. Is it different now? Yes and no. We have no guarantees," Koeser said adding that the Bakken production is more than five times greater than the previous boom (Burnes 2013a). Another distinction drawn is the relative ease at which oil companies are finding oil. "The biggest issue that oil companies faced in the 1980s was failure to strike oil. Now oil is hit more than 99 percent of the time and dry holes are a thing of the past. Thirty years ago, the companies would drill until finding a pool of oil, then begin to drill around the pool but would still find five to six dry wells in the process" (Burnes 2013a). In an attempt to quell disagreement from community members, Koeser has drawn distinctions and has claimed that Williston is in new territory. He also says that once stability is reached the city can better plan and prepare for market collapse (Burnes 2013a). It was thought that oil production had reached its peak (signaling stabilization) in 2009 (Davies 2009), but Koeser thinks it was late in 2012 (Burnes 2013a).

Second, and probably most important in creating a middle voice, community members and new-comers alike have turned to the newspaper to voice open-mindedness about the challenges and opportunities presented by the boom. Many note the opportunity that North Dakota has compared to many economically deprived areas around the country. These opportunities mostly take the form of jobs and economic development. "The boom has created tremendous challenges for many people, longtime locals and newcomers alike. However, it has also created fantastic opportunities for our community and entire state. Williston will be bigger and have more restaurants, retail and recreation venues when it is all said and done. We are not out of the woods, yet, but eventually we will step out" (Brooks 2012). Even those who are looking to step out of the "woods" claim that even more important is to focus on the fact that new residents are likely to stay as compared to previous boom workers. "The many new people coming to town with their families will be part of the next generation of North Dakotans. They will pay taxes, shop in our stores, and invest time and money in the future of our community. They have new energy and new ideas. They have a right and responsibility to use those ideas to try to make this community better" (Yockim 2010). There are others, though, that even if they are attempting to provide a space for a voice of reason seem accusatory in their tone. "How do we use this information? We are going to have the best economy in the country for years to come. This will bring many new people to town. Let's welcome them and work together to make our community better ... Be part of the solution, not part of the problem" (Taylor 2010). However, many are calling for a practical application of open-mindedness. Long-time resident Phyllis Larson reminded people, "We've got to have respect for these people. They want to fit in with us. You have to open your arms" (Ebersole 2013).

One article noted that when one approaches the individuals who have been perceived as the causes of the problems, images of community members and the community in general become more positive as well. This is especially beneficial when wives of oil workers speak positively about the community, as they are likely to have a major stake in staying in the Williston area. "It was comforting hearing them [oil workers' wives] agree that Williston has generally become a safer community. Of course, you must always be aware of your surroundings—this fact is most noted by people from larger cities—but in general, the women felt safe going on their own to grocery stores, restaurants, and other establishments" (Killelea 2014).

Although these attempts to provide a middle voice are made, they are significantly fewer in number. Nearly two-thirds of the articles pulled up by searches about the boom focused especially on the negative aspects. Furthermore, even when more positive stories advocated for a middle or progressive stance, they included similarities between the previous boom and the new boom and the practical difficulties faced on a daily basis. Here is where we find the erasure of the middle voice and a lack of advancement of contingent positions for community members and new comers. However, I think there is hope for providing an alternative view, but only if we begin to recognize the limiting capabilities of current public memories.

Exorcising Demons to Exercise Deliberation

It should be clear that although there are real problems associated with the influx of new individuals to the Bakken and the city of Williston, immigration to the area is not as big a problem as the memories of previous booms that haunt those within the community. Too much of a focus on the previous busts has erased the voice of those who are optimistic about the future of Williston and about the oil boom. One way to explain this phenomenon and to address the future contingencies is through theories of public memory. In addressing the memories, through this scholarship, it is my hope that we can begin to exorcise the haunting demons from the discourse of the community in order to enable all stakeholders in the community to exercise better deliberative practices. This can be done by concentrating on two key items.

First, rhetorical construction of public memory is vital to understanding the contemporary situation people of Williston specifically and the Bakken generally find themselves in. Individuals continue to speak of the current boom in light of the previous busts creating an explicit link and hindering the potential benefits the current boom might be seen as having. As indicated above, many find the economic benefit as positive, but those who have found the inconveniences and disturbances of the influx have drowned out the more centrist view. This is due to the loss of community and identity to many of the long-time residents.

This loss of community and identity has created a desperate situation for community members as they lose what they see as the very essence of what it means to be from rural North Dakota. Even those who had lived through the previous boom had noted that these changes in community and identity were at the cost of a considerable amount of blood and sweat equity paid by those who had continued to live in the area after the busts. As Schulz and Reyes (2008) point out, loss of agency to affect the loss of community leaves stakeholders in an even more marginalized position. This loss of agency is precisely the result of the constructed nature of memory indicated by the literature previously discussed, because these memories form the relationships between historical and contemporary circumstances and stakeholders (Halbwachs 1992).

If constructions of memory were to change, the contemporary stakeholders could change the discourse to better enact civility and deliberation. A concerted effort must be made to draw distinctions between the busts and the booms of past. As I pointed out above, Porter (2009) and Robinson (1966) outline that there were major improvements to the area due to the booms of the past. Increasing economic influence for western North Dakota within state and regional politics allowed communities within the Bakken to better position themselves within the peripheral model North Dakota operates in. Focusing on the positive memories and effects of the previous booms will reconstruct the public memories and alleviate the shutting down of middle voices. A more effective effort must also be made to show that the boom of today is structurally different than previous booms. As indicated above, the current boom is much more successful at finding and securing oil in much larger numbers than the previous cycle. This does not indicate that a bust will be circumvented, but it could indicate the longterm investments that oil stakeholders might be willing to make in the communities where they work. Furthermore, it ought to indicate the even more important role communities will play in the success of oil workers and their families' lives when compared to previous cycles. Constructing memories of the oil booms and busts of the past will reconstruct culture in the area to better facilitate deliberation and decision making for the communities in the Bakken.

Second, reconstructing memories ought to lead to an increased perception of agency for all stakeholders and better facilitate the expansion of middle voice. By providing a discourse that focuses specifically on the positive contingencies of the boom allows stakeholders on all sides to focus more on resource allocation with an eye on the positive effects of the future. This is no easy task, but ought to be the goal of all. Negative consequences will continue to be on the minds of many, but acknowledging the negatives without overemphasizing them will better enable the positives to become more apparent and better able to saturate the public memory discourse. This must be done primarily so that positive discourse or more middle voices can be heard. However, it has the added feature of acknowledging the collective knowledge of long-time community members without stripping them of symbolic agency to dictate the discourse about their home.

Shifting memory will not be an easy task. Culture is bound up in webs of signification. Given the high stakes of identity and community, maybe these webs have been wound more tightly than political issues plaguing the community. Furthermore, those who have immigrated to the area are in a very desperate position as well. In many instances, these individuals have nothing but what they brought with them to the Bakken and are in a frantic subject position attempting to legitimate their worth to community members while trying to meet basic survival needs and improve their quality of life. Those who are advocating the middle voice have acknowledged the difficulty, and in order to better facilitate the middle voice more must recognize the difficulty faced on both sides. "But no amount of planning will change the fact that Williston is divided into a number of factions right now … Balancing those interests is no easy task" (Mayhugh 2010). One way to do this might be acknowledging the humanity of all stakeholders. If we can better acknowledge the human worth of individuals rejecting demonic construction of the boom, we might drive out the phantoms that haunt the Bakken and create the rhetorical situation ripe for middle voice.

References

Bolstad, Jackson. 2012. "Surviving the Boom: Williston Front and Center at Oil Show." *Williston Herald*, May 23. www.willistonherald.com/news/surviving-the-boom-williston-front-and-center-at-oil-show/article_20d6a904-a4f1-11e1-ac5a-001a4bcf887a.html.
Brooks, Jacob. 2012. "A Tale of 2 Winters … and a View After the Boom." *Williston Herald*, February 25. www.willistonherald.com/opinion/columnists/a-tale-of-winters-and-a-view-after-the-boom/article_f2eb6516-6003-11e1-a207-0019bb2963f4.html.
Brown, Ralph B., Shawn F. Dorius, and Richard S. Krannich. 2005 "The Boom-Bust-Recovery Cycle: Dynamics of Change in Community Satisfaction and Social Integration in Delta, Utah." *Rural Sociology* 7, no. 1: 28–49.
Burnes, Jerry. 2012. "Oil Boom Leaves some Senior Citizens Behind." *Williston Herald*, November 8. www.willistonherald.com/news/oil-boom-leaves-some-senior-citizens-behind/article_a9569786-29d4-11e2-b56f-0019bb2963f4.html.
Burnes, Jerry. 2013a. "Could the Boom be Over?" *Williston Herald*, July 25. www.willistonherald.com/news/could-the-boom-be-over/article_

c4dcadfc-f53e-11e2-9364-0019bb2963f4.html.

Burnes, Jerry. 2013b. "N.D. Crime Rate Rises 7.9 Percent." *Williston Herald*, July 31. www.willistonherald.com/news/n-d-crime-rate-rises-percent/article_74bde204-f9f9-11e2-8f4d-001a4bcf887a.html.

Cantarine, Liz. 2012. "Reflecting Back on the First Williston Oil Boom." *Williston Herald*, June 21. www.willistonherald.com/opinion/letters_to_editor/reflecting-back-on-the-first-williston-oil-boom/article_d85847dc-bbc0-11e1-87d1-001a4bcf887a.html.

Davies, Phil. 2009. "After the Oil Rush: In the Williston Basin, Less Drilling Activity has Created Uncertainty About the Future." *FedGazette* 21, no. 5. www.minneapolisfed.org/research/pub_display.cfm?id=4271.

Ebersole, Jenna. 2012a. "Sales Taxes Have Also Boomed." *Williston Herald*, November 3. www.willistonherald.com/news/sales-taxes-have-also-boomed/article_1129c4aa-2601-11e2-8473-0019bb2963f4.html.

Ebersole, Jenna. 2012b. "In the Boom, Many are Left Homeless." *Williston Herald*, November 9. www.willistonherald.com/news/in-the-boom-many-are-left-homeless/article_3a880ade-2a87-11e2-b206-001a4bcf887a.html.

Ebersole, Jenna. 2012c. "Hospitals Facing Possible Crisis Due to Bad Debt." *Williston Herald*, November 30. www.willistonherald.com/news/hospitals-facing-possible-crisis-due-to-bad-debt/article_3105157e-3b08-11e2-beba-001a4bcf887a.html.

Ebersole, Jenna. 2013. "Police Release Annual Report to City." *Williston Herald*, March 2. www.willistonherald.com/news/police-release-annual-report-to-city/article_169a722e-8397-11e2-9434-001a4bcf887a.html.

Ellis, Blake. 2011a. "Crime Turns Oil Boomtown into Wild West." *CNN Money*, October 26. money.cnn.com/2011/10/26/pf/America_boomtown_crime/.

Ellis, Blake. 2011b. "Six-Figure Salaries, but Homeless." *CNN*, October 26. money.cnn.com/2011/10/21/pf/america_boomtown_housing/.

Grambling, Bob, and Sarah Brabant. 1986. "Boomtowns and Offshore Energy Impact Assessment: The Development of a Comprehensive Model." *Sociological Perspectives* 29, no. 2: 177–201.

Halbwachs, Maurice. 1992. *On Collective Memory*. Translated by Lewis A. Coser. Chicago: University of Chicago Press.

Heiser, John A. 2012. "Fed Up with the Oil Boom Way of Life." *Williston Herald*, January 24. www.willistonherald.com/opinion/letters_to_editor/fed-up-with-the-oil-boom-way-of-life/article_1ebafffc-46ab-11e1-94b4-0019bb2963f4.html.

Killelea, Eric. 2014. "Oilfield Wives a Different Side of the Boom." *Williston Herald*, January 23. www.willistonherald.com/opinion/columnists/oilfield-wives-a-different-side-of-the-boom/article_a436c1e4-8465-11e3-8265-0019bb2963f4.html.

Killelea, Eric, and Jerry Burnes. 2014. "Police Playing Catch-Up to Oil Patch Crime Increases. *Williston Herald*, February 15. www.willistonherald.com/news/police-playing-catch-up-to-oil-patch-crime-increases/article_76268ae2-9698-11e3-a282-001a4bcf887a.html.

Macpherson, James. 2014. "North Dakota, in Midst of Oil Boom, Woos Workers." *Portland Press Herald*, April 11. www.pressherald.com/business/North_Dakota__in_midst_of_oil_boom__woos_workers.html.

Mathews, Mark. 2012. "Populations Boom Impacting Schools." *Williston Herald*, June 23. www.willistonherald.com/news/population-boom-impacting-schools/article_a140548a-bd8a-11e1-91f4-001a4bcf887a.html.

Mayhugh, Kyle. 2010. "Struggling to Find a Balance as Bakken Gets Hotter." *Williston Herald*, April 13. www.willistonherald.com/opinion/struggling-to-find-a-balance-as-bakken-gets-hotter/article_7b2bfc03-71cb-512c-b35a-fc53c1377fca.html.

Phillips, Kendall R. 2010. "The Failure of Memory: Reflections on Rhetoric and Public Remembrance." *Western Journal of Communication* 74, no. 2: 208–23.

Porter, Kimberly. 2009. *North Dakota: 1960 to the Millennium*. Dubuque, IA: Kendall Hunt Publishing.

"Potential Signs a Boom Cannot Sustain Itself." 2011. *Williston Herald*, June 18. www.willistonherald.com/opinion/editorials/potential-signs-a-boom-cannot-sustain-itself/article_1104b217-dcf2-5edf-806e-0208386b4511.html.

Robinson, Elwyn B. 1966. *History of North Dakota*. Lincoln, NE: University of Nebraska Press.

Rundquist, Bradley C., Devon A. Hansen, Enru Wang, Stanely D. Brunn. 2012. "Perceptions of the Recent Oil Boom Among Long-

Term Residents of Williston, Stanley, and Watford City, North Dakota." University of North Dakota Geography Department. arts-sciences.und.edu/geography/_files/docs/oil_boom_survey_results. pdf.

Schulz, David P., and G. Mitchell Reyes. 2008. "Ward Churchill and the Politics of Public Memory." *Rhetoric and Public Affairs* 11, no. 4: 631–58.

Scott, Charles E. 2004. "The Appearance of Public Memory." In *Framing Public Memory*, edited by Kendall R. Phillips, 147–56. Tuscaloosa, AL: University of Alabama Press.

Seman, Sara Jean. 2013. "North Dakota Oil Fields Spur Employment and Population Growth." *Town Hall*, December 30. townhall.com/tipsheet/sarahjeanseman/2013/12/30/census-report-north-dakota-employment-and-population-grow-due-to-oil-fields-n1770016.

Smith, Michael D., Richard S. Krannich, and Lori M. Hunter. 2001. "Growth, Decline, Stability, and Disruption: A Longitudinal Analysis of Social Well-Being in Four Western Rural Communities." *Rural Sociology* 66, no. 3: 425–50.

Smith, Nick. 2011. "Oil Has Been Coming Out of North Dakota Since the 1950's But Are We On Track for Another Boom and Bust Cycle Like Previous Decades." *Williston Herald*, August 4. www.willistonherald.com/news/oil-has-been-coming-out-of-north-dakota-since-the/article_5845a9f9-ab7b-5e43-b865-f37d2d812acf.html.

Taylor, Doug. 2010. "When Will the Boom End?" *Williston Herald*, December 24. www.willistonherald.com/opinion/letters_to_editor/when-will-the-boom-end/article_a6315a19-4ade-56ee-b817-dc053955fc69.html.

Ventsch, Shelly. 2012. "It's Not a Matter Of If Something Happens, But When." *Williston Herald*, December 4. www.willistonherald.com/opinion/letters_to_editor/it-s-not-a-matter-of-if-something-happens-but/article_fee6a452-3e29-11e2-ad63-001a4bcf887a.html.

Vivian, Bradford. 2004. "'A Timeless Now': Memory and Repetition." In *Framing Public Memory*, edited by Kendall R. Phillips, 187-211. Tuscaloosa, AL: University of Alabama Press.

Willey, Payton. 2012. "Not All Changes Due to Oil Boom Have Been Positive." *Williston Herald*, November 6. www.willistonherald.com/news/not-all-changes-due-to-oil-boom-have-been-positive/

article_29d2c260-282f-11e2-9cbb-0019bb2963f4.html.

Yockim, Jim. 2010. "There was a Time When Strangers Were Welcome Here." *Williston Herald,* November 4. www.willistonherald.com/opinion/letters_to_editor/there-was-a-time-when-strangers-were-welcome-here/article_0c4e453a-da58-5c44-a27b-8515aa4448dd.html.

Zelizer, Barbie. 2004. "The Voice of the Visual in Memory." In *Framing Public Memory,* edited by Kendall R. Phillips, 157–86. Tuscaloosa, AL: University of Alabama Press.

CHAPTER 5

REVISITED FRONTIERS: THE BAKKEN, THE PLAINS,
POTENTIAL FUTURES, AND REAL PASTS

Sebastian Braun

*Thousands of emigrants, as our magazines have told us again and again,
are thronging annually to the great plains of the Northwest, where wheat-
farming has offered the home-seeker great financial opportunities. All
Americans rejoice that these thousands of home-seekers are able to establish
themselves financially. On the other hand, residents of the East, the South,
or the Pacific Coast, who love a pleasing diversity of hill and dale, grove and
meadow, lake and river, cannot but regret that millions of their fellows are
doomed to live on the monotonous Western plain, and to gaze daily on a view
which includes no hill, no valley, no grove of trees, no water, nothing but earth
and wheat.*

Wallace Craig (1908)

During the Bakken oil boom beginning in 2008, people from all over the
United States would once again flock to North Dakota, lured by economic possibilities. In this boom, however, images of monotonous doom
have had no place. In the curious historical frame of post-terror inse-
curities and anger, of rising, if reluctant, acknowledgment that climate
change has real consequences, of post-Iraq realizations that it might not
be possible to truly control oil abroad, and of living through an economic
depression that wiped away jobs (yet left wealth intact), messages about
the Bakken have been very clear. The oil boom, while a temporary in-
convenience, has helped North Dakota stay out of economic trouble, has
brought a population increase, has revitalized the state, and has put the
state on the map. North Dakota became the poster child for the American dream after having languished in national amnesia, or worse, as the
poster child for lonely abandonment, for decades. The message came
(and comes) from official and unofficial state channels, was (and is, although with more question marks) picked up by the media, as well as
by educational institutions. The Bakken is exciting, it is a chance to start

over, it is a new chapter for the state, and all of this is made possible by new technology: hydraulic fracturing and horizontal drilling. Here, I will not try to evaluate the claims made about economic, ecological, or social impact. I will not attempt to dissect and deconstruct political statements. I will not critique well counts, tax agreements, pipelines, flaring practices, or roads. All of these issues need to be addressed. However, in this text, I will simply put the Bakken into its context as a resource extraction boom. Booms—and busts, which people often forget in the excitement of a developing boom—are nothing new, and so, it would seem, a state undergoing a resource boom would be able to learn a lot from the experiences of past booms—and busts.

Resource booms are nothing new to North Dakota. In fact, the response of many communities in the Bakken region to the developing boom in its early years was guided by the experiences with the last oil boom, in the early 1980s, which ended in a bust very quickly. Not sure whether this new boom would last, experienced residents decided to adopt a wait-and-see attitude. Instead of risking investments into infrastructure that might lead to financial troubles again, perhaps the boom would blow over, and once the workers and their machines were gone, the communities could emerge more or less intact. This attitude, of course, shaped the response by the state, which placed considerable emphasis on the long-term nature of the boom (preferring not to speak of a boom, instead predicting that these developments would increase the population in communities three-fold, for the long term). Local challenges became regional opportunities, and this new boom was nothing like the earlier one. Hence, historical models would only be misleading. A new society was being built, with new technology, opening new opportunities. In fact, even if the events would not benefit the communities they were going to directly affect, they would at least provide security—energy security—to the rest of the nation. The potential futures projected onto graphs and into newspapers, onto whiteboards and screens, and most importantly into dreams and over frustrations, were millennial and sometimes bordering on the messianic.

The history of the United States, is, of course, permeated with the idea of building new societies, a shining city on the hill, the new Jerusalem—communities that would not be linked to historical precedent. Of this mythical American project, and the stories that accompany it, Ziauddin Sardar and Merryl Wyn Davies (2002, 207–8) have written that the "most hateful of all acts of 'knowledgable ignorance' is the failure to examine history and to acknowledge that deeds done to others in the name of virtue have actually done great harm." Working, teaching, and writing as an anthropologist in a department of American Indian Studies, and thus entering into dialogue with those kinds of deeds every day, I have to agree. The world is complex, history is complex, motivations for action are complex. Nobody asks that any action taken cannot hurt anybody. But the painting of a new canvas, no matter how grand, virtuous, or well-meaning, is never isolated from history, nor disconnected from people in communities.

Frontiers

The Bakken boom, far from being something terribly new, is in fact simply a revisitation of the "frontier" to the northern plains, a region that has seen different waves of frontier booms based on natural resource extraction for centuries. Thinking about frontiers in terms of settlement or demographics is to use the wrong category. In a superficial reading of Fredrick Jackson Turner ([1920] 1996) or the Buffalo Commons prediction (Popper and Popper 1987), demographic change might appear to be the factor determining whether frontiers open or close. However, although population changes might be one of the consequences of booms and busts, it is not population density that defines a frontier. What makes a frontier is, most often, a resource boom. Turner ([1920] 1996, 147) actually did connect the frontier to the industrialization of a landscape: "The transcontinental railroad, the bonanza farm, the steam plow, harvester, and thresher, the 'league-long furrow,' and the vast cattle ranches, all suggested spacious combination and systematization of industry." Frontiers do rearrange landscapes, as Fredric Jameson (1998) has pointed out, and it is not simply the physical landscape that is altered: legal, cultural, social, political, and spiritual landscapes are affected as well (Braun 2008, 210–14). Resource frontiers do not simply extract resources and then disappear without a trace. They extract resources and leave a fundamentally changed environment. On the northern plains, the resources have taken diverse forms: in no particular order, fur, gold, water, hides, land, uranium, buffalo bones, coal, and, for quite a while now, oil.

Oil was first sought and found in Montana in the early twentieth century. Between 1915 and 1920, several oil and gas wells became operational in east-central Montana between Lewistown, Billings, and Miles City (Rowe 1920). The discovery of the Cat Creek field in 1920 began a boom that lasted several years. Investors in one company saw a 9,500 percent return on investments over seven years. The boom, however, did not last. No new major fields were discovered, and the onset of the great depression in the late 1920s busted the developments. World War II meant a renewed interest in exploration, which was prolonged into the 1950s (Darrow 1956). In North Dakota, too, oil exploration started in the

1910s, expanded in the early 1920s, and was revived and focused after the war (Thom 1952). While a North Dakota well produced a single pint of oil in 1950, the first commercial well in the Williston Basin was drilled in Manitoba in 1951, followed that same year by wells in North Dakota and Montana (Fox and Matiniuk 1992; Laird 1962). The following boom lasted into the early 1960s, but then production decreased into the 1970s. New discoveries together with the OPEC crisis then led to a renewed oil boom into the early 1980s (Anderson et al. 1982), when it went bust. This was the last oil boom before the current Bakken boom, which started in earnest around 2009. It is this last boom, and the experiences that longtime residents made at that time, that informed at least the initial reactions to the contemporary Bakken boom.

As in most places, frontiers in North America have been waves of expansion and retraction of state control, of procedural landscapes (Braun 2013). States, however, let private companies or individuals interested in resources take the lead and limit their presence to licensing, permitting, and, if necessary, the enforcement of policies, laws, and territorial control. This is an old pattern of European colonial expansion, seen in the *repartimiento* and *encomienda* system of the Spanish conquest (e.g., Service 1951; Pastore 1997), and then its proto-capitalist English, Dutch, and French system of trading companies (MacLeod 1967), and its American descendants of free market governance. As one author points out, "The conquest and colonisation of America, therefore, was a joint venture between the Spanish state and private entrepreneurs" (Pastore 1997, 333). The same is true for most other European colonial efforts, as well as for the United States. On the northern plains, the first encounters with this developing global capitalist market system that brought wealth and power, unknown risks, and ultimately dependency, occurred during the early fur trade, when both British and French companies explored the region, established posts and trade relationships, and began a boom cycle. Native peoples in the region thus have experiences with proto-industrial and industrial extraction economies within a global context that stretch back at least three hundred years (Ray 1998). Different resources created booms and frontiers in different regions in North America. They all, however, demanded adaptations, commodified and stripped the resources, and created dependencies that could be exploited when the booms busted (e.g., Milloy 1988; Braund 1993; Gallay 2002). Frontiers were primarily an economic enterprise. They did not establish total political control at once, nor were they one-sided, as "colonialism was seldom if ever imposed but instead built through interactions" (DuVal 2006, 47). Frontiers, however, returned, often in waves, dependent on the need for new resources (see Braun 2013). While this pattern is observable all around the globe, the northern plains provide a great example of it, and the current Bakken oil boom is but one historical manifestation.

Most booms and frontiers do not originate from the discovery of new resources (unless the value of that resource is, at the time, very high), but from a change in economic value of a known resource. The fur trade was not driven by the existence of fur-bearing animals, but by the fashion demands in Europe. The buffalo hide boom was driven by the new value for hides once they could be industrially processed. The buffalo bones boom was driven by the demand for fertilizer. Energy booms are similarly driven by specific demands. Once the demand or the value falls (which is not always the same thing, as natural resources are extracted in a global context), that particular resource boom goes bust. If the value stays the same, however, the boom goes on for as long as the resource lasts. Particular frontiers thus move over landscapes, and the local boom economies are always dependent on global economic values outside their control. Nobody should understand that better than those who have to estimate property values. "The oil economy can be fickle," as one banker in North Dakota put it (Ustinova and Louis 2013). In the Marcellus Shale gas boom, the more conservative banks are calculating mortgage risks based on the assumption that the boom disappears. Others only value 20 percent of royalty income in their appraisals (Scarborough 2012). Community reactions to the Bakken oil boom at least initially took a similar approach. Communities did not want to invest in new infrastructure if the boom would not last as happened in the 1980s, and as a result communities would become insolvent after the bust. After a while, however, the influx of people and wealth can no longer be ignored because it disrupts and paralyzes life as people knew it.

Studies of social impacts of natural resource extraction on local communities were developed in Canada, Australia, and Alaska, mostly in the 1970s, and mostly in the context of indigenous communities affected by mining, oil extraction, or pipeline construction. The most significant of these studies, and in many ways the model, was the Berger inquiry into the Mackenzie River valley pipeline in the Yukon Territory (Young 1995, 184–88). The report, titled "Northern Frontier, Northern Homeland," demonstrates that frontiers are not wilderness areas becoming settled, but the territories of people making their homes there (Nuttall 2010, 62–70; see also Watkins 1977). In some situations, because of treaties, sovereign status, special legal status, or other considerations, it is important that in many cases, it is indigenous peoples that are affected by resource frontiers. However, implications are the same whether locals are indigenous or not. Frontiers exist as *frontiers* for outsiders, on the same land that is *home* to locals. The imposition of frontiers, then, already showcases that they are an expression of power: the power to transform homes into a frontier. It is by reclassifying and transforming a landscape into a frontier (supposedly free for the taking) that the resources also are transformed from owned to exploitable. The Berger report resulted in a ten year moratorium to clarify land title and prepare for social impacts, but these kinds of setbacks to industry are extremely rare, and only come about through thoughtful governments intent on using power benignly.

Interests and Discourse

Mineral resource and oil or gas booms might be the most visible, and perhaps most infamous, resource booms today. However, they are obviously not the only natural resource booms; probably the most common are land booms. Whatever the desired resource is, these booms and associated frontiers show structural similarities, both in their local manifestations and in their general existence. Historically, one of the primary similarities was that booms and frontiers were temporary, at least in expectation. Once the resource—furs, gold, oil, land—was exhausted, the area no longer held any interest. This was even true for the seemingly most permanent resource: land. As long as the intent is simply to extract value from the land—that is, as long as land is seen as an alienable or alienated commodity, not a place or a home—there is no incentive to expend resources on further investments once the easy returns are gone. Historically, this can be seen with the example of agricultural frontiers in the United States.

The plains, David Danbom (2006, 146, 148) has concluded, were settled as a "postindustrial commercial frontier," and have remained "largely colonial, exporting raw commodities and importing capital and manufactures." Looking at this agricultural frontier as an industrial frontier indeed shows the similarities to other booms, such as the Bakken. Geoff Cunfer (2005, 219) describes the necessity of the constantly moving agricultural frontier in the United States based on soil depletion, "a farm system that mined soil nutrients." Once a particular frontier had run its course, and land as a natural resource had been depleted, a new frontier was opened—"there were the farther free lands to which the ruined pioneer could turn" (Turner [1920] 1996, 148). When there were no more "free lands" suited for agriculture, however, the frontier was transformed. "Rather than adopt one or more of the ancient strategies, farmers (and the industrial nation behind them) created a new option. They appropriated abundant, cheap fossil-fuel energy to import enormous amounts of synthetically manufactured nitrogen onto their fields" (Cunfer 2005, 219). Ultimately, the land frontier and the fossil fuel frontiers are directly linked. This history, however, leaves out several aspects of frontiers and booms, most importantly the legal implications and the global consequences of resource frontiers.

Governments of expanding states are always interested in advancing frontiers, as discussed in part because their frontiers appropriate the homes of others. However, they are not necessarily interested, at least not in the modern, capitalist state, in pouring resources into these frontiers. Just as they are for businesses, frontiers are extractive for governments, too. In the United States, this has historically resulted in government disposing of newly acquired territories to private individuals—"the distribution of the public domain," as one author called it (Klose 1964, 98–104). After all, the "free land," and other "free" resources were only "free" for the taking because the state directly or indirectly imposed and enforced the fact. The political dynamics at work can be seen on the plains in the subsidized, land-grant railroads, beginning with the Pacific Railroad Act of 1862.[1] On a global stage, the quest for fertilizer before the advent of synthetic nitrogen led to the opening of new frontiers with the Guano Islands Act of 1856, which enabled the appropriation of any "island, rock, or key" with guano deposits, for the sole purpose of allowing the commercial extraction of that resource. After the resource was depleted, the United States was in no way obligated to keep the territory (or any responsibilities for it) (Foster 2000, 150–151).[2]

Resource booms do not exist, and never have come into existence, as a function of an essential need for more resources. Such an interpretation leaves out the political, social, cultural, legal, and environmental contexts of booms. It could be argued that the growth-imperative of modern capitalist economies has to lead to constant expansion into territories of cheap resources and labor. However, just like the expansion of the Inca and Aztec empires was not a function of religion, and religion did not have the purpose to serve as a legitimization of expansion (Conrad and Demarest 1984, 191–209), so, too, can we not interpret economics from a functionalist perspective only. The establishment of resource frontiers is a social, cultural, and political choice. It is embedded in other discourses, and partially dependent on them, but it is a voluntary activity. The nature of resource frontiers, too, is dependent on cultural choices. Mississippian buffer zones, for example, were used for resource extraction, but they

---

[1] I have argued elsewhere that 1862 marked the beginning of the true colonization of the plains. In conjunction with the Pacific Railroad Act, the Morrill Act and the Homesteading Act prepared this. See Braun (2009).

[2] See also 2011 U.S. Code, Title 48—Territories and Insular Possessions, Chapter 8—Guano Islands (§§1411–19).

98

looked very different from other frontiers. Their depletion probably led to societal collapse (Anderson 1990, 205–6). This might be true for all resource frontiers, but a global economy can exploit more alternative niches and therefore can hide the collapse longer. While the goal for a buffer zone was to be sustainable, the goal for extractive resource frontiers, especially booms, is not to be sustainable, but to provide as much economic profit as possible. We have to be careful not to infuse local peoples with ecological wisdom (Krech 1999), but the decision to leave intact resources that could be extracted is possible, an available choice.[3]

What resources are extracted, how, and how a frontier should look, then, are choices that are up for debate. However, because resource extraction in boom frontiers is in the interest of the state or of corporations, and because the legality and legitimacy of frontiers are often tenuous at best, an open debate might not be in the best interest of powerful stakeholders. Instead, most frontiers are enshrined in a hegemonic discourse. As mentioned, in the Bakken, and in other oil and gas booms in the early twenty-first century, this discourse is dominated by the idea that these booms save the state and the people. The urgency to extract resources as fast as possible in order to jumpstart the national and regional economy, to provide energy security, and to provide jobs thus merges with the old ideas of the frontier as the bringer or guarantor of American wellbeing and identity. These booms are also positioned in a context in which the "focus of government policy [has] shifted to making the world a more hospitable place for American business." This is nothing new, as in reality, "the heads of US-based corporations" were always the frontiersmen (Byers 2005). The myth of the American frontier is anchored in the lone, individual hero (Sardar and Davies 2002), but in reality, frontiers were controlled (and financed) by private and state capital, from railroad barons to ranch empires, from government agencies to multinational corporations. Local people often experience booms and frontiers as chaotic and uncontrollable, but this might more be a consequence of not being privy to the planning decisions.

The discourse in the Bakken has been stressing that corporations might move somewhere else if the state is not lenient in regulating them. State regulators and legislators have been especially wary of environmental regulations that might slow the rate of development, warning of EPA regulations on hydraulic fracturing (Donovan 2011), just as they have warned against EPA regulations on coal power plant emissions (Nowatzki 2014). This discourse is nationally organized, for example

[3] For example, in the Ecuadorian Amazon; for a general argument on this see Grober (2012).

through groups like the American Legislative Exchange Council (Gold-enberg 2014; Yeatman 2013). "Decades worth of oil, natural gas, coal and uranium are once again within reach—along with many thousands of jobs and trillions of dollars in government revenues," wrote one author; yet, "almost as quickly as technologies and discoveries are announced, national environmentalist groups, local activists, bureaucrats, courts and politicians proclaim their opposition, based on potential to specu-lative risks to air quality, groundwater, endangered species or Earth's climate, or on resistance to energy projects and facilities in their back yards" (Driessen 2010, 3). The discourse is so pervasive that in my own research on boom impacts, I have learned of and met faculty at regional institutions and employees at federal agencies reluctant to engage in any research or data sharing activities that might be seen as directed against the interests of industry. This includes basic research on air and water quality, or the sharing of public satellite images. One of the best examples of this discourse came in the summer 2012, when I attended the *Energy Impact Solutions Conference* at Minot State University. John Hurlimann, the presenter on "Statewide Community Resilience for North Dakota" and working for Dickinson State University, was talking about the dan-gers of terrorism for the Bakken boom, in a passage that merits quoting in full:

> I know, people look at me like I'm crazy when I talk about terror-ists, and we are becoming more of a terrorist target in this country, right now, uh, for a couple reasons. We have two groups that don't want to see a lot of things going on here. One are the environmen-talists, and, trust me, you read the blogs, and I mean they would just as soon close down the coal and everything else we have. The EPA is a good example of that, uhm ... and, sorry, Senator Con-rad's office, but, uhm ... they passed a rule last year that said any power plant that uses coal will be fined unless it changes to a new biodegradable fuel. The problem was, this fuel has not been in-vented yet. But their argument was that they're gonna fine people anyway because that was an encouragement for them to invent the fuel. So, I mean, that's what we're dealing with sometimes with these people.[4]

Maybe because this was North Dakota, nobody raised an eyebrow at this equation of a federal agency with terrorism because the agency is trying to

---

[4] The quote in full is transcribed from the DVD of the conference presentations *Energy Impact Solutions Conference*, Tuesday, August 14, 2012. In possession of author.

regulate the energy industry. The example showcases how hegemonic the discourse of the resource extraction frontier as an economic enterprise in the interest of the state has become. To put this into historical context, the land boom that populated the plains in the late nineteenth century was in part fueled by a discourse of rain-making through "pluviculture" and other schemes, a discourse that "was understandably popular in a land where dreams were much more pleasant than realities" (Danbom 2006, 145).

Realities

In reality, booms are never only pleasant, not the current oil boom, nor the fur trade, nor uranium mining, nor gold rushes, nor the land boom in the nineteenth century. Less than 20 percent of homesteaders on the plains stayed on the plots they settled first. They found that the environments did not adhere to the dreams of pluviculture. However, "such a constrained environment is not likely to be accompanied by limited expectations by people from modern industrial cultures" (Bennett 1996, 261). People who believe in the hegemony of technological and industrial solutions did not and do not expect to have their dreams shattered by local realities. In essence, that is why booms occur: there is a disconnect between the lived realities of local people and the dreams of strangers, who flock to boom regions. Because booms are temporary phenomena, and because capital can be controlled globally, frontier realities of local people also often do not match those of outsiders.

In addition, booms create status divisions. Oil and gas booms, for example, create divisions between those who own mineral rights and earn royalties and those who do not, yet have to live with all the disturbances that are necessary to create their neighbors' new wealth (Hudson and Braun 2013). Simona Perry (2012) describes the impacts by hegemonic discourse, wealth differentiation, and the influx of strangers on communities in the Marcellus Shale as "collective trauma." Her description of local realities under boom conditions are very similar to community impacts in other resource frontier situations. Accounts of the Marcellus fracking boom show how the initial local enthusiasm—fueled by dreams of poverty relief, national recognition, and patriotism—disappeared when it became clear to some in these communities that this development had divided communities and sometimes families, had the potential to create great environmental harm, and would ultimately mostly benefit outsiders (McGraw 2011; Wilber 2012). While in the abstract, booms have a positive economic impact on an international, national, regional, and local level, the impact on local people cannot be captured by general statistics or numbers alone.

Only in very abstract terms can economic growth be used to define development because it is mostly meaningless for people in communities. As has become increasingly evident, economic recovery has been disconnected from employment opportunities, for example. In other words, "the 'trickle-down effect' rarely takes place; growth does not necessarily lead to enhanced standards of living. As societies in the affluent North demonstrate, the increased use of highly sophisticated technology or a fast-growing GNP does not necessarily eradicate poverty, illiteracy or homelessness, although it may well alter the ways these ills are experienced" (Gardner and Lewis 1996, 7). In the case of resource booms like the Bakken, it is easily arguable that homelessness increases and education is disincentivized. Like other booms, the Bakken has in part led to the deterritorialization of locals, who either cannot afford to pay hugely inflationary rents or have their subsistence activities disrupted by mineral rights owners. The lure of quick money is, at least from anecdotal evidence, also leading large numbers of young people to forgo higher education.

The majority of local residents in the Bakken, in my experience, still look at the extraction of natural resources as a positive development. Many have come to see the boom in a different light, though, and question whether extraction has to be hurried, or whether it can be carefully thought through, well-regulated, and supervised. The issue for them is not whether or not extraction should take place. "The key issue is," as Young (1995, 183) pointed out for mining in Australia, "aboriginal [or local] control over deciding where [extraction] can take place and how its benefits will flow through to the community." The loss of local control, "the most serious consequence of 'development'" (Bennett 1996, 347), along with alienation from the earth and from one another have long been recognized as two conditions of capitalism (Foster 2000). They flow as necessities out of the prioritization of economic capital and growth, the simplification of context for the sake of efficiency (Dussel 1998, 13). In frontier situations, this can mean the exclusion of local concerns, as the preexisting local is denied under the assumptions of wilderness; in boom situations, the local is denied under the assumption of overarching economic or political interests.

While some authors may argue for at least the potential of a "sustainable boom" (Parlow 2011), I see that idea as an oxymoron. But even if booms were "sustainable" (what exactly would that mean[5]—and is it

---

[5] See Grober (2012, 17–21) and Boff (1997, 128–29).

not in the definition of "boom" that it will go bust?), they contribute to new inequalities. I have argued that "the proper goal for a contextualized economy is not only materially healthy communities but also spiritually, ecologically, and physically healthy communities" (Braun 2008, 177). In 1869, the naturalist Alfred Russel Wallace wrote that we "should now clearly recognize the fact, that the wealth and knowledge and culture of the few do not constitute civilization, and do not of themselves advance us towards the 'perfect social state'" (Wallace 2000, 457). Poverty, power, and sovereignty are evident factors in the hydraulic fracturing booms of the early twenty-first century. Poor communities need income and jobs, and they do not have the luxury of asking whether they agree with how these are generated, or whether the mode of production will destroy their communities in a few generations' time (Braun 2008). In other words, they do not have, or feel they do not have, the privilege of sovereignty, a good that has increasingly become a luxury of "the few." This can, for example, be seen by an analysis of decision making processes during another energy boom opportunity in North Dakota, the coal-gasification boom of the early 1970s in Mercer County (Tauxe 1993, 138–44). Energy development can be beneficial to local communities. In order for that to happen, however, they need to regain control, which sets up a built in conflict over sovereignty between local and outside interests.

The way these conflicts have been fought may perhaps best be seen by the experience of Native communities, who have been embroiled in struggles over sovereignty for a long time (Ambler 1990). Energy and other resource booms have affected indigenous communities for centuries, and several, especially Fort Peck and Fort Berthold, have been in the center of different oil booms on the northern plains. It is an expression of the ways in which power inequalities are mustered in the interests of the state and industry when local people express feelings of being treated "like Indians" when they feel disappropriated by governments (Tauxe 1993, 145; Wagoner 2002). Patricia Limerick has pointed to western ranchers' self-perception as victims in the wake of the sagebrush rebellion, and Lamm and McCarthy also identified themselves with "the New Indians," refusing to "be herded to the new reservations" (Limerick 1987, 47, 157). In the spring of 2014, militia members from all over the United States participated in a successful armed standoff against the Bureau of Land Management in Nevada, which was trying to enforce grazing fees on public lands against a rancher. These events underscore how much frustration government power still creates (e.g., Eowyndbh 2014). They also recall, however, the long fight by Western Shoshones Mary and Carrie Dann against the BLM and other agencies who do not accept the Treaty of Ruby Valley (Luebben 2002), and faintly echo other ongoing fights against treaty violations. Perhaps more interesting than the effort to paint oneself as a victim (and write the "old Indians off the page"? [Braun 2007, 199]) is that Lamm and McCarthy (1982, 5) start their book with a "nightmare" scenario of energy politics, a hypothetical blockade of Middle Eastern oil:

> The federal government takes immediate action, mandating massive energy exploration and recovery in the American West. State and local laws are overridden as energy profits proliferate across the land. The western states are not consulted. They are ignored. Their rights are abrogated, their sovereignty destroyed. Energy combines, unleashed by the government, invade the West ... Boomtowns mushroom across the West's rural face, disfiguring the land. Cedar breaks crumble to strip miners, waters fill with toxic waste, mountain valleys fall to tractor roads, and evening sunsets blaze through polluted air. Ways of life change forever ... New cities, plagued by crime and violence and nonexistent social and economic services, cannot deal with the change.

Apart from the cedars and the mountains, the scenario seems almost prophetic when compared to the local perception of the Bakken boom, and many other energy booms in the early twenty-first century—except that the government has given the driver's seat to industry, in part under the pressure of political leaders who want to see "energy profits proliferate across the land."

In the last decade of the twentieth century, some authors thought that the western United States had been deindustrialized, that "the federal government succeeded in transforming the colonial economy of the West into a pacesetting technologically advanced economy" (Nash 1999, 145). Others, however, warned that there had been no real structural change. "The form of capital remaking the hinterland may be different, the ensuing pace of change may be more immediate, and the remapping of regional landscapes may be on a much greater scale, but in terms of external influences on local conditions, little has changed. Events in the West today differ only in scope and magnitude from the events of 1893, when decisions made in transatlantic boardrooms brought immediate chaos and suffering to the tiniest of industrial communities in the western outback" (Robbins 1994, 194). Lamm and McCarthy (1982, 5–6), too, saw western history as a continuity of dependence: "In time, the energy rush dies. The boomers disappear. Left behind is a wasteland, its skeletal boomtowns and cratered-out landscape a graphic reminder of days past.

Western people, pawns in an ugly and endless war, regroup and rebuild. And their cyclical history begins again."

The Real Resource: Water

A cyclical nature is not only a marker of settler history on the plains, and of boom-bust economies, but also of the plains ecosystem, especially in regards to drought cycles (Clark et al. 2002). Yet, in early 2012, the predominant water-related metaphor for the Bakken boom did not mention drought. Instead, people were framing the boom as a potential tsunami. This might have been a response to the 2011 tsunami that had devastated the Japanese coast, yet it made perfect sense. The image of an unstoppable wave crashing into and over peaceful communities and leaving nothing but destruction in its wake captured the fears of locals, both Indian and non-Indian. On the Fort Berthold reservation, however, I heard another metaphor, too. Several people used the historic flooding of the Missouri River as an image to describe their fear for their communities. Lake Sakakawea had destroyed communities, livelihoods, and the nation's economy fifty years earlier, leading to lasting dependency (Parker 2011). Those events thus capture, on one hand, the fears of destruction at the hand of outside forces. For others, they are the reason why the tribe needs to invest in and profit from the boom: it presents the chance to finally rebuild something akin to what was lost.

Beyond these metaphors, however, lies a greater truth. All the booms and frontiers on the plains have one thing in common: water is the key resource. Whether it is furs, electricity, gold, uranium, land, or oil that is extracted, the ultimate resource for all activities has always been water. Water is also at the heart of the Bakken boom, and of fracking booms in general. This has two reasons: hydraulic fracturing uses a lot of water, and it produces a lot of wastewater. In 1890, John Wesley Powell pointed out the centrality of water as a resource for the arid lands of the west. He went a step farther, however, and problematized another aspect of water as a critical resource, namely commodification and regulation: "The land itself is valueless without the water. If a company owns that water, unless protected by local, national, or State law in some manner the farmer becomes the servant of the company" (Powell 1890, 252). Even in semi-arid lands, like the plains, interdependent natural resources "are often set in a hair-trigger equilibrium which is quickly upset by uncontrolled use" (Leopold 1991, 112–13). Aquifers across the United States and globally have been depleted by agriculture and industrial usage and population increases (Konikow 2013; Wada et al. 2010).

According to a brief survey of data from FracFocus.org, a typical fracking well in the Bakken needs about two million gallons of water to complete. In southern Mountrail County, the range of water used lies between 700,000 and 30,000,000 gallons of water; at the beginning of June 2014, there were 1,055 wells listed for the county.[6] In October 2013, 809 had been listed. This means that the fracking industry used at least 400 million gallons of water in one county during these nine months. Initial water usage for fracking a well is extended by maintenance usage, which amounts to about 600 gallons a day per well (Kiger 2013). In 2012, the estimated water usage by the oil industry in the state came to 5.5 billion gallons (Dalrymple 2013). In 2010, estimates for total usage needs in 2025 ranged from 4.5 billion gallons to 9.1 billion gallons per year and came to the conclusion that "the only plentiful and dependable supply of water for the oil industry in western North Dakota, at projected rates of extraction, is the Missouri River system" (Schuh 2010, 43–47). Perhaps in part because of the Missouri, water use for fracking is not perceived to create a hugely competitive situation in North Dakota, in contrast to drought-hit regions with fracking booms, such as Texas (Freyman and Salmon 2013). North Dakota also has a more effective regulatory system in place. Anyone with a legal interest in land can apply for a water use permit; these permits are then examined by the State Water Commission. The oil industry has given rise to many water permits being used for "water depots," where the industry buys the water needed for its operations (Schuh 2010; Western Organization of Resource Councils 2013). The system exemplifies the frontier as a place where public resources are commodified for the profit of individuals and corporations. However, permits limit the quantity of water to be extracted.

Because the future of the oil boom in North Dakota hinges on the availability of water from Lake Sakakawea, the state, which is supporting the industry, and the federal government, which is trying to regulate the water usage in the Missouri River watershed overall, have come into conflict. The Corps of Engineers has been playing with the idea of asking for a "storage fee" for water from the lake, a notion that the state is rejecting out of hand, as it claims the water for itself. If the water belongs to the state, water permits could be given for a nominal fee, and the industry would have cheap access to the critical resource it depends on. In 2012, the Corps signed a first water agreement, for 1.6 billion gallons. In 2010, it had applications for easements for about 11 billion gallons, although the amount requested might not be the amount of water that is either needed or would be removed (US Army Corps of Engineers 2010;

---

[6] Data retrieved from FracFocus.org on June 2, 2014.

Springer 2013). The fact that this conflict mirrors frontier water disputes of the nineteenth century, and that water is the actual key resource in the Bakken is also illuminated by the response from the Mandan, Hidatsa and Arikara Nation on Fort Berthold. In 2012, the Three Affiliated Tribes passed a resolution against water agreements by the Corps, noting that the "Corps' proposal to sell or allow the taking of water from Lake Sakakawea for use in the oil and gas industry will undermine the Tribes' current plans to market and sell water to the oil and gas industry and thereby raise needed revenue" (Tribal Business Council of the Three Affiliated Tribes 2012). New communal water delivery systems in northwest North Dakota are also counting on industrial sales of water to finance the infrastructure. Even if there is enough water, competition between water providers to raise revenues for communities is becoming a new economic and sociopolitical reality.

Water usage is only one part of the role water plays in hydraulic fracturing frontiers; however, the other part is the generation and disposal of wastewater. Water is mixed with chemicals before it is injected into wells to frack them. That water, as well as additional water, comes back up the well, and in contrast to water that is used for agriculture or ethanol or coal plants, this water cannot be allowed to reenter the water cycle. The only way to legally dispose of it in the Bakken and in most other oil and gas shale plays, is to inject it deep into the ground. The illegal way to dispose of it is to simply let it drip out of tank trucks while driving along the road. However, in North Dakota, as in other states, the Department of Health "considers oilfield-produced saltwater (brine) to be an effective substitute for commercial dust and ice control products." As such, brine can be spread on dirt roads in winter and summer. The NDDoH notes that "wastes are exempt from waste management rules and are not considered a waste when it is: '(2) Used or reused as effective substitutes for commercial products'" (North Dakota Department of Health n.d.). Brine as a waste product is injected in one of over 30,000 Class II disposal wells in the United States. In early 2013, North Dakota was injecting over 19 million gallons of produced water brine into the "Dakota Formation" per day, or over 7 billion gallons a year (Davisson and Luther 2013).[7]

Deep injection wells are designed to be safeguarding drinking water and aquifers, but the regulations are often based on unproven assumptions (Lustgarten 2012). A study hypothesizing that fracking itself can change the properties of the shale in which it occurs, which could then lead to the permeability of assumed stable geological formations, enabling waste

---

[7] For a discussion of the inconsistencies in nomenclature of formations, see Thamke and Craigg (1997, 12–13).

to travel into other layers, including aquifers, was heavily criticized, in part by a consulting firm (Myers 2012; Saiers and Barth 2012; Cohen and Andrews 2013). However, other studies have postulated that some of the assumed impermeable geological layers might have natural fractures, and that brine has contaminated groundwater (Warner et al. 2012). It seems that deep injection is relatively safe for now, as long as the injection wells are constructed and maintained well. The volume of waste injected, the lack of known data, potential seismic activity caused by injection, and communication between fracked wells, all raise the potential for contamination of ground water over the long term. Recent research by a consulting company rejecting the permeability of layers comes to the conclusion that "where upward flow occurs, both permeability and flow rates are low, and therefore, timescales for transport are long" (Flewelling and Sharma 2013; Flewelling et al. 2013). Thus, if problems occur, they might become noticeable after the industry has left the region.

Most contamination issues exist from improper handling, storage, and well construction. The potential for contamination of drinking water in shallow aquifers on the northern plains is demonstrated on Fort Peck, where brine has contaminated drinking water and the Poplar River since the 1970s. To reduce the threat to groundwater serving three thousand people in the Poplar area, remediation systems were established (Thamke and Craigg 1997; Thamke and Smith 2014). Potential water contamination and other health risks, such as air pollution (McKenzie et al. 2012), have led to calls for the inclusion of a comprehensive public health approach to discussions on hydraulic fracturing development (Mackie et al. 2013). It is, of course, the presence of such planning discussions that mark the absence of a frontier, or a boom. Comprehensive planning and regulations mark not necessarily an economic bust, but the fact that the state is changing its interests from securing resources for individuals and corporations to a public safety enforcement.

Conclusions

Industrial booms are nothing new to the global or national landscapes, nor are they new to the northern plains. Recurrent waves of frontiers, each one extracting resources a little more difficult to get at, have swept the region. As all frontiers, each visitation has disrupted those tied to place, and shifted economic and political power to those not related to the region and those who disentangle themselves from such ties. "Today's disintegration of rural life," wrote Osha Gray Davidson (1990, 159), "the breakup of families, small-town organizations, and whole communities—fits the pattern established by colonial powers throughout the Third World." There is a connection between inequality, dependence, poverty, and frontier resource extraction: the first three create a society where "civic culture" is more likely absent (Duncan 1999), and that enables the establishment of a frontier economy. Frontiers are economic and political patterns that take advantage of and create more inequality. They persist until one of two things happens: either the resources are depleted and capital leaves, or some beneficiaries successfully (re-)build a civic culture. In the first case, local communities are left with depleted resources and nothing to show for it. In the second case, the frontier transforms into a stable, regulated economic and political environment. This transformation, however, also needs to accomplish a successful economic diversification, or the stability will be a delusion. Brian Black (2000, 187) describes the dreams for such a transformation for the region around Petrolia, where "delusions of permanence had been based on a finite resource; it was a lesson about the nature of the oil industry." That lesson has been learned by planners in North Dakota as they attempt to attract families, to build infrastructure and subdivisions, and to advertise the Williston Basin as a sustainable boom. The underlying dependence on a finite resource, however, raises the specter of yet another bust.

Facing the spectacular end of the land boom on the plains in the years after the Dust Bowl, the Great Plains Committee came to the conclusion that hubris and ignorance about geographic, climatic, and environmental conditions had been mainly to blame. Although "an inherent characteristic of pioneering settlement," the assumption that "Nature is something to take advantage of and to exploit" was obviously a mistake. Since natural resources are actually not inexhaustible, the report advocated for conservation instead of temporary economic profiteering. It also, however, pointed out that "under pioneering conditions … if anyone acquired some portion of the free natural resources and turned it into productive use, he was … rendering a service to the entire society"; yet, in hindsight, "only too frequently what appears to be of immediate good to the individual in the long run is not good for the people of the region, and even for the individual" (Great Plains Committee 1947, 63–64). Local control cannot mean handing that control to economic interests that are often not tied to local communities. Local sovereignty over resources needs longterm wisdom and regulations, and outside control needs insight and deference to local needs and wants. Neither is given in frontier situations. In 1924, Aldo Leopold advocated that "uncontrolled use of one local resource may menace the economic system of whole regions. Therefore, to protect the public interest, certain resources must remain in public ownership, and ultimately the use of all resources will have to be put under public regulation, regardless of ownership" (Leopold 1991, 113).

This advice, namely to keep decisions about natural resources outside the influence of economic interests, would end frontiers and regulate booms.

The crux is, of course, as it has been ever since the American settlement of the West, what "public interest" means. For Leopold and others, it was the defense of the community and the environment upon which the community rests against corporate interests and those wanting to exploit "free" resources. This is still the interpretation of communities, for example, that have passed no fracking ordinances in order to safeguard their water. It is hard to reconcile such a notion with contemporary practices of states, however. Providing free resources to individuals and corporations so they can profit from them hardly protects the public interest, unless, of course, the public interest is identical with corporate interests. This is, of course, what lobbying groups such as the American Legislative Exchange Council postulate.

The public interest in natural resource has been interpreted in the interests of the state since the 1930s at least. In the case of water, the Tennessee Valley Authority and the Pick-Sloan dams on the upper Missouri are testimony to that. Energy extraction—with or without fracking—as a national interest follows the same trajectory. However, there is a difference between a resource being appropriated by the state and a state giving free reign over a resource to corporations. The latter, which creates the frontier extraction model, may fall into the current trend for states to clear the way for business interests. I have to admit, however, that this leaves me deeply suspicious. Imagine watching a movie in which the sheriff tells John Wayne or Gregory Peck that they cannot help poor ranchers fight for their right to water because the rich water barons need to make more money off them.

Boosterism has always accompanied frontiers, just as it does in the Bakken today. Yet boosterism works only by abstracting specific positive elements of booms from their contexts, and then claiming they stand for the whole. "Pluviculture" never worked in context; the rain does not follow the plow, even if at times, it might rain after somebody plows. Neither is it true that "the lesson of history is that in free societies individuals produce more energy than they consume" (Bradly and Fulmer 2004). The first law of thermodynamics has something to say about that. Neither is it true that "'non-renewable' energy sources have become more abundant" (Desrochers 2005)—we have just happened to find more, like in the Bakken. But ultimately, no amount of boosterism can realistically deny that the Bakken needs to be analyzed in the appropriate, historical and contemporary, global context of energy, environment, and politics.

References

Ambler, Marjane. 1990. *Breaking the Iron Bonds: Indian Control of Energy Development*. Lawrence: University Press of Kansas.

Anderson, David G. 1990. "Stability and Change in Chiefdom-Level Societies: An Examination of Mississippian Political Evolution on the South Atlantic Slope." In *Lamar Archaeology: Mississippian Chiefdoms in the Deep South*, edited by Mark Williams and Gary Shapiro. Tuscaloosa: University of Alabama Press.

Anderson, S.B., J.P. Bluemle, and L.C. Gerhard. 1982. "Oil Exploration and Development in the North Dakota Williston Basin." In *Williston Basin, Fourth International Symposium*, edited by J.E. Christopher and J. Kaldi. Special Publication Number 6. Regina: Saskatchewan Geological Society.

Bennett, John W. 1996. *Human Ecology as Human Behavior: Essays in Environmental and Development Anthropology*. New Brunswick, NJ: Transaction.

Black, Brian. 2000 *Petrolia: The Landscape of America's First Oil Boom*. Baltimore: Johns Hopkins University Press.

Boff, Leonardo. 1997. *Cry of the Earth, Cry of the Poor*. Maryknoll, NY: Orbis Books.

Bradley, Robert L., and Richard W. Fulmer. 2004. *Energy: The Master Resource*. Dubuque, IA: Kendall/Hunt.

Braun, Sebastian F. 2007. "Ecological and Un-ecological Indians: The (Non)portrayal of Plains Indians in the Buffalo Commons Literature." In *Native Americans and the Environment: Perspectives on the Ecological Indian*, edited by Michael E. Harkin and David Rich Lewis. Lincoln: University of Nebraska Press.

Braun, Sebastian F. 2008 *Buffalo Inc.: American Indians and Economic Development*. Norman: University of Oklahoma Press.

Braun, Sebastian F. 2009. "Developing the Great Plains: A Look Back at Lincoln." In *Papers of the Forty-First Annual Dakota Conference, "Abraham Lincoln Looks West,"* edited by Lori Bunjer and Harry F. Thompson. Sioux Falls, SD: Augustana College .

Braun, Sebastian F. 2013. "Against Procedural Landscapes: Community, Kinship, and History." In *Transforming Ethnohistories: Narrative, Meaning, and Community*, edited by Sebastian Felix Braun. Norman: University of Oklahoma Press.

Braund, Kathryn E. Holland. 1993. *Deerskins and Duffels: Creek Indian Trade with Anglo-America, 1685-1815*. Lincoln: University of Nebraska Press.

Byers, Michael. 2005. *War Law: Understanding International Law and Armed Conflict*. New York: Grove Press.

Clark, J.S., et al. 2002. "Drought Cycles and Landscape Responses to Past Aridity on Prairies of the Northern Great Plains, USA." *Ecology* 83, no. 3.

Craig, Wallace. 1908. "North Dakota Life: Plant, Animal, and Human." Bulletin of the American Geographical Society 40, no. 6.

Cohen, Harvey E., Toomas Parratt, and Charles B. Andrews. 2013. "Comment." *Groundwater* 51, no. 3.

Conrad, Geoffrey W., and Arthur A. Demarest. 1984. *Religion and Empire: The Dynamics of Aztec and Inca Expansionism*. Cambridge: Cambridge University Press.

Cunfer, Geoff. 2005. *On the Great Plains: Agriculture and Environment*. College Station: Texas A&M University Press.

Dalrymple, Amy. 2013. "North Dakota Oil Field Is Thirsty: 5.4B Gallons of Water Used in 2012." *Dickinson Press*, March 17.

Danbom, David B. 2006. *Born in the Country: A History of Rural America*. 2nd ed. Baltimore: Johns Hopkins University Press.

Darrow, George. 1956. "Oil Exploration History of Central Montana, 1915–1952." In *Guidebook: Seventh Annual Field Conference*, edited by Donald I. Foster. Billings: Billings Geological Society.

Davidson, Osha Gray. 1990. *Broken Heartland: The Rise of America's Rural Ghetto*. New York: Doubleday.

Davisson, Len, and Mark Luther. 2013. "Environmental Responsibility Drives Siting of Saltwater Disposal Wells." *Bakken Magazine* 1, no. 4.

Desrochers, Pierre. 2005. "Book Review: Energy: The Master Resource." *Quarterly Journal of Austrian Economics* 8, no. 3.

Donovan, Lauren. 2011. "Helms Says EPA Could Halt Fracking in Oil Patch." *Bismarck Tribune*, November 27.

Driessen, Paul. 2010. "Affordable Energy: The Foundation of Human Rights and Economic Justice." *The State Factor: A Publication of the American Legislative Exchange Council*, April.

Duncan, Cynthia M. 1999. *Worlds Apart: Why Poverty Persists in Rural America*. New Haven: Yale University Press.

Dussel, Enrique. 1998. "Beyond Eurocentrism: The World System and the Limits of Modernity." In *The Cultures of Globalization*, edited by Fredric Jameson and Masao Miyoshi. Durham: Duke University Press.

DuVal, Kathleen. 2006. *The Native Ground: Indians and Colonists in the Heart of the Continent*. Philadelphia: University of Pennsylvania Press.

Eowyndbh [pseud.]. 2014. "BLM and Bundy Ranch—BLM Will Be Back." *Keys to Liberty Blog*, April 14. keystoliberty.wordpress.com/2014/04/14/blm-and-bundy-ranch-blm-will-be-back/

Foster, John Bellamy. 2000. *Marx's Ecology: Materialism and Nature*. New York: Monthly Review Press.

Fox, J.N., and C.D. Matiniuk. 1992. "Petroleum Exploration and Development Opportunities in Manitoba." *Journal of Canadian Petroleum Technology* 31, no. 5.

Flewelling, Samuel A., and Manu Sharma. 2014. "Constraints on Upward Migration of Hydraulic Fracturing Fluid and Brine." *Groundwater* 52, no. 1.

Flewelling, Samuel A., Matthew P. Tymchak, and Norm Warpinski. 2013. "Hydraulic Fracture Height Limits and Fault Interactions in Tight Oil and Gas Formations." *Geophysical Research Letters* 40, no. 14.

Freyman, Monika, and Ryan Salmon. 2013. *Hydraulic Fracturing and Water Stress: Growing Competitive Pressures for Water*. Boston: Ceres.

Gallay, Alan. 2002. *The Indian Slave Trade: The Rise of the English Empire in the American South, 1670–1717*. New Haven: Yale University Press.

Gardner, Katy, and David Lewis. 1996. *Anthropology, Development and the Postmodern Challenge*. London: Pluto Press.

Goldenberg, Suzanne. 2014. "Barack Obama's Emissions Plan Comes Under New Line of Attack." *The Guardian*, May 2.

Great Plains Committee. 1937. *The Future of the Great Plains*. 75th Congress, 1st session, Document No. 144. Washington, DC.

Grober, Ulrich. 2012. *Sustainability: A Cultural History*. Totnes, UK: Green Books.

Hudson, Marilyn, and Sebastian Braun. 2013. "Boom! The Mandan, Hidatsa and Arikara People and Sustainability in the Face of Bakken Oil." *Community Connect: The Journal of Civil Voices* 6.

Jameson, Fredric. 1998. *The Cultural Turn: Selected Writings on the Postmodern, 1983–1998*. London: Verso.

Kiger, Patrick J. 2013. "North Dakota's Salty Fracked Wells Drink More Water to Keep Oil Flowing." *National Geographic*, November 11. news.nationalgeographic.com/news/energy/2013/11/131111-north-dakota-wells-maintenance-water/.

Klose, Nelson. 1964. *A Concise Study Guide to the American Frontier*. Lincoln: University of Nebraska Press.

Konikow, Leonard F. 2013. *Groundwater Depletion in the United States, 1908–2008*. U.S. Geological Survey Scientific Investigations Report 2013-5079. Reston, VA: United States Geological Survey.

Krech, Shepard, III. 1999. *The Ecological Indian. Myth and History*. New York: W.W. Norton.

Laird, Wilson M. 1962. "History of Oil Exploration in North Dakota." In *Oil and Gas Fields: A Symposium*, edited by Charles D. Tyler and Robert S. George. Bismarck: North Dakota Geological Society.

Lamm, Richard D., and Michael McCarthy. 1982. *The Angry West: A Vulnerable Land and Its Future*. Boston: Houghton Mifflin.

Leopold, Aldo. 1991. *The River of the Mother of God and Other Essays by Aldo Leopold*, edited by Susan L. Flader and J. Baird Callicot. Madison: University of Wisconsin Press.

Limerick, Patricia Nelson. 1987. *The Legacy of Conquest: The Unbroken Past of the American West*. New York: W.W. Norton.

Luebben, Thomas E., and Cathy Nelson. 2002. "The Indian Wars: Efforts to Resolve Western Shoshone Land and Treaty Issues and to Distribute the Indian Claims Commission Judgment Fund." *Natural Resources Journal* 42.

Lustgarten, Abrahm. 2012. "Injection Wells: The Poison Beneath Us." *Propublica*.org, June 21. www.propublica.org/article/injection-wells-the-poison-beneath-us.

Mackie, P., C. Johnman, and F. Sim. 2013. "Hydraulic Fracturing: A New Public Health Problem 138 Years in the Making?" *Public Health* 127, no. 10.

MacLeod, William Christie. 1967. "Celt and Indian: Britain's Old World Frontier in Relation to the New." In *Beyond the Frontier: Social Process and Cultural Change*, edited by Paul Bohannan and Fred Plog. Garden City, NY: Natural History Press.

McGraw, Seamus. 2011. *The End of Country: Dispatches from the Frack Zone*. New York: Random House.

McKenzie, Lisa M., et al. 2012. "Human Health Risk Assessment of Air Emissions from Development of Unconventional Natural Gas Resources." *Science of the Total Environment* 424.

Milloy, John S. 1988. *The Plains Cree: Trade, Diplomacy and War, 1790 to 1870*. Winnipeg: University of Manitoba Press.

Myers, Tom. 2012. "Potential Contaminant Pathways from Hydraulically Fractured Shale to Aquifers." *Groundwater* 50, no. 6.

Nash, Gerald D. 1999. *The Federal Landscape: An Economic History of the Twentieth-Century West*. Tucson: University of Arizona Press.

North Dakota Department of Health. n.d. "Guidelines for the Use of Oilfield Salt Brines for Dust and Ice Control." www.ndhealth.gov/WQ/gw/pubs/IceDustControlUsingOilfieldBrine_20130321.pdf.

Nowatzki, Mike. 2014. "EPA Chief Gets Earful on Ethanol, Coal on ND Visit." *Prairie Business*, March 4.

Nuttall, Mark. 2010. *Pipeline Dreams: People, Environment, and the Arctic Energy Frontier*. Copenhagen: IWGIA.

Parlow, A.L. 2011. "This Boom Will be Sustainable" High Plains Reader, October. hpr1.com/feature/article/this_boom_will_be_sustainable/.

Parker, Angela. 2011. *Taken Lands: Territory and Sovereignty on the Fort Berthold Indian Reservation, 1934–1960*. PhD dissertation, University of Michigan.

Pastore, Mario. 1997. "Taxation, Coercion, Trade and Development in a Frontier Economy: Early and Mid Colonial Paraguay" *Journal of Latin American Studies* 29, no. 2.

Perry, Simona L. 2012. "Development, Land Use, and Collective Trauma: The Marcellus Shale Gas Boom in Rural Pennsylvania." *Culture, Agriculture, Food and Environment* 34, no. 1.

Popper, Deborah E., and Frank J. Popper. 1987. "The Great Plains: From Dust to Dust." *Planning*, December.

Powell, John Wesley. 1890. *Eleventh Annual report of the Director of the United States Geological Survey*. Part II: Irrigation. Washington, DC: Government Printing Office.

Ray, Arthur. 1998. *Indians in the Fur Trade*. Toronto: University of Toronto Press.

Robbins, William G. 1994. *Colony and Empire: The Capitalist Transformation of the American West*. Lawrence: University Press of Kansas.

Rowe, J.P. 1920. "Possibility of Oil and Gas in Montana." *Bulletin of the American Association of Petroleum Geologists* 3, no. 3.

Saiers, James E., and Erica Barth. 2012. "Comment." *Groundwater* 50, no. 6.

Sardar, Ziauddin, and Merryl Wyn Davies. 2002. *Why Do People Hate America?* New York: Disinformation.

Scarborough, Melanie. 2012. "Boomtown Banks." *ABA Banking Journal*, September.

Schuh, W. M. 2010. *Water Appropriation Requirements, Current Water Use, & Water Availability for Energy Industries in North Dakota: A 2010 Summary*. Water Resources Investigation No. 49. Bismarck: North Dakota State Water Commission.

Service, Elman R. 1951. "The Encomienda in Paraguay." *Hispanic American Historical Review* 31, no. 2.

Springer, Patrick. 2013. "Western States Coalition Opposes Federal Water Fee." *Prairie Business Magazine*, August 19.

Tauxe, Caroline S. 1993. *Farms, Mines, and Main Streets: Uneven Development in a Dakota County*. Philadelphia: Temple University Press.

Thamke, Joanna N., and Steven D. Craigg. 1997. *Saline Water Contamination in Quaternary Deposits and the Poplar River, East Poplar Oil Field, Northeastern Montana*. Water-Resources Investigations Report 97-4000. Helena, MT: U.S. Geological Survey, in cooperation with Fort Peck Tribes.

Thamke, Joanna N., and Bruce D. Smith. 2014. *Delineation of Brine Contamination In and Near the East Poplar Oil Field, Fort Peck Indian Reservation, Northeastern Montana, 2004–09*. Scientific Investigations Report 2014–5024. Helena, MT: U.S. Geological Service, in cooperation with Fort Peck Tribes.

Thom, W.T., Jr. 1952. "The Importance of Recent Oil Discoveries in the Williston Basin." In *An Introduction to the Williston Basin*. Casper, WY: Petroleum Information.

Tribal Business Council of the Three Affiliated Tribes of the Fort Berthold Indian Reservation. 2012. Resolution No. 12-048-VJB. Fort Berthold, ND: The Council.

Turner, Fredrick Jackson. (1920) 1996. *The Frontier in American History*. Mineola, NY: Dover.

US Army Corps of Engineers. 2010 *Garrison Dam/Lake Sakakawea Project, North Dakota. Draft Surplus Water Report*. Omaha, NE: The Corps.

Ustinova, Anastasia, and Brian Louis. 2013. "The Shale Boom floods Rural Banks with Cash." *Bloomberg Businessweek*, February 7.

Vision West ND. 2014. *Regional Plan for Sustainable Development*. Boise, ID: Building Communities Inc.

Wada, Yoshihide, et al. 2010. "Global Depletion of Groundwater Resources." *Geophysical Research Letters* 37, no. 20.

Wagoner, Paula. 2002. "They Treated Us Just Like Indians": *The Worlds of Bennett County, South Dakota*. Lincoln: University of Nebraska Press.

Wallace, Alfred Russel. 2000. *The Malay Archipelago*. Hong Kong: Periplus.

Warner, Nathaniel R., et al. 2012. "Geochemical Evidence for Possible Natural Migration of Marcellus Formation Brine to Shallow Aquifers in Pennsylvania." *Proceedings of the National Academy of Sciences* 109, no. 30.

Watkins, Mel, ed. 1977. *Dene Nation: The Colony Within*. Toronto: University of Toronto Press.

Western Organization of Resource Councils. 2013. *Gone for Good: Fracking and Water Loss in the West*. Billings: WORC.

Wilber, Tom. 2012. *Under the Surface. Fracking, Fortunes, and the Fate of the Marcellus Shale*. Ithaca: Cornell University Press.

Yeatman, William. 2013. *The U.S. Environmental Protection Agency's Assault on State Sovereignty*. Arlington: American Legislative Exchange Council.

Young, Elspeth. 1995. *Third World in the First: Development and Indigenous Peoples*. New York: Routledge.

CHAPTER 6

PUBLIC DISCOURSE ON THE RISE AND REGULATION
OF THE ILLICIT SEX TRADE DURING NORTH
DAKOTA'S ECONOMIC BOOMS

Nikki Berg Burin

"What is the difference between Grand Forks and ancient Rome? ... Rome had seven 'hills,' while Grand Forks has seven 'hells.'" This riddle was presented by Reverend T. F. Allen of the Methodist Church of Grand Forks in Dakota Territory to a "large and attentive audience" in 1883. The seven hells to which he was referring were seven houses of prostitution that dotted the landscape of the budding city. Noting that a fallen woman was the lowest of the low, Reverend Allen reminded his audience that she brings "destruction and death to all who come her way." While certainly worried about the impact of the so-called "soiled dove" on individual residents and families, the reverend was also concerned about the larger damage such sordid characters could cause. In his mind and that of many others, the reputation of the city was at stake. This was alarming at a time of tremendous economic and demographic growth in what would become eastern North Dakota. In fact, rumors circulated in the official newspaper, the *Grand Forks Daily Herald*, that students were refusing to come to the university because of the immoral character of its host city. It was unacceptable to proud and respectable citizens that prostitutes could sully their fine town on the prairie (*Grand Forks Daily Herald*, September 11, 1883). Nearly 130 years later, as North Dakota experiences a new economic boom, community members and officials are expressing similar sentiments in cities throughout the state. "Locals who have long called these windy plains home are fleeing," warned a 2013 article in the *Star Tribune* of Minneapolis. The rise of illicit sex is one of the factors that has contributed to this flight. Upon being propositioned in Williston, North Dakota, where prostitutes reportedly "troll the bars," a resident lamented, "This is not a small town anymore" (Eligon 2013; Louwagie 2014). A Williams County sheriff's deputy concurred. "This street has gone to hell," he remarked while driving a reporter through a nightclub-lined road in Williston in 2012 (Brown 2013). When reports of prostitution taking place in a Watford City hotel surfaced that same year, the manager exclaimed, "We don't want a reputation for that" (Donovan 2012). Such sentiments are not unreasonable. However, when put in the larger context of popular discourse on the revival of the illicit sex trade in North Dakota, it becomes apparent that the nineteenth century view of prostitutes as a scourge on good communities persists. In local, regional, national, and even international newspapers, North Dakota's general public tends to discuss prostitutes in terms that convey their disapproval if not outright contempt for these supposedly mercenary women. The public's empathy is absent and their outrage is misdirected.

The popular narrative of prostitutes as lascivious troublemakers is simplistic, inaccurate, and harmful to the many women who are engaged in the sex trade not by choice but, rather, by compulsion. The Department of Justice estimates the average age of entry into prostitution in the U.S. is 13–14 years old. As many as 80 to 95 percent of prostitutes are controlled by pimps through various forms of compulsion (Barry 1995). A 1998 study found that 88 percent of prostitutes want to get out of the trade (Farley and Barkan 1998). These statistics collectively form a picture of trafficking, which the U.S. Department of State (2013) defines as "the act of recruiting, harboring, transporting, providing, or obtaining a person for compelled labor or commercial sex acts through the use of force, fraud, or coercion." Trafficking is modern day slavery, and it is on the rise in North Dakota. The influx of men in the Bakken oil fields has served as a magnet for those who sell women and children for sex. As Windie Lazenko, a sex trafficking survivor and victim advocate in North Dakota, told the *Star Tribune* in August 2014, "the pimps are definitely exploiting the community. They can come in and pretty much do whatever they want." According to Lazenko, sex trafficking is happening in bars, strip clubs, and even Wal-Mart (Louwagie 2014). It is also happening online, with a multitude of ads selling sex with women and children across the state on websites like Backpage.com. While sex trafficking is often hidden from plain view, it is becoming increasingly visible in North Dakota. As a result, media outlets in the state and beyond are paying increasing and meaningful attention to the issue. However, when the sentiments of the general public and even some law enforcement officials are conveyed in media reports, it becomes clear that many North Dakotans do not see or wish to ignore the connections between sex trafficking and prostitution.

Like their nineteenth century ancestors, North Dakotans today express great sympathy for victims of trafficking, particularly those who are minors. They tend to draw a distinction, though, between such victims and those they see as willing prostitutes out to make a buck. Upon being propositioned by two prostitutes, a resident of Williston pointed out their seemingly avaricious nature by noting, "The ones that are here aren't too bashful." A local police officer concurred: "It's easier to get a prostitute than it is ordering pizza" (Louwagie 2014). Viewers of *Valley News Live* out of Fargo, North Dakota responded in large numbers when the station reported on a prostitution sting in Grand Forks, which resulted in the arrest of five men seeking to hire a prostitute. Many posted online comments arguing that the "police could better spend their time busting 'real criminals'" ("Are Prostitution Stings Worth Police Effort?" 2014). Each of these examples reflects the longstanding notion that prostitution is a victimless crime. As sociologist Julia O'Connell Davidson points out, the contractual elements of prostitution create a "façade of voluntarism" (Davidson 1998, 121). North Dakota's current laws, which criminalize prostitution as a Class B misdemeanor, support this perception and the misguided vilification of prostitutes. While trafficking victims are deemed worthy of compassion and support, popular opinion holds that prostitutes generally are not.

The false dichotomy between prostitution and sex trafficking perpetuates misogyny and one of its most conspicuous and harmful manifestations: the sexual objectification and exploitation of women. In the wake of a recent mass shooting by a male supremacist in Santa Barbara, California, author and journalist Jessica Valenti reminded us that misogynists are "created by our culture, and by communities that tell them that their hatred is both commonplace and justified" (Valenti 2014). The shaming and censure of prostitutes during North Dakota's first economic boom was so commonplace that a justification for such hatred was hardly needed. And yet this negative community response to prostitutes did nothing to stop the illicit sex trade or the exploitation of women. What it did accomplish was to put a society's most vulnerable population in an even more tenuous position. Such an outcome is no surprise when a community's outrage is directed at the victims of a crime and not at the individuals or circumstances that facilitated their victimization. To avoid going down a similar path today, North Dakotans should be attentive to and critical of these strains in the public discourse about prostitution. They would also be wise to reexamine the nineteenth-century mentality regarding prostitutes. Doing so will help clear the haze of misogyny that continues to distort the public's perception of prostitution and its victims.

* * *

While the newspaper industry may be suffering a decline here in the twenty-first century, at the end of the nineteenth century, it was the most prominent "voice of the community" on all relevant and significant issues, including prostitution. As historian Anne Butler explains, "frontier journals became the instrument through which communities expressed their confusions, ambivalences, and disagreements about prostitution and the local policies that dealt with it" (Butler 1987, 81). Newspapers like the *Grand Forks Daily Herald* set the tone for the public discourse on prostitution with the stories they covered, the frequency of those stories, and, especially, the words they used to describe the women caught in the web of prostitution. Like most other regional and national newspapers, the *Daily Herald* typically referred to prostitutes as inmates, the demimonde, or soiled doves. Words are powerful and those used repeatedly and uncritically by the newspaper editors, writers, and contributors of the time were loaded with harmful connotations.

Inmates is an interesting word choice, for one might interpret it as an expression of sympathy for the women who, through various means of compulsion, were confined and oppressed within so-called "houses of ill-repute." The *Daily Herald* printed a story in 1883 about how the city solicitor was presented with a petition by the "ladies of Grand Forks" in which they requested that he break up the houses of prostitution and "drive the inmates from our city" (September 23, 1883). It becomes clear in statements such as this that when used by the general public, the term inmates was generally not intended to raise awareness about the plight of prostituted women but, rather, to highlight their criminality. Such terms placed the burden of sexual exploitation on the women who suffered from it, rather than placing responsibility on the shoulders of those who deserved it: the madams, pimps, and patrons who objectified women for pleasure and profit.

Equally problematic was the term *demimonde*. This is an eighteenth century French word that described those who challenged traditional bourgeois values by leading a flagrantly hedonistic lifestyle. The demimondaine was composed of women whose hedonism was expressed by unabashed relationships with multiple lovers. Over the course of the century, demimonde became a euphemism for prostitutes. This was an unfortunate development for prostituted women, for the term inherently suggested not only that they made depraved choices, but, even worse, that they found pleasure in them. Demimonde hid the brutality, destitution, and compulsion that shaped the lives of most prostitutes. Moreover, it conveyed consent and choice, both of which were compromised (or at least complicated) by the personal histories and socioeconomic struggles of the majority of prostituted women.

While some late nineteenth century women did willfully and affirmatively choose prostitution as a profession, the vast majority came to it under duress and, for those not held against their will, in a tentative fashion. As legal scholar and feminist theorist Catharine MacKinnon argues, women who are prostituted in the flesh or in pornography "are, in the main, not there by choice but because of a lack of choices." She goes on to explain:

> They usually "consent" to the acts only in the degraded and de-mented sense of the word ... in which a person who despairs at stopping what is happening, sees no escape, has no real alternative, was often sexually abused before as a child, may be addicted to drugs, is homeless, hopeless, is often trying to avoid being beaten or killed, is almost always economically desperate, acquiesces in being sexually abused for payment, even if, in most instances, it is payment to someone else. (MacKinnon 2005, 995).

While MacKinnon is writing from a modern point of view, her assess-ment is relevant to the lives of late nineteenth-century prostitutes as well—an era when women had even fewer choices and little autonomy; when the slightest sexual impropriety was grounds for ostracization; when the absence of inherited wealth or a male supporter almost always invited economic deprivation. Nineteenth century women turned to prostitution for a wide variety of reasons that have remained consistent over time. One of the most pressing compulsions was and continues to be economic hardship and a lack of meaningful and sufficient employ-ment opportunities. As historian Judith Walkowitz argues in her study of British prostitutes in the Victorian era, "some working women regarded prostitution as the best of a series of unattractive alternatives" (Walkowitz 1980, 31). Women did choose prostitution as a profession and some even did so as an expression of empowerment and liberation from restrictive sexual and gender mores. However, the majority of prostitutes came to the choice out of the duress of poverty and countless other challenging personal circumstances. Furthermore, as Walkowitz points out, the deci-sion to enter prostitution "did not free women from a life of poverty and insecurity, and further subjected them to physical danger, alcoholism, ve-nereal disease, and police harassment" (Walkowitz 1980, 31). In short, the "demimonde" rarely lived the free, hedonistic, and lavish lives the term conveyed. Not only were all prostitutes subject to the whims and desires of their patrons who were far from "lovers," but many were also subject to the demands of brothel owners.

Madams were prominent participants in the illicit sex trade in late nineteenth-century Dakota Territory (Engelhardt 2007; Sylvester 1989). The *Daily Herald* frequently reported the happenings of local madams and "*their* girls" or "*their* soiled doves." An article from 1900 relays the story of a Grand Forks farmer's daughter who was arrested for being in an

122

underground saloon (the city went dry in 1890). A local madam offered to pay the girl's fine if she would become "one of the regular occupants" of her brothel. Having no money of her own, the young girl agreed. The article goes on to explain that this was not the first case of entrapment in Grand Forks. Just one week earlier another young girl was lured into the same saloon by a "hack driver" who acted as a middle man between a madam and the girl. After being arrested, her fine was paid by the madam "on condition that she lead a life of shame which she agreed to do, did do, and is still doing" (*Grand Forks Daily Herald*, June 17, 1900).

While the mythology of the Old West conjures up images of the entrepreneurial and independent prostitute, the reality is that most prostituted women were under the control of or dependent upon a madam or pimp. A combination of alcohol, drugs, poverty, unhealthy or nonexistent family lives, histories of abuse, and certainly a lack of meaningful choices contributed to the vulnerability of those recruited or compelled into "the life" and enhanced their submission to and dependence on those who ran the brothels. The individuals with the relatively flush purses tended to be the ones in control, the ones doing the exploiting. In the twenty-first century, we all too often hold nineteenth century madams up as successful businesswomen and do not hold them accountable for their complicity in the sexual exploitation of other women. While the frontier press and public did not applaud the business acumen of madams, they too ignored the coercion inherent in facilitated prostitution and lumped madams and "their girls" into the same category of the demimonde. In doing so, they perpetuated a damaging stereotype about depraved and hedonistic prostitutes and, as a result, misdirected the community's outrage over the illicit sex trade and ignored the forces that compelled women to enter and remain in it. While demimonde and inmate were loaded and influential words, perhaps no term accomplished the task of condemning prostitutes so well as "soiled dove."

The most popular euphemism for prostitute, "soiled dove" was a familiar part of nineteenth century North Dakotans' vernacular. A rather condescending term to prostitutes, it reflects the gender prescriptions of the day in regard to women's required sexual purity and the fouling of their virtue by bad choices—namely the "choice" to engage in commercial sex. The term simultaneously told those who were listening or reading that they should, on one hand, feel pity, for the woman in question was once wholesome and respectable, but, on the other hand, they should feel revulsion in the same way they would when anything that was once fine is spoiled. "Soiled dove" is an artifact of the nineteenth and early twentieth centuries that provides great insight into the sexual scripts and gender norms of that era. Like demimonde and inmate, it masked and even romanticized a brutal and exploitative institution. While the journalists who helped make these terms a permanent part of the historical record and a common part of the day's vernacular should not be judged for using the language of their time, their repeated use of them was damaging and facilitated the strong public bias against prostitutes. It was not, however, just their use of this specific terminology that contributed to a negative public opinion, but also the nature of their reporting. While often the only mention of prostitutes in the papers were straightforward notices of their arrests and fines, there were also many cases of ridicule and scorn.

"Generally, as a social agency with a responsibility to encourage the well-being of the community, the frontier press bungled a unique opportunity," writes Anne Butler. "It possessed neither the personnel nor motivation to become a social champion" (Butler 1987, 82). This is readily apparent in the instances when newspapers incorporated humor into their reports on prostitutes. In October 1883, an article titled "Migratory Birds" appeared in the *Daily Herald*:

> If an early flight of wild fowls to the southward is any criterion to judge by, we may confidently expect winter to be close at hand. For several days past there has been observed birds of various kinds flying south, and yesterday two soiled doves, who have been mating during the past season in this city in order to escape the cold wave, poised their wings and left for the land where the orange blossom blooms. In other words, Kate Gray and her assistant have left the community permanently and for the community's good. (*Grand Forks Daily Herald*, October 3, 1883)

One can imagine the writer feeling proud of this clever piece of writing knowing that his audience probably appreciated his wit. While the specific circumstances of Kate Gray and her associate are unknown, it is likely that local authorities forced them to leave town upon serving jail time or paying fines for prostitution. Earlier that same year, the *Daily Herald* reported on the attempt of "a couple of the demi-monde" to visit the house of a respectable citizen. The newspaper readers likely chuckled at the image of their rude dismissal from the home. "Although no bull-dog is kept about the premises," wrote the reporter, "one of the soiled doves was heard to say, as soon as she reached the street, 'my Lord! What a reception!'" (*Grand Forks Daily Herald*, June 29, 1883) Reporting like this reinforced the public's misconception that prostitutes were villains, not victims. As such, they were susceptible to ridicule and mockery. Everyone in the community was able to have a good laugh at the expense of their most marginalized members, which only enhanced the latter's isolation.

The community's disdain for prostitutes was most transparent in newspaper accounts that went beyond reporting the facts and entered the realm of moralizing. When madams Millie Watson, "Big" Kate, and "three crews of soiled linen" went to a grand ball in East Grand Forks in 1889, a brawl broke out when one of the prostituted women rejected one man and acquired the attention of another. As the *Daily Herald* reported, "considerable indignation was manifested on our streets over the affair, and a determined effort in the future will be made to 'sit down' on such, when they try to mingle with respectable people" (*Grand Forks Daily Herald*, August 27, 1889). The previous year, the *Daily Herald* printed a story about two women who were accused of keeping a "house of ill repute" and were forced out when some unknown persons sprayed a fire hose into their home while they were sleeping. The newspaper reported that it was unlikely that the authorities would try to apprehend the operators of the hose. It condoned their aggression and the authorities' apathy by stating "such women have no business to live in respectable localities" (*Grand Forks Daily Herald*, August 20, 1888).[1] When an African American prostitute became pregnant with a white man's child, the *Daily Herald* took its condemnation to the next level. Their headline read "White caps are needed to punish a bad black woman and a worse white man." The writer lamented that the story had to be written at all. "Depravity—unparallelled [*sic*] comes to light in our midst. Were it not that we consider the newspaper the proper medium for exposing such hybrid deeds of satanic wickedness and bringing the guilty to punishment, we would consign the appended to ignominious oblivion." Ignominious oblivion was not to be and, as a result, the "Ward family of prostitutes" likely endured the wrath of their neighbors (*Grand Forks Daily Herald*, February 13, 1889).

Such wrath was reserved for the women whose stories were unknown, which was the majority of prostitutes. In the absence of any known personal background and any desire to understand the circumstances that brought women into the illicit sex trade, communities throughout the country assumed that prostitutes were always willing participants in the sordid deeds that took place in brothels and that violated female codes of honor. However, the very same communities rallied behind those who were known victims of trafficking, which at the time, almost always included abduction and usually minors.[2] In 1897 the *Daily Herald* reported the tragic story of a young girl who passed through Grand Forks on her

---

[1] The writer stated that the men who patronize brothels also have no business living there.

[2] According to the U.S. Department of State, in the twenty-first century one does not need to be guilty of abduction to be found guilty of trafficking.

way to a new job in a small town nearby. She ran into an old acquaintance who invited her to stay at her home. The young woman did not realize the home in question was a brothel and that her old friend was a prostitute. While there, the young woman was drugged, raped, and then put to work (a common series of events for victims of trafficking then and now). After she was rescued, the *Daily Herald* reported that "one of the prominent ladies of Grand Forks through a generous hearted gentleman in the city was induced to give her a home and the unfortunate, sweet faced stranger left a few days ago for her own home in southern Minnesota" (*Grand Forks Daily Herald*, April 4, 1897).

Fortunately for this young woman, the community was willing to accept that she was the victim of a terrible crime. This widespread compassion for minors who were trafficked into prostitution is, thankfully, still prevalent in the United States and North Dakota today. Efforts are currently being made by lawmakers at both the state and federal level to pass "safe harbor" legislation, which would protect child victims of sex trafficking from being charged with the crime of prostitution. However, the proposed legislation is problematic in its age limitations. It implicitly suggests that when one turns eighteen, he or she is given the gift of empowerment and choice. At age seventeen, a child engaged in commercial sex will be considered a victim of trafficking, but once the same individual is eighteen, the law declares him or her to be a criminal. Eighteen is not a magic number. The forces that coerced one into the illicit sex trade as a thirteen-year-old do not disappear once that teenager reaches the age of majority. While the North Dakota State Legislature is also considering legislation that would create an affirmative defense for adults charged with prostitution if the charge was a direct result of being trafficked, the burden of proof falls on the shoulders of the defendant. This is problematic because fear, trauma, and manipulation by traffickers cause many sex trafficking victims to not identify as such. The decriminalization of prostitution for minors and the creation of an affirmative defense for adults charged with prostitution are steps in the right direction for empowering victims of sex trafficking. However, the limits and flaws contained in these laws reveal the persistence of the narrow and moralistic attitudes regarding prostitution and prostitutes that were so common in late nineteenth century North Dakota.

Those attitudes meant that the majority of women who were locked into "the life," either by falling into or being recruited into it, were not offered the empathy or assistance provided to victims of sex trafficking. As discussed above, they were the targets of ridicule, scorn, and shame on the streets and in the press. A local judge captured public sentiment in his condemnation of houses of prostitution and their inhabitants. As reported by the *Daily Herald*, the judge remarked, "It is unnecessary for the court to depict the baneful and polluting effects flowing from these sinks of filth and crime" (*Grand Forks Daily Herald*, May 26, 1893; cf. Donovan 2012).[3] He was right about it being unnecessary, for nearly everyone was certain that prostitutes were a scourge on their communities. Yet the public discourse that developed from this belief did nothing to stop prostitution. While Grand Forks prided itself on its virtue by eventually ridding its city of saloons and their accompanying brothels, the illicit trade thrived across the river in East Grand Forks, Minnesota where all of the madams and their customers relocated.

In 1891, a special correspondent of the *Minneapolis Tribune* visited Grand Forks and proclaimed it "is the most prosperous of the inland towns and cities of the northwest ... Today it easily outranks every other city between [Minneapolis and Great Falls] in beauty of location, business development and thorough going energy ... no New England village was ever more quiet or dignified." He went on to observe that by simply crossing over the bridge to East Grand Forks one entered a different civilization. "The first building you approach stands upon the bridge itself like a devil-fish meeting you half way, and reaching out its slimy arm to enfold you and drag you into the embrace of death." The correspondent was chagrined by the multitude of brothels and saloons. Who was responsible for such "wickedness and vileness"? Grand Forks was according to the author. He claimed the much larger city used East Grand Forks as a "dumping ground" (Frank Mead, *Grand Forks Daily Herald*, September 5, 1891). Grand Forks's disdain for prostitutes and support for prohibition shaped public policy, which did not end the illicit sex trade, but simply made it someone else's problem and made the lives of the prostituted more tenuous in the process.

North Dakota is once again facing a rise in prostitution and sex trafficking. And, once again, the general public's feelings and attitudes about the illicit sex trade are strong. They are also far too reminiscent of the past. Traces of late nineteenth century moralism are common in today's public discourse about prostitution and prostitutes. However, in the late nineteenth century, such moralizing was informed not only by the gender prescriptions and sexual mores of the time, but also by the public's ignorance of the brutal realities of the sex trade and of the desperate circumstances that often compelled women to enter it. With unlimited

---

[3] Similar sentiments are still expressed today. When discussing prostitution in the Bakken in 2012, one law enforcement official articulated disdain for prostitutes and their customers, noting that some of what he encountered made him "want to take a shower." Lauren Donovan, "Prostitution in the Oil Patch," *The Bismarck Tribune*, March 31, 2012.

access to information and more expansive views of female sexuality, there is no excuse for such ignorance today and no place for such moralizing. Instead of judging those engaged the illicit sex trade by choice or compulsion, twenty-first century North Dakotans would be wise to focus instead on the complex forces creating and sustaining a market for the sexual exploitation of women and children in this state.

The creation of a new anti-trafficking coalition in North Dakota,[4] the commitment of the legislators in the North Dakota Democratic Women's Caucus to pass anti-trafficking legislation in 2015 (Mooney 2014),[5] and the increased attention to and sharp criticism of sex trafficking by the North Dakota press are encouraging signs that the state is ready to take action against the sexual exploitation of women and children. But will the anti-trafficking movement be broad or narrow in its goals and advocacy? Will today's North Dakotans take cues from their nineteenth century ancestors and condemn those coerced into prostitution by a lack of choices, histories of abuse, poverty, drugs, and violence? Will they determine that some exploited women are worthy of our sympathies and aid and others are not? Or will they protect and support all who find themselves selling their bodies for sex—those who were compelled by circumstances or traffickers, as well as those who made the choice of their own free will and desire? Will they target those who are sold as commodities or will they instead target the traffickers who sell them and the johns who buy them? Never has the history of prostitution, sex trafficking, and the efforts to regulate and eradicate both in North Dakota been more pertinent. It is imperative for North Dakotans to reflect on their ancestors' actions and inaction so as to make informed decisions that will not simply relocate traffickers and prostitutes to another state, but that will instead eradicate the seemingly insatiable demand for the bodies of women and children.

---

[4] The coalition is called FUSE (a Force to End hUman Sexual Exploitation) and currently consists of the North Dakota Women's Network, First Nations Women's Alliance, CAWS North Dakota, the National Association of Social Workers—North Dakota, and Prevent Child Abuse North Dakota.

[5] The 2015 legislative session featured widespread, bipartisan support for anti-sex trafficking legislation. The North Dakota Century Code now includes a "Uniform Act on the Prevention of and Remedies for Human Trafficking" (Chapter 12.1–41 of the Criminal Code). This comprehensive legislation includes a "safe harbor" law protecting minors and an affirmative defense law protecting adult victims of sex trafficking.

References

"Are Prostitution Stings Worth Police Effort?" 2014. *Valley News Live*, April 28. www.valleynewslive.com/story/25350233/are-prostitution-stings-worth-police-effort.

Barry, Kathleen. 1995. "Pimping: The World's Oldest Profession." *On The Issues Magazine Online*. www.ontheissuesmagazine.com/1995summer/pimping.php.

Brown, Curt. 2013. "North Dakota Communities Cast Adrift on the Ocean of Oil." *Star Tribune*, December 31.

Butler, Anne M. 1987. *Daughters of Joy, Sisters of Misery: Prostitutes in the American West 1865-90*. Urbana and Chicago: University of Illinois Press.

Davidson, Julia O'Connell. 1998. *Prostitution, Power and Freedom*. Ann Arbor: University of Michigan Press.

Donovan, Lauren. 2012. "Prostitution in the Oil Patch." *Bismarck Tribune*, March 31.

Eligon, John. 2013. "An Oil Town Where Men Are Many and Women Are Hounded." *New York Times*, January 15.

Engelhardt, Carroll. 2007. *Gateway to the Northern Plains: Railroads and the Birth of Fargo and Moorhead*. Minneapolis: University of Minnesota Press.

Farley, Melissa, and Howard Barkan. 1998. "Prostitution, Violence, and Post Traumatic Stress Disorder." *Women and Health* 27, no. 3: 37–49.

Louwagie, Pam. 2014. "Sex Trade Follows Oil Boom Into North Dakota." *Star Tribune*, August 30.

MacKinnon, Catharine A. 2005. "Pornography as Trafficking." *Michigan Journal of International Law* 26: 993–1012.

Mooney, Gail. 2014. "Help Prevent Human Trafficking in North Dakota." *Grand Forks Herald*, January 20.

Sylvester, Stephen. 1989. "The Soiled Doves of East Grand Forks 1887–1915." *Minnesota History* 51: 290–300.

United States. Department of State. 2013. *Tracking in Persons Report 2013*. www.state.gov/j/tip/rls/tiprpt/2013/210543.htm.

Valenti, Jessica. 2014. "Elliot Rodger's California Shooting Spree: Further Proof that Misogyny Kills." *The Guardian*, May 24.

PART 3

HEALTH
AND THE
BOOM

Chapter 7

Nowhere to Run: Impacts of the Bakken Oil
Boom on Domestic Violence Survivors and
Service Providers

Laura Tally

Great innovation led to the booming growth that we see in the Bakken today. Energy development and material progress in the Bakken continue along with innovative solutions to meet the needs of oil patch communities. However, social service providers who work with victims of domestic violence have yet to benefit from a similar level of innovation. This chapter aims to clarify connections between Bakken energy development, state and local fiscal policy, and monumental challenges faced by social service providers.

News reports from the Bakken tend to focus on the abject or brief human interest story. As demonstrated by the previous chapters in this section, what we need are comprehensive assessments that draw clear pictures of health and welfare disparities. Greater clarity then compels us to support Bakken communities by raising public awareness of institutional barriers that hinder lifesaving crisis intervention and violence prevention. As awareness grows, so does our responsibility to fund and conduct academic research that leads to innovative solutions.

According to the North Dakota Council on Abused Women's Services, in cooperation with the Coalition Against Sexual Assault in North Dakota for the state health department, 4,179 new victims of domestic violence were reported in 2007. In 2013, the same collaborators reported 4,807 new victims. Crisis intervention centers reported 4,496 instances of domestic violence called into their centers in 2007, compared with 5,177 calls in 2013 (NDCAWS 2014). During the same time period, housing costs and populations soared while funding for new infrastructure remained stagnant (Headwaters Economics 2012). While the numbers above display a seemingly modest increase in the number of victims and crisis calls, this data must be viewed alongside the capacity of Bakken service providers to respond.

Each day in the Bakken people make the life-saving decision to leave abusive relationships in spite of being uncertain of the support services available to them. At the same time, advocates for these brave people face new obstacles directly tied to explosive growth in the area. Often, the difference between life and death for these victims lies in the strength of the social service providers who frame their safety net. As many Americans benefit from North Dakota's economic growth, it is vital that we develop a national comprehension of the growing challenges to justice for Bakken families impacted by violence and abuse. While the root causes of domestic violence and barriers to healing are complex, the Bakken oil boom provides us with unique opportunity to research and advocate for creative solutions.

The Bakken: Critical Geographic and Demographic Facts for Advocates

The "Bakken" refers to the Bakken shale formation, which consists of an enormous quantity of oil and natural gas buried deep below ground across a vast area in the Northern plains of the United States. The Bakken extends from North Dakota and eastern Montana into Saskatchewan and Manitoba, Canada. This is a very rural area of North America with little or no public transportation in most places. It is not uncommon to drive forty minutes from home to the nearest gas station and further for groceries and community gatherings. It is vital that barriers to affordable transportation be considered when developing innovative solutions for families in crisis.

Energy development is drastically changing this rural landscape, and once-small towns are becoming bustling cities. However, fossil fuel extraction in the Bakken is not a new phenomenon. People have been drilling for oil in the Bakken intermittently since the 1950s, and the area has experienced several economic booms and busts over the years. Recently the technology to extract these fossil fuels has advanced. This new technology is a complex process called hydraulic fracturing or "fracking." Fracking has drastically increased the amount of oil and gas we can extract from the Bakken shale.

The United States Geological Survey (USGS) reports that "recoverable oil reserve estimates have doubled since the area was surveyed in 2008" (2013). The word "recoverable" is key to understanding why the USGS estimates grew significantly in that short time period. Previous oil booms have provided short periods of growth, followed by periods of economic stagnation or "busts." Put simply, we might recover much more oil than we have in the past using conventional technology, which could prolong the boom and stave off the bust. In a report analyzing North

Dakota's fiscal policies regarding oil and gas development, Headwaters Economics, a nonprofit research group based in Bozeman, Montana, highlights energy extraction in the Bakken as fundamentally different from previous instances of energy development. The group reports that "the 'treadmill' of drilling and fracking activity suggests that impacts will be heightened and more continuous throughout the life of the Bakken play" (Headwaters Economics 2012, 1). With that understanding, we should seek innovative solutions to better the lives of new and lifelong Bakken residents alike.

Population Growth in the Bakken: Understanding Impacts on Infrastructure

While the issues surrounding government funding for critical service providers are complex, all community leaders rely on accurate information to guide policy decisions. Unfortunately, due to the speed at which this economy is growing, reliable population data is difficult to obtain in the Bakken. The census numbers reflect estimated population growth, and though often disputed, these numbers guide policy decisions on funding new infrastructure.

The latest oil boom began around 2005, but population growth in the Bakken due to oil extraction increased significantly beginning in 2009. Population and economic growth in this once-quiet place creates unique infrastructure challenges that require sound research and reporting. Official population growth was measured at 4 percent in the state between 2010 and 2012, compared with a 1.7 percent average growth rate for the rest of the country. Williams County, however, has experienced an estimated population increase of 19.1 percent from 2010 through 2012. Williams County hosts the town of Williston, which the United States Census Bureau reports as the fastest growing micropolitan area in the country with a 40 percent population boom between April 2010 and July 2013 (United States Census Bureau 2014).

These population spikes are great news for new businesses, but they pose a challenge for local governments. Accurate population estimates are critical when government leaders create new budgets. These budgets propose funding measures for the public services people rely on. Public services are referred to as infrastructure, which include schools, housing, public utilities, roads, hospitals, and law enforcement. Crisis shelters for domestic violence victims are also counted as infrastructure. Nationally, 27 percent of domestic violence service providers reported a reduction in government funding in 2013. In North Dakota, 21 percent of providers reported the same (NNEDV 2014). Any reduction in funding for these critical services puts lives at risk. Understanding the census measurements that inform policy is vital to protecting those funds. While accurate population estimates are critical to guiding policymakers, we currently lack innovative solutions for measuring how many people live in boom communities.

Researchers with the Agribusiness and Applied Economics department at North Dakota State University conducted a study examining future employment projections for the state. Their aim was to develop a new method for estimating the number of people who might work and live in key areas affected by energy development. They stressed that our standard methods for measuring population are not capable of providing accurate numbers in the Bakken at this time and that housing availability would determine future permanent populations (Bagsund and Hodur 2012, 18). This shortcoming critically reduces our ability to adequately fund social service programs because no one can estimate how many people will depend on those programs from one year to the next. If basic community planning cannot keep pace with growth, it can be assumed that many people in crisis will not receive adequate support.

While planning for the future may be hampered by the speed of population growth, North Dakota is financially capable of meeting the needs of all residents. In the first six months of the 2011–13 biennium, oil tax revenue for the state of North Dakota had exceeded official government projections, and sales tax revenue from the Bakken reached 43 percent beyond the optimistic projections of 347 million dollars (Smith 2012). Despite this abundance of revenue, Headwaters Economics (2012) found that fiscal policy regarding the redistribution of that revenue was not adequate in light of the new and complex process of fracking and its impacts on local infrastructure. In the summary findings of that study, it was stated that "North Dakota stands out among its peers (other energy-producing states) for providing the least direct funding for oil-impacted communities" (2).

The rural location, type of energy development, and unique fiscal policies in place across the Bakken have unveiled particular challenges that must be understood to effectively address the social infrastructure needs of residents. There is a shortage of quality research tools available to measure this booming population and even fewer predictive tools to guide policymakers. Amidst the confusion, teams of dedicated professionals are still trying to meet the needs of domestic violence victims in crisis. It is reasonable to assume that growth in the Bakken has outpaced the capacity of most local agencies to intervene when victims choose to seek help.

Agencies that address domestic violence serve clients in extreme crisis and respond to a host of needs. They are tasked with providing safe shelter, legal assistance, child advocacy, advocate training, and counseling. They collaborate with skilled professionals including nurses, social workers, and lawyers, all of whom are crucial to completing their mission. On shoestring budgets, they strive to prevent domestic violence by lobbying, raising awareness, and providing statistics for academic research. There is no question that these agencies are vital to people across the state. Nationally, it is estimated that one in four women and one in seven men have been victims of "severe physical violence by an intimate partner in their lifetimes" (Breiding et al., 2014).

The North Dakota Council on Abused Women's Services (ND-CAWS) compiled these domestic violence statistics for the state health department for the year 2011. The state reports a 3 percent increase in new victims from 2010, along with a 3 percent increase in reported incidents, which totaled 5,159. Although domestic violence affects whole families, 94 percent of victims were female. Law enforcement referrals increased 4 percent from the previous year highlighting an increased demand on local police forces (NDCAWS 2012).

The National Network to End Domestic Violence conducts an annual survey in September each year. They collect information vital to increasing our awareness of the harsh realities faced by victims and advocates. On September 17, 2013, nineteen of twenty North Dakota service providers participated in the survey. Within twenty-four hours, ninety calls for help rang in to domestic violence crisis lines. Unfortunately, 21 percent of providers reported a reduction in government funding with emergency shelter making up 71 percent of unmet requests for services (NNEDV 2013). Among other unmet requests for services were legal representation and transportation assistance which were not provided at all due to a lack of fiscal or personnel resources. In addition, four direct service staff positions were eliminated in 2013.

These statistics must be viewed along with the evidence that despite ample economic resources population growth in the Bakken has outpaced North Dakota's ability to respond financially to social welfare needs. Most likely, this leaves law enforcement and victim advocates serving more people with staff and funding resources, which were probably inadequate before the oil boom began. Direct crisis intervention requires adequate funding to pay staff, keep the lights on, and pay the rent on office or shelter space. As noted in the NNEDV report, if programs are unable to intervene at the critical point of emergency shelter, it seems unlikely that they can wage effective violence prevention strategies for people in need before they find themselves in the midst of crisis.

To further comprehend how the oil boom is affecting domestic violence agencies and victims in the Bakken, the author contacted several service providers and asked them to relay their experiences. Their testimonies were enlightening and horrific considering the fact that human lives are lost even as we try to compile and understand the statistics. Before we read their stories, it is essential that we examine how providers function to help survivors in a challenging new environment.

Scope of the Crisis According to Bakken Providers

Numbers paint an incomplete picture of the dire situation for victims and those who advocate on their behalf in the Bakken. Linda Isakson agrees with this sentiment. As the assistant director for the North Dakota Coalition of Abused Women's Services in 2013, Isakson graciously corresponded via email for this report. According to surveys of providers statewide, about five hundred more victims were served in 2012 than were served in 2007, before the start of the oil boom. It was also noted that eighty additional victims of sexual assault requested services in the same time frame. Isakson explained that funding was woefully inadequate for all service providers, regardless of services offered, but measuring particular deficiencies among providers was very difficult. It was also stated that few providers had the time or resources to respond to surveys, further complicating research and advocacy efforts. Above all, there was a major concern relayed about a devastating lack of affordable housing in the Bakken.

Affordable housing and domestic violence intersect at two critical points. Victims need affordable emergency shelter while social service professionals and law enforcement need housing as well. Isakson underscored affordable housing as the most difficult barrier for her agencies to overcome at this time:

> There is a woeful lack of housing in oil-impacted counties and what becomes available is unaffordable for those needing immediate and safe shelter. The domestic violence crisis program provides a shelter for victims but survivors stay an extended period of time with little turnover. No safe shelter means victims return to abusers or need transportation to available shelter beds more than one hundred miles away.

Isakson brought cold facts and figures to a terrible light by saying, "The situation in oil country is one of crisis … no safe shelter means victims return to abusers" (personal communication, 2013). This statement underlines the inability of current programs to intervene during crisis, much less prevent violence or heal victims. A report compiled by NNEDV echoes Isakson's comments on inadequate shelter in a summary for North Dakota: "42% of programs report that victims are forced to return to their abuser, 5% report that victims become homeless, and 11% report that the families are forced to live in their cars" (2013).

During a phone interview with an intake counselor at the Fargo-Moorhead YWCA emergency shelter, inadequate transportation and affordable housing were mentioned as substantial barriers for women fleeing domestic violence across the state. Fargo is located at least six hours east of most communities in the oil fields. The counselor claimed that many victims began their escape from abuse on foot because they had no access to reliable transportation, and then traveled across the state because there was nowhere safe and affordable to live in their own communities. It was then noted that many victims endured further violence as hitch-hikers, and often had to leave children and pets behind with the abuser. There was also an observation that more women were suffering sexual exploitation, and that injuries from physical abuse were more serious than what the counselor was accustomed to seeing (personal communication, 2013).

The town of Minot, North Dakota is almost five hours away from Fargo but close to the oil boom. Dena Filler, executive director for the Domestic Violence Crisis Center, shared her struggles about an exploding population and inadequate funding. In 2011, Minot was devastated by a flood, which destroyed all of their transitional housing for survivors. The destroyed transitional housing Filler spoke of comprised eight units intended to serve a regional population of more than 70,000 people. Four thousand homes in the area were also lost due to flooding exacerbating the oil-boom housing shortage. Filler noted that the media portrayed a bustling economy and numerous job vacancies but failed to report on the absolute lack of affordable housing (personal communication, 2013).

Fortunately, media outlets are beginning to highlight the issue of affordable housing in the Bakken. In a brief article that garnered national attention, Samantha Grossman (2014) found that one-bedroom apartments in Williston, North Dakota were renting for an average of $2,400 per month. Similar housing in large cities such as New York or Los Angeles were renting for $1,500 per month around the same time. Victims of domestic violence may delay seeking help in crisis if there is nowhere affordable to live. In addition, professionals who can assist them are also burdened with higher costs of living. Pay for law enforcement, child protection specialists, and community health workers is tied directly to fiscal policies that have been shown to lag behind the pace of growth in North Dakota today.

A Lack of Adequate Law Enforcement and Legal Assistance

While the failure of local and state leaders to provide affordable housing in the Bakken exacerbates the crisis for many people, there are many more institutional barriers to justice that impact domestic violence victims. The events that precede an escape from domestic violence usually involve law enforcement. According to the NDCAWS (2012) domestic violence fact sheet for 2011, police were called to 50 percent of the 5,159 cases, and of those, 1,083 arrests were made. Linda Isakson had this response when asked which occupation was most lacking in the Bakken:

> The number of law enforcement officers needed to provide public safety is currently inadequate in many ways ... the turnover rate is very high. The amount of money being paid to drive truck, provide security or supervise a [construction] crew is extremely tempting to officers working long hours for little money (personal communication, 2013).

A lack of pay for law enforcement commensurate with state revenue growth can certainly be viewed as an institutional barrier to justice that must be reformed. In addition to police officers, many professionals are dissuaded from social justice work in the Bakken due to the high cost of housing.

Those with legal experience are critical to defending the rights of victims. They assist with child custody, property and financial rights, and the criminal prosecution of abusers. Regarding the advocacy barriers she struggled with most, Dena Filler explained that attorney fees in her community are too expensive for women in crisis. She claimed that family law attorneys in the area commonly charge a $5,000 retainer fee for services regarding child custody or immigration and take little pro-bono work. Her program in Minot, the infrastructure center for about 70,000 people in the region, has no professional staff to address mental health issues or substance abuse (personal communication, 2013). While unjust barriers to affordable housing, legal services and adequate mental health professionals surely exist throughout our society, according to this investigation, they are severely exacerbated in the Bakken for victims and the advocates who serve them.

A Lack of Quality Research to Guide Policymakers

Barriers to affordable housing also prevent our universities from collecting the data that will influence effective policy. Academic institutions are trying to understand the unique challenges to social welfare communities where energy development is booming. Their research efforts, including the housing and transportation of surveyors can be hampered by the accessibility of funds to conduct quality assessments. A 2011 study conducted by the Center for Community Vitality at North Dakota State University in Fargo asked university employees from their extension service about various quality of life issues in their specific regions. All extension officials mentioned affordable housing as the most pressing concern. The average cost to rent a studio apartment in some places went from $300 to $900 dollars per month in the span of two years. Affordable housing was also a barrier to hiring adequate extension service employees to gather the data for the report and was mentioned as the lead concern for employers in all sectors. Notably, the social service professions were among those that could not compete with salaries offered by oil companies (Bohenkamp et al. 2011).

Conclusion

Amidst record state revenue growth, victims of domestic violence in the Bakken are being turned away from safe shelter, and advocates can barely keep up with crisis intervention much less attend to prevention measures. This illustrates a critical health disparity that merits immediate action. Domestic violence is a serious public health issue, and the infrastructure to prevent and end this violence must be strengthened whenever possible. Beyond funding for crisis intervention, we should seize opportunities to conduct quality research on family violence in a place where innovation has changed many lives for the better. Failure to do so, either by ignoring the voices of Linda Isakson and Dena Miller or remaining silent when policymakers set budget priorities, amounts to tolerance of violence.

In her essay "The Five Faces of Oppression," Iris Marion Young explains that toleration of violence, demonstrated clearly when Bakken policymakers fail to support Bakken families in crisis, is unjust. "To the degree that institutions and social practices encourage, tolerate, or enable the perpetration of violence against members of specific groups, those institutions and practices are unjust and should be reformed" (Young 1990, 39–65). She goes on to note that reform needs to begin within our culture by recognizing institutional and social barriers to justice. We have effectively established that government, academic, and corporate institutions within the Bakken tolerate fiscal policies that send victims back to abusers. The "specific group" is represented by families and children in crisis. However, women are overrepresented as victims of family and sexual violence as illustrated throughout this section on health in the Bakken.

Reform begins when we study the connections between North Dakota fiscal priorities, fracking, and victims of domestic violence. To seek justice for domestic violence survivors in the Bakken, we must recognize extraordinary challenges posed by the population boom and tailor innovative solutions. Without funding for quality research to accompany public outcry, survivors in future booms will be left behind while policymakers remain ignorant to the needs of their communities. Furthermore, neglecting the opportunity to develop new and sustainable service delivery methods, both in domestic violence intervention and prevention, amounts to a societal tolerance of violence. Academic institutions across the country must collaborate on funding quality research intended to educate and inform policy makers today and the students who will be the policy makers of the future.

The economic prosperity some feel from the Bakken oil boom has led to a crisis situation for many others. If we are to strive toward social justice in this area addressing the needs of people who must escape domestic violence is a good place to start. Census numbers, victim statistics, and market values tell only part of the story. To facilitate understanding of the social injustices occurring in North Dakota, we need to ask more questions. The opportunity for research abounds in the Bakken for all social disciplines and should be funded at the same rate we fund research into energy development. The quality of life for everyone hangs in the balance, and must be treated with greater respect or greed and economic disparity threaten future prosperity. We can acknowledge the scars, bruises, and broken families by raising awareness about domestic violence in the Bakken, but our obligation to support survivors does not end there.

We need to gather the testimony of dedicated social workers, nurses, and teachers and share it with our academic institutions, governments and social justice organizations. We need to demand that our media give equal time to covering the positive aspects of domestic energy *and* the negative effects the oil boom has on our communities. The people who allow oil and gas corporations to influence the way a community functions must demand that they uphold the human rights of citizens above profits. However, without compelling social research that attracts public attention and creates a demand for justice, they will not be able to do so. Quality research initiatives with an emphasis on service learning must begin immediately and span a multitude of disciplines in order to effectively patch the safety net for victims of domestic violence in the Bakken.

There are complex economic, social, and cultural forces exacerbating injustice for victims in the Bakken at this time, but academia can focus on two main components immediately. We need to further examine how social welfare agencies suffer when infrastructure needs such as affordable housing or adequate law enforcement go unmet and the consequences of inadequate government funding for social services on rapidly growing populations. This examination must be detailed and accurate, with no speculation on the value of defending the rights of victims of violence. Victims of family violence come from all socioeconomic, race and ethnic backgrounds. We can match the remarkable innovation that made the Bakken boom possible by creating new ways to help our friends and neighbors. To facilitate a more just society on the rural high plains, we must further expose the complex roots of domestic violence along with the institutional barriers that prevent victims from receiving the services they need to heal and thrive.

References

Bagsund, Dean, and Nancy Hodur. 2013. "Williston Basin 2012: Projections of future Employment and Population North Dakota Summary." Agribusiness and Applied Economics Report 704. North Dakota State University Department of Agribusiness and Applied Economics. purl.umn.edu/142589.

Bohnenkamp, Shelby, Alex Finken, Emily McCallum, Audrey Putz, and Gary A. Goreham. 2011. "Concerns of the North Dakota Bakken Oil Counties: Extension Service and Other Organizations' Responses to These Concerns." North Dakota State University Center for Community Vitality. www.ag.ndsu.edu/ccv/documents/bakken-oil-concerns.

Breiding, M.J., S.G. Smith, K.C. Basile, M.L. Walters, J. Chen, and M.T. Merrick. 2014. "Prevalence and Characteristics of Sexual Violence, Stalking and Intimate Partner Violence Victimization—National Intimate Partner and Sexual Violence Survey, United States, 2011." *Mortality and Morbidity Weekly Report* 63, no. 8: 1–18. www.ncbi.nlm.nih.gov/pubmed/25188037.

Gold, Russell. 2012. "North Dakota Enjoys Oil Boom But Girds for Slowdown." *Wall Street Journal*, December 23.

Grossman, Samantha 2014. "The Highest Rent in the U.S. Is Not in New York or San Francisco." *Time Magazine*, February 18. time.com/8731/highest-rent-in-us-williston-north-dakota/.

Headwaters Economics. 2012. "Benefitting from Unconventional Oil: State Fiscal Policy is Unprepared for the Heightened Community Impacts of Unconventional Oil Plays." headwaterseconomics.org/wphw/wp-content/uploads/ND_Unconventional_Oil_Communities.pdf.

NDCAWS (North Dakota Council on Abused Women's Services). 2014. "North Dakota Council on Abused Women's Services: Get the Facts: Domestic Violence: Domestic Violence Statistics." www.ndcaws.org/facts/.

NNEDV (National Network to End Domestic Violence). 2013. "2012 Domestic Violence Counts: A 24-Hour Census of Domestic Violence Shelters and Services." Washington D.C.: National Network to End Domestic Violence. nnedv.org/projects/census.html.

NNEDV (National Network to End Domestic Violence). 2014. "Nationwide Survey Reveals Urgent Need for Increased Funding for Domestic Violence Service Providers." *National Network to End Domestic Violence*. March 6. nnedv.org/news

Smith, Nick. 2012. "North Dakota Exceeds Economic Goals, Breaks Oil Production Records." *Bismarck Tribune*, February 24. bismarcktribune.com/special-section/news/.

United States Census Bureau. 2013. "Oil and Gas Boom Driving Population Growth In the Great Plains, Census Bureau Estimates Show." March 14. www.census.gov.

United States Census Bureau. 2014. "North Dakota Quickfacts from the US Census Bureau." quickfacts.census.gov.

United States Geological Survey. 2013. "USGS Releases New Oil and Gas Assessment for Bakken and Three Forks Formations." United States Dept. of the Interior. May 2. www.usgs.gov/blogs/features/usgs_top_story/usgs-releases-new-oil-and-gas-assessment-for-bakken-and-three-forks-formations/.

Young, Iris Marion. 1990. *Justice and the Politics Of Difference*. Princeton, NJ: Princeton University Press.

CHAPTER 8

OIL BOOMS AND BABIES! WOMEN'S HEALTH
PROFESSIONALS EXPLAIN THE CHALLENGES OF
WESTERN NORTH DAKOTA'S OIL BOOM

Heather Jackson

Introduction

The Bakken oil boom in North Dakota is well known. The oil drilling has
had a large impact on the health system, education system, environment,
and criminal activity (see Nikki Berg Burin's and Laura Tally's chapter in
this volume) in North Dakota. The influx of population and the accompanying challenges have introduced substantial changes to the state and
its residents.

Public health officials are overwhelmed. More immunization clinics
are opening, sexually transmitted infections are increasing, substance
abuse and mental health issues are increasing, and there are healthcare
staff shortages (Dwelle 2013). The North Dakota Department of Health
has also found that there is a lack of affordable housing and that many
oil workers or their families are homeless, and many do not have access
to a primary care provider (Bullinger 2012). The increase in patients
has forced directors to discontinue walk-in services at clinics. (Bullinger
2012).

The main purpose of this chapter is to understand the impact of the
oil boom on women's health professionals and on issues surrounding
pregnancy in particular. However, before exploring this particular issue,
this chapter examines research about maternal health impacts and stress
on healthcare workers following oil booms and gas drilling. Additionally,
it provides an overview of the changing birth rate, prenatal risks, prenatal visits, and distance traveled to give birth in North Dakota pre- and
post-oil boom.

Lastly, this chapter discusses the results of semi-structured interviews
with five birth and women's health professionals. The interviews focused
on the research question, *What are the positive and negative changes of*

patients, clinics, and hospitals that women's health professionals have seen as a result of the oil boom? The findings suggest that staff are overrun because of the population increase, hospitals are not as equipped as they can be, and parents are confused and uninformed as they prepare for delivery.

Impacts of Oil Booms and Oil Spills

Earlier studies have explored the impacts of oil booms and oil spills, in particular on maternal and child health and healthcare provider stress. They point to potential consequences for North Dakota's oil boom and the state's future. They also demonstrate the need for more research.

Maternal and Child Health

The following studies focused on physical health outcomes of pregnancies on the fetus or the baby. There are very few studies on the emotional and psychological experiences of pregnant mothers.

In Taiwan, researchers found a correlation between increased risk of preterm delivery and air pollution in areas with a petroleum refinery plant. Each study adjusted for potential confounders and still found a correlation (Yang 2002; Yang et al. 2002; Tsai et al. 2003). Another study described a link between mothers who were exposed to untreated environmental wastes and the likelihood of miscarriage (San Sebastián et al. 2002). This is an important consideration for the Bakken area because we are unaware of the air pollution near the drilling. These studies point to an important consideration regarding the consequences on maternal and child health. Drilling is occurring where people live. How is the health of vulnerable populations being affected?

One study of 124,842 births between 1996 and 2009 analyzed correlations between natural gas development and postnatal defects (McKenzie et al. 2014). It found an association of congenital heart defects and neutral tube defects in babies living within ten miles of a natural gas development. Researchers attributed the correlation to exposure to teratogens, which can cause neonatal defects, emitted by natural gas developments. Hill (2013) compared birth weights of babies in areas of Pennsylvania where wells were permitted but not drilled and areas where they were drilled. It found that babies born within 1.5 miles of the drilled wells were 25 percent more likely to have a low birth weight (5.5 pounds or less). These findings indicate the importance of considering the health of the population who lives in these areas. Not only do they demonstrate an association related to birth, but they force us to ask, do these consequences affect babies in the long term? And if so, how? Will children being born in the Bakken have health consequences further down the road?

While some of these results may be attributable to other factors, there are still significant findings related to oil booms and pregnancy. This is not an exhaustive list of the maternal and child health impacts after oil booms and gas drilling, but there are recent studies of impacts found in other areas of the world. These are issues to be aware of, since these issues could occur in North Dakota.

Stress on Healthcare Workers and Providers

Few studies have looked at stress on healthcare providers during an oil boom. However, there are many articles in newspapers regarding the strains healthcare workers face. John Eligon (2013) reports that hospital debt at McKenzie County Healthcare System in Watford City, ND, has climbed more than 2,000 percent over the past four years, and the average number of emergency visits has increased to four hundred a year (up from one hundred a year). Moreover, ambulance calls have increased by 59 percent from 2006 to 2011, and traumatic injuries in the oil patch have increased 200 percent in the first six months of 2007. Furthermore, rates of debt at the twelve medical facilities in western North Dakota have increased by 46 percent in 2011–12. Additionally, Philip Bump (2013) states that ambulance vehicles have a hard time finding where injured oil workers are located. Fellow oil workers have been driving with the injured worker to meet the ambulance in another location.

Patrick Springer (2011) reports that Mercy Medical Center in Williston has experienced an increase in birth rates and lacks the necessary staff to keep up with the young families moving there. Trinity Hospital in Minot has also experienced changes since the oil boom, as emergency visits have doubled in six years to 40,000 cases a year. The visits include burns, falls, chemical inhalations, explosions, crushing injuries, and accidents. Dr. Jeffrey Sather, director of Trinity Hospital's emergency department, states that three of every four burn transfers from North Dakota to Minneapolis are from Trinity.

Data Methods

The North Dakota birth rate was derived from birth data from 2006 to 2012 provided by the North Dakota Department of Health. Birth certificate data from the North Dakota Department of Health were analyzed to examine potential prenatal risk associations and prenatal visits in western and eastern North Dakota. SAS software V9.3 (SAS Institute, Cary, NC,

Hospital	Year	Birth rate (per 1000)	Vaginal births		Cesarean births	
			N	%	N	%
Williston	2012	31.74	382	64.97	206	35.03
	2006	28.85	286	79.22	75	20.78
Hettinger	2012	39.47	73	72.28	28	27.72
	2006	60.44	124	60.49	81	39.51
Grand Forks	2012	24.63	1207	72.54	457	27.45
	2006	30.21	1088	73.02	402	26.98
Fargo	2012	23.17	1752	71.63	694	28.37
	2006	24.32	1695	76.77	513	23.23

Figure 1. Birth Rates in Williston, Hettinger, Grand Forks, and Fargo, 2006 and 2012 (source: North Dakota Department of Health 2013b; United States Census Bureau 2014)

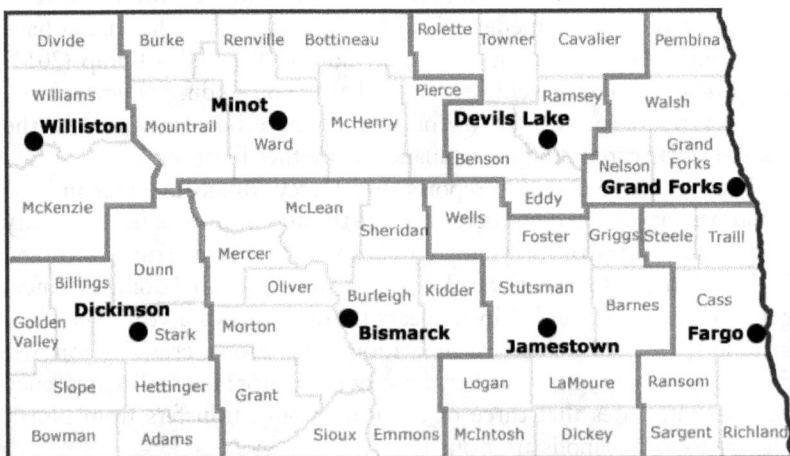

Figure 2. Cities included in study.

USA) was used and chi-square tests were performed. The *p*-values of the tests were analyzed. For comparison purposes, data from 2002 to 2005 (pre-oil boom) and 2006 to 2009 (post-oil boom) were used.[1]

North Dakota Birth Rates

The birth rates of Williston, Hettinger, Grand Forks, and Fargo are described in Figure 1. Williston and Hettinger are near the oil boom and have been affected by an increase in population. Grand Forks and Fargo have not been as affected by the oil boom because they are on the other side of the state. These cities provide an illustration of how the oil boom is affecting western cities more than eastern cities.

In 2012, there were just over 10,000 live births in North Dakota (North Dakota Department of Health 2013b). In 2012, the overall birth rate for North Dakota was 14.4 per 1,000. The birth rate for the United States was approximately 12.7 per 1,000 (Centers for Disease Control and Prevention 2013). The North Dakota birth rate is slightly higher than that of the United States. According to the 2010 census, the population of North Dakota was about 672,000. In 2012, the population of North Dakota was just over 700,000 and in 2013 the population about 723,000. This is an increase of about 7.6 percent. In the United States, the population change was 2.4 percent (United States Census Bureau 2013).[2]

Figure 1 displays the total number of births, vaginal births, cesarean births, and birth rates in 2006 and 2012 for Mercy Medical Center in Williston, West River Regional Medical Center in Hettinger, Altru Health System Health System in Grand Forks, and Essentia Health in Fargo. The total number of births increased for each hospital, probably because of the increase in the total population in North Dakota. Other factors explaining the increase are increased fertility rate and increased population of childbearing age. However, these factors also relate to the increase in population.

Although the total number of births increased for each city, the birth rate itself showed variation. The birth rate is the total number of births per 1,000. Williston shows an increase in the birth rate, which could be due to the population increase. However, Hettinger does not show an increase in the birth rate. One factor that contributes to the increase in the birth rate is that the total population in North Dakota has increased, as previously explained. However, the decrease for Hettinger might be

[1] Data past 2009 were not yet available.

[2] These estimates came from information from the United States Census Bureau.

City		No risk		Risk		
		N	%	N	%	Chi-square
Hettinger	Pre	101	53.72	87	46.28	0.29
	Post	119	56.40	92	43.60	
Valley City	Pre	223	63.17	130	36.83	0.40
	Post	124	60.49	81	39.51	
Williston	Pre	525	55.91	414	44.09	0.35
	Post	738	54.67	612	45.33	
Jamestown	Pre	582	55.96	458	44.04	0.42
	Post	653	54.60	543	45.40	
Fargo/Grand Forks	Pre	7,509	59.89	5,030	40.11	6.90
	Post	8,388	58.31	5,998	41.69	

Figure 3. Association between pre-natal risk and the number of births pre- and post-oil boom (sources: North Dakota birth certificate data, 2002–2009, North Dakota Department of Health)

City		0–8 visits		9–11 visits		12 or more visits		
		N	%	N	%	N	%	Chi-square
Hettinger	Pre	89	47.34	83	44.15	16	8.51	14.17
	Post	84	39.81	80	37.91	47	22.27	
Valley City	Pre	82	23.50	105	30.09	162	46.42	8.37
	Post	70	34.15	46	22.44	89	43.41	
Williston	Pre	164	17.56	451	48.29	319	34.15	45.80
	Post	175	13.36	820	62.20	315	24.05	
Jamestown	Pre	124	11.92	558	53.65	358	34.42	18.74
	Post	169	14.13	532	44.48	495	41.39	
Fargo/ Grand Forks	Pre	1,727	13.87	6,470	51.97	4,252	34.16	16.92
	Post	2,192	15.52	7,325	51.87	4,606	32.61	

Figure 4. Association between number of prenatal visits and number of births pre- and post-oil boom. (source: North Dakota birth certificate data, 2002–2009, North Dakota Department of Health)

due to the fact that fewer people are moving to Hettinger because of the oil boom. Further, oil workers and their families are moving to Williston rather than Hettinger or other towns. Prenatal risk, number of prenatal visits, distance the mother traveled to give birth, and post-natal problems were analyzed. Hettinger and Williston were compared to Valley City and Jamestown as controls because of their similar populations. The eastern cities of Fargo and Grand Forks were also analyzed. Figure 2 shows the location of each city. These cities are not comparable in size to the oil boom cities, but they help clarify the different effects of the oil boom in western cities and eastern cities.

Figure 3 shows the association between pre- or post-boom prenatal risk for Hettinger, Valley City, Williston, Jamestown, and Fargo/Grand Forks. Prenatal risk was a variable created that included alcohol use during pregnancy, low gestation, maternal risks, previous fetus death, previous terminations, multiple births, breech, long labor, omphalocele/gastroschisis, spinal bifida, birth weight between 550 and 2,500 grams, gestational diabetes, gestational hypertension, hypertension, ruptured membrane, or eclampsia. Did these prenatal risks increase after the oil boom started? The risk has not significantly changed, as there were no significant p-values. In other words, there is no demonstrated increased risk when looking at the pre- and post-oil boom data in these cities.

For the number of prenatal visits and the number of births, data from 2002 to 2005 and 2006 to 2009 for Hettinger, Valley City, Williston, Jamestown, and Fargo/Grand Forks were analyzed. Figure 4 describes the association between the number of prenatal visits (0–8, 9–11, 12 or more) pre- and post-oil boom. Prenatal visits are the number of times women see their physician during their pregnancy. The differences for each city were statistically significant. Hettinger showed a significant increase in the number of mothers who had 12 or more prenatal visits and a decrease in 0–8 prenatal visits and 9–11 prenatal visits. Williston also showed a decrease in 0–8 prenatal visits and a large decrease of mothers who had 12 or more prenatal visits. However, Williston showed a large increase of mothers who had 9–11 prenatal visits.

West River Regional Medical Center in Hettinger is a small center that serves a large area. The increase in the number of people in an area served by such a small hospital may explain the increase in appointments later in pregnancy. Additionally, it is possible some of the women are not getting to an appointment until later in their pregnancy because of the increase in population—healthcare providers are too busy to get pregnant women into an appointment at an earlier time. The fact that there

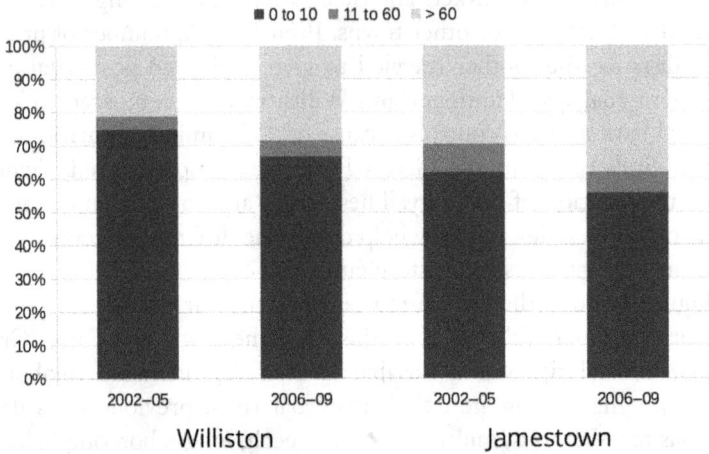

Figure 5. Miles traveled to give birth between 2002-2005 to 2006-2009, Williston and Jamestown (source: North Dakota birth certificate data, 2002–2009, North Dakota Department of Health)

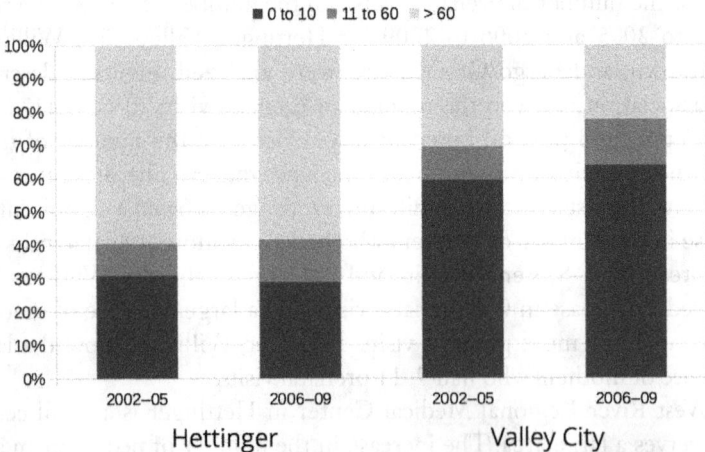

Figure 6. Miles traveled to give birth between 2002-2005 to 2006-2009, Hettinger and Valley City (source: North Dakota birth certificate data, 2002–2009, North Dakota Department of Health)

has been no increase in prenatal risk factors may also explain the decrease in earlier prenatal visits.

Mercy Medical Center in Williston is a larger hospital and has a few clinics. However, the increase of population is possibly driving the decrease in prenatal visits to clinics and the hospital. This could be due to the lack of healthcare providers and appointments available. It is also possible that there is reduction in the availability of appointments, thus making fewer times available for patients to be seen. Furthermore, mothers may be moving to the area at various points in their pregnancy, a fact that may affect how often they see a provider.

For miles to travel, data from 2002 to 2005 and 2006 to 2009 for Williston, Jamestown, Hettinger, and Valley City were analyzed (Figures 5 and 6). The distance traveled was divided into three categories: less than 10 miles, 11–60 miles, and more than 60 miles. Overall, women in Williston traveled more miles in the post-oil boom years than in the pre-oil boom years. The increase in traveling could be due to lack of healthcare providers, lack of birthing options, or lack of housing in the city, which forces people to live further from the hospital. For Hettinger, the miles traveled stayed fairly consistent pre- and post-boom. This could be because the oil boom did not affect the number of miles traveled for women to give birth, but it does not mean that the oil boom, as demonstrated previously, affects other issues.

Lastly, for postnatal problems, a variable was created that included birth injuries, seizures in the infant, infant on ventilation, or high or low birth weight. The data compared came from 2002–5 and 2006–9 for the cities of Hettinger, Valley City, Williston, Jamestown, Fargo/Grand Forks (Figure 7). The numbers are reported in percentages. The percentage of postnatal problems was about the same in Williston and in Hettinger for each year group. Reasons for the percentage consistency are that the oil boom does not appear to be affecting postnatal problems. Perhaps women are prepared, healthcare providers are ready for the issues that may occur after birth, or prevention of the postnatal problems is continuing to work.

Interviews

Participants and Procedures

The additional data for this paper came from interviews with five women's health professionals. All participants lived and worked in western North Dakota. One participant was a nursery nurse training to be an obstetrics delivery nurse; one was a public health nurse; two worked as birth doulas and had their own birthing business; one worked as a birth doula and

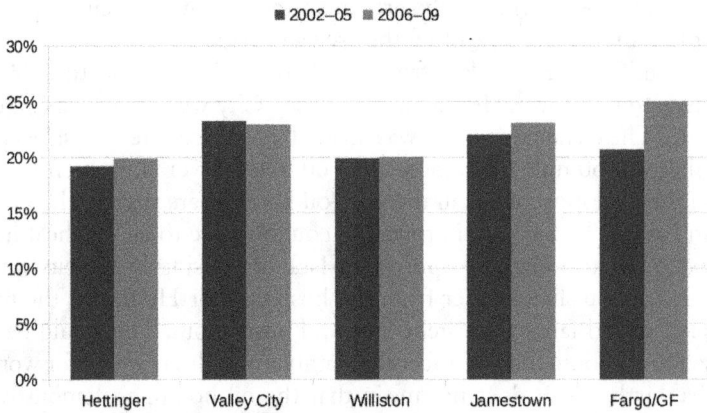

■ 2002–05 ■ 2006–09

Note: $X^2 = 70.2$, $p < .001$

Figure 7. Births with post-natal problems between 2002-2005 and 2006-2009 (source: North Dakota birth certificate data, 2002–2009, North Dakota Department of Health)

childbirth educator and had her own business; and one participant worked as a birth doula, childbirth educator, and Certified Breastfeeding Specialist and had her own business. No further identifiable information was collected, and they are identified here by pseudonyms, per institutional review board guidelines at the University of North Dakota. Participants were recruited via posts on Facebook and North Dakota doula websites. A snowballing technique was used to collect names, phone numbers, or emails. When a potential participant responded and wanted to do the interview over email, the author emailed the informed consent and survey to the participant. If the researcher called the participant, a voicemail was left. When the participant called back, the option was given to do an interview over the phone or an email. Regardless, the informed consent was always emailed.

Interview Protocol and Analysis

The author transcribed each interview verbatim. The transcriptions are presented in this paper in abbreviated form and with a few direct quotes. The interviews included a review of the informed consent. After this, the interviews were conducted and lasted about thirty minutes, if done over the phone. Because the format was interview-based, there were several questions that the researcher asked. Examples include: Have you experienced or seen any positive or negative changes regarding pregnant and birthing patients with whom you work since the oil boom began? Have you experienced or seen any positive or negative changes with how hospitals or clinics handle pregnancy and birth since the oil boom began? The author attempted to make the interviews conversational if they were done over the phone.

Results

Themes of the Interviews

Participants discussed the following themes: (1) parents feel they cannot make their own birth choices because they do not understand them, and (2) hospitals and clinics lack staff and resources. Both themes overlapped with one another. While each participant held different positions and roles in their communities, each talked about similar issues they faced with patients concerning the local clinics, hospitals, and hospital staff. However, there were some differences in opinion between the birth

doulas and the nurses regarding birthing options, why changes have occurred, and where the frustration was directed.

Parents and Birth Choices

Each participant felt that parents often came into appointments not fully
understanding their choices related to the birth process. The birth doulas,
Carol, Sarah, and Jada, felt that the vaginal birth after cesarean (VBAC)
regulations were so restrictive that parents were going through with cesarean births, even when they did not want to. Sarah explained:

> [Parents are] completely unaware that they have rights, that they
> don't have to consent to everything. They have been terribly
> misinformed about the safety and dangers of certain procedures
> ([being told without education that] a cesarean is always the safest
> option, a VBAC is the most dangerous thing you could do). The
> resources available to parents who birth here are pretty slim. Par-
> ents were not always told about other options.

The birth doulas were frustrated with having to refer patients to other
hospitals or to take on patients from other cities and towns who wanted
other options. On the other hand, the nursery nurse, Helen, stated they
follow guidelines by the American College of Obstetricians and Gynecologists and if women wanted to have a VBAC, they could choose to
travel somewhere else. Most of the patients who wanted more or different
birthing options went to Minot, Bismarck, or Sidney, Montana.

Carol also added, "One [concern] that I hear mothers struggle with a
lot is not being able to choose their provider. Because the clinic receives
such an overload of patients, they divide them up among themselves
and don't allow mothers to choose or change." She continued, "The one
choice in town was a family practice MD who recently became sick and is
no longer taking patients, so now there is an OB/GYN practice with four
doctors, and they don't allow women to choose. You get who you get, and
if you throw a fit, you might be out."

Carol's first statement was consistent with what Helen explained:
"[Providing birthing options] makes it difficult when we are don't have
the staff to [meet client's needs] ... we are on [the] shorter side for staff."
She added that because of the traveling nurses,[3] constant change in staff,
and unexpected increased population, it is difficult to meet a client's

---

[3] Traveling nurses work at particular locations for short amounts of time. Their
main purpose is to help hospitals and clinics fill the need of healthcare staff
shortages (Padgett 2009).

needs. The public health nurse, Elsa, added that she has read reports of patients feelings rushed through appointments and not feeling that they are getting their healthcare needs met.

It appeared that the lack of understanding and education, paired with the lack of resources, made for difficult and confusing experiences for the parents and healthcare providers. There also seems to be tension between the birth doulas and the nursery nursing regarding VBAC options. The restrictions are due to the guidelines by the American College of Obstetricians and Gynecologists, which birth doulas felt were too restrictive.

In short, doulas described mothers' lack of control over their birth experience. Not being able to choose one's own provider is stressful, but also it is stressful being on the staff side, as providers are dealing with an influx of population and increased birth rate. Not only has the oil boom affected mothers' abilities to choose how their birth takes place, but it also puts healthcare providers in a difficult position of wanting to provide the best healthcare while being limited by a lack of resources. It also makes it difficult for the birth doulas, who do not work in the hospitals but run their own businesses, since they have to work more diligently to offer resources to their patients in other locations. Furthermore, the quantitative data show that women are traveling further for appointments and birth, and there is a lack of appointments available. If there were more appointments available, parents would have more time and resources to explore their options. Being that appointments are fewer at the beginning of pregnancy, options may not be laid out clearly for the parents.

Lack of Staff and Resources

This theme presented issues similar to the previous one. Helen explained that the hospital in Williston has many traveling nurses and that makes it difficult to keep up with the increasing number of patients, because new traveling nurses need to receive training in each hospital's policy. She also explained that they are averaging fifty to sixty births a month and there were approximately twenty to thirty births a month before the oil boom. Lack of staff and increased rates of births have made it difficult to keep up with the medical and health needs of the patients.

The birth doulas felt that the rise in population has restricted resources and information and has made the obstetricians more restrictive about birth choices. They felt there was not enough time to go through all of the potential options a parent can choose. Furthermore, Elsa explained that it was difficult for patients to get questions answered about their pregnancy: "When calling the hospitals with questionable [birth] labor or concerns, people complain of being brushed off as they are too busy in the OB unit at the time and try to keep unnecessary admits off the unit."

Helen added that women who do not have health insurance and are new to the area come to the hospital instead of clinics for regular prenatal care appointments. She stated that they do run labs and check the fetus. She stated that hopefully the Affordable Care Act will push women to clinics for prenatal appointments instead of hospitals.

Elsa and Helen brought up the issue of discharging patients. Helen explained that they only keep patients in the hospital for twenty-four to thirty-six hours after birth, unless there are other concerns with the mother or baby. Some of the reasons were the lack of rooms and the increase of patients coming into birth. Elsa stated that patients have been complaining because they do not feel ready to leave. Sarah added, "The hospital is so nervous about the potential amount of births and the shortage of workers that they are trying to push mommas and babies out too quickly." She also added that she had her child by cesarean birth in 2011.

Sarah explained that her hospital experience was:

Bad … But where I noticed issues directly related to the population increase was the amount of time it took them to remove my catheter post-surgery. My son was born at [time] am on August 3rd. They did not remove my catheter until after [time] pm on August 4th. I was unable to get up and move for that entire time, despite my requests to move. I feel it was just because they were busy and didn't want to have to deal with getting me up to walk, use the restroom or need anything. I wasn't much trouble to them while stuck in bed.

Carol also added, "the biggest change I have seen is that as they have become busier and busier—the OBs in Williston have restricted choice more and more, mostly due to increasingly limited time and resources."

Jada brought up a similar concern. She explained that the clinics and hospitals are so busy, her patients feel reluctant to ask hospital and clinic staff questions or explore some of their potential options. She added that the patients felt shuffled through appointments, which was similar to what Elsa explained, as well.

Helen explained that babies sometimes have to go to another hospital. The hospital staff often refers these patients to Minot, Bismarck, or Billings, Montana. Mercy Medical Center does not have the resources to handle women who need an immediate operating room team for emergency cesareans. However, she stated they have not had to refer women and babies to another hospital due to lack of birthing rooms.

The theme of lack of resources was very similar to that of the newspaper articles cited above. The lack of resources included lack of hospital staff, patients feeling shuffled through appointments, and lack of choices and education. The participants made links to the population increase and the lack of choices and resources on their own. They felt the drastic changes in the environment were forcing healthcare providers to do what they needed to do to get patients through, instead of taking the time to work with the patients. These issues appear to make the hospital staff make strict decisions without exploring more options with the mothers. Some of this could be because they have no other choice and they have to get patients through, or they are not open to other options related to birth.

On a Positive Note

The two themes pulled from the interview related mostly to negative or challenging issues the health professionals had faced. However, there were some positive things in each interview. While the issues are challenging to everyone, Elsa noted, "I have heard that staff are still amazing most of the time. Much of the staff at the hospital was reported as traveling staff in Williston." Sarah had a similar thought about the travel staff: "there have been a lot of new staff coming in who have experienced birth elsewhere. Who will listen, understand and try with moms. Who will do everything in their power to give moms their desired births." So while there has been difficulty in training and switch over in staff, as Helen had described, the traveling nurses are experienced and from different areas of the country. This was a positive thing for Sarah and Elsa. Helen also had this sentiment. She stated that the members of the permanent staff learn a lot from the traveling nurses, since they have experience in different situations and can bring their experiences to situations the staff come across. She added that the traveling staff balance out the permanent staff.

Discussion

The interviews were eye-opening with respect to the many issues western North Dakota is facing in the health field. One well-known issue even before the interviews was the healthcare staff shortage, and it was something that each participant brought up. Patients reported feeling shuffled through appointments, and they felt they had fewer choices and options. This is concerning, first because important health issues could be missed, and second because women might want other options for birth. This is also concerning as the feeling of being shuffled through appointments could make patients feel less inclined to bring up issues and make it harder to establish trust with providers.

Tensions were clear between the nursing staff and birth doulas about VBAC births and other birth options. This was not a surprising find, as this is a fairly common concern. Regardless, alternative options for patients included referring them to other hospitals (which would do a VBAC birth, for example). However, questions arise from this option such as: is this a sustainable, long-term option? And how does this affect mothers who do not have the resources to travel to another city? Does this affect the health of the mother or baby? What about the increase in traffic?

The interviews also shed light on larger, systemic issues. The oil drilling, the influx of population, and the lack of funding are driving healthcare providers to make the choices they need to make. While healthcare providers are educated on the various options women have in birth, alternative options do not seem possible in this environment. There is no time to discuss alternatives nor are there resources to provide them.

An obvious fix for this situation is to hire more obstetrics and gynecology staff, midwives, and other healthcare providers. Jessica Sobolik's chapter in this volume explores potential solutions to these problems even further. This approach would give more resources and options for patients. It would also be an opportunity to offer more advocacy for birth doulas and their patients. However, this is more complex than simply hiring more people. There is a lack of housing, and it is more expensive to live in Williston generally. Traffic jams exist and crime has increased. People are probably not as inclined to move there because of the changing environment.

These interviews were only a snapshot in time of particular issues in western North Dakota. They did not shed light on many long-term issues. What about the environmental health issues related to newborns and pregnancy? Previous studies have found concerning issues such as babies born with low birth weight, increased risk of prenatal problems, and increased risk and preterm deliveries associated with living near drilling sites. Do these findings repeat in the Bakken?

Lastly, it is important for healthcare providers to work with their patients to the best of their ability. The interviewees stated that the healthcare providers are working to the best of their ability, but the environment and structural issues are also informing their decisions. This may not change soon, either. It will be important to continue addressing these issues and putting the resources and money toward the issues to change them.

Acknowledgements

Dr. Marilyn G. Klug and Mandi-Leigh Peterson from the Center for Rural Health obtained institutional review board approval from the North Dakota Department of Health and the University of North Dakota.

References

Bullinger, Kenan. 2012. "Public and Environmental Health Impacts of the North Dakota Oil Boom." Presentation at the annual North Central Association of Food and Drug Officials, October 16, 2012. Accessed February 18, 2014. www.ncafdo.org/default/assets// File/K%20Bullinger%20-%201%20Public%20%26%20Environmental%20Impacts%20of%20Oil%20Boom%20%2010-16-12.pdf.

Bump, Philip. 2013 "North Dakota's Oil Boom Strains Healthcare System." *Grist* (Seattle, WA), January 28. Accessed March 21, 2014. grist.org/news/north-dakotas-oil-boom-strains-healthcare-system/.

Centers for Disease Control and Prevention. 2013. *Births and Natality*. Accessed February 18, 2014. www.cdc.gov/nchs/fastats/births.htm.

Dwelle, Terry. 2013. "North Dakota's Oil Boom Results in Population Growth Across the State and Public Health Challenges." Accessed February 18, 2014. Association of State and Territorial Health Officials. www.astho.org/Programs/Infectious-Disease/ North-Dakota%E2%80%99s-Oil-Boom-Results-in-Population-Growth-Across-the-State-and-Public-Health-Challenges/.

Eligon, John. 2013 "An Oil Boom Takes a Toll on Health Care." *New York Times*, February 27. Accessed March 21, 2014. www.nytimes.com/2013/01/28/us/boom-in-north-dakota-weighs-heavily-on-health-care.html.

Hill, Elaine L. 2013. "Shale Gas Development and Infant Health: Evidence From Pennsylvania." Working Paper, Charles H. Dyson School of Applied Economics and Management. Accessed February

25, 2014. dyson.cornell.edu/research/researchpdf/wp/2012/Cornell-Dyson-wp1212.pdf.

Little, R. L. 1997. "Some Social Consequences of Boom Towns." *North Dakota Law Review* 53: 401–26.

Liu, Yuting, Shenjing He, Fulong Wu, and Christ Webster. 2010. "Urban Villages Under China's Rapid Urbanization: Unregulated Assets and Transitional Neighbourhood." *Habitat International* 34: 135.

McKenzie, Lisa M., Roxana Z. Witter, Lee S. Newman, and John L. Adgate. 2012. "Human Health Risk Assessment of Air Emissions from Development of Unconventional Natural Gas Resources." *Science of the Total Environment* 424: 79–87.

McKenzie, Lisa M., Guo Ruixin, Roxana Z. Witter, David A. Savitz, Lee S. Newman, and John L. Adgate. 2014. "Birth Outcomes and Maternal Residential Proximity to Natural Gas Development in Rural Colorado." *Environmental Health Perspective* 122, no. 4. doi: 10.1289/ehp.1306722.

North Dakota Department of Health. 2012. "Environmental Incident Reports." September 2012. Accessed January 25, 2014. www.ndhealth.gov/EHS/Spills/.

North Dakota Department of Health. Division of Vital Records. 2013a. "C-Section Reports." Accessed January 25, 2014. December 2013. www.ndhealth.gov/vital/pubs.htm.

North Dakota Department of Health. Division of Vital Records. 2013b. "Fast Facts." December. Accessed January 25, 2014. www.ndhealth.gov/vital/pubs.htm.

Padgett Barry W. 2009. *Travel Nurse Insights*. 1st ed. Mobile, AL: Buffalo Nickel Publishing.

San Sebastián, Miguel, Ben Armstrong, and Carolyn Stephones. 2002. "Outcomes of Pregnancy among Women Living in the Proximity of Oil Fields in the Amazon Basin of Ecuador." *International Journal of Occupational and Environmental Health* 8: 312–19.

Springer, Patrick. 2011. "Oil Patch Health-Care Facilities Stressed as Populations Grow." *Dickinson Press*, November 13. Accessed March 23, 2014. origin-www.thedickinsonpress.com/event/article/id/52909/.

Tsai, Shang-Shyue, Hsin-Su Yu, Chia-Chia Liu, and Chun-Yuh Yang. 2003. "Increased Incidence of Preterm Delivery in Mothers Residing

In an Industrialized Area in Taiwan." *Journal of Toxicology and Environmental Health: Part A* 66: 987–95.

United States Census Bureau. 2013. "State & County QuickFacts." Accessed January 25, 2014. December. quickfacts.census.gov/qfd/states/38000.html.

United States Census Bureau. 2014. "State and County Facts." March 27. Accessed January 25, 2014. quickfacts.census.gov/qfd/states/38/3886220.html.

Yang, Chun-Yuh. 2002. "Increased Risk of Preterm Delivery in Areas with Air Pollution From a Petroleum Refinery Plant in Taiwan." *Journal of Toxicology and Environmental Health: Part A* 64: 637–44.

Yang, Chun-Yuh, Hui-Fen Chiu, Shang-Shyue Tsai, Chih-Ching Chang, and Hung-Yi Chuang. 2002. "Increased Risk of Preterm Delivery in Areas with Cancer Mortality Problems from Petrochemical Complexes." *Environmental Research* 89: 195–201.

CHAPTER 9

DOCTORS WANTED: HOW THE BAKKEN CHANGED NORTH DAKOTA HEALTH CARE DELIVERY

Jessica Sobolik

We often hear through the news media that a physician shortage is occurring in the United States (Association of American Medical Colleges
2014a). Headlines warn that the number of doctors needed to treat
aging baby boomers is insufficient. Furthermore, many physicians are
approaching retirement. However, in rural states like North Dakota, distribution of health care is a larger problem (UND School of Medicine
and Health Sciences 2012, vii). The state's relatively small population
(700,000) is spread out over a large geographic area, and there are not
enough physicians to adequately serve everyone. Thus, people who live
in rural areas often travel more than one hundred miles to receive specialized health care.

During the latest oil boom in western North Dakota, the growing population has strained the state's health care system even further. The new
challenge is twofold: not just a sharp increase in population in general,
but a change in demographics that were not prevalent in North Dakota
since the 1930s (U.S. Census Bureau 2014). Young men doing dangerous
work, often requiring visits to the emergency room (Eligon 2013), have in
many cases brought young families to the state. Hospitals are scrambling
to provide the services that this new demographic requires, among other
challenges. This chapter will explore North Dakota's current health care
system network, the state's demographic changes, the challenges the network is facing, and solutions that may result in better health care for all.

North Dakota's Health Care Network

North Dakota's health care network includes six tertiary hospitals, or the
Big Six: Altru Health System in Grand Forks, Essentia Health in Fargo,
Sanford Health in Bismarck and Fargo, St. Alexius Medical Center in
Bismarck, and Trinity Health in Minot (UND School of Medicine and

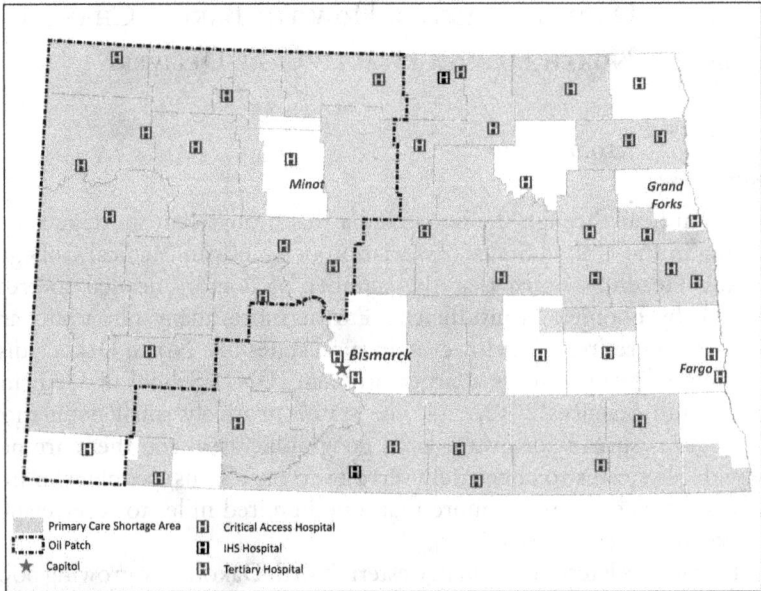

Figure 1. North Dakota's hospital system network (source: UND School of Medicine and Health Sciences 2012, 66).

Health Sciences 2012, 66). Tertiary hospitals offer specialized medical care involving complex procedures and treatments by medical specialists (as opposed to primary or secondary care). The Big Six are located in the four largest cities in the state. In other words, if you were to divide the general rectangle shape of North Dakota into four quarters, each city would serve a quarter (see Figure 1).

The state also has thirty-six critical access hospitals (CAHs, pronounced "caws"). CAHs serve rural areas of the state and must meet federal guidelines such as no more than twenty-five short-term care beds, an average length of stay for patients of ninety-six hours or less, and a location with thirty-five miles of another hospital (not necessarily a tertiary hospital). In addition to various clinics and the tertiary hospitals, CAHs form a network of health care across the state. This does not include the state's three psychiatric hospitals (Fargo, Jamestown, and Grand Forks), two long-term acute care hospitals (Fargo and Mandan), two Indian Health Service hospitals (Ft. Yates and Belcourt), and one rehabilitation hospital (Grand Forks) (North Dakota Department of Health 2014a). Physicians from the Big Six often travel to the CAHs one or two days per week or month to provide specialized care for those who might not be able to travel to the Big Six.

In addition to tertiary hospital Trinity Health in Minot, twelve CAHs are located within the Bakken oil patch: Community Memorial Hospital, Turtle Lake; Garrison Memorial Hospital, Dickinson; Kenmare Community Hospital, Kenmare; Mercy Medical Center, Williston; McKenzie County Hospital, Watford City; Mountrail County Medical Center Hospital, Stanley; Sakakawea Medical Center, Hazen; Southwest Medical Clinic, Bowman; St. Andrew's Health Center, Bottineau; St. Joseph's Hospital, Dickinson; St. Luke's Hospital, Crosby; and Tioga Medical Center, Tioga (UND School of Medicine and Health Sciences 2012, 66). CAHs more centrally located in the Bakken oil field, such as Mercy Medical Center in Williston, are more affected than those on the outskirts, such as Sakakawea Medical Center in Hazen. A closer look at the challenges faced by individual centers later in this chapter may better illustrate how each facility is being affected differently by the oil boom making it difficult to come up with a blanket solution that would fix all health care delivery problems across the state.

Population Changes

Several population and demographic changes have occurred in North Dakota since the Bakken oil boom began, which greatly affect health care delivery. Because many changes have occurred after the U.S. Census in

2010, it is difficult to pinpoint exact population and demographic statistics for the western part of the state today. Still, the U.S. Census Bureau, the authority for demographic statistics, makes projections between census years. Those projections are used in this chapter.

Overall, the state's population tallied 672,591 in 2010 (U.S. Census Bureau 2014). Since then, the U.S. Census Bureau has projected a 4.3 percent increase in population in 2012 and a 7.6 percent increase in 2013 for a record total of 723,393. The previous record of 680,845 was tallied in 1930, right before the Great Depression derailed the state's burgeoning agricultural industry (UND School of Medicine and Health Sciences 2012, 10). In general, the state's population is increasing rapidly, three times more than the national rate (U.S. Census Bureau 2014).

Demographically, North Dakota is the second-oldest state in the nation behind Rhode Island in the percentage of its population over eighty-five-years-old (defined as "elderly") (UND School of Medicine and Health Sciences 2012, 5). Based on 2012 Census Bureau population projections, people over age sixty-five made up 14.4 percent of the state's population (U.S. Census Bureau 2014). Older populations use more health care workforce resources than younger populations requiring more ambulatory services and more family physician visits (UND School of Medicine and Health Sciences 2012, 5).

However, 22.1 percent of the state's projected 2012 population (701,345) consists of children under age 18 (U.S. Census Bureau 2014). Children and their mothers require physicians of different specialties, primarily pediatrics and obstetrics/gynecology. As far as gender goes, according to 2012 projections, the state's population is still split roughly 50/50, although more men are working in the oil fields.

North Dakota counties that saw the largest population increase from 2000 to 2010 were primarily in the western part of the state: Burleigh (Bismarck), Mountrail (Stanley), Williams (Williston), McKenzie (Watford City), Morton (Mandan), Stark (Dickinson), and Ward (Minot) (UND School of Medicine and Health Sciences 2012, 11). Burleigh, Mountrail, Williams and McKenzie counties increased their populations by more than 10 percent.

Generally speaking, the population in western North Dakota will continue to grow and demographics will continue to change as oil production in the area increases. In order for hospitals to provide adequate health care to the growing population, they must understand the area's changing demographics.

Physician Specialties

Primary care physicians are most in demand in North Dakota and across the nation, followed by general surgeons. Various health care entities categorize primary care specialties differently; this chapter uses the most generally accepted definition of primary care as family medicine (basic health care), internal medicine (prevention, diagnosis, and treatment of adult diseases) and pediatrics (development, care, and diseases of babies and children). There are 550 primary care physicians practicing in North Dakota (UND School of Medicine and Health Sciences 2012, 52). Fifty-nine percent of them specialize in family medicine, 28 percent are internists, and 13 percent are pediatricians. Primary care physicians do not earn as much compensation as other specialists (Association of American Medical Colleges 2014b), a fact that likely has some effect on workforce shortages in western North Dakota.

Aside from primary care, physicians can specialize in a number of areas. More popular specialties include: anesthesiology, dermatology, emergency medicine, neurology/psychiatry, obstetrics/gynecology, ophthalmology, otolaryngology, pathology, radiology, surgery (orthopedic, plastic, thoracic), and urology (American Board of Medical Specialties 2014). One can also subspecialize in a particular specialty. For example, cardiology is a subspecialty of internal medicine.

Specialists in North Dakota are more often found at the tertiary hospitals where patients requiring those specialties are expected to go (see Figure 2). However, recognizing that sometimes patients are unable to travel long distances, some specialists travel to the CAHs on a limited basis.

Workforce Needs

In 2011–13, CAHs responded to a survey that helped form individual community health needs assessments compiled by the Center for Rural Health at the UND School of Medicine and Health Sciences. Of the twelve CAHs in Bakken oil country, all identified "health care workforce shortage" as one of their significant health needs (Center for Rural Health 2014). Less than one-third of all CAHs *did not* identify this need, indicating a statewide challenge as opposed to a Bakken challenge. Assuming all CAHs were already facing this challenge, the oil boom only made the issue worse.

It is important to note that not all twelve western North Dakota CAHs feel affected by the Bakken oil boom. "We are impacted, but not nearly to the degree that those in the center of the activity are," said Darrold

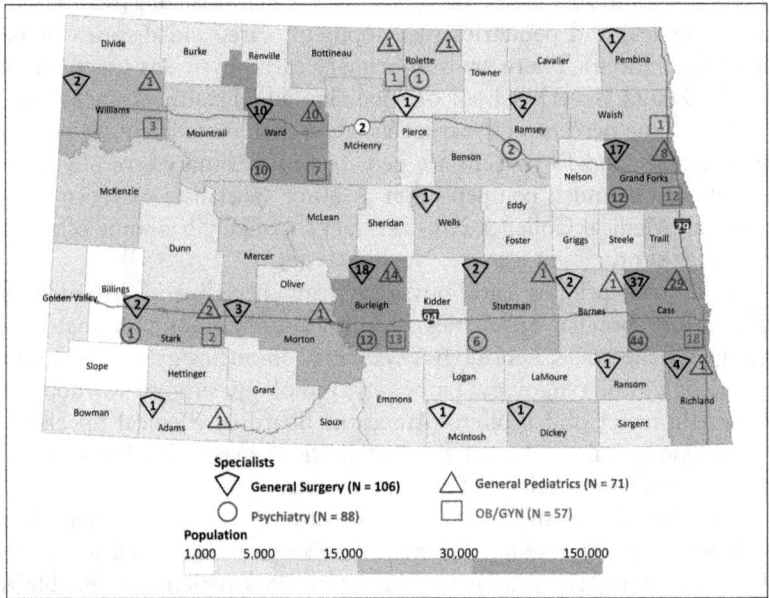

Figure 2. Location of specialty physicians in North Dakota (source: UND School of Medicine and Health Sciences 2012, 55).

Bertsch, CEO of Sakakawea Medical Center in Hazen, in an email to this author. However, facility administrators are still hoping to restart obstetric services and add specialized pediatric services (Hall 2012, 52–53). The number of young families is increasing in western North Dakota, and patients living in Hazen, for example, currently travel seventy miles to Bismarck to receive those services.

Southwest Medical Clinic in Bowman was one of few facilities that did not indicate oil field challenges at all in its community health needs assessment. In fact, it predicted a slight decrease in total population between 2000 and 2017 (Eide Bailly 2013, 10).

Clearly, not every CAH has the same needs when it comes to specialties. Some have more of a need for family medicine physicians. Others agree that pediatricians and obstetricians/gynecologists are needed (Jackson, current volume). But almost all CAHs in the Bakken have indicated workforce challenges tied to the oil industry, even at St. Andrew's Health Center in Bottineau in the far northeast corner of the Bakken oil patch. In its community health needs assessment, the facility's community members and health care providers acknowledged a growing population and a similar increase in emergency room visits (Hall and Becker 2012, 33). In addition to the specialists mentioned above, health care providers in the area also expressed interest in expanded radiology services (e.g., ultrasound and MRI) (Hall and Becker 2012, 40).

As cited in his facility's community health needs assessment, Tioga Medical Center CEO Randall Pederson also reported a growing number of emergency room visits. "In 2007, we would see 600 patients in ER per year," he said. "In 2012, we anticipate seeing over 2,000. So in a five-year period, we have more than tripled our emergency room visits" (Becker and Hall 2013, 58). The assessment also indicated an interest in adding surgeons (general and orthopedic) (Becker and Hall 2013, 60).

For this chapter, administrators at the twelve CAHs were interviewed in order to identify challenges being faced since the community health needs assessments were completed. Out of the twelve, four administrators completed the interview questions, one responded briefly in general, two declined participation due to other commitments, and five were unreachable. The following is a closer look at four specific facilities, their communities and their physician needs, along with a brief indication of how the facilities plan to fill those needs (e.g., recruitment agencies).

Spotlight on Williston

Williston has been identified as the center of oil boom activity (Rocco 2013). In its community health needs assessment, respondents addressed the demographic changes taking place in the community. "Lifelong residents are bitter about the influx of residents due to the oil boom and they feel their needs are not being met," one said. Others mentioned that elderly residents were moving away because of the increase in the cost of living (e.g., housing, food) (Hall and Becker 2013b, 43).

In an email to this chapter's author, Mercy Medical Center CEO Matt Grimshaw confirmed the demographic challenges facing his facility in Williston. "The most significant change in our region, apart from the increase in population, has been the changing demographics," he said. "Williston is getting younger faster than any city in America, and because of that, the kind of services needed here have changed dramatically. Demand for the many services needed by younger people have increased 100 percent in the past four years (ER, obstetrics, pediatrics), while other services have only increased slightly (inpatient surgery, intensive care)."

Grimshaw confirmed that his facility was facing a physician shortage before the oil boom began. He estimates the current shortage in Williston is approximately six full-time primary care physicians, and he projects that shortage to increase to more than twenty providers over the next five years. Specialties currently needed include emergency medicine, orthopedics, general surgery and oncology. Future needs include cardiology, urology, and critical care. Mercy Medical Center is actively recruiting to fill open positions with physicians who are a good fit with the facility's existing team and who are "fully committed to providing the highest quality of care possible," according to Grimshaw. The facility utilizes online recruiting resources and multiple recruiting firms. In the meantime, the facility brings specialists in from multiple neighboring facilities. These specialists focus on cardiology, neurology, neurosurgery, and oncology.

Spotlight on Garrison

Garrison is located between Minot and Bismarck on the eastern border of the Bakken oil patch. According to its community health needs assessment, St. Alexius Garrison Memorial Hospital has seen an increase in acute and emergency room visits because of the oil boom (Howe Enterprises LLC 2013, 5). In an email to this author, hospital administrator Tod Graeber confirmed that the oil boom has greatly stressed his facility's emergency medicine department, similar to St. Andrew's Health Center in Bottineau and Tioga Medical Center. "Our emergency department has seen increases of 25 to 30 percent in volume in the past five years," he said.

He also mentioned the challenge of collecting payments from patients after services were provided. "There are a lot more transient patients," he said. "These patients are often hard to track down to find an address to send a bill to. There are a lot of good-paying jobs, but often a lot of these workers do not have health insurance."

In the community health needs assessment, Garrison community members and health care professionals indicated the number one reason patients seek health care services in other towns is because of a lack of specialists (Howe Enterprises LLC 2013, 47–48). According to Graeber, the hospital only provides primary care and emergency care, for which he feels the facility is adequately staffed. The hospital used to provide specialty services via visiting physicians one or two days per month. However, since western North Dakota's population has grown, Graeber said the hospital has lost access to some of its visiting specialists who are being called elsewhere. These included urologists, podiatrists, neurologists, and psychologists. Graeber is hoping to restore some of these services in the future. The facility posts its job openings on its website, on related industry websites, and in relevant professional publications.

Spotlight on Kenmare

Located 50 miles northwest of Minot, Trinity Kenmare Hospital is located on the eastern edge of the Bakken oil patch. Still, the community has felt significantly affected by a growing population according to its community health needs assessment. Young single males make up most of the influx, and their chosen profession in the oil fields is requiring more emergency services (Trinity Kenmare Community Hospital 2013, 4).

In an email to this author, hospital administrator Shawn Smothers said her facility only has one physician who rotates with a family nurse practitioner every other week. She would like to hire another family medicine physician, but the hospital cannot afford one. Instead, it is considering hiring a midlevel provider—a family nurse practitioner—to cover clinic hours, as well as the emergency room and overnight shifts. Smothers also pointed out that it has been difficult to keep adequate hospital staff on the payroll. Either they are leaving for higher paying jobs in the oil fields, or they have spouses making enough money in the oil fields making a second income unnecessary.

Outside of primary care, the hospital does not have any specialists except a podiatrist who visits the facility once a month and a physician who covers the emergency room up to ten days a month. Smothers did not feel additional specialists were needed, although community members have expressed interest in having more access to an oncologist (Center for Rural Health 2013, 10). The hospital utilizes recruitment agencies to fill job openings.

Spotlight on Watford City

Watford City, like Williston, is more centrally located in the Bakken oil field. Forty-five miles southeast of Williston, McKenzie County Healthcare System has a greater need for emergency medicine, just like in Tioga and Garrison. According to CEO Dan Kelly in an email to this author, the county's hospital was seeing fewer than one hundred emergency room patients per month in 2007. Today, that number exceeds five hundred per month. "In addition, we're seeing more trauma patients," he said. Further, according to the hospital's community health needs assessment, there are not enough outpatient clinic doctors to see patients in a timely manner, so patients are using the emergency room as a walk-in clinic (Hall and Becker 2013a, 60).

In particular, Kelly does not feel his facility has the need for a full-time pediatrician or obstetrician/gynecologist just yet, but as the population increases, he acknowledges that will change. However, he would like to recruit one more family or internal medicine physician. Currently, the ratio of McKenzie County residents to primary care physicians is five times the state average and six times the national average (Hall and Becker 2013a, 60). On the other hand, community members indicated a need for more "birthing services/obstetrics" and pediatric services in the community health needs assessment (Hall and Becker 2013a, 44). So while some community members desire these specialties, there are still not enough patients to justify bringing these full-time specialists on board. In addition, cardiologists, pediatricians, and orthopedic surgeons operate separate specialty clinics in the area.

Solutions

This chapter has identified a number of challenges facing health care facilities in western North Dakota today. In summary, there has been a swift increase in population, changing patient demographics, a shortage of specialists and physician recruitment. Particularly CAHs are seeing a greater need for pediatricians, obstetricians/gynecologists, and emergency medicine providers.

In light of this information, solutions are being identified and action plans are being formed across the state. CAHs are drafting their implementation strategies based on the community health needs assessments. Also, the UND School of Medicine and Health Sciences has developed the

Health Care Workforce Initiative, which aims to reduce disease burden, increase retention of graduates, increase student class sizes and improve the health care delivery system overall (UND School of Medicine and Health Sciences 2012, 108–10). According to its purpose statement, the School of Medicine and Health Sciences, the only medical school in the state, is responsible for educating future physicians and other health professionals and enhancing the quality of life for all North Dakotans (UND School of Medicine and Health Sciences 2013).

By reducing disease burden, or encouraging disease prevention, fewer people would get sick and therefore require fewer health care services. Specific to the Bakken oil fields, for example, educating workers about preventing sexually transmitted infections could reduce the number of future health care visits. Public health officials already provide these educational services to physicians (North Dakota Department of Health 2014b). The UND School of Medicine and Health Sciences created a Master of Public Health program in 2012 to educate more public health officials (UND School of Medicine and Health Sciences 2012).

Retaining graduates is perhaps the most challenging goal, but also one of vital importance. All medical school graduates are required to complete residency training, which lasts three to seven years depending on the specialty (Association of American Medical Colleges 2014c, 11). Yet most residencies are located outside the state, and statistics indicate that medical students are more likely to practice in the state where he or she completed residency training (UND School of Medicine 2012, 104). In-state residency programs include family medicine, internal medicine, psychiatry, and surgery. Discussions are underway to resurrect the state's obstetrics/gynecology residency program. Furthermore, the North Dakota Legislature approved funding for a RuralMed Program, which defrays tuition costs if the graduate agrees to practice family medicine in a rural area of the state for five years (UND School of Medicine 2012, 109).

Increasing student class sizes would increase the likelihood of more graduates choosing to practice in North Dakota. Therefore, the state legislature approved funding to allow the School to increase its class sizes starting in summer 2012 (UND School of Medicine 2012, 109–10). Using medical students as an example, the first expanded class would graduate in 2016 and finish residency training no earlier than 2019.

Improving the health care delivery system would encourage the tertiary hospitals to work cooperatively with the CAHs across the state to ensure that all areas of the state receive quality health care.

To get a better idea of how long it takes to produce certain specialists, it may be helpful to look at the latest graduating class of medical students at the UND School of Medicine and Health Sciences. Out of a class of sixty-four students graduating in May 2014, nine plan to go into family medicine, four are going into obstetrics/gynecology, five are going into emergency medicine, and four are going into pediatrics (UND School of Medicine and Health Sciences 2014). The rest have chosen other specialties. Comparing these numbers to the needs identified in Williston and elsewhere (e.g., Mercy Medical Center needing six primary care providers), this year's class cannot fill current shortfalls, so physicians must be brought in from out of state or outside the United States. Midlevel providers (e.g., nurse practitioners, physician assistants) could also help fill the gaps. No matter what solutions or action plans are identified as the best, it is certain that inaction would only make the physician shortage worse and the health care delivery system in western North Dakota more strained.

Summary

In conclusion, the delivery of health care via CAHs across North Dakota was already strained before the latest Bakken oil boom occurred. Now, CAHs are lacking the appropriate workforce to provide the necessary health care for their communities. In general, the specialists most needed or desired are pediatricians, obstetricians/gynecologists and especially emergency medicine providers. However, just because community members desire additional services or providers, it may not warrant actual hiring of those providers.

Each community has been impacted differently. By taking a closer look at four specific CAHs and their communities (Williston, Garrison, Kenmare, and Watford City), it is evident that each facility must develop unique strategies to follow in the near future.

By identifying the changing North Dakota demographics and the parallel needs of the state's CAHs, the UND School of Medicine and Health Sciences and other health care partners can then develop the most effective ways to improve health care delivery statewide, which is especially challenging when the state's population increases so quickly. As history has shown, North Dakota's health care network will work together to ensure that everyone is entitled and has access to high-quality health care.

References

American Board of Medical Specialties. 2014. "Specialties and Subspecialties." www.abms.org/who_we_help/physicians/specialties.aspx.

Association of American Medical Colleges. 2014a. "Physician Shortages to Worsen Without Increases in Residency Training." www.aamc.org/download/153160/data/physician_shortages_to_worsen_without_increases_in_residency_tr.pdf.

Association of American Medical Colleges. 2014b. "Starting Salaries for Physicians." www.aamc.org/services/first/first_factsheets/399572/compensation.html.

Association of American Medical Colleges. 2014c. "The Road to Becoming a Doctor." www.aamc.org/download/68806/data/road-doctor.pdf.

Becker, Karin, and Ken Hall. 2012–13. "Community Health Needs Assessment: Tioga Medical Center, Tioga, North Dakota." Grand Forks: University of North Dakota Center for Rural Health. ruralhealth.und.edu/projects/community-health-needs-assessment/pdf/2012-2013-tioga-medical-center.pdf.

Center for Rural Health. 2014 "List of Most Significant Health Needs by North Dakota Community." Grand Forks: University of North Dakota Center for Rural Health. ruralhealth.und.edu/projects/community-health-needs-assessment/pdf/most-significant-health-needs-by-community.pdf.

Eide Bailly. 2013. "Southwest Healthcare Services Community Health Needs Assessment 2013." Grand Forks: University of North Dakota Center for Rural Health. ruralhealth.und.edu/projects/community-health-needs-assessment/pdf/2013-southwest-healthcare-services.pdf.

Eligon, John. 2013. "An Oil Boom Takes a Toll on Health Care." *New York Times.* www.nytimes.com/2013/01/28/us/boom-in-north-dakota-weighs-heavily-on-health-care.html.

Hall, Ken. 2012. "Community Health Needs Assessment: Sakakawea Medical Center; Custer Public Health Unit, Coal Country Community Health Center; Knife River Care Center; and Mercer County Ambulance, Hazen, ND." Grand Forks: University of North Dakota Center for Rural Health. ruralhealth.und.edu/projects/community-health-needs-assessment/pdf/2012-beulah-hazen-center.pdf.

Hall, Ken, and Karin Becker. 2012. "Community Health Needs Assessment: St. Andrew's Health Center, Bottineau, North Dakota." Grand Forks: University of North Dakota Center for Rural Health.

ruralhealth.und.edu/projects/community-health-needs-assessment/
pdf/2012-st-andrews-health-center.pdf.

Hall, Ken, and Karin Becker. 2013a. "Community Health Needs Assessment: McKenzie County Healthcare Systems, Watford City, North Dakota." Grand Forks: University of North Dakota Center for Rural Health. ruralhealth.und.edu/projects/community-health-needs-assessment/pdf/2012-2013-mckenzie-county-healthcare-systems.pdf.

Hall, Ken, and Karin Becker. 2013b. "Community Health Needs Assessment: Mercy Medical Center, Williston, North Dakota." Grand Forks: University of North Dakota Center for Rural Health. ruralhealth.und.edu/projects/community-health-needs-assessment/pdf/2012-2013-mercy-medical-center-williston.pdf.

Hall, Ken, and Karin Becker. 2013c. "Community Health Needs Assessment: St. Joseph's Hospital and Health Center, Dickinson, North Dakota." Grand Forks: University of North Dakota Center for Rural Health. ruralhealth.und.edu/projects/community-health-needs-assessment/pdf/2013-st-josephs-hospital-and-health-center.pdf.

Howe Enterprises LLC. 2013. "St. Alexius Garrison Memorial Hospital Community Health Needs Assessment." Grand Forks: University of North Dakota Center for Rural Health. ruralhealth.und.edu/projects/community-health-needs-assessment/pdf/2013-st-alexius-garrison-memorial-hospital.pdf.

North Dakota Department of Health. 2014a. "Facility Directory." www.ndhealth.gov/HF/PDF_files/Hospital/hospital_feb_2014.pdf.

North Dakota Department of Health. 2014b. "Sexually Transmitted Diseases." ndhealth.gov/std/.

Rocco, Matthew. 2013. "North Dakota Oil Boom Driving Economic Development." Foxbusiness.com, 11 February. www.foxbusiness.com/economy/2013/02/11/north-dakota-oil-boom-driving-economic-development/.

Trinity Kenmare Community Hospital. 2013. "Community Health Needs Assessment Report and Implementation Strategy." Grand Forks: University of North Dakota Center for Rural Health. ruralhealth.und.edu/projects/community-health-needs-assessment/pdf/2013-trinity-kenmare-community-hospital.pdf.

UND School of Medicine and Health Sciences. 2012. "Second Biennial Report 2013." Last modified December. www.med.und.edu/community/files/docs/second-biennial-report.pdf.

UND School of Medicine and Health Sciences. 2013. "Purpose Statement." Last modified May 31. www.med.und.edu/about-us/purpose-statement.cfm.

UND School of Medicine and Health Sciences. 2014. "Residency Sites: Class of 2014." Last modified March 21. www.med.und.edu/enews/documents/document201403261197028.pdf.

U.S. Census Bureau. 2014. "State and County Quick Facts: North Dakota." Accessed March 21. quickfacts.census.gov/qfd/states/38000.html.

PART 4

ENVIRONMENTS
AND THE
BOOM

CHAPTER 10

THE ARCHAEOLOGY OF MAN CAMPS:
CONTINGENCY, PERIPHERY, AND LATE CAPITALISM

William Caraher

One of the most visible and discussed aspects of the Bakken Oil Boom is the proliferation of so-called "man camps" in Williams and McKenzie Counties in North Dakota. The term "man camp" is a colloquialism for the temporary workforce housing associated with the Bakken oil boom and other similar booms across the world and throughout history. It is a general term encompassing a range of housing types from clusters of squatters in public parks to RV and mobile home parks and relatively luxurious transportable compounds provided by and for global companies. The range of habitation in the Bakken and the influx of workers into this remote corner of the world captured the attention of the global media and put a human face on the challenges and opportunities of this 21st century oil boom. The contrasting figures of the remote, forbidding, and abandoned northern plains and the eager arrival of workers from around the country attracted global interest (Bowden 2008; Brown 2013). Few images capture this contrast better than the NASA photographs showing the light from drill rigs, equipment, and the flaring of natural gas to emphasize the shocking scale of development in the Bakken and its relative remoteness from the bright lights of the coasts and regional centers like Chicago and Minneapolis (NASA n.d). The juxtaposed remoteness of the Bakken and the influx of workers has provided a provocative perspective on the character of extractive industries, contingent labor, and global capitalism.

As the contents of this book show, the bright lights of the oil patch not only lured oil works to the Bakken, but researchers as well seeking understand that challenges and opportunities associated with the transformation of the Bakken region. Since 2012, the North Dakota Man Camp Project has focused on the architecture, material conditions, and human aspects of workforce in the Bakken oil patch. Our research combined interviews with the careful documentation of the material culture around temporary workforce housing sites to produce an extensive dataset of attitudes, objects, and architecture in the Bakken. Our goal was to locate the Bakken Boom in a global and historical context. My contribution to this volume uses tools associated with archaeology of the contemporary world to situate workforce housing in the Bakken in a global context. An archaeological focus provides a way to integrate both contemporary and historical perspectives on architecture and space in late modernity, the dynamics of core-periphery interaction, and the ongoing discussion of the western frontier in American historiography (Harrison and Schofield 2010; Graves-Brown et al. 2013; for the archaeology of capitalism see: McGuire 2014; Cowie 2011; Shackel 2009; Johnson 1996).

My position in writing this essay (and editing this volume) is both as an insider and as an outsider. As a North Dakotan, I have a front row seat to the ongoing discussions about the prospects, potential, and pitfalls of the Bakken boom. I am distinctly aware of the economic, environmental, and human costs of the boom on both the standard of living in present and the future generations in the state. My physical proximity to the oil patch, regular conversations with friends, colleagues, and students who feel its direct impact on their communities, and access to ongoing research and policy discussions among residents of the state has certainly shaped my opinions and complicated the influence of the national media's generally polarized coverage of the oil boom. On an academic level, the history department at the University of North Dakota stands in the long shadow of Frederick Jackson Turner's frontier thesis. The first professional historian in the department was Orin G. Libby, a student of Frederick Jackson Turner, who established an important foundation for the study of North Dakota (Caraher 2009; Iseminger 2001). Libby's successor, Elwyn B. Robinson produced the landmark *History of North Dakota*, and suffused it with Turnerian views on the challenges of the western frontier (Robinson 1966).

At the same time, I am an outsider to the basic narrative of North Dakota history and many of the disciplinary tools necessary to analyze such a complex, modern phenomena like the Bakken boom. I was not trained in U.S. History, anthropology, or even the archaeology of the contemporary world. My background is in intensive pedestrian survey in Greece and Cyprus, Early Christian architecture, and the ancient and early Medieval Eastern Mediterranean. Translating these experiences and training to North Dakota, I attempted to combine the rigorous data collection models from intensive Mediterranean survey with more ad hoc practice reflecting the complexity of particularly dynamic, modern historical assemblages. Moreover, my experiences working both on Cyprus with its long history of extractive industries and at peripheral and short-term habitation sites in Greece and Cyprus has encouraged me to consider the archaeological signature of short-term habitation at sites from the Hellenistic period to the early 20th century (Knapp et al. 1998; Caraher et al. 2006; Caraher et al. 2010; Caraher et al. 2014). Many of these sites stand at the periphery of settlement in the region and reflect interests of a regional core to project their power into their own frontier zones (Hall et al. 2011). My experiences, then, in the Mediterranean informed both the methods that we used to document workforce housing in the Bakken, as well as my tendency to interpret short-term housing in western North Dakota as characteristic of a historical and global periphery.

Methods and Typology

My rather unorthodox background freed our research project from a commitment to any particular disciplinary tool kit and this proved valuable for understanding the geographically dispersed and constantly changing landscape of the Bakken oil boom. North Dakota Man Camp Project travelled to the Bakken counties with a team of archaeologists, historians, architectural historians, and photographers. Our methods for documenting the various camps followed procedures developed by archaeologists working in across a wide range of historical periods, but particularly the newly emerging field of archaeology of the contemporary world. We complemented these methods with approaches drawn from the social sciences and oral history to gather interviews with the residents of the camp. Most of these interviews were quite long and relatively unstructured.

This paper draws upon evidence collected from over 50 workforce housing sites through architectural and archaeological methods. Each site received a number, a basic description, and a sample of individual units from each camp received more thorough documentation. Whenever possible we took systematic photographs of the camps from the air using a kite and from the ground using a camera mounted to a slow moving vehicle. In many cases, we also sketched plans of the camps and individualunits. The photographs, detailed descriptions, and sketches became part of an archive uploaded to the cloud and accessible to all the participants in the project. Eventually, this archive will be part of a permanent record for the project.

As the first step in analyzing this data, we produced a typology of workforce housing that sought to describe the variation within the larger phenomenon of workforce housing in the Bakken and summarized a range of features and institutional characteristics that distinguished various kind of facilities. We refer to the largest and most prominent "man camps" in the Bakken as Type 1 camps. These are constructed and administered by large corporations like Target Logistics who contract with the large oil services companies like Halliburton or Schlumberger (Rothaus 2013 for a survey of a Type 1 camp). These camps represent a kind of international vernacular architecture that would be familiar to short term workers around world as well as soldiers and Olympic athletes. They often house thousands of workers who travel to diverse worksites by bus. Type 2 and 3 camps are RV parks or other spaces where residents generally bring their own units. Type 2 camps are probably the most common form of workforce housing in the Bakken and can accommodate anywhere from over 300 lots for RVs to as few as 10. These camps provide metered, 30 or 50 amp electrical hookups and in most cases water and sewage. Type 3 camps tend to be ad hoc, scattered, and rare. They lack electricity, water or sewage hookups. Many Type 3 camps stand on short-term construction sites or on sites occupied by squatters.

This typology was both practically useful in that it allowed us to describe the phenomenon of workforce housing facilities in a more or less consistent way, but it also echoes historical descriptions of workforce housing. For example, in the East Texas oil boom of the mid-1930s, the Humble Oil company (which would later become Exxon) arranged for housing for their employees near the town of Kiglore, Texas (pop. ca. 500) (Weaver 2010). The facilities ranged from five room houses for supervisors with electricity and gas to lots where hourly employees could build or move more modest homes in the so-called "poor boy camp." A similar division between individuals with supervisory roles who lived in wood cabins, and those involved in manual labor, who lived in canvas tents, existed in the camps set up to accommodate workers on the Los Angeles Aqueduct project or at any number of other large scale construction or extractive industries in the American west (Van Bueren 2002). This division between individuals in supervisory roles and those who provided labor does specifically correspond to the division between Type 1 and Type 2 camps in North Dakota, but the basic material divisions between temporary housing sites in the Bakken does reflect different functions (and pay rates) in the boom.

There is also a long tradition of short term, ad hoc settlement associated with extractive industries. Around Kilgore, Texas, workers looking for work or filling the myriad lower-paying or more contingent positions in support of the work in the East Texas fields often squatted in wooded or marginal areas. Over three hundred people lived illegally in a camp known as "Happy Hollow" despite regular raids by the police. Steptoe City, Nevada represents a particularly long-lived example of this kind of squatters' camp which accommodated a range of workers and "hangers on" that did not fit into the company towns provided by the mining firms (Goddard 2002). In the early days of the Bakken boom, squatting in Williston, ND, city parks or in the Walmart parking lot was a common practice. While our study commenced after most of these activities were dispersed by law enforcement and new ordinances, there were still a handful of Type 3 camps visible in the Bakken. Like the squatters in Happy Hollow in miniature, these small camps were generally hidden, accommodated unemployed new arrivals or workers otherwise on the margins of the extractive industries.

Our typology, then, reflected the historical development of workforce housing in construction and extractive industries. The use of housing to distinguish between classes of individuals, responsibilities on the worksite, and corporate employment represents longstanding practices in the American west.

Workforce Housing and the American West

While traditional depictions of the American West present rugged, independent prospectors who set out to conquer the wilds in the hope of untold riches, scholars have increasingly viewed the American West as space for male wage labor and the westward movement of industrial capitalism and its attendant social expectations (Turner 1893; for a recent historiographic overview see Aron 2005). In this analysis, Frederick Jackson Turner's "frontier" became less of an untamed wilderness and more of an extension of longstanding eastern interests committed to deploying capital, workforce, and infrastructure in their search for profit (Schwantes 1994; Cronon 1992). This "wage-earner" frontier, as described by Carlos Schwantes, presents the historical development of the west as part of a larger trajectory of American and, indeed, global capital (Schwantes 1987 but with earlier formations by Goodrich and Davison 1935; 1936). Thus, inscribing the American West with mining camps, timber camps, and oil camps, contributed to expansion of a set of domestic values, hierarchies, and class relations nurtured in the East and then pushed out with the expansion of industry.

That the Bakken formation is geographically part of the American West (as typically defined) and subjected to a kind of extractive economy most closely associated with historical processes taking place in the American West is a coincidence and should not necessarily determine how we understand this phenomenon. At the same time, the historical study of North Dakota has long recognized certain themes fundamental to the development of an underpopulated state and region. Elwyn Robinson famously articulated 6 themes: remoteness, dependence, radicalism, economic disadvantage, the "too-much mistake," and the climate of a sub-humid grassland (Robinson 1959; Robinson 1966). While the application of these themes to every historical problem is perhaps ill-advised, the influence of these ideas on how North Dakotans imagine themselves and understand their history remains important. For example, the challenges of adapting existing infrastructure to the growing workforce in the Bakken counties could easily be articulated in the context of the "too-much mistake" which recognized the overly ambitious investment in infrastructure at the foundation of the state. Moreover, Robinson's understanding of the remoteness, dependence, and economic disadvantage of the sparsely populated North Dakota prairie fit well within later understandings of periphery favored by scholars committed to core-periphery models (McGuire and Reckner 2002; Hardesty 1988; Malone 1989).

Articulating workforce housing in the Bakken as part of the American West likewise frames how we understood settlement in the area from an archaeological and architectural perspective. Historically, scholars have used archaeology to document temporary settlements associated with extractive industries and construction in the West (Knapp et al. 1998 especially Hardesty 1998; See the various contributions to *Historical Archaeology* 36 [2002]). As William Cronon reminds us in his remarkable study of the town and mine at Kennecott, Alaska, the remains of these sites serve as physical reminders of the increasingly integrated global economy of the early 20th century. This expansive network of technologies and economic relationships made it possible to extract copper from veins deep within the earth, transport a workforce, supplies and ore via rail, and sustain these activities at a remote location in central Alaska (Cronon 1992). In the Bakken, workforce housing camps, particularly the Type 1 variety, represents a century-old tradition realized in distinctly 21st century materials, infrastructure, and plans.

John Bickerstaff Jackson, another great 20th century student of the American West, recognized in the mobile homes of the four corners region the direct predecessors of our Type 2 camps (Jackson 1960). He described the sudden appearance of trailer courts with their unadorned cinderblock common room designated for laundry. These settlements arrived on the border of New Mexico, Colorado, Utah, and Arizona often to house a pipeline or construction crew and lasted only as long as the project. For Jackson, these mobile homes represented part of long tradition of housing in the New World that began with the temporary wooden houses of the first European settlers on the East Coast and continued through the balloon frame homes of the 19th century to the box houses and mobile homes of the 20th century (Jackson 1984). The latter forms moved west with the surging population and soon became a defining feature of the Western landscape. While the power of Jackson's essays are in their poetic landscapes grounded in vivid observations, he, nevertheless, recognized the economic importance of mobile housing for wartime production (Foster 1980; Jackson 1984; Mitchell 2012), post-war shifts in settlement, and pressures brought about by the baby boom.

The RV came to represent capitalism in the American West in two ways. First, RVs and mobile homes express the speculative, extractive industries and massive construction projects fueled by a highly mobile workforce and the absence of persistent infrastructure across the region. Today Type 2 and 3 camps form the twenty-first–century version of "wage-earners frontier" populated by an itinerant workforce for whom mobility is a crucial aspect of their economic survival in a region still characterized by vast distances, short-term booms, and low population density. The automobile age has produced a mobile workforce to match the speed and fluidity of economic capital.

If the RV and mobile homes have become an important source of housing in the American West, they also represent a tradition of leisure practice that came into its own in the parks and landscapes of the American West. The RV, in particular, embodied the desire of the middle class to get away from their place of work and home and to have adventures in nature (Hart et al. 2002). Of course, the division between the spaces of work and spaces set aside for the experience of nature represents the same capitalist impulse as the mobility of capital and the workforce (MacCannell 1976). State and national parks provided some basic infrastructure for residents, but part of the leisure experience of the American West revolved around a contrast with developed amenities of the settled "East." Historically, the American West, then, embodied a space of contingent settlement whether in response to dynamic workforce needs of western industries or on account of the recreational mystique of the same open places and opportunities.

Negotiating the Periphery

Scholars have often seen the development of the American West as the projection of the core into the periphery (McGuire and Reckner 2002; Hardesty 1988; Malone 1989). The core-periphery model developed as a tool for understanding global economic and political relations in the context of World Systems Theory (or World Systems Analysis) (Hall et al. 2011 for an overview of this; for a more historical survey see Wallerstein 2000). The core possesses capital, social organization, and infrastructure to extract and monetize natural resources from the periphery. For most of its history, the Bakken counties have fit into a classic geographic model of the periphery. The main artery and the impetus for the development of the region was the "The Highline" of the Great Northern Railway linking St. Paul, Minnesota to Seattle, Washington. This rail route moved agricultural produce of the region to the major milling centers of Minneapolis or Duluth with its port on Lake Superior. The distance from markets, challenging climate, and extensive agricultural practices ensured that the region had a low population density with settlements mainly clustered in small towns near rail sidings (Robinson 1966). The historic structure of the region persists today as the Route 2 corridor (along the Highline) continues to guide traffic through the region, attract settlement, and anchor infrastructure.

There exists little scholarship on the economic or political impact of the North Dakota oil boom of the 1950s or late-1970s (Schaff 1957). Historically, these communities benefited in only very limited ways from the transfer of wealth from the core to the periphery. The short term nature of past booms, the region's dispersed settlement patterns, and small populations discouraged outside investment and preserved a relatively stable small town landscape with slowing dwindling populations. The absence of outside investment deprived the peripheral space of western North Dakota of the capital necessary for rapid upgrades to infrastructure. Since the 1970s, scholars like Andre Gunder Frank saw the absence of investment in peripheral areas as part of a strategy of the core to maintain the underdevelopment of the periphery and foster politically and economically expedient patterns of dependence (Frank 1966).

This is not to imagine the residents of the Bakken region as passive recipients of a dominating core. The concept of "negotiated periphery" recognizes that the myriad individuals who occupy the periphery participate actively in the core-periphery relationship (Kardulias 2007). In the Bakken, for example, local communities through their municipal governments have pushed back against the rapid expansion of workforce housing facilities across the area with periodic bans on Type 1 camps, ordinances managing the appearance of Type 2 camps, and limits on the various ad hoc arrangements of camps within city limits and on private land. Some of these ordinances reflect the long shadow of the "too much mistake" and regard the infrastructural and housing needs of the population boom as short-term inconveniences rather than long-term challenges. The small agricultural communities developed risk averse strategies in their interaction with the core as a way to mitigate the asymmetrical power relationships between the two poles. The result of this dynamic between the core and periphery is that the periphery remained fundamentally underdeveloped, but this involves strategic decision making on the part of both parties (Frank 1966).

The result of these strategies directly influenced the form of workforce housing. Type 1 camps with their highly modular designed can appear fully functioning in the region after only a few months work. Moreover, these increasingly sophisticated units have their own sewage treatment facilities, generators, and water supplies to manage the strain on local utilities (Rothaus 2013). These facilities are designed both to leave a very light footprint on the ground and to provide cost, energy, and space efficient lodging. The expectation of the core that the periphery could provide little in the way of infrastructure intersects with the periphery's desire to manage outlay of civic capital and risk. While the Bakken area received an influx of development capital since 2008 and construction starts, including hotels and apartments, increased rapidly, it remains significant that temporary workforce housing facilities continued to appear throughout the region as frequently as periodic bans on their spread. In other words, the interaction between core and the periphery continues to be negotiated mutually.

The residents of Type 2 and 3 camps also have agency in the creation of the "wage-earners" frontier. The absence of big box or large scale retail outlets outside of local market centers of Williston and Dickinson has shaped discard practices adopted by residents of Type 2 camps and the ways that residents of these camps reused a range of objects common to the industrial environment in the Bakken. Many of the larger Type 2 camps have areas set aside for the discard of PVC pipes, scrap wood, chicken wire, and other common building material. Most of this material comes from departed residents of the camp who left behind objects that have relatively little value outside of the underdeveloped area of the Bakken. Large cable spools and especially shipping pallets are ubiquitous in Type 2 and 3 camps. Shipping pallets serve as fences, walkways, and decks where they kept furniture and walkways above the mud of the Bakken spring. The shipping pallet represents common features in the industrial landscape of the Bakken where almost all activities involve moving bulk goods into sites across the region. The Bakken lacks both centralized distribution facilities and pallet recycling shops common in areas with well developed distribution infrastructure. As a result, the shipping pallets that arrived on various sites throughout Bakken owing to the decentralized circulation of goods simply pooled in the region. The area lacked a local recycling and repair center, and despite the large number of pallets, they remained too inconvenient and unprofitable for collection and transport to Bismarck, Fargo, or Grand Forks. As a result, they remained widely available for adaptive reuse.

The most dramatic example of provisional discard in the Bakken is the abandonment of built mudrooms by departing residents of the camp.

These three-sided structures with shed roofs were leaned against the side of RVs to provide space to take off muddy clothing, additional storage, and an air barrier between the frigid North Dakota winter and the heated RV. Residents typically construct these rooms out of plywood and two-by-fours and shingle roofs. The more elaborate mudrooms have built in storage spaces, windows, and weatherproof doors. Larger Type 2 facilities have a brisk trade in built mudrooms offered for sale by departing residents. Abandoned Type 2 camps are fields of abandoned mudrooms left behind by departing residents.

Non-Places and Beyond the Periphery

While circumstances and conditions in the Bakken intersect to produce a space historically and geographically defined as a periphery, the economic organization of Late Capitalism or Late Modernity offers challenges to just this kind of straightforward core-periphery dyad. Multinational corporations, for example, no longer present clear "cores" asserting dominance over geographic or political peripheries. Just-in-time manufacturing techniques and a globalized workforce of contingent labor has produced a world made up of a kaleidoscopic mosaic of cores and peripheries following the eddying flow of transnational capital. Like the "cubical farm" offices, the peripheral and contingent workforces no longer assemble and disperse at the physical or even political margins, but wherever global capital dictates (Ngai and Smith 2007). In keeping with the speed and transience of (late) capitalism, the austere nature of these units present a phenomenon that Marc Auge has termed "non places" that can appear in any context globally without distinguishing characteristics, regional styling cues, or obvious orientation (Auge 2008).

Nothing captures the fluidity of the late 20th and 21st workforce and population more than the emergence of "the camp" in its various forms. C. Hailey's exhaustive study of the camp as an architectural form both locates this within the history of vernacular architecture, the rise of leisure activities, and the emergence of substantial, mobile populations displaced by war, natural disasters, or economic need (Hailey 2009). Like the mid-century tourists who towed their RVs to parks of the American West, the lack of infrastructure associated with camps, their contingent residents, and their temporary status have marked these spaces as peripheral no matter where they emerge (Hart et al. 2002; Sumrell and Varnelis 2007). The use of "blue tarp," modular housing units, shipping pallets, and other mobile, readily available, and ad hoc approaches has produced a common form of temporary settlement suitable to accommodate diverse situations and populations around the world (Hailey 2009, 377–83).

This reconfiguring of the core-periphery relationship and the emergence of the camp as ubiquitous form of temporary settlement are manifest in our reading of workforce housing in western North Dakota. For example, the mobile, modular units constituent of Type 1 camps appear in contexts ranging from the Olympic Village to housing for refugees of the Hurricane Katrina. Similar units appear as housing for Nepalese guest workers in Qatar and NGO officials, military forces, and diplomats in Iraq (Bruslé 2012). The regularized appearance of these units, their mobile and modular design, and the efficient arrangement of the interior space presented a domestic analogue to the structured life of work, military service, or security in a dangerous or vulnerable place.

The RVs and mobile homes of Type 2 and 3 camps might initially present an even more dislocated notion of peripheral space as their very form embodies varying degrees of transience and independence from geographic constraint. From a historical perspective, John Bickerstaff Jackson observed in his classic essay that the mobile home continues a long tradition of short-term, temporary housing that has followed the western frontier from the first settlements on the Atlantic (Jackson 1984). Even if we accept that the late modern world has globalized the character of both cores and peripheries and the contingent character of the mobile workforce, the residents and units in Type 2 and Type 3 camps in North Dakota nevertheless appear to view the tradition of domesticity that recognizes the home (in whatever form) as an expression of identity. Residents in the well established Type 2 camps add mudrooms, surround their units with potted plans, fence simple lawns, build paths and decks, and maintain picnic tables and outdoor living spaces. While one could argue that outdoor living spaces and mudroom additions are concessions to the cramped conditions of RV life, residents often take pains to beautify their space, introduce landscape cues like paths, gardens, patios, set apart from, say, the parking areas for vehicles or storage. Hints of ethnic identities appear as well in the choice of color schemes for the plywood mudrooms or the statue of the Madonna in the small garden. In other words, the contingent nature of workforce housing did not prevent residents of the Bakken from investing in their surroundings in ways that echo the more settled domesticity of the suburban neighborhood.

It is worth noting that at least one model for the Type 2 man camp is the destabilizing modern periphery of the suburb. Taking names like "Foxrun" that capture the settled countryside of a bygone age, the largest Type 2 camps offer community spaces for residents to gather, landscaped entrances, and well ordered rows of RVs. They also have a sense of neighborhoods and community that comes from shared experiences and the physical proximity of the RVs. In fact, the arrangement of lots in the camp and their locations often reflect the development of the camp over time. It was not unusual for residents to Type 2 camps to stop us during our reconnaissance tours to ask what we are doing, and in most cases they were free with information about their neighbors and friends in the camp. If suburbs represented a simulacrum of country life, then the Type 2 camps of the Bakken represent the countryside at two removes. Thus, the more elaborate Type 2 camps provide the orderly appearance of non-spaces, while preserving space for individualization.

In smaller Type 2 and Type 3 camps, efforts to appeal to suburban models of domesticity frequent break down in the contingent space of temporary workforce housing. The dirt and grime of the industries related to oil work cover vehicles and equipment parked close to mobile homes and RVs. In many cases Type 2 and Type 3 camps stand at worksites and violates the traditional distinction between space for work and space for domestic pursuits. Ironically, it is Type 1 camps that distinguish more clearly between space for work and space for sleeping and eating. They present a warped model of domesticity that adapts the early 20th century company town to contingent character of the late 20th century workforce. They are an efficient and industrialized, twenty-first–century echo of the company towns set up by the Humble Oil Company in Kilgore, Texas.

In a provocative essay, Talal Asad described the power relationships that forged the modern world. He noted that the currents of modernity and capitalism fused in the discourse of colonial and, later, postcolonial nationalism (Asad 1992). He noted that the terms of resistance and accommodation as strategies could not exist outside of the terms set by capital and the nation-state. In this era of late capitalism, the basic structures anticipated by Asad in the 1980s are in sharp decline. The center is no longer the capital or the nation, but the company that exists outside of national boundaries and outside of space entirely. If the postcolonial world had become "Conscripts of Western Civilization," the oil patch, full of non-places and contingency have become the "conscripts of the postmodernity." Workforce housing becomes the locus of for enforcing and resisting this new conscription.

Conclusion

As an outsider, workforce housing in the Bakken presents a model for understanding the practices and structures of temporary settlement on a global scale. Narratives of the American West and the history of North Dakota provide an easy point of departure for a historical reading of the Bakken. Low population density, limited infrastructure, and the distance from major urban centers, have caused communities within the Bakken counties to struggle to accommodate the influx of workers associated with large-scale oil exploration and extraction. The struggles encountered by the Bakken counties provide a domestic parallel for global peripheries studied under World Systems Analysis models. The strategies used by the core, whether it was grain millers in Minneapolis or global corporations, to exploit the resources and communities of this region allow us to easily recognize the Bakken as part of historical processes that shaped the distribution of wealth around the world. In these contexts, temporary, workforce housing becomes the human manifestation of the increasingly fluid and fast-paced flow of global capital. Our Type 3 squatter camps in shelter belts and city parks, rows of RVs in Type 2 camps, or even the corporate uniformity of the Type 1 lodges, all reflect historical approaches to accommodating workers engaged in extractive industries around the world.

Type 1 camps are particular indicative of the increased speed of capital and the dynamism of labor markets in a world filled with a growing number of indistinct "non places" that resist characteristics of local places or resident identities. The multinational companies themselves with their myriad subsidiaries remain remarkably indistinct and placeless. It is hardly remarkable, then, that they offer a similarly homogenized vision of workforce housing. For the historian and the archaeologist, these non-places present a distinct challenge and raise serious questions about our disciplinary assumptions at the dawn of the 21st century. Both disciplines came of age with the rise of the nation, and the expectations of both fields depend in part on the coherence of the archive, the stability of the object of study, and the existence of recoverable expressions of place. Absent these features, a history or archaeology of a post-national landscape populated by multinational companies, like the Bakken flickers at the edge of our current methods. The workforce housing, capital, and contingency of the Bakken resists the formation of a clear object in both temporal and spatial terms.

Whatever the ambiguity and indeterminacy that might exist on the global and systemic level in the Bakken, the encounter with the contingent workforce of extractive industries has refracted in distinct ways among both the residents of the Bakken and the workers who make North Dakota home for however short of a time. Workforce housing is continuously being negotiated by innovative residents, intrepid municipalities, and contingent labor. My position on the eastern side of North Dakota resident has given me a first hand perspective on various efforts to negotiate the periphery and to resist the alienating spread of non-places. It is this very sense of place that locates my perspective on the Bakken.

References

Agger, B. 1989. *Fast Capitalism: a Critical Theory of Significance*. Urbana: University of Illinois Press.

Aron, S. 2005. "What's West, What's Next." *OAH Magazine of History*, 19 (November): 22–25.

Asad, T. 1992. "Conscripts of Western Civilization?" In *Dialectical Anthropology: Essays in Honor of Stanley Diamond*, vol. 1, edited by C. Gailey, 333–51. Gainesville, FL: University Presses of Florida.

Auge, M. 2008. *Non-places: Introduction to an Anthropology of Supermodernity*, translated by John Howe. New York: Verso.

Bowden. C. 2008. "The Emptied Prairie: North Dakota Ghost Towns Speak of an Irreversible Decline." *National Geographic* 213, no. 1: 140–57.

Brown, C. 2013. "North Dakota Went Boom." *New York Times Magazine*, February 3.

Bruslé, T. 2012. "What Kind of Place is this? Daily Life, Privacy and the Inmate Metaphor in a Nepalese Workers' Labour Camp (Qatar)." *South Asia Multidisciplinary Academic Journal* 6. samaj.revues. org/3446.

Caraher, W. 2009. "History at the University of North Dakota, 1885–1970." Unpublished manuscript. Elwyn B. Robinson Department of Special Collections, Chester Fritz Library, University of North Dakota.

Caraher, W., D. Nakassis, and D.K. Pettegrew. 2006. "Siteless Survey and Intensive Data Collection in an Artifact-rich Environment: Case Studies from the Eastern Corinthia, Greece." *Journal of Mediterranean Archaeology* 16: 7–43.

Caraher, W., D.K. Pettegrew, and S. James. 2010. "Towers and Fortifications at Vayia in the Southeast Corinthia." *Hesperia* 79: 385–415.

Caraher, W., D.K. Pettegrew, and R.S. Moore. 2014. *Pyla-Koutsopetria I: Archaeological Survey of An Ancient Coastal Town*. Boston: American Schools of Oriental Research Archaeological Research Series.

Cowie, S.E. 2011. *The Plurality of Power: An Archaeology of Industrial Capitalism*. New York: Springer.

Cronon, W. 1992. "Kennecott Journey: The Paths Out of Town." In *Under an Open Sky: Rethinking America's Western Past*, edited by W. Cronon, G. Miles, and J. Gitlin, 28–50. New York: Norton.

NASA (n.d.) Suomi NPP. npp.gsfc.nasa.gov.

Frank, A.G. 1966. *The Development of Underdevelopment*. Boston: New England Free Press.

Foster, R.H. 1980. "Wartime Trailer Housing in the San Francisco Bay Area." *Geographical Review* 70, no. 3: 276–90.

Goodrich, C., and S. Davison. 1935. "The Wage-Earner in the Westward Movement I." *Political Science Quarterly* 50, no. 2: 161–85.

Goodrich, C., and S. Davison. 1936. "The Wage-Earner in the Westward Movement II." *Political Science Quarterly* 51, no. 1: 61–116.

Goddard, R. A. "Nothing but Tar Paper Shacks." *Historical Archaeology* 36, no. 3: 85–93.

Hailey, C. 2009. *Camps: A Guide to 21st Century Space.* Cambridge, MA: MIT Press.

Hall, T.D., P. Nick Kardulias, and C. Chase-Dunn. 2011. "World-Systems Analysis and Archaeology: Continuing the Dialogue." *Journal of Archaeological Research* 19, no. 3: 233–79.

Hardesty, D. 1988. *The Archaeology of Mining and Miners: A View from the Silver State.* Pleasant Hill, CA: Society for Historical Archaeology. Special Publication Series 6.

Hardesty, D. 1998. "Power and the Industrial Mining Community in the American West." In *Social Approaches to an Industrial Past: The Archaeology and Anthropology of Mining,* edited by A. Bernard Knapp, Vincent C. Pigott, and Eugenia W. Herbert, 81–96. London: Routledge.

Harrison, Rodney, and John Schofield. 2010. *After Modernity: Archaeological Approaches to the Contemporary Past.* Oxford: Oxford University Press.

Hart, John Fraser, Michelle J. Rhodes, and John T. Morgan. 2002. *The Unknown World of the Mobile Home.* Baltimore: Johns Hopkins University Press.

Harvey, D. 1982. *The Limits to Capital.* Chicago: University of Chicago Press.

Iseminger, G. L. 2001. "Dr. Orin G. Libby: A Centennial Commemoration of the Father of North Dakota History." *North Dakota History* 68, no. 4: 2–25.

Jackson, J. B. 1953. "The Westward Moving House." *Landscape* 2, no. 3: 8–21.

Jackson, J. B. 1960. "The Four Corners Country." *Landscape* 10, no. 1: 20–26.

Jackson, J. B. 1984. "The Moveable Dwelling and How It Came to America." In *Discovering the Vernacular Landscape,* 91–101. New Haven, CT: Yale University Press.

Johnson, M. 1996. *An Archaeology of Capitalism.* Cambridge, MA: Blackwell Publishers.

Kardulias, P.N. 2007. "Negotiation and Incorporation on the Margins of World Systems: Examples from Cyprus and North America." *Journal of World-Systems Research* 13, no. 1: 55–82.

Knapp, A. Bernard, Vicent C. Pigott, and Eugenia W. Herbert. 1998. *Social Approaches to an Industrial Past: The Archaeology and Anthropology of Mining*. London and New York: Routledge.

MacCannell, D. 1976. *The Tourist: A New Theory of the Leisure Class*. New York: Schocken.

Malone, M.P. 1989. "Beyond the Last Frontier: Toward a New Approach to Western American History." *Western Historical Quarterly* 20: 409–27.

Mcguire, R. 2014. "Won With Blood: Archaeology and Labor's Struggle." *International Journal of Historical Archaeology* 18, no. 2: 259–71.

McGuire, R., and P. Reckner. 2002. "The Unromantic West: Labor, Capital, and Struggle." *Historical Archaeology* 36, no. 3: 44–58.

Mitchell, D. 2012. "*La Casa de Esclavos Modernos*: Exposing the Architecture of Exploitation." *Journal of the Society of Architectural Historians* 71: 451–61.

Ngai, Pun, and Chris Smith. 2007. "Putting Transnational Labour Process in its Place: The Dormitory Labour Regime in Post-Socialist China." *Work Employment Society* 21, no. 1: 27–45.

Graves-Brown, Paul, Rodney Harrison, and Angela Piccini, eds. 2013. *The Oxford Handbook of the Archaeology of the Contemporary World*. Oxford: Oxford University Press.

Rothaus, Richard. 2013. "Return on Sustainability: Workforce Housing for People, Planet and Profit." *Target Logistics White Paper* 08-13. www.targetlogistics.net/1_pdfs/white-papers/ReturnOnSustainability.WorkforceHousingForPeoplePlanetAndProfit.pdf.

Robinson, Elwyn B. 1959. "The Themes of North Dakota History." *North Dakota History* 26: 5–24.

Robinson, Elywn B. 1964. *The History of North Dakota*. Norman: University of Oklahoma Press.

Schwantes, C.A. 1987. "The Concept of the Wageworkers' Frontier: A Framework for Future Research." *Western Historical Quarterly* 18, no. 1: 39–55.

Schwantes, C.A. 1994. "Wage Earners and Wealth Makers." In *The Oxford History of the American West,* edited by Clyde Milner and Carol O'Connor, 431–68. New York: Oxford University Press.

Shackel, Paul A. 2009. *The Archaeology of American Labor and Working-Class Life*. Gainesville, FL: University of Florida Press.

Sumrell, R., and K. Varnelis. 2007. *Blue Monday: Stories of Absurd Realities and Natural Philosophies.* Barcelona: Actar Editorial.

Tauxe, C. S. 1993. *Farms, Mines, and Main Street: Uneven Development in a Dakota County.* Philadelphia: Temple University Press.

Turner, F.J. 1893. "The Significance of the Frontier in American History." *Annual Report of the American Historical Association*: 199–227.

Van Bueren, Thad. M. 2002. "The Changing Face of Work in the West: Some Introductory Comments," *Historical Archaeology* 36, no. 3: 1–7.

Wallerstein, I. M. 2000. *The Essential Wallerstein.* New York: New Press.

Weaver, B. 2010. *Oilfield Trash: Life and Labor in the Oil Patch.* College Station, TX: Texas A&M Press.

CHAPTER 11

EXTRACTIVE INDUSTRIES AND TEMPORARY
HOUSING POLICIES: MAN CAMPS IN
NORTH DAKOTA'S OIL PATCH

Carenlee Barkdull, Bret A. Weber, and Julia C. Geigle

Covered in a luxurious coating of hoar frost, the trees sparkled on a strikingly beautiful, frigid North Dakota morning in February 2013. Standing in the bright sunlight, Chris Wiedmer surveyed the scene outside of his man camp "home" just northwest of Tioga in the heart of North Dakota's oil boom. From Coeur d'Alene, Idaho, Wiedmer had been working in the patch and living in man camps since 2010. Man camps range from barracks-style lodges, to cluttered collections of recreational vehicles built for a week's worth of camping fun—not perennial survival in North Dakota's winters. Almost the first thing Wiedmer said in his interview was, "Build more apartments!" In the face of the intractable housing shortage in North Dakota, the need and the solution both seem obvious and simple.

Too little investment and communities miss the chance to build new schools, upgrade aging infrastructure, or the opportunity to develop longterm, sustainable economies independent of unstable, extractive industries. But housing policies and related infrastructure decisions have another side. Locals who remembered the short-lived oil boom in the late 1970s and early 1980s may fiercely resist making investments in infrastructure. Large amounts of additional housing require building not just houses or roads, but also water and sewer lines, longterm investments in personnel and other infrastructure supports, and twenty-year municipal bonds to pay for it all. Communities that had tried to capitalize on the earlier boom often found themselves holding the bill for surplus, redundant infrastructure in the aftermath of what was a devastatingly rapid and unexpected crash. Too often, the people left with the responsibility to pay longterm loans may have enjoyed only minimal benefit from the boom in the first place. While only some share in the wealth, all local residents have to live with the high prices, bad roads, and crowding. Perhaps most importantly, the reluctance to build adequate housing—on the part of local governments, the state, and industry—means workers and their families too often live in substandard and even potentially dangerous temporary housing. And yet a letter to the editor in the *Grand Forks Herald* praised the cautious approach of western North Dakota's communities "this time around," noting that local governments in the western half of the state were left "holding the bag" in the 1980s as they found that those willing to share in the boom's dividends were less anxious to share in the costs of the bust (Hennessey 2014).

One of the defining characteristics of the boom has been the proliferation of temporary labor housing structures, referred to by the more commonly-used and admittedly problematic term *man camps*, which is the term used throughout this chapter. Indeed, it could be argued that man camps would be more accurately described as human camps, since all the various forms of workforce housing in western North Dakota include lodging for men, women, and children. In September 2011, the county commissioners in Williams County drew up a moratorium to control the spread of man camps ("County Puts" 2011). The moratorium defined man camps as all forms of temporary housing including the large institutional camps, trailer parks, and more ad hoc situations, and this chapter shares that broad use of the term.

E. Ward Koeser, President of the Tioga city commission in Williams County stated, "I look at man camps as being somewhat a necessary evil" (quoted in Klimasinska 2013). The majority of policymakers seemed to share that view. The main response to the housing crisis was to impose minimalist safety standards alongside ad hoc efforts to limit the spread and longevity of man camps. The policies were generally focused on short-term, financial considerations. This chapter argues for the recognition of the social justice issues inherent in housing policy and the need for a more balanced and human-centered approach.

It is a daunting task to determine the right mix of temporary and permanent housing in the unpredictable face of any boom, especially booms related to extractive industries such as oil. Decisions require more than just the wisdom of local policymakers or the industriousness of workers. A complex array of factors causes fluctuations in the price of oil, which in turn makes the difference between needing thousands of new workers or shutting down an entire oil play.

North Dakota's response to its oil boom-related housing crisis offers important policy lessons regarding temporary worker housing. This chapter examines state policies relevant to temporary labor housing in North Dakota; accompanying recommendations are viewed through a social justice lens and a concern for human wellbeing, congruent with the social work values framework of its authors. While theories of social justice are many and varied, they share core concerns about inequities that are unfair or unjust (e.g., Sen 2006; Hankvivsky 2012). In other words, the differential effects of macro-level forces on communities, groups, or individuals possessing less advantage or privilege are a necessary consideration of policy analysis (Van Wormer 2004).

The following section provides a brief introduction to North Dakota's twenty-first century oil boom and the resultant housing crisis. This is followed by a brief description of the temporary labor housing typology developed by the North Dakota Man Camp Project and the state policies affecting temporary labor housing. The chapter then considers the problems that relevant policies attempt to address or solve and describes the manner in which those policies are supposed to function. The conclusion offers a series of recommendations that considers human wellbeing as a necessary primary objective of housing policy. The intent is to offer informed context for North Dakota policymakers (at the state and local levels) and for other communities around the globe facing similar situations.

Contextual History of North Dakota's Twenty-First Century Oil Boom

With the development of the Parshall Oil Field in 2006 (Johnson 2011), the twenty-first century oil boom in the rural, agricultural state of North Dakota was underway. Lying beneath most of the western half of the state, exploitation of the Bakken formation's oil shale deposits was made possible by the convergence of high oil prices and new hydraulic fracturing ("fracking") and horizontal drilling technologies.

Prior to the boom, population loss had been the defining demographic characteristic of much of the state since the Great Depression. Indeed, this remote state with a 2011 population of less than 700,000 people had lost more than half of its population over the previous century. At the start of the boom, more than two-thirds of its counties were classified as "frontier," with thirty-seven of fifty-three counties having a population density of seven or fewer people per square mile (U.S. Census Bureau 2012). Population loss was one of North Dakota's most pressing economic challenges. In dramatic contrast, soon after the start of the boom, North Dakota became the fastest-growing state in the nation (U.S. Census Bureau 2012).

By 2014, North Dakota had become the country's second largest oil producer (Associated Press 2012), bringing a number of economic benefits to the state and shielding its economy from the Great Recession of 2008. North Dakota recorded the highest gross domestic product (GDP) growth rate of any state in 2013, coming in at 13 percent, compared to the sluggish national rate of 2 percent (Hess and Frohlich 2014). In the first quarter of 2014, North Dakota also reported the country's lowest unemployment rate of 2.6 percent (U.S. Bureau of Labor Statistics 2014). The state's director of mineral resources, Lynn Helms, estimated that 65,000 new oil-related jobs would be created by 2020, resulting in a state population of 1 million (Dalrymple 2012). The twenty-first century boom cycle has been predicted to last thirty years or more (North Dakota Petroleum Council 2011), and yet North Dakota's generally conservative state and local governments have proven reluctant to invest in permanent infrastructure—especially for housing—given the hardships that followed the oil industry's boom-bust cycles of the 1950s and 1980s (Weber et al. 2014).

Housing Needs Accompanying North Dakota's Oil Boom

Extractive industries have long been connected to periods of expansion and decline, including rapid population growth, unprecedented job opportunities, and heavy demands on community services and facilities (Camassia and Wilkinson 1990). With their small political constituencies and underdeveloped infrastructures, rural communities bear the brunt of rapid and unplanned boom economy development.

In the long recession that followed the economic downturn of 2008, the arrival of thousands of workers from neighboring states and across the country resulted in dramatic impacts on the state's western communities. Critical housing shortages and intense pressures on social service systems created hardships for both newcomers and longterm residents. Oil industry workers' pay outpaced the wages of those outside the industry, and the rising costs of living, particularly for housing, disproportionately affected vulnerable populations including low-income residents and those on fixed incomes (Weber et al. 2014). The lack of housing also directly affected incoming workers and job-seekers.

Some of these hardships were documented in 2012 through focus groups with North Dakota county social service directors and regional human service center staff (Weber et al. 2014). Triangulating the focus group data with extensive archival data, the study identified housing as the "nexus" issue deserving the highest level of attention and energy by policymakers, citizens, and advocates for vulnerable populations (Weber et al. 2014). The general lack of housing and shortage of affordable housing connect to more specific problems including: (1) price gouging, sub-standard living conditions, and homelessness; (2) difficulties in hiring due to a lack of available housing; and (3) challenges related to temporary labor housing. Indeed, issues related to housing were deeply intertwined with a host of other challenging social conditions in western North Dakota.

The affordable housing shortage created hiring challenges for companies generating the wealth, the construction companies that could help build housing, and for community service agencies. Resident surveys gathered by researchers at Minot and Dickinson State Universities, along with testimony given during legislative hearings, confirmed that more employees were essential to meet the rapidly growing "demand for law enforcement, emergency response, public health, social services, public works, and medical services" (DSU, MSU, and GPEC 2011, 4).

As in any boom economy in rural areas, attempting to plan for infrastructure needs based on employment projections presents considerable difficulties as additional workforce data is needed to refine models used to predict growth (Hodur et al. 2013). For example, although 60 percent of oil industry workers were classified as "temporary" in a study released in 2013 (Hodur et al. 2013), determining to what extent temporary workers might also be accompanied by spouses and minor children poses a significant challenge to infrastructure planning.

Community Resistance to Building More Housing

North Dakota has a history of oil and natural gas exploration dating back to 1892, although the first period characterized as a "boom" occurred in the early 1950s with the discovery of oil in Williams County in the northwestern part of the state (North Dakota Energy Forum 2013). Of more direct salience to the communities in the twenty-first century boom is the boom-bust cycle of the 1980s. Longtime western North Dakotans carry vivid memories of the bust that followed the boom when oil prices plummeted and could no longer support oil development activities in the 1980s. One Watford City resident shared that the oil company workers pulled out so fast they left their breakfasts uneaten on the table. This colorful anecdote captures both the sudden and rapid nature of the economic decline that abruptly followed the bust, and the attendant impacts on the small rural communities that had invested in infrastructure during that period. Williston, the county seat of Williams County, was left holding a debt of $25 million after making considerable infrastructure investments for housing. Additionally, county government was forced to assume ownership of undeveloped lands abandoned when developers fled to avoid property tax obligations they could no longer meet (Holeywell 2011).

While oil development in the Bakken is projected to last as long as three decades (Clark 2014), the intensive labor needs of the earlier stages of exploration and drilling abate as oil rigs come online and require fewer people to maintain extraction processes (Hodur et al. 2013). Predicting population flows around oil development is a mix of art and science as best estimates for managing dynamic and rapidly changing infrastructure needs must consider historical precedents, the best understanding of current trends, and the need to respond to numerous and conflicting demands from various constituents. One economic development official in McKenzie County stated that his rule of thumb for planning for the growth was to accommodate 20 percent, as opposed to 100 percent of the growth, but he was also candid in stating, "My guess is no better or worse than anyone else's" (Gene Veeder, quoted in Holeywell 2011).

Watford City (McKenzie's county seat) is illustrative of the housing challenges facing communities at the epicenter of the patch. The formerly sleepy town at the gateway to Theodore Roosevelt National Park's North Unit had enjoyed only very modest economic development success and narrow escapes from the tide of population loss typical to rural North Dakota towns. Its census count of 1,435 in 2000 (U.S. Census Bureau 2012) had grown by just slightly more than 300 individuals to 1,744 in 2010 (Monke 2014). As a result of the boom, the population quadrupled over a four-year period to an estimated 7,500 residents early in 2014, with growth projections planning for up to 17,000 permanent residents by some estimates (Monke 2014).

Dick Gardner, an economist working with estimates supplied by the North Dakota Department of Minerals and other data (e.g., Hodur et al. 2013), estimated that McKenzie County's oil industry workforce would grow to about 14,000 in 2015 and then begin to level off after 2019, to a figure close to 9,000 workers over the remaining decades of the boom (Shipman 2013). These figures did not include employees in secondary occupations. Gardner also predicted the construction of more permanent housing and anticipated a doubling of housing units from 3,672 in 2013, to 8,956 by 2036 (Shipman 2013).

These figures were questioned by Watford City's Mayor Brent Sanford, who found the projections low in relation to anticipated oil rig construction and experience with unmet housing demands (Shipman 2013). The mayor questioned the assumptions of the study, asserting that basing projections on what county governments provided to oil field workers during the previous boom was logically flawed (Shipman 2013). Given the limits of data available to social scientists and others attempting to assist local officials with timely and useful information, developing models that more accurately predict demand for housing and other infrastructure needs remains a challenging proposition (e.g., Hodur et al. 2013).

Limiting investments in more housing infrastructure to meet the needs has meant skyrocketing rents and housing costs throughout western

North Dakota. According to one source, the city of Williston topped the list of most expensive entry-level rentals in the country early in 2014, outpacing New York City, San Francisco, and Honolulu (Craig 2014). While some benefited from skyrocketing home values, more vulnerable residents were displaced and both newer- and longer-term residents grumble bitterly about "price gouging."

Some hoped the institutional man camps would be an attractive solution. Large companies like Target Logistics are contracted to remove all infrastructure and return property to preexisting conditions. Others noted that the existence of these camps—some large enough to be included among the state's twenty largest cities—did little to keep housing costs down or to prevent the proliferation of more ad hoc housing arrangements with their related social, safety, and environmental concerns (Weber et al. 2014). Additionally, the large crew camps do not always mesh with the needs of many oil industry workers and job seekers as these lodges charge relatively high fees, enforce strict rules (including drug screening and prohibitions on alcohol), and prohibit residents from personalizing their living spaces.

The North Dakota Man Camp Project

In early 2012, a diverse group of researchers from the University of North Dakota began a multidisciplinary project to better understand the impacts of the boom on various communities and systems. Those efforts quickly affirmed media reports about the extent and centrality of the housing crisis. The North Dakota Man Camp Project (NDMCP) evolved to take a closer look specifically at temporary worker housing. The NDMCP brought together techniques of archaeology, architectural history, and the social sciences to document the social, material, and environmental conditions of workforce housing in the Bakken. Led by Professors William Caraher and Bret Weber, the NDMCP sought to develop an up-to-date set of perspectives on the longterm costs, benefits, and impacts of various forms of labor housing (Caraher current volume; Cassidy current volume).

In August, 2012, the first full field team began systematic data collection including photographs, architectural drawings, inventories of the material culture in and around housing units, and interviews with camp operators, the inhabitants, and local and state officials. Over the next two years more than fifty camps were documented in this fashion, leading to the development of an initial typology of temporary labor housing that continues to be refined in an attempt to capture the rapidly changing nature of such housing in western North Dakota.

Types of Man Camps

As noted earlier, while acknowledging that men comprise the majority of individuals occupying North Dakota's temporary labor housing, women and children also reside there. Each form of man camp presents unique advantages and challenges to their residents, the surrounding communities, and the physical environment.

The NDMCP identified three types of temporary labor housing in western North Dakota. Although this typology is original to this project, patterns are remarkably similar to written descriptions and photographs of man camps documented since the earliest U.S. oil booms in Pennsylvania and Texas (Weaver 2010).

Type I housing, sometimes referred to as "crew camps," consist of uniform, institutional housing, primarily in the form of dormitory-style rooms and communal dining and recreational facilities. Veterans from Iraq and Afghanistan frequently remark about the similarity with military barracks, which is not surprising since companies like Target Logistics own and manage housing both for the military and for industry. Type I housing makes the most efficient use of resources and has the smallest and least permanent environmental footprint in relation to the number of beds provided (Caraher et al. 2015). By addressing worker needs in a collective manner it can be argued that Type I housing minimizes the impacts from transportation and water and sewage infrastructure. Type I camps also may be more positively regarded by local community residents as they are largely self-contained with strict rules about alcohol, drugs, and resident conduct.

The rigidly standardized nature of life in Type I man camps evokes a sense of laborers as a temporary and replaceable commodity, rather than as North Dakota's newest residents or future citizens. Despite the common presence of community rooms complete with wide screen television, pool tables, and video games, these shared spaces receive surprisingly little use. People work long, hard hours in the patch, often in seven-days-per-week, three-week schedules, with a week off before starting all over again. In Type I housing, it is common for workers to be assigned a different space after returning from their week "at home." This schedule, along with the material realities of the spaces themselves, limits opportunities for personal expression and individual freedoms, and offers only a limited, generally artificial sense of community (Caraher et al. 2014). For these reasons, Type I housing is not always the most attractive to workers. The earliest Texas oil booms tended to include camp housing similar to this primarily for middle and upper management, or for the most skilled and valued workers. Those camps, like many of the present Type I camps, offered communal cooking and cleaning services, but with strict restrictions about alcohol and social activities.

Essentially ad hoc RV parks, units in Type II camps are a mix of individually owned recreational vehicles manufactured for only temporary use. Most units are neither built to provide habitation over the course of years nor to withstand the harsh weather typical to the northern plains including persistent winds, prolonged sub-zero temperatures (with potential windchills exceeding -100°F), and un-shaded heat.

The opportunity for workers to personalize their living spaces (both inside and outside their units), while still limited, far exceeds the situation in Type I camps. Additionally, the living environment attempts to replicate the sense of community found in working-class suburbs, or that of retired "snowbirds" living seasonally in the Sunbelt. Residents are more likely to be familiar with neighbors, tend to know and watch out for one another, and generally enjoy greater freedom of self-expression including small garden plots, outdoor grills, and few-to-no restrictions about alcohol or socializing (Caraher et al. 2014).

Type II camps make greater demands on existing infrastructure, and, with less tightly controlled administration, they create more environmental impacts (Caraher et al. 2014). Additionally, units originally built for temporary living have increasingly become near-permanent housing structures, although they are not covered by the building and safety codes that cover motels and Type I camps. The precedent for Type II camps set a century earlier in Texas included company land that was set aside for workers who would bring or build their own ad hoc housing.

Type III camps can be best described as "living rough" with no fixed electrical, water, or sewage infrastructure. From a strict material perspective, this is the least desirable form of housing both for workers and host communities. Type III camps have the greatest per capita environmental impact and offer the lowest quality of physical existence, especially in relation to harsh weather. Additionally, the ad hoc nature of Type III housing is the least controllable from a community perspective creating the highest potential for health concerns and the least possibility for social control. Type III camps, somewhat ironically, seem to have the strongest sense of community with residents more directly intimate and even dependent on one another. In one Type III camp documented by the NDMCP, residents cooked communally, organized shared recreational activities, and often gathered in the evenings to socialize around a bonfire.

Bobby Weaver's (2010) book *Oil Field Trash* describes parallels between Type III camps in today's Bakken oil play and the situation in East Texas nearly a century earlier:

Those hands not so fortunate as to be employed by majors had to continue as best they could under poor circumstance. At first many of them slept in fields, using old newspapers for cover during good weather, and when it rained or turned cold they sought shelter in churches, abandoned barns, or whatever was available ... One place in particular became known as living quarters for destitute people. Known as "Happy Hollow" ... at any given time between one hundred and three hundred people called the place home. It was raided on a regular basis by local law enforcement officers who always managed to arrest a hundred or more citizens on each occasion. Nevertheless, by the next day or so it would refill with desperate people in need of work. (Weaver 2010, 97)

By the time the NDMCP was documenting camps in North Dakota, much of the Type III activity had been curtailed. And it was never as extreme as the case in East Texas' Happy Hollow, though newspaper accounts and anecdotal evidence indicate that city parks throughout the area were similarly inhabited during the earliest phases of the boom, and some of the Type II parks in existence in 2014 had originated as Type III squatter camps.

While many of the camps documented by the North Dakota Man Camp Project tended to fit neatly into the three categories of the typology, others tended to be mixed or existed on a continuum. Archetypal Type I camps have security and fences with neatly structured lines of connected modules, complete with all necessary services including independent water treatment facilities. Other Type I camps might include multiple rows of identical modules alongside a smattering of irregular cabins, or even with an area of RVs appearing to share the same space and administration. Classic Type II camps tend to include an administrative office and a playground to identify the unity of the place amid a vast collection of uniquely decorated and appointed RVs, each masted according to the required efficiencies of the Montana-Dakota Utilities company. More "blended" Type IIs sometimes included either a handful or an entire line of Type I-style uniform modules, or, on the other end of the spectrum, they might include trailers off to the side with no water or electrical connections. Type III camps, inherently "off the grid" both literally and metaphorically, tended to be particularly ephemeral and difficult to find. Sometimes they would include extension cords strung from neighboring farm buildings or were serviced by a water tank. The man camp typology is utilized below as a tool of analysis to help illuminate the dynamic policy context of temporary labor housing in western North Dakota.

Policy Description and Analysis

The most directly relevant man camp policies connect to lodging (i.e., motel and hotel regulations), or mobile home and recreational vehicle (RV) parks. This section begins with an overview of the basic policies in relation to the various forms or types of man camps. More specifically, this section describes the key problems that the policies are designed to address. The existing framework for administrative policies pertaining to North Dakota's man camps focuses fairly narrowly on what state officials summarize as "fire, life, and safety" (K. Bollinger, personal communication, February 21, 2014).

The policies governing temporary labor housing emerged with the development of mobile homes in the 1950s, and federal designations created by the Department of Housing and Urban Development (HUD) in the 1970s. The major portions of the North Dakota Century Code (NDCC) related to the lodges, mobile home parks, trailer parks, and campgrounds that host the various forms of temporary labor housing in North Dakota's oil boom were already enshrined in the NDCC prior to the boom in the 1980s. There were some minor revisions during the oil boom of the 1980s, primarily setting deadlines for existing mobile home parks to comply with changes in state code.

The major revisions encoded during the twenty-first century boom include clarifying the definition of temporary work camp housing as a "modular residential structure used to house workers on a temporary basis for a maximum period of five years," and the requirement that owners of such housing are legally obligated to remove the housing and "all related above-grade and below-grade infrastructure within one hundred twenty days after the temporary work camp housing is vacated" (NDCC 54-21.3-02.8 and 54-21.3-04.3). By 2014, many camps had already outlived the five-year limit, and by September of that year, headlines in the *Williston Herald* announced, "Companies facing millions in fines for temporary housing," with twenty-nine separate housing units approaching locally imposed expiration dates (Bell 2014).

Policies Covering Type I Camps

Beyond the modest changes in state law made in relation to the 1980s boom, in 2011, North Dakota joined the Interstate Industrialized Buildings Commission (IBC), which provides oversight on the modular units used in Type I camps. These larger, institutional-style camps are generally referred to as lodges.

As defined in the NDCC, lodges are technically any building or structure provided to the public "where sleeping accommodations are furnished for pay" (NDCC 23-09-01.8). While governed by many of the same inspection and building laws as motels and hotels, Type I camps consist of manufactured "industrialized/modular" buildings, and include the requirement noted above that all traces of their existence are to be removed within four months after being vacated. These units are all factory-built and are generally brought in either by rail or on flat-bed trailers. In the spring of 2011, North Dakota Governor Jack Dalrymple signed Senate Bill 2284 into law, making the state the fourth member of the IBC (created in 1991 by New Jersey, Minnesota, and Rhode Island). The IBC works with the industrialized (modular) buildings industry to oversee and implement uniform rules and regulations governing the manufacture, delivery, and installation of these units with the intention of eliminating the "costly reviews and inspections by multiple jurisdictions" (North Dakota Department of Commerce 2014).

In relation to state law, one important distinction between lodges and RV parks (Type II camps) is the ability of state health workers to inspect the interior of each unit. Fire safety inspections address smoke detection devices or other approved alarm systems, as well as proper posting of safety procedures and the provision of adequate fire escapes and exits (NDCC 23-09-03 to 23-09-07). Inspectors also consider provision of safe drinking water, adequate washroom facilities, clean bedding, appropriate refuse disposal, and protection from insects (NDCC 23-09-04 to 23-09-10). State inspectors must review lodges at least biennially except in cases where county departments are deemed sufficient.

The presence of food services offers an additional opportunity for bureaucratic oversight, which also relates to a key part of the designation as a lodge: the use of corridors to connect individual, modular units. Corridors afford some of the conveniences of a motel by joining individual rooms to food services, communal showers (though most units include individual bathrooms), or recreational rooms. The distinction between Type I lodges and Type II RV parks can be blurred when standardized, modular units lack corridors. Camps where units are spaced apart from each other are not technically lodges and are sometimes licensed as RV parks, especially when they are co-located with RVs and campers.

However, the goal of state and county officials, along with some camp owners, is to provide to the greatest extent possible the minimal safety standards afforded by state law. A state health department official states that in the case of Type I camps lacking corridors:

We apply some spacing requirements between the units so that if one starts on fire, the whole group doesn't start on fire. That's how we license them. That would be considered a mobile home or manufactured home park as those would be considered relocatable-type structures—your Type I's as you've called it—but to give them the best protection, we license them as a lodging establishment … [and require] lighted fire escapes, fire extinguishers, and all those other things in place to afford the tenants protection.

Some Type I camps are co-located with RVs and campers and lack corridors. Indeed, some of the modular units include wheels (usually hidden by some sort of apron or skirting) and are technically similar to trailers found in Type II camps; however, there is a standardized, institutional uniformity to these structures that results in characteristics closer to the crew camps than RV parks. According to the health department official, state inspectors and owners strive to license these camps as lodges so as to provide the greater degree of bureaucratic oversight and to enforce safety regulations related to fire, life, and safety.

Policies Covering Type II Camps

Just as there are Type I camps that include RVs, there are also Type II camps that include some modular units but that are nonetheless licensed as RV parks. RVs are distinct from modular units in that they include permanent wheels and can either be mobilized under their own power with a driver's cabin, or pulled behind a truck or car. Mobile homes (also referred to as trailers or trailer homes) are also prefabricated in a factory, but while they have the frames and mechanisms by which they can be moved, they are generally used as permanent homes and are often situated so as to appear more or less as homes built in place. They do not include a driver's cabin or any means for self-propulsion and must be moved by professional trucking services. The North Dakota Century Code groups all of these under the legal umbrella of Chapter 23-10 "Mobile Home Parks, Trailer Parks, and Campgrounds"; however, there are two different license categories for RV parks and mobile home parks. As one state official explains:

If it's not a lodging-style establishment [that's] not pieced together with central corridors, then we'll do it as a mobile home park. An RV park is when it contains travel trailers or recreational vehicles. We have a separate requirement for that, because there are differing requirements, like electrical demands. Sometimes they're different from a mobile home park. The pedestals have to be different, the spacing requirements are different, so we have two different license categories for mobile home parks versus RV parks.

As is the case with the regulations governing Type I camps, North Dakota's state Department of Health has "general supervision over the health, safety, sanitary condition, and legal compliance" with North Dakota Century Code's Chapter 23, the statute overseeing mobile home parks, RV parks, and campgrounds (NDCC 23-10.02). While those attempting to establish or enlarge any property intended for such use must apply with the state, the statute also authorizes local units of government to inspect and enforce regulations, provided that the state has determined that the local government's standards meet or exceed those of the state (NDCC 23-10.02.1). Inspections are required by statute at least biennially (NDCC 23-10.04), and licenses must be renewed annually (NDCC 23-10.06). Upon review of the application and the completed inspection, a license is granted if it is determined that the park or campground is not "a source of danger to the health and safety of the occupants or the general public" (NDCC 23-10-04).

Other relevant rules for mobile homes are found in Chapter 54-21-3, the Uniform Standards Code for Mobile Homes. The stated intent of the code is basically twofold: (1) to "eliminate restrictive, obsolete, conflicting, and unnecessary construction regulations that tend to increase construction costs unnecessarily ... or provide preferential treatment to types or classes of materials or products of methods of construction" (54-21.3.2); and (2) to ensure that such structures "adequately protect the health, safety and welfare of the people of this state" (54-21.3.3). Interestingly, a statute providing for energy efficiency in mobile homes was repealed in 1979 (Chapter 54-21.2).

Similar to Type I regulations, the emphasis is on basic fire, life, and safety issues. More specifically, the statute requires that mobile home park owners follow state code with regard to electrical installations, that parks have adequate roads and lighting, and that sanitary conditions be maintained (primarily drinking water, plumbing, sewage removal, and garbage containment and removal) (NDCC 23-10.07-1-10). This subsection of the code also states that "every mobile home park must be established and maintained upon dry, well-drained ground." Type II camps throughout the Bakken include varying amounts of gravel and scoria. One telling anecdote loosely related to this issue of drainage is that the "patch has three seasons: ice, mud, and dust." Since the vast majority of current oil boom-related Type II camps are rapidly set up in recently cleared agricultural land, paving is essentially nonexistent. With those conditions, the frequently flat terrain means that attempts to deal with mud and standing water are at best an ongoing battle.

With regard to fire, safety, and sanitation issues, the provisions of Chapter 23 apply to mobile home park inspection; inspection of individual units is not addressed. Thus, while a modular unit in a Type I is inspected for smoke alarms and fire escapes the same way that motel rooms and apartment rentals are, Type II units escape this level of scrutiny.

Chapter 23 does contain modest provisions related to quality of life issues, including consideration of children. In addition to language explicitly referring to the "health, safety, and comfort of its occupants" under the sanitation and safety subsection (NDCC 23.10.07), there are requirements for provision of playground space equivalent to one lot for every twenty-five lots (NDCC 23.10.11). In the NDMCP documentation, the playground requirement appears to be only weakly enforced, especially the ratio of one playground space for every twenty-five lots.

Policies Covering Type III Camps

Type III camps, essentially squatting arrangements, fly "under the radar" of the enforcement mechanisms described for Types I and II, which means that complaints about such arrangements are typically addressed, at least initially, by overworked and understaffed law enforcement authorities. While living arrangements in a Type III mean limited or no access to fresh water, electricity, and sewage, camps might consist of one or two units parked, with permission, on private land. Often that could be land owned by one of the oil companies, as in this example given by a state official:

> Some of them may be on private property and there may be an oil company that's housing their employees and it's not just an open camp or park where just anybody can come in. As long as they're providing restroom facilities or something for them, something like this would be kind of unregulated, as long as they weren't violating environmental laws by having septic and so forth running onto the ground and into the ditches and things like that.

As noted earlier, the NDMCP has recently documented the abandonment or disappearance of Type III camps. At the onset of the boom, some of these camps were quite large.

Beyond the fact that most are inherently illegal and therefore intentionally hidden, current Type III scarcity may largely be a function of the widespread adoption of planning and zoning laws that were minimal or largely absent in the rural towns and counties of western North Dakota before the boom. Once enacted in particular jurisdictions, local governments addressed the risk of losing revenues by tightening regulations as business interests rapidly adjusted to move their activities to less-regulated environments a few miles up or down the road. For instance, as Williams County tried to initiate its moratorium on man camps, there was a proliferation of camps just outside the county border, as described by one state official:

> There wasn't always planning and zoning authority in those counties. McKenzie County is the perfect example—where Watford City is located. They never had planning or zoning prior to about two or three years ago. And then everybody, because they were getting shut down or maybe restricted in Williams or Mountrail County, where they had more strict planning and zoning laws in place, said, "Okay, we'll take our business down to McKenzie County and they don't have planning and zoning, and we'll just do what we want to do." Well, it didn't take long for McKenzie County to say, "Hey, we've got to put a stop to this."

Applying the "fire, life, safety" policy framework that characterizes the existing regulatory environment for temporary labor housing, Type III man camps are certainly the most problematic, placing a strain on existing, generally inadequate rural infrastructure, and running a higher risk of creating unsafe and unsanitary conditions for their residents and the larger community.

A Reactive Versus Proactive Stance

As noted, highly impacted communities in the heart of the oil boom have tried to regulate man camp proliferation, especially in those cases where infrastructure capacity was overwhelmed. State officials noted marked improvements in the ability of local governments to plan and control these developments, as exemplified in the statement by this interviewee:

> Now the planning and zoning folks decide if they can handle new (man camp) proposals. If they can handle it, they will probably give the approval. If they can't and they're getting maxed out, which some of those cities—I think Stanley and Williston had some real infrastructure problems—they now may say "no" because they

have to limit the number of people who could tap into their municipal systems.

Essentially, North Dakota's response to temporary labor housing pressures that accompanied the oil boom was to simply apply regulations that were already in place, many of which were initially passed in the 1970s or earlier. While the state was awash in oil revenue, local governmental entities were clearly on their own with only limited state funding. According to one long-term state official:

> [T]here was no state funding for any of this. The counties and cities came up with their own money to put their own inspection departments in place. Most of them are using contracted people for doing the inspections, and some of them—like Williams County and Williston, Watford City—have hired their own inspectors. A lot of the smaller towns use contracted people. There are lots of different arrangements, like Stanley has their own building inspector, but the county does not. They're kind of new to that. Same with McKenzie County. Stark County kind of ran with Dickinson and formed their own inspection service.

The speed with which local entities were able to develop local ordinances and administrative staffing and support for inspection and enforcement varied greatly. With generally insufficient funding and policy support, local and state officials developed new collaborations and communicated with one another in novel ways to help local officials deal with the explosion of temporary labor housing. For example, state and local officials developed rapid-response processes for ensuring that various officials and boards were notified across the patchwork of affected boards, commissions, and other entities. This process begins with application to the state for new developments, which, in turn, triggers a series of e-mail notifications and communications, as described by this state official:

> We license all of them, so they start here a lot, and we require their plans. We don't just let them set up, and then we go out and take a look. They have to meet certain requirements first, and show us how they're going to construct or lay out that facility ... We also copy a variety of other agencies, because there's got to be good communication between all the government entities that may have a say in this—and that's local officials for planning and zoning purposes. We don't want them going to great extremes to satisfy our needs if they haven't got local approval first. And then

we'll copy those folks. We'll also copy the State Plumbing Board, the State Electrical Board, the municipal facilities, and another division within the Health Department that's going to have to approve their wastewater handling system ... Through the years we've developed good communication, and we copy everybody when somebody's approached.

State officials also discussed marked improvements in the capacity of local entities to address issues related to temporary labor housing, as noted by this interviewee:

When this first hit there were a lot of problems because a lot of cities and counties had no oversight and no local building codes. Since then, just about every place out west has adopted building codes and has people in place to do inspections, assert authority, and keep track of things. Now things are working very well and people have a handle on these things.

When asked what might have been done differently, the same individual contrasted the case of two Boom cities, Williston and Dickinson:

There's two completely different ways of handling things. Williston just let everything go, they just let everything in, and they didn't really get a handle on things and it kind of got away from them. Dickinson, on the other hand, from the beginning, slowed everything down and said, "We're going to get some things in place here," and they've had a lot less problems. I think when these types of things start up it's important to slow down, get the infrastructure, get things like inspection all in place.

While this example illustrates the need for local entities to do all they can to control the pace of development, there were key distinctions between the two communities. First and foremost, Williston's central location to oil activity was beyond the control of the city or Williams county officials, whereas Dickinson sits on the edge of the oil patch in a way that creates a different opportunity to profit from, while not being overrun by, the oil activity. For instance, the interstate freeway and much of the oil activity are both on the northern side of Dickinson, while most of the city's housing and retail tend to the south. In contrast, the city of Williston, including its downtown, is almost evenly dissected by highways 2 and 1804, and the formerly sleepy community dealt with extraordinary truck traffic without the benefit of a bypass for more than the first five years of the boom. Additionally, Williston had been particularly hard hit with expensive municipal bonds in the aftermath of the 1980s crash, leaving the community understandably cautious about investing in growth and development, especially amid the uncertain atmosphere of the first years of the oil boom.

Making Ideological Assumptions Visible

The man camp typology, juxtaposed with the framework of policies that regulate temporary workforce housing, demonstrates that the response of state and local municipalities was largely an ad hoc attempt to stretch the existing policy framework—the fire, life, and safety regulations of motels, trailer parks, and campgrounds—to address novel conditions. State and local officials attempted to carry out their charge—to guarantee at least a minimal standard of fire, life, and safety regulation—in the face of enormous challenges and insufficient financial resources. Officials expressed encouragement that, across a variety of approaches, local communities were beginning to develop the capacity to better regulate existing development, and to better shape future development. However, these efforts can still be critiqued for their inadequacy as overcrowded conditions, price-gouging, dismal living conditions, and attendant social problems persist in North Dakota's oil patch.

While one significant challenge for communities was a lack of building codes, they also lacked resources to hire local inspectors. Perhaps more importantly, there was insufficient state funding to support the local communities (municipal and county entities). In response, they either banded together or faced the challenges alone. The decision was generally between starting up and staffing their own inspection departments or contracting with individuals to perform this critical work. While concerns about the lack of state response to local problems is well documented (Holeywell 2011), North Dakota's Governor Jack Dalrymple announced his second biennial "no growth" budget, stating that, while the state has "the nation's strongest economy," its strong growth requires the state government to "become more creative and more efficient" (quoted in Smith 2014).

"What can you do?" is a familiar question uttered by long-term and newer community residents and government officials when asked about boom-related housing challenges. This oft-repeated question, once unpacked, reveals assumptions nested within the larger neoliberal, socio-economic, and political contexts of North Dakota's oil patch. The neoliberal welfare state is characterized by the view that market forces provide the best possible means of addressing human wellbeing (e.g.,

Abromovitz 2012). Additionally, the growing power of global corporate capital increases the difficulty of addressing local issues of social and economic justice when other countervailing forces (such as the governor or the state legislature) cannot or will not act (e.g., Sewpaul 2013).

The oil boom has been a blessing and a curse for western North Dakota. Having lost population for decades, many towns were unable to even keep grocery stores open, let alone schools or medical services. Brad Bekkedahl, a Williston City Commissioner declared, "This is a time of opportunity. It's a time of growth. And it's a time of amazing prosperity and wealth coming into our community" (quoted in Holeywell 2011, 1). Others lament the challenges brought about by the market-fueled inflationary economy. "Anything you can think of that a person would consume is also being consumed by folks in the oil industry," says Dennis Lindahl, a city councilman in Stanley (Holeywell 2011, 1). "Merchants are able to charge an increased rate. Folks in town sometimes get a little upset from supporting the industry while not receiving benefits." And clearly, even for oil boom boosters like Bekkedahl, the market does not have all the answers. In the fall of 2014, Republican candidate for state senate Bekkedahl was supportive of a change in the state's oil production tax to address continuing and growing financial needs. With Williston projected to need more than $1 billion in infrastructure needs by 2020, Bekkedahl noted, "We need $180 million to $200 million just to keep up with demand in the next five to six years" (quoted in Burnes 2014). Of all the economic struggles and challenges, the nexus issue in the oil patch remains the shortage of housing—a phenomenon that continued to be framed primarily as a local problem.

Lesson Drawing and Recommendations Through a Social Work Lens

The sheer insufficiency of policies to address temporary labor housing in the face of the challenges brought by North Dakota's oil boom is the most important lesson drawn from this policy analysis, and it may be of greatest relevance to other communities that are now or may soon experience similar activity as a result of hydraulic fracturing or other twenty-first century extractive industry booms. North Dakota's sleepy rural agricultural communities were overwhelmed in the face of the massive development brought by oil companies and the panoply of support industries that followed. This was compounded by the Great Recession, which brought large in-migrations of economic refugees from the rest of the nation to western North Dakota, compounding already severe housing shortages.

Lack of a centrally coordinated state response to support local communities comprises the second key lesson, leaving many unanswered questions about problems that might have been avoided or better managed if communities had the policy tools, technical expertise, and adequate funds at their disposal from the outset. Lack of vision for a state role in the face of the housing challenges caused by the boom is closely related to this issue.

Finally, this analysis addressed the inadequacy of the minimalist fire/life/safety framework of existing policies that were "stretched" to cover the novel housing conditions of the oil boom. This framework arguably limited the ability of policymakers, state and local officials, and community members to imagine anything other than a reactive response to a narrow and proscribed range of safety concerns. Rather than expending considerable effort to predict how much housing will be needed by the oil companies over the coming decades, communities might be better served by state policies that more proactively consider the possibility of extending the pace of oil development. It might even make sense to plan in reverse by first determining desired levels of local housing and infrastructure development, and then gearing oil production to those benchmarks, rather than allowing oil production to drive those decisions.

Viewed through a social work lens concerned with human wellbeing, this analysis concludes with recommendations regarding policy actions and policy-related research in North Dakota's oil patch. First, the state (through the governor's office or by action of the state legislature) should appoint a special commission to gather existing data related to housing issues in the oil patch and utilize this information to make data-driven decisions to advise local communities and state policymakers. Proposed outcomes should explicitly include quality of life considerations, with indices that can be tracked in relation to both individual and community levels. Such a commission could also act as a clearinghouse to share information about regulations that help cities and counties control the pace of development and promote remedies to ameliorate some of the seemingly inevitable, but unnecessary harmful effects.

Current planning around temporary labor housing is largely driven by economic models that attempt to predict—based on current and projected drilling activity—how many "units of housing" will be needed in various western North Dakota communities. Quality of life issues for workers might gain more traction in the neoliberal sociopolitical context if such concerns were introduced as essential human capital investments, supported by evidence that connects worker wellbeing with productivity and increased workforce stability. More research is also needed among residents of Type I camps, although tight corporate control over such

220

lodging makes it challenging to gain access. Some of North Dakota's Type I man camps would be among the twenty largest communities in the state; however, these "communities" have no mayor or city council, electoral, or legal representation. Ideally, planning processes and housing policies should include not only financial calculations, but also considerations that housing is an inseparable aspect of community and that community is essential to social wellbeing.

Community residents are a natural constituency that can be tapped to increase policymaker attention to the impacts of temporary labor housing on quality of life at the community level. Statistics that indicate increasing levels of crimes related to drug trafficking, human trafficking, and other attendant social problems such as domestic violence and child abuse and neglect, are increasingly well documented through research as well as journalistic reports, as are rising resident fears about crime (e.g., Archbold 2013). Reports of these problems have garnered a national audience, and the enormous challenges for law enforcement officials, given the transient nature of life in North Dakota's man camps, have made their way into national headlines as some of the larger Type I man camps have been the subject of unfavorable national news reports (e.g., Associated Press 2014). As the state is heavily concerned with projecting a positive image with its newfound wealth, concern for negative reports about the darker side of the boom may provide political leverage for advocates of improved housing conditions.

Comparative studies of temporary worker housing in other states, Canada, and beyond North America are also needed to inform communities of potential strategies for better controlling housing costs, conditions, and the pace of development. Within North Dakota, selected case studies of communities may also shed light on the costs and benefits associated with varied policy responses, including environmental impacts.

Somewhere between the pleas of man camp residents to simply build more housing and the concerns of local taxpayers about getting stuck paying for municipal bonds lie opportunities to implement a more optimal balance of permanent long-term development with a suitable amount of temporary labor housing. A social justice framework requires that judgments regarding economic activity and housing be pursued to benefit human beings, and compels us to remember that neither temporary laborers nor long-term residents deserve to be treated like inventories of widgets, with no more consideration than corporate ledgers.

However, the language of social justice is unlikely to gain much traction in the current economic and political context. Despite the oil boom, North Dakota's landlocked and remote geographic location, legendary winters, lack of high-profile tourist attractions, and largely agrarian economy combine to maintain its distinction as the least visited state in the continental U.S. (e.g., Holdman 2013). Prior to the oil boom, North Dakotans frequently pointed with pride to the high quality of life (Conway current volume) as a potential lever for much-needed economic development in a rapidly depopulating state; despite the boom, this ethos remains, and, indeed, constitutes the foundation of a North Dakota Economic Development Foundation Division campaign (Hageman 2014) to lure new residents—the flip side of North Dakota's lowest-in-the-nation unemployment rate means that numerous jobs go unfilled.

North Dakotans' historic and continuing pride in their quality of life provides a potential avenue for seeking better solutions to the daunting housing-related challenges of the oil patch, and a better balance between robust economic activity and matters affecting quality of life. Policymakers will hopefully make decisions based on the best available data. Similarly, corporate interests will understandably attempt to shape the policy context in ways that serve their best interests, including narratives that further perpetuate neoliberal beliefs that markets hold the best answers to all economic-related problems. That is where researchers must address their responsibility to provide both the quantitative and the qualitative data necessary to consider not only the economics, but also the human side of extractive industries and the resulting impacts on local communities.

References

Abramovitz, M. 2012. "Theorising the Neoliberal Welfare State for Social Work." In *The SAGE Handbook of Social Work*, edited by M. Gray, J. Midgley, and S. Webb, 33–51. London: SAGE.

Archbold, C.A. 2013. "Policing the Patch: An examination of the oil boom on small town policing and crime in Western North Dakota." www.ndsu.edu/fileadmin/cjps/Policing_the_Patch_Report_-_Final_Draft_August_4th_-_Archbold.docx

Associated Press. 2012. "ND Becomes Nation's Second Leading Oil Producer." *Alaska Journal of Commerce*, May 15. www.alaska-journal.com/Alaska-Journal-of-Commerce/May-Issue-2-2012/ND-becomes-nations-second-leading-oil-producer/.

Associated Press. 2014. "Dark Side of ND's Oil Boom: Meth, Heroin, Cartels: All Part of Growing Drug Trade." *Fox News*, April 12. www.foxnews.com/us/2014/04/12/dark-side-nd-oil-boom-meth-heroin-cartels-all-part-growing-drug-trade-1418696252/.

222

Bell, Tyler. 2014. "Companies Facing Millions in Fines for Temporary Housing." *Grand Forks Herald*, September 23.

Burnes, J. 2014. "Formula Change Proposed." *Williston Herald*, September 25. www.willistonherald.com/news/formula-change-proposed/article_a1499a64-44e6-11e4-9579-5fb60f0cde06.html.

Camassia, M.J., and K.P. Wilkinson. 1990. "Severe Child Maltreatment in Ecological Perspective." *Journal of Social Service Research* 13, no. 3: 1–18.

Caraher, W. R., B.A. Weber, K. Kourelis, and R. Rothaus. 2015. "North Dakota man camp project: The archaeology of home in the Bakken oil fields." Unpublished manuscript.

Clark, M. 2014. "Decades of Life Left in North Dakota Bakken Crude Oil Shale, Petroleum Producer President Says." *International Business Times*, March 5. www.ibtimes.com/decades-life-left-north-dakota-bakken-crude-oil-shale-petroleum-producer-president-says-1559668.

"County Puts 6-Month Moratorium on New Man Camps." 2011. *Williston Herald*, September 12. www.willistonherald.com/news/county-puts--month-moratorium-on-new-man-camps/article_8d-444cb0-a0b2-5767-9b7b-cb16167f741f.html.

Craig, C. 2014. "What's the Most Expensive Town in the U.S.? The Answer Might Surprise You." *Apartment Guide*, February 17. www.apartmentguide.com/blog/williston-nd/.

Dalrymple, A. 2012. "State Official Says Oil Development Will Push Jobs, Population Growth." *Oil Patch Dispatch*, May 24. oilpatchdispatch.areavoices.com/2012/05/24/state-official-says-oil-development-will-push-jobs-population-growth/#sthash.tnpcW8R3.dpuf.

DSU (Dickinson State University), MSU (Minot State University), and GPEC (Great Plains Energy Corridor). 2011. "Energy Impacts in North Dakota 2011." www.ag.ndsu.edu/ccv/documents/energy-impacts.

Hageman, J. 2014. "ND Workforce Recruitment Campaign Aims to Fill Jobs." *Prairie Business Magazine*, April 28. www.prairiebizmag.com/event/article/id/18873/.

Hankvivsky, O., ed. 2012. *An Intersectionality-Based Policy Analysis Framework*. Vancouver, BC: Institute for Intersectionality Research and Policy, Simon Fraser University.

Hennessey, M. 2014. "Left Holding the Bag." *Grand Forks Herald*, March 5, 3A.

Hess, A., and T.C. Frohlich. 2014. "Ten States with the Fastest-Growing Economies." *24/7 Wall Street*, June 12. 247wallst.com/

special-report/2014/06/12/10-states-with-the-fastest-growing-economies/.

Hodur, N.M., D.A. Bangsund, R. Rathge, and K. Olson. 2013. "Estimates of Enrollment Projections: Ray, Stanley, Watford City, Williston and Dickinson." Agribusiness and Applied Economics Report No. 708-S. ageconsearch.umn.edu/bitstream/146659/2/schoolExecutiveSummaryPrintDraft.pdf

Holdman, J. 2013. "The Least Visited State in Mainland U.S. Is Having a Tourism Boom, Thanks to Oil." *Bismarck Tribune*, March 31. skift.com/2013/03/31/the-least-visited-state-in-mainland-u-s-is-having-a-tourism-boom-thanks-to-oil/.

Holeywell, R. 2011. "North Dakota's Oil Boom Is a Blessing and a Curse: The State's Oil Boom Is Bringing Unmatched Growth and Unanticipated Problems." *Governing the States and Localities*, August. www.governing.com/topics/energy-env/north-dakotas-oil-boom-blessing-curse.html.

Johnson, M. S. 2011. "Discovery of Parshall Field, North Dakota." In *The Bakken-Three Forks Petroleum System in the Williston Basin*, edited by J. W. Robinson, J. A. LeFever, and S. B. Gaswirth, 418–27. Denver, CO: The Rocky Mountain Association of Geologists.

Klimasinska, K. 2013. "No Kids, No Booze, No Pets: Inside North Dakota's Largest Man Camp." *Bloomberg News*, February 12. www.bloomberg.com/news/2013-02-12/no-kids-no-booze-no-pets-inside-north-dakota-s-largest-man-camp.html.

Monke, D. 2014. "Oil Patch Hub Watford City Adjusts to Burgeoning Population, Financial Questions." *Grand Forks Herald*, March 3. www.grandforksherald.com/content/oil-patch-hub-watford-city-adjusts-burgeoning-population-financial-questions.

"North Dakota Leads Nation in GDP Growth." 2013. *Bismarck Tribune*, June 7. bismarcktribune.com/business/local/nd-leads-nation-in-gdp-growth/article_f9d9a51c-cfac-11e2-8ec3-001a4bcf887a.html.

"North Dakota Department of Commerce." 2014. *Third party inspection*. Retrieved from www.communityservices.nd.gov/buildingcode/ThirdPartyInspection/.

"North Dakota Energy Forum." 2014. North Dakota Oil and Gas History. Message posted to www.ndenergyforum.com/topics/north-dakota-oil-and-gas-history.

North Dakota Petroleum Council. 2011. *E-News 2011*, December 14. www.ndoil.org/?id=214&ncid=9&nid=188.

Sen, A.K. 2006. "What Do We Want From a Theory of Justice?" *Journal of Philosophy* 103, no. 5: 215–38.

Sewpaul, V. 2013. "Neoliberalism and Social Work in South Africa." *Critical and Radical Social Work* 1, no. 1: 15–30.

Shipman, N. A. 2013. "Study: Decades of Oil Development Ahead." *McKenzie County Farmer*, January 23. watfordcitynd.com/?id=10&nid=2004.

Smith, N. 2014. "Governor: Hold Even on Budget." *Bismarck Tribune*, May 7. bismarcktribune.com/news/local/govt-and-politics/governor-hold-even-on-budget/article_6012380a-d662-11e3-bfc1-0019bb2963f4.html.

U.S. Bureau of Labor Statistics. 2014. "Regional and State Employment and Unemployment Summary." *Economic News Release*, October 21. www.bls.gov/news.release/laus.nr0.htm.

U.S. Census Bureau. 2000. "Census 2000 Data for the State of North Dakota." www.census.gov/census2000/states/nd.html.

U.S. Census Bureau. 2012. "North Dakota Is Nation's Fastest-Growing State Since 2011." www.census.gov/newsroom/releases/archives/population/cb12-250.html.

U.S. Census Bureau. 2012. *State and County Quickfacts*. quickfacts.census.gov/qfd/states/38000.html.

U.S. Energy Information Administration. 2013. "North Dakota Sees Increases in Real GDP Per Capita Following Bakken Production." July 12. www.eia.gov/todayinenergy/detail.cfm?id=12071.

Van Wormer, K. S. 2004. *Confronting Oppression, Restoring Justice: From Policy Analysis to Social Action*. Washington, DC: Council on Social Work Education.

Weaver, B. D. 2010. *Oilfield Trash: Life and Labor in the Oil Patch*. College Station, TX: Texas A&M University Press.

Weber, B.A., J. Geigle, and C. Barkdull. 2014. "Rural North Dakota's Oil Boom and Its Impact on Social Services." *Social Work* 59, no. 1: 62–72.

Chapter 12

100 Miles of Wild: North Dakota Badlands Transect

Richard Rothaus, Simon Donato, Andrew Reinhard, and Melissa Rae Stewart

The North Dakota badlands are little visited not just because of their distance from large populations, but also because they are physically challenging. What look like rugged but traversable hills from a roadside overlook quickly become a maze of endless ups and downs that twist upon themselves, exposed to the sun, without shade or water. Little infrastructure has been put in place to support travelers by foot. Thus the areas between the roads remain almost unvisited. This project has its origins in the half-formed plans of Richard Rothaus and Andrew Reinhard for a "simple" backpacking trek in the badlands just for fun, to try to capture some of the inspiration felt by the young Theodore Roosevelt when he visited the badlands.

In their planning, as Rothaus described the impact of the Bakken oil boom to Reinhard, the duo came up with a vision for something greater than a trip: a transect, cutting cross-terrain, to see how many inspiring areas of wild were still out there in the middle of a boom. While not particularly hazardous, the badlands are difficult, and the transect envisioned called for individuals at the peak of physical conditions, and this is where the juncture with Adventure Science was formed. Adventure Science is a collective focused on citizen-scientist explorations of rugged and remote places to answer questions out of the reach of the casual traveler. Rothaus had previously participated in Adventure Science expeditions, and he and Reinhard worked with Adventure Science founder Simon Donato to create 100 Miles of Wild: North Dakota Badlands Transect

The 100 Miles of Wild project had a simple aim: go to a little visited area of North Dakota and discover firsthand the condition of the wild that inspired Roosevelt's effort to preserve wilderness for all Americans and the world. But to do that, the team devised a series of difficult transects, across rather than with the rugged terrain, matched with a systematic collection of quantifiable and impressionistic data, photos and video. The

Figure 1. North Dakota Badlands, Courtesy of EcoFlight.

Adventure Science project was self-funded and self-organized, to ensure that we could remain an unbiased voice as we discuss these sensitive areas. As teams hiked a collective 270 miles of transects it became apparent that the difficult geography of the badlands have shielded the landscape from large-scale development. The transects ran primarily through the federally managed Little Missouri National Grasslands. The Grasslands are not a designated wilderness area, and the mandate of the U.S. Department of Agriculture is to use the lands for the public good, a use that currently includes grazing and oil development. The rugged nature of the Grasslands has, however, led to an area largely undisturbed except by ranching until the current oil boom.

Team members were Jane Davis (Community Health Educator), Dr. Simon Donato (Geologist), Jessica Kuepfer (Writer), Tyler LeBlanc (Paramedic), Dr. Tim Puetz (Biomedical Researcher), Andrew Reinhard (Archaeologist), Dr. Richard Rothaus (Archaeologist and Historian), Keith Slater (Search and Rescue), and Melissa Rae Stewart (Public Relations). North Dakotan Aaron Barth (Historian) provided assistance at a critical juncture when one team member (Rothaus) became ill.

The terms "wild" and "wilderness" are, of course, somewhat subjective. In a strict definition as an area untouched by human hands, true wilderness areas in the continental United States are uncommon and highly fragmented. The word "wilderness" itself is loaded with cultural connotations and conventions; the sublime religious experience, rugged frontier individualism, an area untouched by human hands (Cronon 1996). In this document we have tended to use the word "wild" to avoid these issues. The parlance among the team members, who were not, after all, scholars debating such issues, included both "wild" and "wilderness." But for a group of pragmatic individuals with extensive experience in the "wild," we used the a definition of "wild" or "wilderness" not as a place untouched, but rather a place where the touch is not a dominant feature of the landscape. This type of wild varies based on the perception of individuals, and the team was carefully chosen to include only participants who had worldwide travel experience in exceptional wild areas. Thus when the team notes say something "felt like wilderness," their point of reference is more likely to a place such as Borneo rather than a local park.

Introduction and Rational for Project

North Dakota's historic legacy is rooted in its character as "wilderness," and recent tourist campaigns tout the openness of the western half of the state, usually with golden sunlight and the tagline "Legendary." North Dakota is indeed a vast state with scattered outposts of small towns, but

Figure 2. Adventure Science Team (left to right, Tyler LeBlanc, Andrew Reimhard. Tim Puetz, Jessica Kuepfer, Jane Davis, Keith Slater, Richard Rothaus, Simon Donato). Photo courtesy of the Adventure Science Team.

it is also a state that is currently facing a significant land use challenges. Now a star of oil boom stories, until recently, the State was best known for its wide open spaces, ranching and agriculture. The wilds of the internationally famous badlands of North Dakota offered inspiration and consolation to a young Theodore Roosevelt, reeling from the deaths of his mother and wife in the early 1880s. As President, Roosevelt, remembering his life-changing experiences as a temporary cowboy and ranch owner, vigorous established his legacy of conservation by establishing five national parks, creating the U.S. Forest Service, and signing into law the Antiquities Act (Brinkley 2010, Morris 1979, Morris 2010). North Dakota today still shares much with the Dakotas of the early nineteenth century. The state has the fourth lowest population density in the U.S., with less than 10 people per square mile. North Dakota has a long history of progressive, independent, self-sufficiency, and is the homeland of several Native American Tribes that still thrive there today (Robinson et al. 1995).

North Dakota is also in the midst of a shale oil boom. This is not North Dakota's first oil boom, but it is by far its largest. The boom has brought with it road construction, drilling, pipelines, and infrastructure throughout the oil rich Bakken Formation, which underlies northwestern North Dakota, North Eastern Montana, and a large swatch of southern Saskatchewan. This boom is driven by new technologies, with oil extraction accomplished by drilling lengthy horizontal wells, and then fracturing the shale formation (fracking) to release trapped oil.

The rapid pace of the massive industry behind the oil boom has caused a breathtaking expansion of drilling pads and roads into the previously "empty" interior of North Dakota. Questions about the environmental impact abound. While the oil companies adhere to the state and federal regulations on development, the growth and rapid advance of the drilling front is at a scale that is difficult for anyone to perceive and understand. This has created significant polarity among North Dakota residents— some opposed to the rapid growth, others in support of it, all deeply affected by it. Our project sought to understand that impact through experiences that paralleled the way Roosevelt immersed himself in the land, to see if we could or would have similar experiences and feelings.

The Transect Route and Methodology

From 22 April to 2 May 2013, Adventure Science undertook the 100 Miles of Wild: North Dakota Badlands Transect, the only project of its kind across the rugged badlands. Rather than take the established Maah-Daah-Hey Trail, the team navigated primarily off-trail through areas of

Figure 3. Badlands Oil Pad Photo courtesy of the Adventure Science Team.

interest. To tie itself to the history of the region, the trek started at the North Unit of Theodore Roosevelt National Park (TRNP), headed to Theodore Roosevelt's Elkhorn Ranch, and concluded at the South Unit of TRNP near Medora (Kaye et al. 1993; Rogers 2006). The teams traveled on foot to seldom visited, isolated places within the badlands, typically staying within the boundaries of the federally administered Little Missouri National Grassland. Three two-person teams were deployed daily and tasked with covering distances between 10–25 miles each day. These teams, Team Tortoise, Speed Deer, and Mountain Kitty, were assigned routes designed to cross varied and difficult landforms, with an emphasis on traveling to places no one goes to on foot. For this project, the journey, not the destination, was important.

While deployed, the teams were charged with observing and recording their impressions of the native flora and fauna, as well as any manmade features. Documentation was done with the goal of establishing a description and personal sense of this landscape. The data also was collected so that it can be used to create a "baseline" impression of the land. While certainly not the equivalent of an environmental or archaeological inventory, the record is sufficient to capture a snapshot view of current conditions in the badlands. This can be used, for example, as a point of comparison to the state of the badlands when Roosevelt visited in the nineteenth century. More deliberately, we have consciously sought to collect a record that can be used in the future to gauge the impact of the Bakken Oil Boom. A redocumentation of the transect in the future, for example, would reveal much about the impact of the oil boom.

Team routes and recordation locations were carefully tracked with GPS units. While making their transects, teams were required to stop every few hours to record their experiences and observations. Each of these locations was designated as a log point, and at each of these team members recorded a photo and video panorama, and took notes on what they observed and felt. Team notes included an assessment of their location and signs of "civilization" they could see, the sounds and smells of the location, and perhaps most importantly the feeling of their location. Teams also recorded natural and anthropogenic features, and included a narrative of their travels between log points. This method of recordation was designed in part to overcome the inability to collect quantifiable data from a quick pedestrian transect, and in part out of recognition that the project aim was to collect the feeling of the landscape, which is inherently personal and non-quantifiable. Additionally, this data was appropriate for collection by individuals with extensive wilderness experience but lacking discrete scientific skills applicable to this landscape. At the end of each

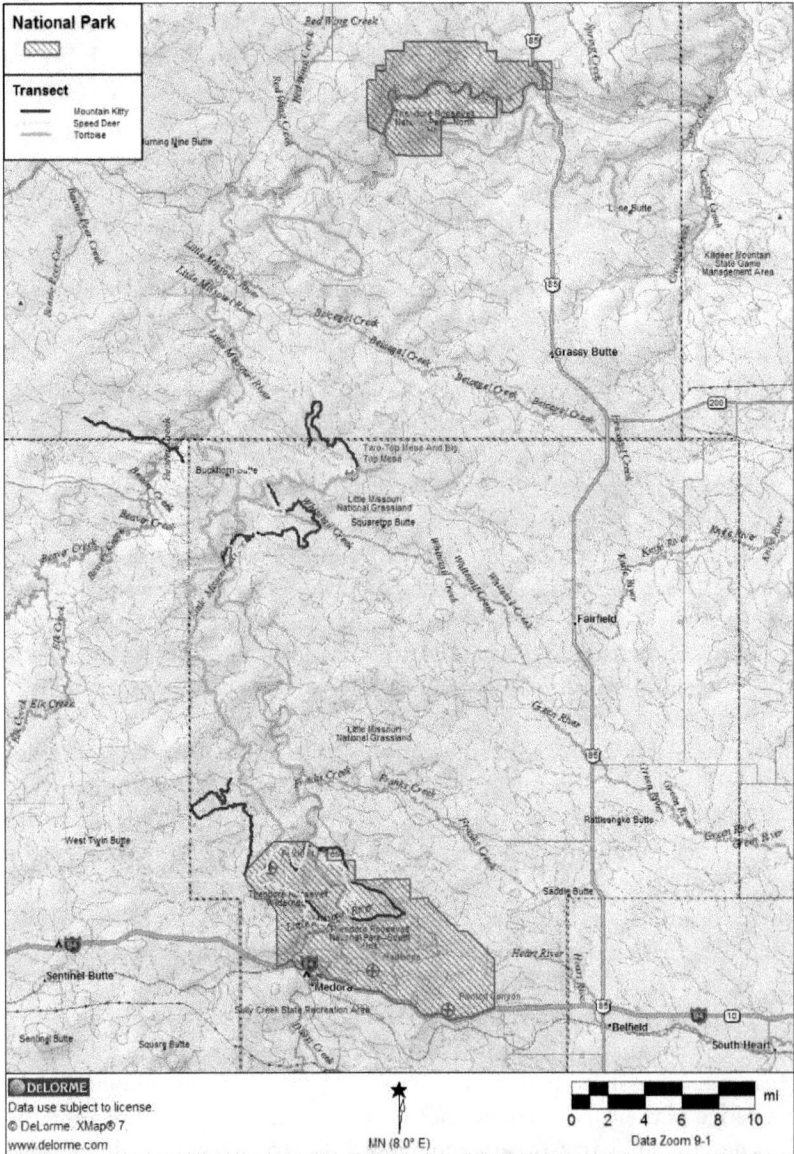

Figure 4. Transect Routes.
Map courtesy of the Adventure Science Team.

day, a debriefing was held, and each team shared what they learned about the state of they found to be an inspiring wild place.

Team Tortoise, led by Andrew Reinhard, who personally walked over 200 miles, spent the most time in the badlands, traveling 185 miles from Lone Butte east of the North Unit of TRNP to the TNRP South Unit. Team Tortoise was charged with traveling slowly and recording their impressions with more detail than the other teams. The transect for Team Tortoise began in one of the most remote locations and slowly transitioned into a route paralleling the Mah-Daah-Hey Trail. This team began during a heavy snow melt, and the route was modified and truncated in part by areas made impassable. In the spring, when the slick clays of the badlands are saturated, it becomes impossible to climb many slopes that would be only moderately challenging in dry conditions. Team Tortoise gained a total of 16,415 feet of elevation over the course of the transect, an indicator of the extreme ruggedness of the territory. While no single climb or peak is particularly notable, the repeated ups and downs equated to climbing more than three-fourths of the elevation of Mt. McKinley.

Team Tortoise spent the first two days traveling from log points T1 to T10 through difficult terrain that was farthest removed from oil development and ranching. Usually the only sign of human impact was very faint highway noise. Days three and four saw a marked increase in the evidence of historic and active ranching, which, despite the absence of oil development, made those areas feel less wild. As the team made its way south from the fifth day onwards, evidence of man became more frequent, with generally ubiquitous evidence of ranching, and more frequent observance of oil development and infrastructure. Finding areas with a truly wild feel became far less common due greater fragmentation. The area where the transect began (T1 to T4), Lone Butte, which has been proposed for designation as a roadless area, was perhaps the most "wild" of all the areas encountered by the teams. Team Tortoise recorded thirty-three log points (T1–T33) (North Dakota Wilderness Coalition 2008).

Team Speed Deer, led by Dr. Timothy Puetz, was a fast moving team and covered a total of eighty-six miles from Magpie Creek Camp to TRNP South Unit, with 14,530 feet of elevation gain. Using the same parameters for determining "wilderness" as Team Tortoise, the team found "wilderness" in a very fragmentary state from log points S1 to S18. Team Speed Deer found signs of the oil development common, as well as variable levels of disturbance of the ecosystem through ranching. As the team neared the TRNP South Unit, the landscape did become wilder, and far less developed (log points S19–S22). Team Speed Deer recorded twenty-two log points (S1–S22).

Team Name: *Speed Deer* Date (D/M/Y): _____ Time (24hr): *2:54*

Team Members: *Tim & Jane* Location (UTM NAD 83): *13T 0602518*
                                                  UTM 5205578

Describe the view of where you are. What can you see? Be sure to include signs of "civilization" (roads, oil pads, cattle...):

Tim & I are currently kneeling beside a deceased golden eagle apparent death caused by electrocution from the ~~wires~~ wires above. This sight is heartbreaking & fascinating at the same time. Below us is a ravine we chose to avoid leading to this spot

Describe the sounds and smells of where you are. Can you hear or smell "civilization"

The smell is of a freshly deceased carcass is the very pungent smell

Describe the feel of where you are. Does it feel like you are in the wilderness (why or why not)?

Interestingly enough after traveling through "a large number of pasture land & "civilized" homesteads these powerlines seem to divide the boundary between our return to the "wild"

Describe wildlife, plants and natural features you encountered in the last hour:

Since our last journal entry this poor eagle has been has been the only natural wild creature we have seen.

Describe cultural or fossil resources (archaeological and historic sites over 50 years old) you encountered in the last hour:

We did come across a section of mounds that had petrified stumps approximately 5.

Provide a brief narrative of the last hour of travel. Be sure to includes encounters with impressive or interesting natural features, civilization, people, obstacles in your travel, and your general feelings. Did it feel like you were in the wilderness?

Our travels since last entry have continued through the monotany of cow pastures In its wake erosion & poor vegetation. 2 more barbed wire fence crossings for a total 15 (RICHARD) As we left the pastures the hills have broadened & led us to Mr Eagle

As you consider your sense of wilderness and the section you completed, remember to think of about it in the context of what you see locally, but also how it compares to your larger experiences in other places.

CHECKLIST

☑ Photo of this page (do this first)	☑ Photos that capture the vegetation coverage of your location
☑ Photos of your GPS, showing coords	☑ Photo a 360° panorama (START at north, rotate clockwise)
☑ Photos that capture the feel of your location	☑ 1 minute video of sites and sounds (video this page at start)

[CONTINUE ON PAGES AT BACK OF NOTEBOOK AS NECESSARY]

Figure 5. Sample Log Entry.
Image courtesy of the Adventure Science Team.

Mountain Kitty was led by Dr. Simon Donato, and covered seventy-nine miles with 16,474 feet of elevation gain from April 28 to May 2, 2013. Their data corroborates the Team Tortoise and Speed Deer findings, in that between log point M1 to M10, areas of true wilderness were highly fragmented, discontinuous, and not geographically extensive. From log point M11 to M17 the landscape showed less signs of impact from ranching, oil development significantly declined, and the sense of wild grew. Mountain Kitty recorded 17 log points (M1–M17).

The consistent thread amongst all three teams was that wild areas are still present albeit variable. These areas however, are severely fragmented and discontinuous. Teams traveled into and out of areas of wild, with the transition sometimes being quite abrupt as canyons would lead to new, scoria topped roads, and active well pads. All the transects experienced a situation where the wild could still be encountered, but immersion was short-lived.

Overview of Findings

The challenge of blending the semi-impressionistic records of a large team is significant, so here we have tried to present a mix of informed interpretations and data summaries. Using the log point data, we have been able to describe how frequently the teams encountered oil development, roads, ranching, paleontological and archaeological sites, wildlife, manmade noise and other people. Not only does this information provide a context that allows readers to determine if our overall impressions are reasonable, it also provides a base data set that can be checked in future years, by different people. One unique aspect of this dataset is that it is tied to experience on the ground. While similar information can be gathered remotely, from satellite images for example, the translation of those datasets to what a human might experience, much less their emotional reaction, is difficult.

Oil Development

The most direct and obvious measure of the impact of the current boom in remote areas is well pads and roads. While the team was on the lookout for obvious major unregulated impacts (e.g., illegal dumping, oil spills), we knew that a handful of people were unlikely to stumble across such on Federal lands, and indeed we found none. Through the transect data, however, the team gained a good overview of the impact of the most critical above ground infrastructure of access roads and well pads.

Figure 6. Andrew Reinhard. Photo courtesy of the Adventure Science Team.

The transect was conducted in the earliest days of spring when minimal drilling activity occurs. Thus our impression of wild via the transect lacks the impact of active drilling and fracking, and the associated very heavy truck traffic. As those who live or work near a well being actively drilled or fracked have reported, the noise and traffic are significant. That said, our data reflects the more permanent infrastructure that will be left behind when active drilling is reduced or over.

The teams did not record every pad that they passed by on their respective transects, but only those that they were able to see during their observational stops. Stops were determined at team discretion, as determined by time (about every 60 to 120 minutes), changing terrain, and the instructions that, for an impressionistic study, stopping at interesting landforms was more important than regular spacing. Well pads and derricks that were visible in the far distance (typically more than one or two miles) were not recorded as present at the observation point.

Pad construction was generally basic, with holding tanks, derrick, several small out buildings, and a containment berms of varying heights. Litter was rare at most sites visited, and most pads were free of spills, odor, and noise. No unconfined liquids were encountered. In addition, Federal Grasslands regulations require derricks to be painted a matte taupe, which works well to minimize the visual impacts. Not all impacts are visible, of course, and teams carried Hydrogen Sulfide (H2S) monitors to detect this deadly colorless gas sometimes emited by wells. No H2S sources were recorded during the expedition. Members of the team who had experience in other oil fields noted that the well pads we encountered were among the neatest and cleanest they had seen, presumably a result of regulations and oversight by the USFS. Team member without oilfield experience reported that the paths were much cleaner and trash-free than they anticipated. There was some thought, however, that containment berms were rather uncommon compared to other areas.

Oil pads were typically clustered in valley bottoms, which is normal when producing an oil field, and when a team would encounter one pad, they would encounter several. Overall, the transect taken by team Mountain Kitty resulted in the lowest percentage of wells viewed at their observation stops (24 percent), while Speed Deer encountered the most (41 percent), and Tortoise was at the low end of the spectrum (27 percent). The results indicate that the presence of well pads is a significant and now permanent part of the experience for any recreational user of the badlands. As Tim Puetz expressed it, the omnipresence of the well pads is significant: "We knew [oil] was always with us, like we were walking hand-in-hand."

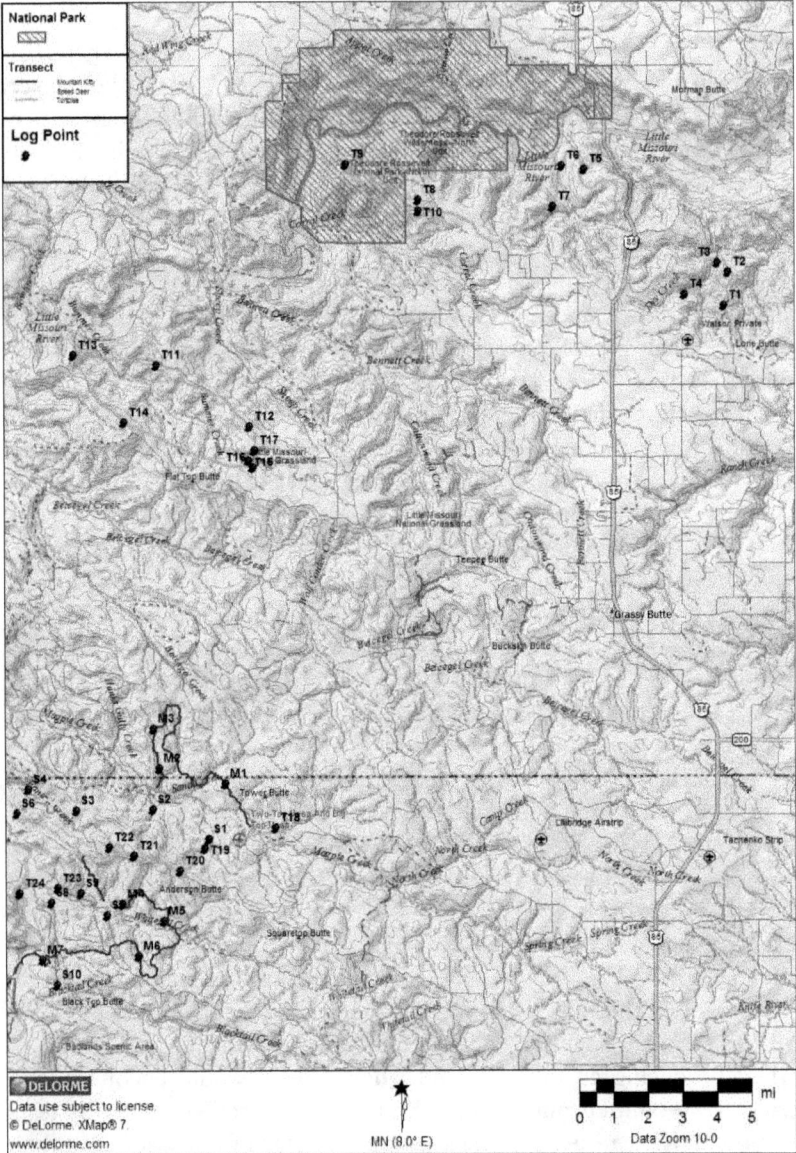

Figure 7. Log Points, North
Map courtesy of the Adventure Science Team.

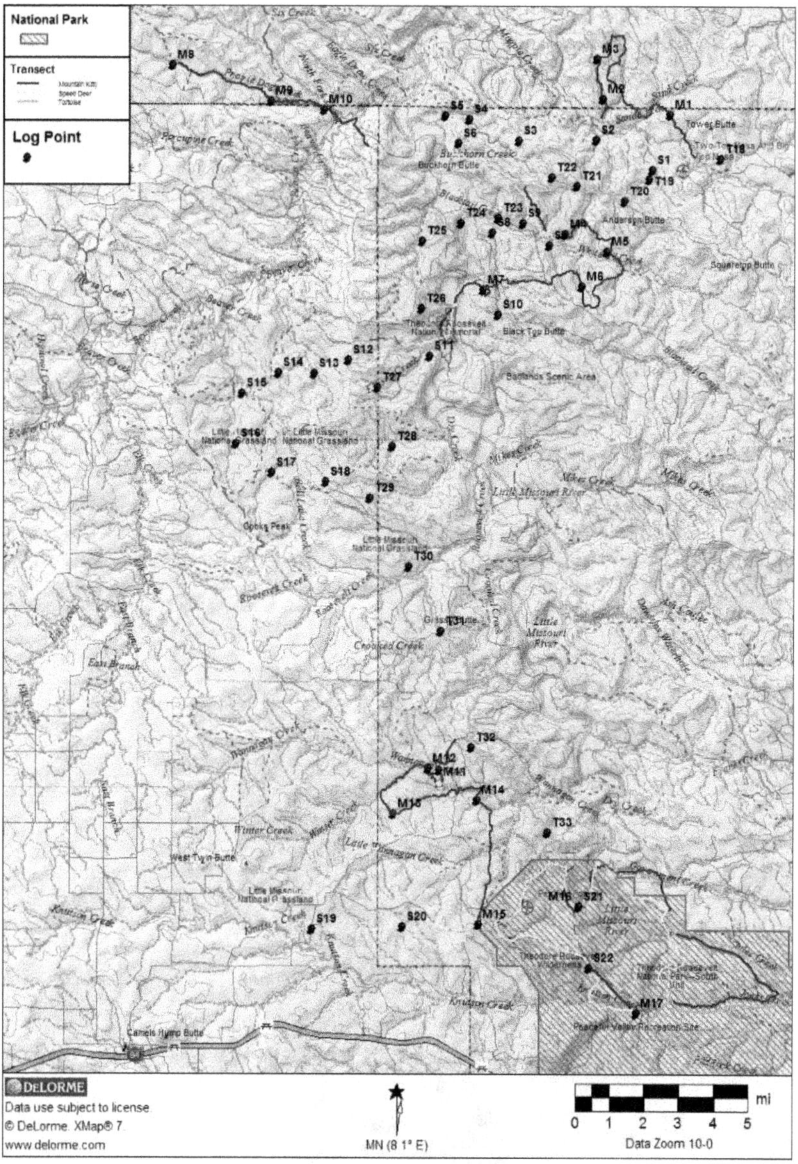

Figure 8. Log Points, South.
Map courtesy of the Adventure Science Team.

Figure 9. Kuepfer Navigates a Ridgeline. Photo courtesy of the Adventure Science Team.

By far, the most vivid evidence of the oil industry along the transect routes were the scoria topped roads. Scoria, or clinker, is a locally available sedimentary rock that is baked in the ground following natural fires in adjacent coal seam. Lightning strikes are the most common cause of such fires. The fragmented scoria is a striking red color, and natural beds of it bisects numerous badland valleys. With local gravel sources few and far between, clinker is the default road construction material, as it is hard and relatively durable. Those who drive on it will tell you that it is sharper than gravel, wreaks havoc on tires, and wears out quickly. But it works well enough to stabilize the bentonite clay soils, which otherwise becomes impassable during wet periods.

The bright red clinker topped roads snaking through isolated valleys boldly announce the presence of pads, and on their own have created a major visual impact on the badlands. As with well pads, roads that were visible in the far distance (typically more than one or two miles) were not recorded as present at the observation point. Speed Deer observed roads at 68 percent of their observational stops, while Mountain Kitty and Tortoise saw roads at less than half of their stops (41 percent and 36 percent respectively). These numbers indicate that for the badland traveler trying to avoid civilization, a road will be visible more than a third of the time. Moreover, these roads are predominately made of the red scoria, which marks a strong contrast with the surrounding landscape, as the long roads reach to the horizon. Consensus among the team members was that the roads were by far the more visible indicator of oil development, and also had the larger impact on their sense of wild. The bright red color of the network of roads led the team to refer to them as "scars."

Ranching

Ranching is synonymous with North Dakota. With a history stretching back into the 1800s, even Theodore Roosevelt was drawn to North Dakota as much for its ranching as for its wild. His Elkhorn home was, during its time, his attempt at a cattle ranch. Ranching is still alive and well in the badlands, and all teams consistently encountered evidence of this. Fences, watering and feed stations, cattle tracks, and the ubiquitous cow pats were the obvious signs, and they appeared in such quantities that only their absence was notable. Most ranching areas were simply grazing lands, and few structures, aside from watering stations, were observed in these areas. While there was some historic farming in the area, such land usage is increasingly uncommon.

Even though there still was snow on the ground in places, grazing was evident nearly everywhere. The difference between ungrazed and

Figure 10. Workover Rig.
Photo courtesy of the Adventure Science Team.

moderately to heavily grazed areas was obvious by the flora present. Ungrazed or lightly grazed areas were strongly dominated by grasses—the native flora of the non-wooded regions in the badlands. Areas where grazing pressure was high displayed a mixed flora, with thistle and other inedible plants common or even dominant. Since it was calving season during our expedition, the cattle had withdrawn to sheltered locations, and were not often observed in pasture.

All teams recorded a strong presence of ranching, with evidence in nearly all badland environs and landscapes. Mountain Kitty identified ranching evidence in 82 percent of their observation stops, while Tortoise observed it in 61 percent, and Speed Deer in only 46 percent. The patterning reflects, presumably, grazing leases on the Federal lands, which are likewise determined in part by proximity to roads and private lands. Participants found that ranching had a major impact on their experience in traversing and camping in the badlands. A daily and continual nuisance was the ubiquitous cow manure. In areas where grazing was ongoing, there was nary a place to stand, sit, or pitch a tent that was not covered in manure. All areas with standing water were trampled and contaminated. One participant explained the situation in comparison with oil development: "we can turn our backs back on oil pads and forget about them for a while, but the never-ending slipping and dodging manure made some areas more akin to feedlots than wilderness."

Geology, Paleontology, and Archaeology

The geology of this region is generally well understood, and the North Dakota Geologic Survey (www.dmr.nd.gov/ndgs/) has published a significant amount of detailed information online. Briefly, the stratigraphy that outcropped in the badlands, forming the buttes and ridges observed during the expedition is predominantly composed of Paleocene (66 to 56 million years ago) sandstones, silts, clays, coal, and clinker. In the valleys and ranch lands, especially near the Little Missouri River, Pleistocene (3 million to 12,000 years ago) to modern aged alluvial sediments dominated. Paleocene and Pleistocene fossils are numerous throughout the area covered by the transect. Prehistoric archaeological sites in the badlands (which are not overly abundant) can be difficult for the non-expert to identify, as they usually are expressed by small lithic scatters. A number of 30–50-year-old farming, ranching, and mining implements were noted during the survey, but these were not recorded individually. Fences were ubiquitous.

Subject matter experts instructed teams on how to recognize common fossils, stone artifacts or tools, historical implements, landform

Figure 11. Fence Line.
Photo courtesy of the Adventure Science Team.

modifications, and similar features to identify paleontological, archaeological, or cultural or historic sites of potential significance. Despite this, it is a challenge to recognize many of these in the field, even for the experts, and especially during a rapid survey. Team members were instructed in the legal and ethical necessities of non-disturbance. In hindsight, we wished we had trained all team members to identify erosional bone beds. These are one of the more easily identifiable sites, and we learned *en route* that while our team members were not at first noticing these, a brief onsite training brought them up to speed quickly.

Most of the exposed rock, clay, and bentonite explored during the transect were devoid of vertebrate or invertebrate fossils. No vertebrate fossils of Mesozoic age (252 to 66 million years ago) were identified, but invertebrates (marine bivalves, presumably Paleocene) were regularly observed during the trek. By far, the most abundant large fossils in this area are fossilized tree trunks, which are very common and in some areas litter the surface for several hundred square meters. Fossil trees were so numerous they were not individually documented, and only large fossils or clusters tended to be recorded in the notes.

Stratified Pleistocene and Holocene (12,000 years ago to the present) alluvial deposits were common as fill in the valleys. These deposits record fluvial activity and tend to be highly fossiliferous, with well preserved bison material weathering out of creek banks in numerous locations visited. Exploring creeks proved worthwhile, as their eroded banks yielded some excellent bison dominated bone clusters. The oldest bone fragments were found at the boundary of the conglomerate-sandstone interface. Above this, bones were more common, often with clusters of several bones weathering out from a certain interval. Bison bones dominated the assemblage, and lower limb bones were most prevalent. Several locations yielded intact bison skulls. These bone bed sites were recorded with GPS, photos, and brief descriptions. No collection of artifacts or materials occurred.

No definitive prehistoric archaeological sites were identified. Abundant skeletal remains of bison, horse, and other plains mammals were observed and recorded during the expedition. A possible chert scraper found in association with a bison bone bed (log point M12), suggests that this may be an archaeological site. At this location, bone density increased upwards in the column, before vanishing abruptly in the upper meter of sediment. This abrupt disappearance may coincide with the extermination of bison by hunters in the late 1800s (Hornaday 1889; Lueck 2002).

The observance of fossil or cultural material suffered an educational training bias, as only one team leader is a paleontologist, and only two team members were archaeologists. This aside, Team Mountain Kitty

Figure 12. Cattle.
Photo courtesy of the Adventure Science Team.

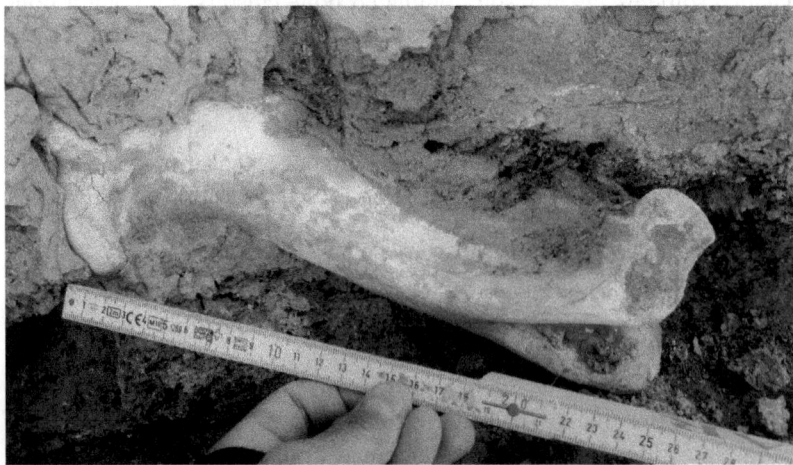

Figure 13. Bison Bone in Bone Bed.
Photo courtesy of the Adventure Science Team.

(which had a paleontologist as a leader) saw fossil or cultural material at 53 percent of their stops, while Tortoise saw it at 24 percent, and Speed Deer 23 percent. These relatively high numbers as tallied by nonspecialists only hint at the abundance of the fossil an archaeological resources in the area of the transects.

Wildlife and Environment

A late spring limited the wildlife visible, as birds were just returning to the landscape, and many mammals were still in secluded areas. Evidence for wildlife included animal and bird sightings, tracks, and the discovery of skeletal remains and antlers. A number of species were directly observed including big horn sheep, mule deer, eagles, coyote, rabbits, beaver and pronghorn. Bison, wild horses, and elk were observed only in the TRNP. Mountain Lion tracks were ubiquitous in any area near streams or springs, and wolf or coyote tracks were not uncommon. Possible bear scat was noted near the North Unit of the park. A number of bird species were observed, although not identified.

Due to the time of year and cold temperatures, insects, amphibians, and reptiles were not very active, although frogs were heard. Two Golden Eagles were observed during the survey—one alive, the other recently deceased, apparently by electrocution as it was found directly under live power lines connected to an active oil well.

Teams recorded evidence of wildlife presence at most of their stops (Mountain Kitty 94 percent, Tortoise 84 percent, and Speed Deer 68 percent). Wildlife was present in areas with well pad activity, although the only evidence observed of mountain lions and large wolf/coyote were made in more isolated, harder to reach areas.

The Human Presence

This landscape is generally unpopulated. Encounters with humans were rare, and they were restricted to service vehicles heading to well pads, or workers on pads. Outside of the TRNP South Unit, no other hikers or recreators were encountered. The North Dakota badlands can be a very windy landscape. The predominant sound for all the teams during this project was the wind. Occasionally, vehicular traffic from a nearby highway or a passing jet could be heard, but for the most part the auditory experience was thus one of moderate to near total isolation. The ubiquity of oil pads, roads, or ranching meant one never was far removed from a reminder of humans on this landscape, but the humans themselves

Figure 14. Kuepfer and Davis at Petrified Tree with Explorer's Club Flag. Photo courtesy of the Adventure Science Team.

Figure 15. Bison. Photo courtesy of the Adventure Science Team.

were rarely seen. There were also pockets where no human influence was readily detectable, especially in lowland areas. It should be remembered, however, that we did the transect during early spring, when roads were soft from meltwater and truck traffic was extremely limited.

Conclusions and Ideas

The badlands, referred to by General Alfred Sully as "Hell with the fires gone out," seem an unlikely place for a trip on foot, and that is precisely why the team undertook this project (Chaky 2012). While difficult, the terrain was not impossible. The main challenges, all anticipated, were navigating the confusing, rough terrain, temperature extremes, and the steep, unstable slopes. In the past, these challenges, combined with terrain unsuitable for horseback travel, and the sparse occupation of the area, generally kept people out. Off-road motorized vehicle travel is prohibited in much of the Federal land, and the inhospitable remoteness of the badlands has left the area largely undocumented and unexplored. Adventure Science's self-funded and self-organized transect has given us a unique window to view these badlands.

This expedition found that the wild that Theodore Roosevelt described so long ago does exist, but is highly fragmented. Ranching remains common, and the new change in the form of oil resource development is increasing. From the perspective of the Adventure Science team, the impact of ranching was far greater and more immediately visible than the impact of the boom. The most visually unappealing and perhaps major impact of oil development is the expansion of roads through these beautiful areas. Obviously the risk of oil spills, pipeline leaks, H2S release, and other accidents are real, but our expedition encountered none of these. The reader should note, however, that if oil development in this area continues, this situation could and will change significantly. This transect provides an excellent baseline for a followup expedition that will be able to analyze and document change at a level of detail previously not possible.

Adventure Science is not an activist group, and our goal was documentation, not recommendations. All participants were struck, however, by the rather shocking recent fragmentation of the areas between the North and South Units of TRNP. While these Federal Grasslands were never intended to be wild, the level of fragmentation at a point when most oil exploration is still on private land is astonishing. The roads to oil pads and other areas have spread like a chaotic web. This fragmented state seems not only detrimental to the conservation and recreational mandates of the Grasslands, but unnecessarily damaging to the area. The

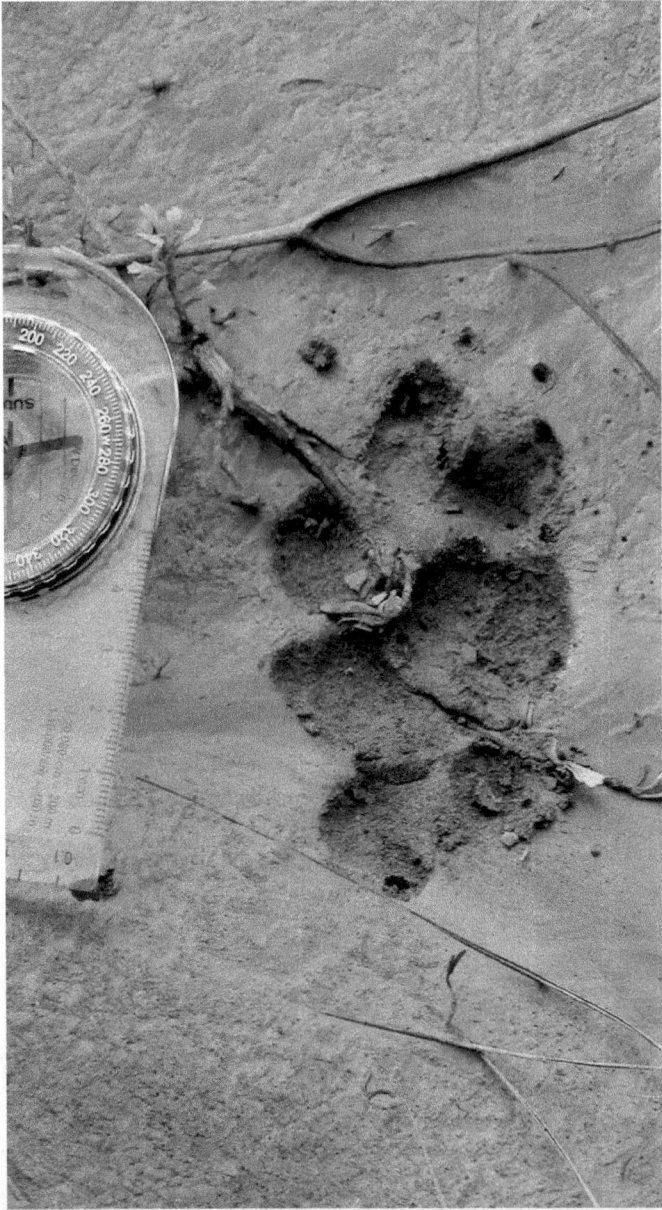

Figure 16. Mountain Lion Track
Photo courtesy of the Adventure Science Team.

myriad of roadways provide access for invasive species throughout the Grasslands, and during drilling season we are told they create a great deal of noise and dust. Just as the Adventure Science Team was never far from a road, it is increasingly difficult for wildlife to navigate this area without exposure to road disturbance and hazards. For the reticent and skittish key species of the area such as Bighorn Sheep and Golden Eagles, this is most problematic.

Given that the area remains quite wild, and this wildness could be preserved with some relatively small steps, it seems obvious to act on the part of preservation. This need is amplified by the relatively small sizes of the North and South Units of TRNP. Our work not only supports the already proposed idea for some roadless areas within the Grasslands, but suggests a most obvious need: centralized planning of access roads with an eye toward minimizing the spreading web, and maintaining open corridors for the natural inhabitants of the region (North Dakota Wilderness Coalition 2008). Equally obvious, albeit more difficult to achieve, would be the creation of a protected wild corridor linking the TRNP North and South units. While this idea probably is not politically feasible in an area with entrenched ranching interests in the midst of an oil boom, the reality remains that it could be achieved. Such a corridor could serve to allow the wild to expand, and return to its natural state, as well as give wildlife ways to move freely, unimpeded by fences, drilling activity, and busy roads. While we have doubts whether such a corridor will ever be created, we have little doubt that future residents will look back upon this period as a lost and last opportunity to have done so.

Afterword: The Badlands Transect Saved My Life

On the very first day of the transect I (Rothaus) started having trouble breathing and I assumed it was a flareup of asthma. I had suspected I would have trouble because training had gone hard. The first several days of the transect were just to be Reinhard and me, and we had asked Aaron Barth to come out and man a vehicle and to shuttle gear to increase my chances of success and be ready to get me just in case. With the help of inhalers and steroids, Reinhard and I struggled out of Lone Butte in freezing temperatures that first night, and we were pretty glad I was able to make it out before the cold really hit. I quit the ambitious transect plans and started consuming a maximum dose of steroids to keep going. Reinhard trekked alone until Tyler LeBlanc arrived and joined him, instead of being medical reserve as was the initial plan. I managed to walk about forty miles on boring, easy roads, each night moving my camp away

Figure 17. Scoria Roads and Well pads, Courtesy of EcoFlight.

Figure 18: Pipelines and Badlands.
Photo courtesy of the Adventure Science Team.

from the others so my coughing and inevitable retreat to a running truck for warm air would not disturb the others.

By the end of the transect I was a wreck. When my family arrived at the end for the victory celebration they were told "Wait till tonight; you'll see how bad he gets." I called ahead to my doctor at the University of Minnesota and told him, "I'm coming out of North Dakota. I can't breathe. I'm almost out of steroids. There is no way this will end well." Within a few days of return I was at the pulmonologist for treatment and testing. But this is not the interesting part. The pulmonologist tested away, and determined that I do not have asthma, which was quite the shock after a lifetime of trying to treat it. She found the pharmaceuticals that made my lungs work again, and we continued searching for a cause beyond some vague idiopathic inflammatory issue. We never have identified a discrete cause, but treatment is keeping me going. But this is not the part where the badlands saved my life.

While searching for a cause, my pulmonologist sent me to a gastroenterologist to get my throat scoped. Sometimes acid reflux can get into the lungs and cause breathing problems. I knew I had acid reflux, and I knew I was overdue for a checkup. I knew I had Barrett's esophagus, a condition where acid reflux causes the lining of the throat to convert into a lining more like that of the stomach. And I knew Barrett's esophagus was an indicator of cancer risk. The endoscopy found a small tumor, the biopsy found esophageal cancer, and I found that I am (so far) one of the lucky 5 percent who survive because we found it early, while looking for something else. The badlands transect broke me, sent me wheezing to the hospital, and saved my life. That is the interesting part.

References

Brinkley, Douglas. 2010. *The Wilderness Warrior: Theodore Roosevelt and the Crusade for America.* Reprint edition. New York: Harper Perennial.

Chaky, Doreen. 2012. *Terrible Justice: Sioux Chiefs and US Soldiers on the Upper Missouri, 1854–1868.* Norman, OK: University of Oklahoma Press.

Cronon, William, ed. 1996. *Uncommon Ground: Rethinking the Human Place in Nature.* 1st edition. New York: Norton.

Hornaday, William Temple. 1889. *The Extermination of the American Bison.* Washington, DC: Smithsonian Institution.

Kaye, Bruce M., Henry A. Schoch, and K. C. DenDooven. 1993. *Theodore Roosevelt National Park: The Story Behind the Scenery,* edited by

Mary L. VanCamp. Revised edition. Las Vegas, NV: KC Publications, Inc.

Lueck, Dean. 2002. "The Extermination and Conservation of the American Bison." *The Journal of Legal Studies* 31, no. S2: 609–52.

Morris, Edmund. 2001. *The Rise of Theodore Roosevelt*. New York: Random House.

Morris, Edmund. 2002. *Theodore Rex*. New York: Random House.

North Dakota Wilderness Coalition. 2008. "Prairie Legacy Wilderness: North Dakota Citizens' Proposal for Wilderness on the Dakota Prairie Grasslands." Bismarck, ND: North Dakota Wilderness Coalition.

Robinson, Elwyn B., D. Jerome Tweton, and David B Danbom. 1995. *History of North Dakota*. Fargo, ND: North Dakota State University Institute for Regional Studies.

Rogers, Hiram. 2006. *Trail Guide to the Maah Daah Hey Trail, Theodore Roosevelt National Park and the Dakota Prairie Grasslands*. 1st edition. Boulder, CO: Johnson Books.

PART 5

MEDIA
AND THE
BOOM

CHAPTER 13

COVERING THE BOOMTOWN: HOW MEDIATED
COMMUNICATION HAS SHAPED LIFE IN THE
BAKKEN OIL REGION

Angela Cary

Introduction

The captivating, yet increasingly challenging, narrative of western North
Dakota continues to be molded by the journalists, newsmakers, and residents who turn the gears in this ever-developing region. From coffee
shop regulars who chat about local headlines over a steamy cup of joe to
researchers scanning online news articles about oil shale extraction, the
media has tailored new approaches to teach their audiences about the
Bakken's tale. This chapter attempts to define North Dakota's changing
media roles in light of the latest oil boom, and examine how the explosion of media attention has affected this quiet state since the latest boom
began.

For a glimpse inside the inner workings of a western North Dakota
boom town, *Williston Herald* readers need only begin with the online
classified section. Page after page of neatly printed copy offers valuable
insight about life in this rapidly-growing city of over 26,000 since the
latest oil madness began. For both the skilled and unskilled, the region
has blossomed into a job haven. Large display ads beckon job seekers of
all kinds with alluring benefits and bonuses—drivers, electricians, rental
property managers, healthcare workers, oil workers, and diesel techni-
cians. Smarter employers go a step beyond with promises of available
housing or college tuition reimbursement. According to the North Dakota Job Service website, over 12,000 positions were listed in the state's
twenty-eight western counties in March 2014 (North Dakota Job Service 2014). In a region where jobs are plentiful, but potential employees
and housing are not, companies are forced to up their ante to attract the
highest bidder.

Another click to the *Herald*'s housing link brings readers to a page
where $31 nabs you a sleeping spot in a four-bedroom mobile home.

258

That's the *nightly* rate. A three-bedroom home listed in Cavalier, North Dakota for $40,000 sounds like an unbelievable dream until an out-of-state buyer realizes that Cavalier and the oil patch are 5½ hours apart. In a study conducted by Apartment Guide, an online source for apartment hunters, Williston had the highest rental rates in America, topping all major metropolitan cities to receive the dubious honor (Burnes 2014). Maybe, just maybe, the five-hour cross-country trek every other weekend isn't such a bad idea after all.

In the Bakken oil region the local media have shaped stories as often as they've reported them. Every apartment listing produces a relieved renter. Every employer hopes his or her "help wanted" ad yields a dependable employee. Radio stations offer vital road reports to the estimated 17,500 drivers who travel busy Highway 85 between Williston and Watford City each day (Norman 2014). Current crude oil prices are announced as regularly as the weather. Young reporters cut their teeth on every reportable aspect of the boom assigned by their news editors. Niche publications fill grocery store newsstands and internet search engines—*Bakken Breakout Weekly*, *The Drill*, and *Bakken Oil Business Journal*, to name a few. It's all about oil. And it's the biggest story most Bakken journalists will report—and most likely remember—during their news careers.

However, some of the best Bakken storytelling is shared through social media, which creates a new voice for a younger, digitally-connected audience. One example: newcomers to the Bakken can find friendly lifestyle advice or warnings on blogs and YouTube videos. A blog entry bemoans the lack of retail outlets and high prices. "There is a larger grocery store coming to Watford City. Perhaps it will create some of that healthy competition so that people can buy a quart of cream without having to get a second mortgage" (Arias 2013).

Capturing life in the Bakken has spurred a fascination that stretches worldwide. When a tornado ripped through a Watford City man camp in May 2014, residents recorded amazing close-up video of the funnel that was viewed around the globe on YouTube. As the findings in this piece suggest, all forms of traditional and new media have been bolstered by the state's oil development with users playing a significant role in the dialogue.

Print Journalism and Online News

Small-town news has been a staple of the North Dakota newspaper industry. County weeklies devote column space to "chicken dinner news"—neighborhood coffee parties, family visitors from distant lands (such as Minnesota), and charity benefits held at the American Legion club. The *Divide County Journal*'s "Noonan News" and "Fortuna News" sections provide readers with a weekly "who's who" in communities of fewer than five hundred people. The prospect of seeing your grandson's latest achievement in print is well worth the price of a subscription.

Focusing on localism is still key for smaller newspapers, no matter how large the story is. According to Cecile Krimm, publisher of the *Divide County Journal* and *Tioga Tribune*, their approach to covering the Bakken's distinctive story is the same as any other story: what's the local angle? "Everything we do is done from the standpoint of how it plays out in Crosby, North Dakota or Divide County," said Krimm. "The one premium we have is the news that no one else has, so we don't just want to do the story everyone else is doing. We want to do the story that brings it home" (interview with author, 2014).

Krimm notes, however, that the *Journal* and *Tribune* were momentarily caught up in the boomtown fervor when the Bakken story first began. Stories about housing, school enrollment, and increased traffic dominated the pages in 2012. "The *Journal* has always been a paper that's been known for features, personalities and people. In the process of having to cover an oil boom our paper became much less about individual people and about how the oil impact was playing out collectively on the community. It was often hard to personalize that oil impact story" (interview with author, 2014). She added that both papers have since returned to more of a people-centric focus.

Like other traditional media forms, the demise of newsprint-and-ink journalism has been well documented over the past decade. Pew Research found that full-time professional newsroom employment declined another 6.4 percent in 2012 and the trend is expected to continue (Mitchell 2014). Media downsizing is no different than downsizing in any other field—fewer employees are responsible for producing essentially the same product.

The surplus of jobs in the Bakken region has presented its own set of challenges and benefits for both media management and personnel. Newspapers, like other oil patch businesses, have had to increase employees' salaries to stay competitive, but revenue has not increased at the same rate. "People were making $10 an hour. We're now paying them $15 an hour, and we have to offer housing stipends to employees to help them be able to live here," said Krimm. The positive side is that better wages have enticed a wider pool of qualified applicants than ever before. "Right now we've just hit a sweet spot where our money is attractive, the story is interesting, and so we're able to attract some people with some skill" (interview with author, 2014).

One of those skilled reporters is Amy Dalrymple, another contributor to this volume. She and her husband moved to Williston two years ago when her company, Forum Communications, posted a job listing for an oil patch reporter. "I immediately started working on my husband to see what he would think if I were to apply for the job. I definitely pursued the opportunity out here and was fortunate enough to be selected," she said (interview with author, 2014). While it's sometimes difficult to work around oil company policies or the busy schedules of public officials, Dalrymple finds that residents are eager to clear up the misconceptions, expose the complications, and break through the Bakken mystique. "People want their story told to (readers in) Fargo and Grand Forks," said Dalrymple. "They want more people in the state to understand what's happening here. They want them to understand the challenges" (interview with author, 2014).

Most newspapers have increased their online and mobile presence, even in the smallest communities. A study conducted by the Missouri School of Journalism showed 47 percent of online users choose local newspaper websites as their preferred source for local news, compared to just 24 percent who preferred local television stations' websites (Fleming and Schwartz 2013). During a controversial one-month period in October 2011, the *Williston Herald's* website reached 1.1 million page views, fueled by unusually juicy stories of prostitution, skyrocketing apartment rentals, and the region's unprecedented national media attention (Jacobs 2011).

The paradox is that numerous online newspapers have added video resources to keep their websites user friendly and interactive. Print journalists have taken off their proverbial PRESS hats and picked up video cameras as they've diversified their news gathering efforts. The *Tioga Tribune's* website features a five-part video series titled *Oil in the Street*, giving residents from different backgrounds an opportunity to share how the boom has affected their part of the community ("Oil in the Street" 2011). The web series was fashioned to look like a typical television news series: interviews, edited cover video, and name and locator graphics. Across the North Dakota/Montana border, the online *Sidney Herald* featured a video story about spring ice jams written and shot by a *Herald* newspaper reporter ("Ice Jams and Floods" 2014). The rudimentary video demonstrated the icy impact far better than a quality news photograph could have. When breaking news or feature stories happen, multimedia journalists in smaller communities now have the resources to make the action come alive for their readers. They also have quicker access to nearby news than a television news team traveling from a major city. The benefit for

rural residents is simple: they don't have to wait until tomorrow's issue—
or next week's issue—to get the community news they need.

As cities develop ways to solve housing, education, and infrastructure
issues, local media outlets appear to be trending more towards the "silver
lining" stories rather than gloom and doom. This is significant because
headlines and news photos stir conversation in a community.

A survey of Bakken-related headlines in three regional online newspapers—*The Williston Herald*, *The Dickinson Press*, and *McKenzie County
Farmer* (Watford City, ND)—revealed a mix of community progress and
challenges. The daily Williston and Dickinson papers were chosen because they cover two of the largest cities in the region. The third paper
reflects the perspective of a smaller weekly newspaper in one of the fastest-growing communities in the region, Watford City.

Fifty-seven headlines from the three newspapers were selected for
examination. The two daily newspapers (*Williston Herald* and *Dickinson Press*) were reviewed during a two-week period, while the weekly
McKenzie County Farmer received a month-long review to compare approximately the same number of headlines. Headlines that didn't include
any noticeable link to either primary or secondary oil activity were not
considered for this study.

Based on the story's direct relationship to oil activity, four categories
were used to evaluate the news headlines. "Positive primary news" included headlines related directly to oil production progress and solving
oilfield issues, like improved technology or new oil-related legislation.
The "negative primary news" category included headlines related directly
to oil industry challenges and regressions, like oil spills or rail service
problems. "Positive secondary news" included headlines related to civic
growth indirectly resulting from the boom, like the addition of new
community buildings or services. "Negative secondary news" included
headlines about unsavory community effects caused indirectly by the
boom, like increased traffic and infrastructure overload.

The composite headlines from all three online newspapers showed a
higher percentage of positive headlines (68 percent) than negative news
headlines (32 percent) in both categories:

Total percentage of positive primary headlines:
   25 percent *(14 stories)*
Total number of positive secondary headlines:
   43 percent *(25 stories)*
Total number of negative primary headlines:
   14 percent *(8 stories)*
Total number of negative secondary headlines:

18 percent *(10 stories)*

Positive secondary headlines were by far the most prevalent (43 percent), with most stories showcasing new facilities, community efforts, or economic development ventures:

> "City looks to build $56 million events center" (*McKenzie County Farmer*, April 8, 2014)
> "Airport to get $3.5 million facelift" (*McKenzie County Farmer*, March 18, 2014)
> "Baseball is back: Ray adding activities with rising enrollment" (*Dickinson Press*, April 12, 2014)
> "Commission agrees to expand 11th Street" (*Williston Herald*, April 10, 2014)

Positive primary headlines followed at (25 percent). These stories featured progressive topics related directly to the oil industry and its subsidiaries:

> "State looks to capture more natural gas" (*McKenzie County Farmer*, April 8, 2014)
> "State clamps down on oilfield waste: rules specify leak-proof containers for filter socks" (*Dickinson Press*, April 10, 2014)
> "Ground broken on truck bypass in North Dakota oil patch" (*Williston Herald*, April 9, 2014)

Negative secondary headlines placed third (18 percent). The theme of these stories included unwelcome community issues resulting indirectly from oil boom activity:

> "Buried under pending court cases, County State's Attorney seeks more help" (*McKenzie County Farmer*, April 1, 2014)
> "Traffic accidents spike upward in February" (*Williston Herald*, April 8, 2014)
> "The dark side of black gold" (*Williston Herald*, April 12, 2014)
> "Sanford mobile clinics illegal in Williston: city commission could lift moratorium on businesses" (*Dickinson Press*, April 2, 2014)

Only 14 percent of the headlines fit into the negative primary category. This category included negative stories tied directly to oil production:

> "Tank overflow reported at oil well near Alexander" (*Dickinson Press*, April 9, 2014)

"Study of oil from deadly derailment points to Bakken crude's vola-
tility" (*Dickinson Press*, April 4, 2014)

While environmental issues and worker safety will always be a newsworthy source of concern for the region, these results suggest that new
perceptions of growth and progress now outweigh the often-reported
negativity and problems of the past.

Any gaps in online content have been filled by those who have the
most sentimental stake in the survival of a local newspaper—the readers
themselves. Like most sites, the *Williston Herald* welcomes online comments to its columns, like Jerry Burnes's *A Newcomer's Guide to Williston*
(Burnes 2014). Online contributors are required to abide by several
"North Dakota Nice" rules: Keep it clean. Be truthful. Be nice. When
the columnist penned congenial tips like, "Go out, meet people around
town, get involved in some great organizations like the Salvation Army,
the Moose Lodge and others," and "If you're fighting bad landlords, the
rest of the city will be too," he wasn't met with much resistance from
either side.

The *Divide County Journal's* video page offers a place where high
school prom-goers can upload their comical Grand March video shorts
("DCHS Prom 2012"). Another clip features a community rib cook-off
and car show ("Rib Cook-off" 2011). For those looking to relocate from
across the country, these amateur videos have an added benefit: they
offer a friendly, hometown slice-of-life which may appeal to potential
oil patch workers and their families. Giving online readers an editorial
voice and allowing users to create their own content are two ways smaller
newspaper can service their readership while keeping in step with what's
happening in their communities.

Today's online content producers might be compared to the home-
makers-turned-journalists who emerged during their small town's heyday.
Had these local correspondents—often housewives—had the power of
the internet back in the 1940s or 1950s, they might have taken to writing
an online blog about their bridge parties or hospital auxiliary luncheons.
Facebook would have exploded with selfies of stylish women playing
cards on a weekday afternoon. They wrote about what they cared about,
and just like today's online contributors or video uploaders, they wanted
their material to create a buzz in the community.

Niche publications have also flourished in the region. Bismarck's
monthly *Inspired Woman Magazine* features a special "Western North
Dakota Women" tab leading readers to articles about fearless females
who live, work, and thrive in oil country. *Bakken Living*, a publication of
the *Sidney Herald*, offers a lifestyle primer for newcomers. This, however,

is not your typical woman's magazine. Articles like "Surviving Camper Living" and "Winter is Coming" present nontraditional, yet necessary, information designed for strangers entering a strange land. Those readers who choose to skip camper-dweller Chelsea Neihaus' advice, "It's also a good idea to know where you can take a shower if need be," can't say they weren't warned.

Research has shown that media operations with an active online presence have the potential to expand their demographics as well as their audience (Mitchell 2014). Half of internet users who watch some kind of online video are watching news videos, with 18–29-year-old users making up the greatest portion of these viewers. The next generation *is* getting their news. The print media's challenge is to find innovative ways to keep the information fresh enough for younger users to pursue.

As for reporter Amy Dalrymple, telling the Bakken's tale in print or online is simply another day at the office. "One day I missed a celebration for a gas plant that had been completed in Williston because I was at the groundbreaking for a refinery in Forth Berthold. I thought, 'Wow, how many reporters in the country have this problem?' I sometimes forget I'm in the middle of a big story and I'm the middle of history" (interview with author, 2014).

Television

Long before the first derrick of the new boom appeared on North Dakota's recumbent landscape, longtime residents remember the state's *other* major environmental event that captured national headlines: a massive spring flood that overtook the communities along the Red River Valley in 1997. Hardest hit was the city of Grand Forks, with nearly 50,000 citizens evacuated from their homes virtually overnight (City of Grand Forks 2011).

As families moved out, television satellite trucks rolled in, lining the streets near the sand dikes to report the region's fate to the nation. News videographers navigated the city streets by boat, giving anxious viewers a peek at their own neighborhoods, now surrounded by cold, murky, brown floodwater. Television news directors secured local pilots for exclusive bird's-eye tours of the flooded farmland. Frenzied anchors wrote copy and edited video for hourly updates, grabbing sleep in their offices, unable to go home. Like most natural disasters, it was a shockingly visual story. Television was the best medium to tell the tale.

The media coverage of the Red River flood and the Bakken oil boom has certain similarities. The magnitude of both events certainly caught many North Dakota communities by surprise. While no one expected the river levels to rise as high as they did, few could have predicted the even higher level of national attention the oil story has brought to western North Dakota. Suddenly *National Geographic*, the *New York Times*, and NBC News knew about Williston. Tioga and Watford City were more than dots on the map. However, when the floodwaters in the Red River Valley receded, the national spotlight did too. This isn't the case in the Bakken where the oil, and the storylines surrounding it, could remain active for an unbelievably lengthy period of time. How much oil is there? All anyone knows is that *no one* knows for sure how much shale lies beneath the surface. While the legend of the Red River rolled through as quickly as the floodwater, the newsworthy Bakken has the potential staying power of a pump jack—churning out story after story, year after year.

According to a 2013 Gallup poll, Americans continue to rely on television as their main news source for national and global news (55 percent), followed by the internet (21 percent), newspaper (9 percent) and radio (6 percent). This trend is consistent across all age, educational, and political demographics, and it also extends to local news (Saad 2013). A Pew Research Journalism Project study found that local newscasts were the overwhelming choice for news-seeking adults who categorized their viewing habits as "often" (46 percent), beating both print (27 percent) and radio (26 percent) in the same category (Pew Research 2013).

Twelve stations in western North Dakota serve as television outlets for regional news and entertainment. A two-week survey of news story links posted to KFYR-TV reaped similar results to the newspaper headline survey in each of the same four categories. Of the thirty-one Bakken-related news stories selected for analysis, positive story links (74 percent) prevailed over negative story links (26 percent) by nearly a 3-to-1 margin:

Total percentage of positive primary story links:
  19 percent *(6 stories)*
Total number of positive secondary story links:
  54 percent *(17 stories)*
Total number of negative primary story links:
  12 percent *(4 stories)*
Total number of negative secondary story links:
  12 percent *(4 stories)*

As with the online newspaper survey, stories that didn't correlate to primary or secondary oil activity were not considered for this study. Story links were selected from the KFYR-TV website, and its sister stations in Minot (KMOT-TV) and Williston (KUMV-TV). According to news director Monica Hannan, the probable length of the oil boom has caused her stations to take permanent action. "We've added a full-time energy reporter in Williston," Hannan said, (interview with author, 2014). Like the *Divide County Journal*, the station provides a housing allowance, but they also take it one step further and keep an apartment in Williston due to the housing shortage. "Rent is so high in Dickinson that our Dickinson reporter drives from Bismarck," she noted (interview with author, 2014).

To attract the transient oil patch audience North Dakota television stations also secure viewership through an accessible communication source: cell phones. On-the-go viewers are urged to download KFYR-TV's mobile news or "First Warn" weather apps for breaking news and weather throughout the day.

With more resources to devote to in-depth reporting and fewer daily deadlines, Prairie Public Broadcasting, the state's public television network, has produced and aired a number of longer-length programs about the latest boom. The documentary *Faces of the Oil Patch* introduced viewers to people who live in the "changing vernacular landscape of northwestern North Dakota" ("Faces of the Oil Patch" 2013). *Black Gold Boom* is an independent, award-winning, multimedia project, which explores oil country's many voices through both television and radio ("Black Gold Boom" 2013). Just like the numerous video chronicles that followed the 1997 flood, television continues to be fascinated by the Bakken's changing land and the people who have been changed by it.

Radio

With the advent of satellite radio and short commute times, local radio stations are decidedly more creative with their approaches to oil branding and programming. KTGO Radio of Tioga, ND now brands itself as the "Bakken Beacon." Dickinson's classic rock station Z-92 (KZRX) uses the familiar tagline "Rockin' the Bakken" to promote its format. Despite the increase in traffic, most Bakken-area communities still report commute times of fifteen minutes or less (Zipatlas 2014). Reaching out to those short-term traveling listeners with a clever hook is key.

However, the amount of regular programming tailored to Bakken-specific issues is less than most listeners might think. This is due in part to a decrease in locally-owned radio stations. Media conglomerates, like Clear Channel, have purchased many local stations in smaller markets across the country resulting in complaints from listeners who decry the company's cookie-cutter corporate radio image and the decline of live and local news (Lee 2003). As of this writing, Clear Channel owns eighteen of the 126 radio stations in the state, including several in some of the state's largest cities: Bismarck/Mandan, Dickinson, Grand Forks, and

Minot (Clear Channel 2014). Only one Clear Channel station in western North Dakota, Bismarck's news-and-talk KFYR-AM, offers regular programming targeted to oil patch issues with its weekly, two-hour *Energy Matters* show.

This is where broadcast veterans have stepped in, expanding beyond their station's signals to produce their own Bakken-focused radio programs. Rigger-turned-radio-host Bill ("Wild Bill") Palanuk produces *The Mon-Dak Oilfield Review*, a three-minute daily interview segment heard on twenty-four select stations throughout the state, plus online podcasts. His sponsored pieces focus on the business side of the boom, featuring interviews with local and national newsmakers, experts, and pundits. "The whole world has an eye on the Bakken," he said proudly (interview with author, 2014). For listeners in the Dakotas, Montana, and Wyoming, programs like Jason Spiess's *Building the Bakken* seeks to "tell the story of the people and the businesses that make up the communities building the Bakken everyday through topical and in-depth dialogue" (Building the Bakken 2014).

Offering these mini-program packages to local radio stations provides them with topical oil patch content they couldn't replicate on their own. Equally important, these programs give local account executives a high-quality, pre-produced product to sell to their potential advertiser base. While many local radio stations struggle to maintain local advertisers, *Mon-Dak Oil Review* has garnered stable sponsorships from car dealerships and oil-related businesses, like trucking companies, looking to recruit workers. Palanuk noted that advertisers are also approaching his radio station like never before. "It's like drinking water out of a fire hose," he quipped, (interview with author, 2014). Despite the negative spin that often plagues Bakken news, "Wild Bill" believes residents are seeing the economy strengthen through the new hotels and home building centers popping up in the region. "It's moved them into a mode of acceptance" (interview with author, 2014). Where new business grows, advertising is sure to follow.

With corporate radio's stronger signals and its tighter squeeze on the competition, smaller stations have had to engage listeners with a combination of costly digital upgrades and hometown charm. Well-worn features like the local "trading post," live birthday wishes, and recaps of last night's high school prep sports keep listeners tuning in and keep a community's radio signal at full power.

Public broadcasting has opened the door to the Bakken through the ears of its listeners. *Northern Great Plains Oil Rush* is a 10-part radio series produced by contributors from National Public Radio, and North Dakota and Montana public radio ("Northern Great Plains Oil Rush" 2013).

With stories like "Pitting Oil against Agriculture" and "Commuting for Oil Dollars," radio journalists offered a more comprehensive look at some of the oil patch's best and least-known issues. Another multi-state public media initiative, *Inside Energy*, describes itself as "the spot where people and power intersect," looking beyond simple production to see how humans are "making, moving, (and) using energy" (Inside Energy 2015). The website offers story transcripts, and audio and video links from the nation's leading energy-producing states. Again, a strong online presence assures listeners that these features are still available anytime, anywhere.

While local radio has increased its use of oil as a marketing tool, it's important to note agriculture remains at the heart of many rural stations. North Dakotans have prospered from agriculture far longer than they have from oil. According to the North Dakota Department of Agriculture, the state still boasts an estimated 30,000 farm and ranching operations. Nearly one quarter of North Dakotans work in ag-related industries (Jantzi 2013). In the middle of oil country, the programming schedule for Williston's news-and-talk station KEYZ reads more like the Farmer's Almanac and less like an oil field report. Ag shows like *Harvest USA*, *Dakota Prairie Outdoors*, and area livestock updates fill the airwaves from sign-on until sign-off. The American Ag Network also offers a heavy programming schedule and market updates to KEYZ and its nineteen other statewide affiliates throughout the day.

Satellite radio also continues to peck away at the local radio market share. In 2013, Sirius XM launched a new channel *Rural Radio* devoted exclusively to agribusiness news, commodities updates, and rural lifestyle. Designed for listeners "driving a tractor cab equipped with satellite radio or driving in city commuter traffic," the network puts a nationalized spin on a traditionally local product (Schupf 2013).

Although farm numbers are decreasing nationwide, there's still a mighty force of western farmers and ranchers who depend on cattle and durum wheat to make a living. In a business that prospers or falls with the weather, many farmers start their days with local forecasts and market updates provided in part by local radio and television broadcasters. The state's rural roots will likely remain after the last oil barrel is gone.

Advertising

One change that all local media sources have noticed is an increase in advertising that the boom has produced, both in terms of revenue and the promotion of Bakken-related items. Kris Vendsel, a twenty five-year advertising veteran and current production director of KXMC-TV of Minot, has noticed differences in all phases of the industry. For a region filled with truckers and roughnecks, work gear means big business. "They're doing a bigger push on flame-resistant clothing. We've seen more promotions on outerwear, like Carhartt, the work duty clothing. You start doing more of the professional work boot ads," she said. "With the bigger companies, it's not just television, it's billboards, it's flyers, it's radio" (interview with author, 2014).

Advertisers are also focused on available housing or filling the surplus of jobs in the western part of the state. According to Bill Palanuk, radio recruiting has increased through station promotions like his KXDI "On-Air Job Fair." Billboards touting employment opportunities line the well traveled highways of the region. Kris Vendsel observed, "When this all started, you would drive down Broadway and every single fast-food restaurant's marquee would say 'Now hiring! $300 signing bonus!' not 'Try our double cheeseburger'" (interview with author, 2014).

For the *Divide County Journal*, the oil boom advertising flurry was created in a different way. "Definitely our classified advertising has been more vibrant with help wanted and housing ads," said Cecile Krimm. "What's had a greater impact is the amount of legal notices. We've had more planning and zoning activity requiring hearing notices that need to be published in the paper. Our legal notices have expanded from one page most weeks to sometimes three pages of legal advertising" (interview with author, 2014). As an official county-seat newspaper, this increased revenue helps to offset the production and personnel costs the business has endured because of the boom.

Vendsel notes that many oil companies try to convey a "family friendly" message to their audiences of potential workers through their websites and videos. "That's a big message: we want you to have your family here, we want you to make this your home" (interview with author, 2014). For western North Dakota communities trying to woo families, this is the positive message *they* want to convey too.

Social Media Connections

As the ancient Chinese philosopher Lao Tzu once said, "The journey of 1,000 miles begins with one step." For anyone whose quest for a better life has taken them far from the security of their home, family, and friends, social media has undoubtedly made taking that first step a little easier. Any new North Dakotan armed with a laptop, tablet, or cell phone can begin his or her adventure without completely letting go of life back home.

While many bemoan the impersonal side of technology, research has shown it keeps personal connections intact. A study published by

Pepperdine University determined that couples who used various forms of "computer technology" to maintain their long-distance relationships reported high levels of openness and positivity, despite the distance (Kirk 2013). Technology that offered immediate feedback, like Skype or Facebook chat, received the highest marks for keeping couples connected. A nightly Facetime session with a loved one might make life in the lonely oil patch a little easier.

Facebook breeds imagined communities within real communities. For wives, girlfriends, and children who chose to accompany their oilfield workers to western North Dakota, the social media site has offered a strong support system. Williston's Oil Field Wives Club depends on their Facebook page to inform other families of weekly coffee meetings, children's play groups, GNO (Girls Night Out) gatherings, and regional events. The page also includes photos from the group's annual charity ball and online fundraisers. When sentimental lifelines are hundreds or thousands of miles away from Williston, these mediated connections help bring together a welcome neighborhood of new friends.

On the other side is Facebook's *Bakken Oilfield Fail of the Day* page, which "documents highway crashes, oilfield mishaps, and events illustrating life in the booming area" according to an article by Tom Lutey in the *Billings (MT) Gazette* (Lutey 2013). Lutey goes on to say, "It has more thrills and spills than Evel Knievel and the University of North Dakota men's hockey team combined, and nearly as many social media likes as World Peace" (Current tally: 86,425 vs. 79,331). Facebook's *Missing Persons and Property from the Bakken Oilfield* page has had mixed results in helping to recover lost items, lost pets, and persons misplaced from the community. The Pew Research study found that half (50 percent) of social network users share or repost news stories, images, or videos while nearly as many (46 percent) discuss news issues or events on social network sites (Mitchell 2014).

For those who follow anything "Williston" or "Dickinson" or "Bowbells," Twitter has offered the perfect opportunity to share news and views from inside or outside county lines. Type in a town name and you're sure to find extreme fans and haters. The hashtag #boomtownprobs attracts those who question the cold weather and safety issues, challenged by staunch defenders of the rural lifestyle. The hashtag #onlyinwilliston uncovers a host of unnatural oil town oddities. However, some of the most frequent messages have come from corporate communicators themselves. Buzz-worthy tweets tout Bakken newspaper and magazine articles, television docs, job opportunities, and company news to a perfectly targeted audience.

While native North Dakotans take lefse, winter driving, harvest season, ice fishing, and other cultural aspects of the upper Midwest for granted, out-of-staters may be left shaking their heads. These folksy props and traditions create fodder for newcomers who have expressed their amazement through online blogs like *Real Oilfield Wives*, *Sven's Bakken Blog*, and *Wildcatting: A Stripper's Guide to the Modern American Boomtown*.

Of all the Bakken blogs, *My Life in Williston* has gotten the most attention. Author Robin Arias created the blog to give other women the advice she never received when she moved to the heart of oil country. "There was not a lot of support or information for women in my position when I moved here so I'm doing my best to provide a little now," she notes (Arias 2011). Telling her story, Arias's writing swings between pessimism, optimism, and all points between. Some posts, like "Embrace the Positive, but Don't Ignore the Negative" offer the brilliant insight of a worldly outsider. Others, like "Bottles of Liquid and Freezing Temps Just Don't Mix" leave North Dakota pros shaking *their* heads. The blog isn't a love fest—although she admits she loves North Dakota. Like all bloggers who feel comfortable enough sharing their thoughts for the blogosphere, she tells it like it is.

Often with social media, it's not about what *you're* doing—it's letting everyone *else* know what you're doing. Connecting with old and new friends through Facebook. Connecting almost-in-person with spouses and families via Skype and Facetime. Connecting with an imagined community through personal blogs and feedback. These types of connections make the "boomtown probs" a little less tragic, if only in Williston.

Seeing the National Spotlight in a Different Light

Since word got out about the billion-dollar wealth lying beneath the Bakken oilfield, flocks of journalists from regional, national and international media outlets have descended on North Dakota to see the oil rush for themselves. The 2011 debut of the NBC News magazine *Rock Center* featured a story titled "Now hiring: North Dakota oil boom creates thousands of jobs" in its premiere episode (Kim 2011). A New York Times website search for "North Dakota Oil" yields thousands of results. *Boomtown Girls*, a reality series about four Williston sisters was produced, but never made it to air (Piazza 2012).

Small towns not used to this Cinderella-like attention were suddenly the belles of the ball. But the glamor soon faded. Despite the oil production and economic growth, stories surfaced of a "wild west" mentality permeating the prairie. Tales of man camps, downtown dangers, and Wal-Mart woes became the norm. After a CNN Money story about local dancers pulling in $2,000 per night at a Williston strip club, the female co-owner, tired of being hounded by so many news outlets, refused to grant any more press interviews (Johnson 2012). Enough was enough. It was just the kind of attention a boomtown community didn't need.

Sidney Herald columnist Susan Minichiello offered her perspective on the national spotlight. "It bothers me when I find unbalanced stories in the media covering the Bakken," she noted in her column. "Depending on the news source, the angle may be how 'scary' it is here, or how glorious it is for families to have oil money right now. Either angle is skewed and doesn't show the complete truth" (Minichiello 2014).

Still, the publicity about western North Dakota has filled jobs and brought people and prosperity to the state. The outmigration trend has turned, and midwest college graduates are now finding reasons to stay closer to home. Arguments can be made on both sides, but no one can deny the population explosion has been necessary for the state's survival. There simply aren't enough North Dakotans here to fill the jobs themselves. Whether the national perception is positive or negative, it's still enough to entice many people with a dream.

Conclusion

Three Gallup polls conducted in 2013–14 showed North Dakotans to be a very happy, optimistic bunch. According to the Gallup-Healthways Well-Being Index, North Dakota residents had the highest well-being in the nation at 70.4 percent in 2013 (Witters 2014). Another Gallup survey revealed 77 percent of North Dakotans polled trust their state government, the highest level of confidence in the nation (Jones 2014). A third poll indicated that 87 percent of North Dakotans surveyed were satisfied with the state's public schools (Sorenson and Kafka 2014). Citing these statistics in an editorial, *Fargo Forum* opinion page editor Jack Zaleski wrote, "North Dakotans see government and schools in a positive light likely because state and local governments and schools show mostly good results. Citizen involvement is high. For the most part, elected local and state officials are accessible and responsive" (Zaleski 2014).

The happiness factor contradicts a 2012 survey of longtime northwest North Dakota residents who claimed their quality of life hadn't improved since the boom, despite their economic gains. The University of North Dakota study included persons who had lived in Williston, Stanley, or Watford City for six years or longer, Seventeen percent agreed that the oil boom had improved their quality of life, while 52 percent said they disagreed or strongly disagreed (North Dakota Associated Press 2012). When the boom first began, stories emerged from the west of fed-up longtimers leaving their beloved hometowns behind. North Dakotans may be happy, but they're not always happy about change.

Those who have stayed, however, have started to see some real changes in their communities. "Just thinking about all of the changes I've seen in two years, it's really amazing," said Amy Dalrymple. "There are complete neighborhoods that weren't here when I moved here. There's been significant improvement in housing for teachers, and police and medical personnel. That's been really important to recruit those people to our community" (interview with author, 2014).

Then perhaps it's no surprise the surveyed headlines waxed optimistic. We can't assume all Bakken-area residents have grown complacent about the heavy traffic, high retail prices, increased crime, and dust issues that concern their communities, but maybe, just maybe, hearing more about these positive changes from the media is shifting the focus away from the negative ones.

Ultimately, it's up to the reader, listener, or viewer to uncover his or her own truths behind the Bakken coverage. Perhaps locals have learned to take the glorified news reports in stride, separating sensationalism from their everyday reality. Maybe new North Dakota residents can see beyond the online warnings of cold winters to embrace their brand-new adventure. Possibly someone thousands of miles away will read a magazine article that shapes their perception of North Dakota in an entirely different way. Mediated coverage undoubtedly affects the way western North Dakota residents, newcomers, or observers view their Bakken experience, shaping their own outlook for the future.

References

Arias, Robin. 2011. "About Me." *My Life in Williston* blog. Accessed April 14, 2014. lifeinwilliston.com/index.php/about/.

Arias, Robin. 2013. "Grocery shopping at its best" *My Life in Williston* blog. Accessed March 29, 2015. lifeinwilliston.com/index.php/grocery-shopping-at-its-best/.

"Average Commute Time in North Dakota by City." 2014. Zipatlas.com website. Accessed April 13, 2014. zipatlas.com/us/nd/city-comparison/average-commute-time.4.htm.

Bakken Living. 2014. Accessed April 12, 2014. www.sidneyherald.com/bakken_living/bakken-living-magazine-vol-issue/article_6254e242-7a1f-11e3-a058-001a4bcf887a.html.

"Black Gold Boom." 2013. *Prairie Public Broadcasting* video series. Accessed April 12, 2014. blackgoldboom.com/about.

Brooks, Jacob. 2011. "Herald Website Nets One Million Page Views in October." *Williston Herald*, November 3. Accessed April 10, 2014. www.willistonherald.com/news/herald-website-nets-million-pa-geviews-in-oct/article_217fbfb5-edba-56bc-bb41-426d3b6a21e2.html.

Burnes, Jerry. 2014. "A Newcomer's Guide to Living in Williston." *Williston Herald*, April 9. Accessed April 11, 2014. www.willistonherald.com/opinion/columnists/a-newcomer-s-guide-to-living-in-williston/article_16e6233e-bffc-11e3-aca6-0019bb2963f4.html.

Burnes, Jerry. 2014. "Williston Rent Highest In Nation." *Williston Herald*, February 15. Accessed April 10, 2014. www.willistonherald.com/news/williston-rent-highest-in-nation/article_b0d5b4b4-9699-11e3-8b68-001a4bcf887a.html.

"Clear Channel Station Search—North Dakota." 2014. *Clear Channel.com* website. Accessed April 13, 2014. www.clearchannel.com/CCME/Pages/StationSearch.aspx.

"DCHS Prom 2012." 2012. *Divide County Journal* video, April 29. Accessed April 11, 2014. www.journaltrib.com/?id=123&form_data_id=2145.

"Faces of the Oil Patch" 2013. *Prairie Public Broadcasting* video. Accessed April 12, 2014. www.prairiepublic.org/television/prairie-public-on-demand/faces-of-the-oil-patch.

Fleming, Kenneth, and Sam Schwartz. 2013. "Survey: Community Papers Still Tops for Local News." *Donald W. Reynolds Journalism Institute*, March 21. Accessed April 10, 2014. www.rjionline.org/news/survey-community-papers-still-tops-local-news.

"Grand Forks Flood Disaster and Recovery Lessons Learned." 2011. *City of Grand Forks, ND*. Accessed April 12, 2014. www.grand-forksgov.com/Reports/lessonslearned.pdf.

"Ice Jams and Floods" 2014. *Sidney Herald* video, March 11. Accessed April 10, 2014. www.sidneyherald.com/news/ice-jams-and-floods/youtube_b7c9da26-a980-11e3-a03e-0019bb2963f4.html.

Inside Energy. 2015. "About the Project." Accessed March 29. insideen-ergy.org/about/.

Inspired Women Magazine. 2014. Accessed April 12, 2014. inspiredwoma-nonline.com/category/western-north-dakota-women/.

Jantzi, Darin, 2013. "North Dakota Farm Numbers and Land in Farms." *United States Department of Agriculture*. Accessed April 13, 2014. www.nass.usda.gov/Statistics_by_State/North_Dakota/Publications/Land_Values_and_Farm_Numbers/rel/farms0213.pdf.

Johnson, Robert. 2012. "North Dakota's Boomtown Strippers Wish the Media Had Never Found Them." *Business Insider*, March 6. Accessed

April 14, 2014. www.businessinsider.com/north-dakotas-boomtown-strippers-wish-the-media-never-found-them-2012-3.

Jones, Jeffrey M. 2014. "Illinois Residents Least Trusting of Their State Government." *Gallup Politics*, April 4. Accessed April 14, 2014. www.gallup.com/poll/168251/illinois-residents-least-trusting-state-government.aspx.

Kim, Catherine, and Jessica Hopper. 2011. "Now Hiring, North Dakota Oil Boom Creates Thousands of Jobs." *NBC News*, October 26. Accessed April 14, 2014. rockcenter.nbcnews.com/_news/2011/10/27/8495501-now-hiring-north-dakota-oil-boom-creates-thousands-of-jobs.

Kirk, Allie. 2013. "The Effect of Newer Communication Technologies on Relationship Maintenance and Satisfaction In Long-Distance Dating Relationships." *Pepperdine Journal of Communication Research* 1, article 2. Accessed June 8, 2015. digitalcommons.pepperdine.edu/pjcr/vol1/iss1/2/.

Lee, Jennifer S. 2003. "Media: On Minot, N.D., Radio, A Single Corporate Voice." *New York Times*, March 31. Accessed April 13, 2014. www.nytimes.com/2003/03/31/business/media-on-minot-nd-radio-a-single-corporate-voice.html.

Lutey, Tom. 2013. "Oilfield Follies: Bakken Thrills and Spills Are a Facebook Hit." *Billings Gazette*, November 15. Accessed April 14, 2014. billingsgazette.com/news/state-and-regional/montana/bakken-thrills-and-spills-are-a-facebook-hit/article_18f69fd8-36d8-546c-9575-5a16ec923478.html.

Minichiello, Susan. 2014. "Media portrayal of Boomtowns Inaccurate." *Sidney Herald*, January 21. Accessed April 14, 2014. www.sidneyherald.com/opinion/columnists/media-portrayal-of-boom-towns-inaccurate/article_044554ce-8312-11e3-a75d-001a4bcf887a.html.

Mitchell, Amy. 2014. "2014 State of the News Media." *Pew Research Journalism Project*, March 26. Accessed April 10, 2014. www.journalism.org/2014/03/26/state-of-the-news-media-2014-overview/.

Norman, Stephanie. 2014. "County Roadways Get Attention From County, State Officials." *McKenzie County Farmer*, March 25. Accessed April 10, 2014. www.watfordcitynd.com/?id=10&nid=2642.

North Dakota Associated Press. 2012. "Survey: Some Not Happy with North Dakota Oil Boom." *North Dakota Associated Press*, September 4. Accessed April 15, 2014. www.wday.com/event/article/id/68466/group/homepage/.

North Dakota Job Service. 2014. "Online Job Openings Report." *North Dakota Job Service.com*. Last modified March 20. www.

ndworkforceintelligence.com/admin/gsipub/htmlarea/uploads/
lmi_ojorreg1.pdf.

"Northern Great Plains Oil Rush." 2014. *Prairie Public Broadcasting*
audio series. Accessed April 13, 2014. www.prairiepublic.org/radio/
oil-rush-series.

"Oil In the Street, Parts 1–5." 2011. *Tioga Tribune* video series, July 5. Accessed April 10, 2014. www.journaltrib.
com/?id=119&form_data_id=1755.

Piazza, Katie. 2014. "The Bakken Sisters: 'Boomtown Girls' Reality
Show Focuses On 'Brave and Bold' Williston Women." *Williston
Herald*, February 28. Accessed April 14, 2014. www.willistonherald.
com/news/the-bakken-sisters-boomtown-girls-reality-show-focuses-
on-bold/article_98edc3e2-622e-11e1-9fd9-0019bb2963f4.html.

"Rib Cook-Off and Car Show." 2011. *Divide County Journal*
video, October 11. Accessed April 11, 2014. www.journaltrib.
com/?id=123&form_data_id=1880.

Saad, Lydia. 2013. "TV Is Americans' Main Source for News."
Gallup Politics, July 8. Accessed April 12, 2014. www.gallup.com/
poll/163412/americans-main-source-news.aspx

Schupf, Hiliary. 2013. "Rural Radio to Launch on Sirius XM." June 26.
SiriusXM website. Accessed on April 14, 2014. investor.siriusxm.com/
releasedetail.cfm?ReleaseID=773897

Sorenson, Susan and Stephanie Kafka. 2014. "North Dakota Residents
Most Positive About Their Schools." *Gallup Politics*, April 9. Accessed
April 14, 2014. www.gallup.com/poll/168413/north-dakota-resi-
dents-positive-schools.aspx.

Witters, Dan. 2014. "North Dakota No. 1 in Well-being, West Virginia
Still Last." *Gallup Well-Being*, February 20. Accessed April 14, 2014.
www.gallup.com/poll/167435/north-dakota-well-being-west-virgin-
ia-still-last.aspx.

Zaleski, Jack. 2014. "Trusting, Happy and Satisfied: Really?" *Dickinson
Press*, April 14. Accessed April 15, 2014. www.thedickinsonpress.com/
content/zaleski-trusting-happy-and-satisfied%E2%80%88really.

Radio and Television Websites:

American Ag Network: americanagnetwork.com/network-affiliates/
Building the Bakken: www.buildingthebakken.com/about/
Mon-Dak Oil Review: wildbillsranch.podomatic.com/
KFYR-TV (Bismarck, ND): www.kfyrtv.com/
KMOT-TV (Minot, ND): www.kmot.com/
KUMV-TV (Williston, ND): www.kumv.com/
KEYZ-AM (Williston, ND): www.keyzradio.com/

CHAPTER 14

"COWBOY LOGIC": LESSONS FROM NORWAY

Ryan M. Taylor

I published these pieces in the *Dickinson Press* after I had been invited by one of the editors to write about my fellowship with the Bush Foundation. I had gone to Norway as a Bush Fellow to study their policies and see what could be learned from a country with a long history as a major oil exporter.

I wrote in a style that was personal and practiced due to my part-time vocation as a columnist for agricultural newspapers across the western U.S. and Canada since 1994. My long-running Cowboy Logic column has always dealt with living on a ranch, being part of a tight-knit rural community, and raising a young family in the midst of it all. When I wrote these pieces about the topic of oil development and a handful of global lessons, I kept my same Cowboy Logic voice. I figured the readership of the *Dickinson Press* in western North Dakota would understand and appreciate that. Plus, it allowed me to be myself. My voice is my Cowboy Logic voice.

There is generally a lot of support for oil development in North Dakota, including western North Dakota where the brunt of the impacts are felt—the good, the bad and the ugly. The jobs and the economic development (the good) is something North Dakota has been looking to find for years. The deterioration and the critical shortage of infrastructure (the bad)—roads, highways, housing, emergency services, law enforcement, schools, you name it—seem to be challenges continually faced a day late and dollar short. Then there's the large-scale wasteful flaring of natural gas, the saltwater brine and oil spills onto productive agricultural lands, the diminished feeling of safety in once secure communities, and the surge in traffic fatalities (the ugly). One of the problems in our public discourse, though, seems to be that any mention of the bad or the ugly will bring accusations that you don't appreciate the good, or it'll get you labeled "anti-oil."

As a public figure, I've faced my share of accusations when it comes to the booming oil and gas sector of North Dakota. Having served in the state senate for ten years from 2002 to 2012, I pushed the green (yes) or red (no) button at my desk thousands of times on thousands of legislative bills and issues. I support the harvesting of energy in North Dakota, but I've never been willing to give away our one time harvest or step back from our responsibility to be good stewards of the land and water while we do it.

I remember voting against a tax break for oil companies in the 2009 legislative session. It looked to me like a giveaway; it was pitched as an "incentive." I figured the incentive to drill for oil in North Dakota hinged squarely on the quality of the resource, the world market price for oil, and the technology available to go get it. So I voted no on the oil tax reduction and in my 2010 reelection for the district senate seat, opponents ran radio ads across the state, well beyond my district borders (foreseeing that I would probably be a statewide candidate in the future) that said I was "against the Bakken."

I laughed at the ludicrous spin they were making—that voting against a tax giveaway to oil companies made someone against the Bakken. As a Republican ranching friend and supporter of mine from McKenzie County chuckled and said, "Gosh, Ryan, I didn't think anyone could be against a geological formation!" For the record, I'm not against any of our geological formations or tapping energy from them. I do believe we need to work very hard to do it in a way that respects our land and water, and the communities and people in the middle of the development. And yes, that means maintaining a reasonable oil extraction tax rate to provide the needed investments in those communities and having something to show for the future when this one-time harvest is complete.

In politics today, there seems to be little respect for the idea of middle ground or thoughtful compromise, unfortunately. When I ran for governor of North Dakota in 2012, and later, for state agriculture commissioner, oil development was a fundamental topic of the debate about North Dakota's future and our legacy as a people and an agrarian culture. And, while I won my senate election in 2010 handily in spite of the "against the Bakken" radio ads, that narrative of false choices was continued by my opponents in my two statewide races both of which proved unsuccessful at the ballot box. The attacks were amusing, though. When the Brighter Future Fund (and you can imagine whose bright future they were worried about funding) took to the radio airwaves in my race for ag commissioner to say that I had admitted to being a "tree hugger" in one of my Cowboy Logic columns (gasp), I had to laugh, because I knew the column they were referencing.

The exact words in my July 20, 2009, column were, "Even though I'm a child of the generally treeless plains, I'm a tree lover. I reckon you could call me a tree hugger, although being a Scandinavian Midwesterner with well-managed emotions makes me an unlikely hugger of anything. As with people, I'd be more likely to give a tree a firm handshake or a hearty pat on the back, but not a hug." There you have it. I went on to write about the grove of ponderosa pines my father planted in one of our pastures, and how I built my house next to those trees after they grew so nice and tall. I don't know that I've hugged them—the pine needles are kind of bristly, you know. I have stood on the south side of them when a brisk north wind is blowing in January and felt quite content, however.

I failed to find much derision in Norway for people who appreciate the outdoors and who are willing to advocate for the environmental side of the equation when there are potentially harmful tradeoffs with industry. On the contrary, there is a common Norwegian term, *friluftsliv*, meaning, "the open air life," an ingrained, cultural Norwegian appreciation of the outdoors and outdoor recreation. Understanding the Norwegian *friluftsliv* makes it easy to see the cultural basis of their fourth commandment in the 1971 "Ten Oil Commandments" for Norwegian oil and gas development. It lifted up protection of nature and the environment as a guiding value from the very beginning of their off shore oil and gas extraction activities.

Norway is not perfect—no country is—but it does have policies and experiences that we can learn from. My experience as a policy maker in the state senate and as a candidate for statewide office tells me there is room for improvement in the way North Dakota manages and finds its way through this oil boom. As a Bush Fellow, I believe I have identified some of those possible improvements on the other side of the Atlantic. And as a fourth generation cattle rancher and agrarian who holds our prairie in very high esteem, I believe many of us know what we should be doing and where we must improve. Maybe some Cowboy Logic will help remind us what that is.

Across the Pond: Looking for Lessons in the Old Country

Towner. N.D. — It was 1910, 103 years ago, when a grandfather I never knew packed up all that he had, bought a ticket to America on a ship called the Lusitania and left his home, never to return.

He died long before I was born and that's why I never knew him. And I never really had the opportunity to travel back across the pond, as they say, to get to know his homeland. But this fall, I got to make the trip, and by seeing his country I think I learned a little about both him and his home.

The home he left in Norway was a mountainous valley called Hallingdal, and the place he came to in North Dakota was a significantly less mountainous valley along the Mouse River. The ship that Syvert came over on would become famous five years after his journey in a sinking that would eventually bring the U.S. into World War I, but when he was on board, it was just another long, hard trip to Ellis Island to add his name to a long list of immigrants seeking a life less hard in America.

His trip took weeks just to get to New York, mine took about 12 hours of flying time on three jet planes to get all the way to North Dakota. Syvert never got to see his family again. When I was in Norway, if I wanted to see my family, I simply found a wireless internet connection for my iPad and dialed them up on Skype.

I didn't get to Hallingdal on this trip, but I saw a lot of Norway, and I saw a lot of beautiful country. It's a place that has always been beautiful, but, in 1910, Syvert knew you couldn't eat scenery, so, along with what would be 900,000 of his countrymen and women over a 100 year period they struck out for places with more land and opportunity.

I was in Norway to study the lessons of their policies and practices in the area of oil extraction as part of a Bush Foundation Fellowship that I was awarded. In an interesting turn of fate, the country that was so poor that one third of their citizens had to leave its shores less than 100 years ago is now one of the world's wealthiest, with vast pools oil and gas beneath the waters of the seas they've sailed since the time of the Vikings.

Syvert left a poor country that became a wealthy country with oil. He moved to North Dakota which had more space and opportunity, but was still a hard place to survive, especially through the years of the Depression as a small farmer caring for a family of seven children along with his wife. And now that state is becoming wealthy with oil. The place he left has handled the prosperity pretty well, committed to the geological windfall being a long term benefit to its people for generations to come.

The Norwegians are the same people who ate sheep's head, "smalahove," because they didn't waste anything. Know that, and it's easy to understand that one of the first hard rules they laid out when they started granting permission for companies to drill for oil in their sea was that there would be no unnecessary flaring of natural gas.

It's like eating the sheep's head. They weren't going to light a match to perfectly good natural gas and put it up in smoke. They waited for the pipelines and the plants, they found uses and markets for it or they reinjected it, pressurized the wells and got more oil. No waste.

I learned a lot in the short time I was back in Norway. And even though it was my first time, it felt more like a homecoming than a maiden voyage. I wasn't just a North Dakota cowboy roaming Norway.

I was the grandson of Syvert from Hallingdal, the great grandson of Hans and Ragnhild from Gudbrandsdal. And I ate the gamalost and the lutefisk, and, if it's put in front of me, I'll raise a skol of aquavit and try some smalahove as I listen to their lessons on prudent petroleum management for the long haul.

Hard Work and a Good Rest

Towner, N.D. — Around the world, work is work. Some work is harder, some places definitely have better working conditions, but in the end it's all a trade of time and toil for money, or something else of value.

I grew up knowing full well the old saying, "an honest day's work for an honest day's pay," and it's western companion, "you have to ride for the brand." I knew a lot of people who lived by them. When I went to work in the animal health business years ago my regional manager stood up, said those two things and said that's what he expected of us. I knew I was in the right region and that I had the right manager.

I've had a lot of friends and neighbors go to work in the oil patch, and I know they put in an honest day's work for an honest day's pay, and they rode for the brand because the company logo was on their coveralls, their chore gloves, and their baseball caps! And I'm pretty certain it was hard work. Several of them worked a few years and decided to come back and ranch instead of roughneck. Ranching's no walk in the park so if raising cattle is more tempting than the oil rig, it must be demanding.

They may not have made a lifelong career on the oil rig, but they took the money they made to buy some cows, pick up some land or pay cash for a more modern feeding tractor to make life a little easier on the ranch. Others have made a career out of it, and are working their way up the ladder from worm to driller to who knows what.

When I was in Norway visiting with people in their oil industry the subject of careers in oil came up, of course. I distinctly remember a drilling supervisor tell me that no one looked down on the oil rig jobs, he said there was no such term as 'oil field trash', "these are respected careers," he said, "Lifelong careers that allow people to be with their families."

A lot has changed in oil field jobs, everywhere I think, and that has changed the once held stereotype. Most people can probably remember the bumper sticker from oil booms past, "Don't tell my mother I'm working in the oil patch, she thinks I'm a piano player in a brothel (actually it didn't say brothel, I'm just trying to find a term acceptable for print in a widely circulated paper)." At any rate, the message on the sticker was that 'mother' would put oil patch work below other, shall we say, less respected jobs.

In Norway, the oil is all off shore, so when you go to work on a platform, you are out to sea and on the job for two weeks. The biggest point of pride for the drilling supervisor I talked to was the Norwegian mandate of "two weeks on, four weeks off" for their workers. That, he believed, helped make the careers respectable, sought after, and most important to him and his workers, family friendly.

A parent or spouse might be out to sea for two weeks, but they come back and have a whole month to be a full time parent and a partner before they have to leave again. The supervisor believed that work schedule helped change the status of oil platform work in Norway to one of career and not just cash.

I'm certain the pay was excellent, as it is in much of the industry. I didn't ask anyone the exact pay scale. I still have a hard time doing that because it strikes me as similar to asking a rancher how many cows he has, or how big a place they have. Anyone in the cow business knows those questions are taboo. It'd be like asking someone to show their W2 form and lay out all their personal finances.

Every policy has pros and cons. The supervisor saw a lot of pros to the two on, four off, schedule for family. I'm guessing family holds a high place in Norway because they're also the country with 36 to 46 weeks of mandated, paid parental leave for new mothers or fathers.

I suppose a drawback could be having to recruit more workers to accommodate the job needs during the longer time off, especially in Norway, a country with low unemployment and a short supply of workers similar to North Dakota. However, the policy could make the work that much more attractive across a bigger geographical area and give them more candidates for the work.

The supervisor said his workers can live "wherever they want," and fly in from all parts of Norway, or Europe for that matter. It probably reduces the housing crunch somewhat for the communities closest to oil activity and the heightened demand that increase rents and prices beyond reach.

Whether this is a policy that fits places other than Norway is hard to say. But like everything we learn when we go abroad or talk to others, we discover there's more than one way of accomplishing an honest day's work.

Leadership, Learning and Adaptive Challenges:
Lessons Taught, Experiences Studied

Towner, N.D. — When I was awarded a Bush Fellowship from the Bush Foundation of St. Paul, Minn., the most common question asked, hands down, was if it came from the family of George W. Bush and George H.W. Bush. And, if so, why on earth would they award one to me?

First off, no, the Bush Foundation was established by 3M company executive Archibald Bush, and his wife Edyth, in 1953. And here's a piece of trivia for you. The 3M company which now makes us think of "Post-it" notes and Scotch brand tape, was originally known as Minnesota Mining & Manufacturing (get it? 3M) and started as a mining company that moved into the production of sandpaper.

The fellowship's stated goal in its leadership category is "To support and develop more leaders who are better equipped and better networked to effectively lead change." They mention things like being a "catalyst for courageous leadership" and they "support efforts to expose proven and emerging leaders to new ideas and new people."

The fellowship has certainly done that for me. Most recently, it allowed me to go to Harvard University for a week to participate in a course called "21st Century Leadership: Chaos, Conflict and Courage." Sounds applicable to western North Dakota, especially on the days when the chaos seems to outpace the courageous leadership.

I'd have never guessed I'd have a chance to sit in a classroom at Harvard, in a group of 66 people coming from more than 25 nations around the world. As one of my personal heroes, Will Rogers, said, "A man learns by two things. One is reading. The other is association with smarter people." I got to do both at Harvard.

Some of my readings were in "Leadership on the Line," a book who's author happened to be one of the smart people I got to associate with at Harvard. I guess you'd call that a Will Rogers double.

One of the concepts in the book is the work of differentiating between technical and adaptive challenges. Technical challenges can usually be fixed with a tool or technology. Go get the hammer or the microchip. Adaptive challenges require a change of mindset, require courageous leadership. The hammer won't work, and neither will the newest whiz bang fix.

It brought to mind another lesson from my fellowship when I was in Norway, learning about their oil production practices and policies. I was visiting with a production supervisor for one of their major oil companies. As it goes, whenever a person talks about off shore drilling, the BP oil spill, or the Macondo spill, as some call it, in the Gulf of Mexico in 2010, came up. It resulted in the death of 11 workers and spilled 206 million gallons of oil into the gulf.

We talked about possible technical solutions—blow out preventers, remote triggers, protocols, casings and such. I'm no expert in any of this but I asked him about one piece of blow out technology that I remembered hearing about—one that Norway had mandated since the early 1980's that was still not required in the United States in 2010.

He conceded that it may have helped, but that he thought there was more to the tragedy than mere missing technology. He then drew the distinction for me between technical challenges/solutions, and adaptive challenges/leadership, in his own understated Norwegian way.

He said that his company had a platform operating in the Gulf of Mexico quite close to the Macondo well of BP's. They had lots of trouble too, he said, pressures and disruptions and difficulties with their well. It was a hard go.

But, he said, "we are Norwegians and in our culture sometimes we just back off, and take it easy, and slow down," spoken with his open hands in front of him signaling a backing off. And I had to remind myself that the Norwegians have held that mentality and have still harvested 37 billion barrels of oil and gas (in oil equivalents) off their own shores. Taking it easy did not mean standing idle.

I've thought about that conversation many times. The difference between a continued search for a technical fix in hardware or software, and the seemingly simple, but courageous, adaptive leadership that could have possibly prevented a 206 million gallon oil spill by backing off from the go-go mentality and just "taking it easy." Adaptive leadership could have saved lives, billions and billions of dollars of financial loss and untold environmental challenges and clean-up costs.

And I begin to connect the dots from that visit over a cup of strong coffee in a Norwegian break room to the discussions in a classroom at Harvard University to my place in this fast rising oil state that seems to be searching for courageous leadership in the midst of chaos.

Dance with the One Who Brought You
But Everyone Else is Welcome to Waltz Too

Towner, N.D. —When I came out of NDSU in 1992, the parchment in the nice black folder that the university president handed me said bachelor's degree in agricultural economics. I got a second degree (nearly a two for one in the days when you didn't pay per credit) at the same time that said bachelor's in mass communications.

So I was one of those 'right brain/left brain' anomalies, someone who was good at math and liked economics, but could also write a story, or even draw a picture or recite a poem if need be. But, even though both sides of my brain work, I still shoot my rifle right handed, rope calves right handed and the only time I ever wrote with my left hand was the 12 weeks of healing when I broke my right wrist back in seventh grade basketball. I can spin a Will Rogers-style flat loop with my right or left hand thanks to that wrist-induced period of ambidextrousness.

Anyway, back to ag economics. By training, I'm one of those guys. I can plot supply and demand on the two axis of a graph and identify the intersecting price. I could have taken up ag banking or aspired to corporate management after college graduation, but my Dad had been diagnosed with Parkinson's Disease, the family ranch needed me, and, honestly, I felt I needed to be with my family and back on the ranch as we began to fight Dad's battle together.

But I've always followed economics, and kept economics and business on my reading list. I even had the Wall Street Journal delivered to my mailbox three and half miles from the ranch every day for a year after college. I won it as part of an academic scholarship. The paper was always a day late, but that seemed timely enough in the days before the internet.

Now, after 22 years of post-college cattle ranching, 10 years serving in our state senate, a campaign for governor and a new campaign to be the state's agriculture commissioner, I find myself reading about the economics of agriculture and oil, which, today, are the two main economic movers in North Dakota.

One economic principle that kept popping up in my reading was one called the "Dutch Disease." Not Dutch Elm Disease, that's a nasty one that took out some nice trees in a pasture just north of my house, but just Dutch Disease. It's the identified relationship between an increase in an area's exploitation of natural resources and a correlating decline in that area's agriculture and industry. The term was coined in a magazine, "The Economist," in their description of the decline of the manufacturing sector in the Netherlands after they discovered a large natural gas field in the North Sea.

Now stick with me while I try to nutshell the theory without getting too eggheaded. There's a non-tradable sector and two tradable sectors. Non-tradable is service, tradable is the booming (natural resource) sector and the non-booming (agriculture or manufacturing) sector. Eventually the booming sector increases the demand for labor and so does the service sector in order to meet the needs of the booming sector, the non-booming sector pays higher local prices for both services and labor to the detriment of their business, and deals with shortages from the increased

boom and booming service demand. It sounds familiar, even with the economic jargon.

My brother-in-law is flying in his farming help from South Africa because no local labor is available. It's not an inexpensive venture. Across
North Dakota, railroads have increased rail rates and local elevators can
hardly get grain cars on the tracks laden with oil tankers to get the grain
to market. It forced shutdowns and slowdowns of the state's mill and el-
evator in Grand Forks and sugar beet plants in the Red River Valley. A
long standing livestock sale barn in Minot was scrapped to make room
for boom sector infrastructure. These are economic symptoms of the
Dutch Disease. History shows it has caused the diminishment of pre-
boom manufacturing and agriculture in other countries.

Ways to treat the disease, according to lessons from others, include investments in education and infrastructure for the non-booming sector of
agriculture. Some countries have outright supports for the non-booming
sector. Many nations have large savings funds to hold the taxes and revenues collected from the booming sector to insulate their economy for
future generations and protect them from overheating the economy to
the detriment of their historical agricultural and manufacturing sectors.
Norway's $800 billion sovereign wealth fund is one I got to study to some
extent in my Bush Foundation Fellowship.

It's interesting economics, worth reading about in the Economist or
the Wall Street Journal when it comes to a dusty mailbox three and a half
miles from a remote ranch. Better yet, worth discussing by policy makers
who, first, realize the symptoms, and, second, believe that both agriculture and oil, as well as tourism, technology and manufacturing, are worth
having as contributors to the North Dakota economy.

It's nice to have a new dance partner (oil), but remember the old adage
that also instructs us to dance with the one who brought us (agriculture).

People and Oil, and Stories

Towner, N.D. — I grew up in a community, and in a family, with a strong
appreciation for stories and the storytelling culture. It may be a cowboy
trait that gives birth to cowboy poetry and music and the gatherings at
brandings where a lot of folks who'd rather take a beating than step in
front of a microphone entertain others with tremendous storytelling
talent.

My father was one of those soft spoken cowboys who was full of good
stories. One of my favorites was about a colt he raised on the ranch that
was a year or two old when he was drafted into the army in WWII and
went to fight and serve in the South Pacific. By the time he came home

from the war years later that colt was plenty big, a big one to geld and a big one to break.

He got him broke and a nearby rancher named Morris decided he wanted to own that big gelding. He asked Dad how much he wanted for the horse and Dad told him $75, a decent sum in the late 1940's. Morris dug a check out of his pocket that was written to him for $1,200.

He asked Dad if he could cash that check so he could buy that horse. Dad looked at him and said, "Hell, if I could cash a $1,200 check, I wouldn't be selling the horse!"

That's an honest piece of cowboy logic about buyers and sellers, and ranch finance.

Stories of Norway and oil

I thought about the stories that make up a places economic history when I was in Norway on my Bush Fellowship to study that country's successful practices and policies in oil development.

They have many. There's the story of the geologist in the early stages of analysis who completely discounted the possibility of their being any oil off Norway's shore beneath the sea. He confidently claimed he would drink all the oil that anyone would bring up from the Norwegian Continental Shelf. Lucky for him, 37 billion barrels of oil and gas (in oil equivalents) later, no one held him to it.

A famous letter in the Oil Museum in Stavanger, Norway, is that from Phillips Petroleum in 1962 requesting an exclusive license to explore and develop the Norwegian Continental Shelf. History records the offer to have been $160,000 per month for that exclusive right. Wisely, the government and leaders declined the offer, and they now have some $800 billion in a sovereign wealth fund belonging to all Norwegians derived solely from oil taxes and revenues.*

As another story goes, a fellow Scandinavian country had a similarly low offer for exclusivity at a point in their history. Their chief negotiator, under the influence of a fair bit of alcohol, accepted the offer, and, so, that country has realized a lot less benefit from their petroleum in comparison to Norway. I don't mention the country by name because I was only told the Norwegian version of the story by a friend over a shotglass of aquavit and I can't cite any academic sources for it!

Drawing lines between nations under the sea, spawned another story directly related to the offshore oil field called Ekofisk that I was fortunate

---

* These figures date to 2013, today the Norwegian sovereign wealth fund is $882 billion.

enough to visit, thanks to the hospitality of Conoco Phillips and their helicopter, on my trip to Norway.

By negotiating a starting point beyond their physical shoreline for the demarcation of the boundary with the United Kingdom that put British oil on one side and Norwegian oil on the other, Norway found itself just inside the line for its first major productive oil field, Ekofisk, a field that continues to produce superbly today as technology and recovery methods advance and evolve. I'm guessing the Norwegian negotiator was both shrewd, and sober, when he struck that deal.

North Dakota's Storied History

When the story of North Dakota's oil history is written, it will revolve around some often repeated stories as well, I'm sure. The story of the Iverson well near Tioga that started it all is sure to be among them. I have a copy of a Life magazine from Aug. 13, 1951, with a story headlined "Wheatland Oil Boom," complete with photos of the "Wildcat Headquarters" at Bismarck's Grand Pacific Hotel and of an oilman bargaining with a North Dakota farmer sitting on the seat of his tractor.

Individual farms and ranches will likely have stories of regret when their mineral rights were sold outright to get them through a hard time. Others will have stories of gladness of mineral rights leased and royalties retained to benefit generations forward.

Will the stories of North Dakota's policymakers who were in charge during this boom be stories of wise negotiating and policy-setting on behalf of the all its people, and their children and grandchildren? Or will it be a story told with eyes downcast of missed opportunities and a windfall sold short?

By studying, and sharing, the stories of Norway, afforded to me by the Bush Foundation and their fellowship awarded to me, I hope we'll write stories with happy endings, complete with a little pragmatic, Norwegian cowboy logic.

Chapter 15

Bakken Boom! Artists Respond to the North Dakota Oil Rush[1]

Rebecca A. Dunham

Introduction

In the art exhibition *Bakken Boom! Artists Respond to the North Dakota Oil Rush* (Plains Art Museum, Fargo, ND, January 29–August 15, 2015), Curator Rebecca A. Dunham presents the largest group exhibition in a museum to date that critically examines the rapid development and transformative impact of the Bakken oil boom on North Dakota (Figure 1).[2] Using the Chaordic Stepping Stones to organize this groundbreaking project, Dunham invited twenty-two artists and three collaborative groups to display artworks responding to this hot and divisive topic.[3] The artists are an equal number of local, regional, and national artists, providing a wide range of perspectives, and works from the Museum's permanent collection supplement their contributions.

Ranging from photography and film to sculpture, artist's books, printmaking, paintings, costume design, mixed media works, and site-specific installations, the artworks in *Bakken Boom!* reflect the many ways visual

[1] In memoriam Joel Jonientz.

[2] *Bakken Boom!* is supported by lead sponsor Doris Slaaten with additional contributions from Yvonne Condell, Linda Olson, Walter Piehl, and B. J. Zander. The exhibition and programs are also funded in part by the North Dakota Humanities Council, a nonprofit, independent state partner of the National Endowment for the Humanities. Any views, findings, conclusions, or recommendations expressed in the exhibition and programs do not necessarily represent those of the North Dakota Humanities Council or the National Endowment for the Humanities.

[3] The Chaordic Stepping Stones are a tool to outline a clear path in project planning. For more information, please read Chris Corrigan, "The Chaordic Stepping Stones: Planning Just the Right Amount of Form For Invitation, Gathering, Harvest and Wise Action," chriscorrigan.com/Chaordic%20 stepping%20stones.pdf.

Figure 1. The Plains Art Museum. Fargo, ND.

artists are investigating and commenting on the social, political, economic, and environmental dynamics of the current oil boom. The artists tackle their content with viewpoints ranging from contemplative to confrontational and through various modes of communication such as fictional and nonfictional storytelling, sharing personal experiences, asking questions, or challenging assumptions and beliefs about the Bakken boom. However, all of the artists are united in their roles as *activists*.

Within the last few decades, artists have increasingly utilized their art practices as a means to actively engage the public about controversial socio-political issues. In turn, contemporary art galleries, museums, and other such spaces have increasingly provided forums for artists to explore contentious issues like oil culture in America. When Dunham developed *Bakken Boom!*, it was with these principles in mind. She viewed the artists and collaborative groups as partners, working closely with them to select pieces for display to serve as vehicles for dialogue and debate. Dunham also challenged artists to create new work exclusively for the exhibition, and many did.

It is important to note that Plains Art Museum has no stance on the Bakken oil boom. In this exhibition, Dunham offers artists and collaborative groups a platform to exhibit artworks that encourage North Dakotans and visitors from around the world to ponder the oil and gas industry's past, current, and future presence in the state. She understands visitors may disagree with the artists' opinions and views. In fact, she hopes visitors will have strong reactions to the artworks and encourages them to openly express their responses to the artworks as this action contributes to the goal of the project: foster public discussions about the Bakken oil boom.

Dunham is a relatively new resident of North Dakota, having relocated to Fargo from Houston, Texas, in October of 2013 to become Curator of Plains Art Museum. She quickly noticed that many North Dakotans talk about the Bakken boom in private settings but refrain from public conversations. Moreover, she believes there is a lack of communication between citizens and local and state leaders and representatives from the oil and gas companies. Therefore, she believed (and continues to believe) that the need for projects like *Bakken Boom!* is immediate and conceived of the exhibition as a means to provide visitors with a forum to discuss the current oil boom.

To further fulfill this need, Dunham and the Museum's Director of Education, Kris Bergquist, organized a series of public programs with particular emphasis on socially engaged art practices entitled "Community Conversations." Both the exhibition and the program series encourage discussion in the Museum's galleries and beyond, inspiring visitors to voice their opinions, engage in civil dialogue, and take ownership of how the Bakken oil boom is shaping their community, state, and nation. The remainder of this essay presents the artworks featured in the exhibition and concludes with data culled from the exhibition's program series.

Summary of Exhibition Checklist

A "checklist" is the complete list of artists and artworks displayed in an exhibition. While museums plan their exhibitions years in advance, Dunham only began working on *Bakken Boom!* upon her appointment in October of 2013. Due to the timely nature of the project, it was imperative for her to establish a set of principles to guide the selection of artists and artworks to be included in the exhibition. In order to create a dynamic checklist that reflected the complexity of the Bakken oil boom, she invited artists (no unsolicited proposals were reviewed) from different geographic regions, a mixture of generations, and a combination of emerging, mid-career, and mature artists. She also only considered artists who had a history of exploring the oil and gas industry in their practices. Lastly, all of the artists' artworks are contemporary to the Bakken oil boom (made in the mid-2000s and later) and represent a variety of art materials and media, styles, and subjects.

Summary of Exhibition Design

An exhibition's checklist greatly influences its gallery design. *Bakken Boom!* is installed in two of the Museum's main galleries, the William and Anna Jane Schlossman Gallery and the Fred J. Donath Gallery, which together total 545 linear wall feet and 5,225 square feet. Identical rectangular-shaped rooms with the exception of ceiling height—the former is ten feet high while the latter is sixteen—both galleries also have moveable "L" shaped walls to facilitate the flow of space by dividing the galleries into rooms and enhancing dramatic effects.

Due to the eclectic nature of the exhibition's checklist, Dunham chose to paint the walls white and installed the artworks formally, which means the formal qualities of the artworks (line, size, color, pattern, texture, etc.) provided the basis for their placement in relation to one another. With Bergquist's assistance, she also created information centers in both galleries containing iPads with bookmarked websites about the Bakken boom, copies of relevant publications, and information about the exhibition's program series "Community Conversations." She also made the galleries more comfortable and inviting to visitors by placing cushioned benches around the rooms, on top of which she placed bound gallery guides about the artworks on display.

Exhibition Checklist

The text below consists of the didactic materials Dunham wrote to accompany the artworks on display in *Bakken Boom!*. After Alec Soth's photographs, one of the impetus for the exhibition, the remainder of the artists and collaborations are presented in alphabetical order. In addition to this material, Dunham also wrote information panels about the Bakken Shale Formation and the drilling and extraction technologies utilized at the formation, specifically horizontal drilling and hydraulic fracturing (fracking), to contextualize the artworks and their content. Dunham installed these panels strategically around in the galleries, but these are omitted from this essay because of other authors' contributions about this material to the anthology.

1.
Alec Soth, Minneapolis, Minnesota
Selections from *North Dakota Went Boom*, 2013, printed 2014, Pigment prints

Bakken Boom! was partially inspired by the *New York Times Magazine* February 3, 2013 cover story, "North Dakota Went Boom." Written by Chip Brown with black-and-white documentary style photographs by Alec Soth, it brought national and international attention to the Bakken oil boom. Originally intended for publication in the magazine, Dunham asked Soth to print a selection of these photographs for display in *Bakken Boom!*. Figure 2, which depicts a young male "roughneck," or a laborer in the oil and gas industry, serves as the visual identity of *Bakken Boom!*, having been featured in marketing and promotional materials for the exhibition.

A project-based photographer who likens his process to filmmaking, Soth traveled around North Dakota in the winter of 2012 to capture his subjects. Quite striking individually, the photographs transform into a narrative about life in the oil patch when viewed together (Figures 3). As illustrated in Figure 3, Soth's photographs surround another artwork in the exhibition, a film by Isaac Gale. Gale shot his film—also a black-and-white project—while accompanying Soth on his assignment for the *New York Times Magazine* article and their works feature some of the same individuals. Together, their monochromatic palettes enhance the

Figure 2. The visual identity of *Bakken Boom! Artists Respond to the North Dakota Oil Rush*, a photograph of an oil worker by Alec Soth (2012, printed 2014, pigment print. Photo courtesy of the artist).

documentary nature of their artworks, offering glimpses into their subjects' worlds with an unbiased perspective.

Minneapolis-based photographer Alec Soth is known for his large-format photographs portraying the people and landscapes of suburban and rural communities in the Midwest and the South. He often publishes his series as monographs, including *Sleeping by the Mississippi* (2004), *NIAGARA* (2006), *The Last Days of W* (2008), and *Broken Manual* (2010). After achieving international acclaim in the 2004 Whitney and São Paulo Biennials, the Galérie nationale du Jeu de Paume (Paris) and Fotomuseum Winterthur (Switzerland) held mid-career retrospectives of his work in 2008 and 2010, respectively. The artist is represented in prominent collections, including the Brooklyn Museum of Art, Los Angeles County Museum of Art, Museum of Contemporary Art (Chicago), San Francisco Museum of Modern Art, Walker Art Center, Whitney Museum of American Art, and Museum of Fine Arts, Houston, among others.

2.

Kyle Cassidy, Philadelphia, Pennsylvania
Selections from *North Dakota Man Camp Project*, 2013, printed 2014, C-prints

Photographer Kyle Cassidy is a member of the North Dakota Man Camp Project (NDMCP), an interdisciplinary team of researchers investigating "man camps," or living accommodations for itinerant workers in the oil and gas industry and related services.[4] Cassidy's vivid photographs capture portraits of men in and around their domiciles and portraits of the structures themselves. Originally created as documentary photographs, Dunham invited Cassidy to print a selection of his hundreds of photographs specifically for *Bakken Boom!* Rather than dressing the c-prints with mattes and frames, Dunham hung the intriguing works from clips on wires to underscore their documentary nature (Figure 4). The images present the most common forms of man camps—RV camps, mobile home communities, apartment complexes, and gated company compounds—and the most touching ones depict the workers with their pets (Figure 5). Man camps have historical precedents in the western United States, and Cassidy's imagery reveals their continued development in the Bakken region.

Photographer Kyle Cassidy has been documenting American culture since the 1990s in contextual portraits of politicians, scholars, goths, punks, and metal-heads. Based in Philadelphia, Pennsylvania, the

---

[4] For more information about the North Dakota Man Camp Project, please visit www.northdakotamancamps.com.

Figure 3. A selection of Alec Soth's photographs on display in the Fred J. Donath Gallery. In the center of Soth's photographs is a television for screening Isaac Gale's *Sweet Crude Man Camp* (2013, Film, 10:34 min.). Photo courtesy of Rebecca A. Dunham.

Figure 4. The installation of Kyle Cassidy's photographs (2013, printed 2014, C-prints) in the Fred J. Donath Gallery. Using simple hardware purchased at Ikea, the photographs are clipped to wires in a grid of five photographs on three rows. Photo courtesy of Rebecca A. Dunham.

acclaimed artist earned a BA in English from Rowan University, and also holds an MCSE (Microsoft Certified Solutions Expert certificate). He has published several monographs, most recently *War Paint: Tattoo Culture & the Armed Forces* (Schiffer Publishing, 2012), and has authored several books on information technology. A contributing editor for *Videomaker* magazine, Cassidy's work has appeared in the *New York Times*, *Vanity Fair*, the *Sunday Times* (London), *Marie Claire*, *Photographers Forum*, *Asleep by Dawn*, and *Gothic Beauty*.

Bret Weber, assistant professor of social work at the University of North Dakota (UND), and William Caraher, associate professor of history at UND, founded the North Dakota Man Camp Project in 2012. The research team has grown to include Aaron Barth, a North Dakota State University doctoral candidate in history, Richard Rothaus, CEO of Trefoil Cultural and Environmental, Kostis Kourelis, assistant professor of art history at Franklin and Marshall College, and artists Kyle Cassidy and John Holmgren (also in the exhibition). Together, this group of scholars seeks to document and contextualize the material and social environment of man camps associated with the Bakken oil boom in western North Dakota.

3.
Sarah Christianson, San Francisco, California
Selections from *When the Landscape is Quiet Again*, 2013, printed 2014, C-prints (AP):
Lone Butte, ND
The Skogens' Bedroom Window, Cartwright, ND
Vertical Well Abandoned in 1983, South of Williston
Saltwater Pipeline Spill, Murex Petroleum Corp., Antler, ND
Bottomlands at the Confluence of Missouri and Yellowstone Rivers
Gullickson Gravel Pit #1, Near Cartwright, ND
Drilling Rig near Little Missouri National Grasslands, Charbonneau, ND
Tioga Lateral Pipeline, White Earth River Valley
Natural Gas Flare, White Earth River Valley
Pipeline construction, McKenzie County, ND
Saltwater pipeline rupture, Antler, ND
LK-Wing Wells, near Killdeer Mountains
Two Million Gallons of Water to Frack One Well
Burning Spilled Oil off Jensen's Wheat Field, Tioga, ND
Staked out Location for Future Waste Pit, near Lake Sakakawea
Saltwater-Damaged Farmland, Antler, ND
Natural Gas Flaring at My Family's Wells, Watford City, ND

Figure 5. 1 photograph from Kyle Cassidy's series *North Dakota Man Camp Project* depicting a oil laborer with his pet dog, a common sight in the Bakken oil patch. Photo courtesy of Kyle Cassidy.

In her ongoing series of photographs, *When the Landscape is Quiet Again*, Sarah Christianson communicates her belief that the past and current oil booms are irreparably damaging the landscape. She created the series in response to the strong stance former North Dakota Governor Arthur A. Link took during a coal-mining boom in the 1970s. He pledged to protect the state for future generations: "When we are through with that and the landscape is quiet again ... let those who follow and repopulate the land be able to say, our grandparents did their job well. The land is as good and, in some cases, better than before." Christianson's powerful imagery expresses appreciation for Link's standpoint, thereby challenging those of current politicians and inviting us to do the same. One of her most poignant photographs is the aptly titled *The Skogens' Bedroom Window, Cartwright, ND*, which depicts an idyllic view of the landscape interrupted by a pump jack and oil storage tanks (Figure 6).

Now based in San Francisco, California, photographer Sarah Christianson grew up on a four-generation family farm near Cummings, North Dakota. Her background deeply informs her artistic practice. She creates photographic series with strong narratives about personal experiences with the Midwestern landscape. The artist earned a BFA from Minnesota State University Moorhead (2005) and an MFA from the University of Minnesota (2009). Christianson published her first monograph, *Homeplace*, in 2013.

4.

Jessica Christy, Minot, North Dakota
Through the Window, 2014–15, Mixed media installation: Found objects, lithographs, hand-built shadow boxes, and glass

Through the Window is an all-encompassing installation by Jessica Christy, who lives on the eastern edge of the Bakken region. Installed in a room-like environment, the pieces include 150 shadow boxes, the contents of which represent the oil boom's impact on Christy's daily life and surrounding environment (Figure 7). Each box contains a relic—a found object symbolizing her experiences—and a lithograph depicting related imagery or text (Figure 8). While Christy's installation is highly autobiographical, it also explores the juxtaposition of the "old West" and the "new West."

Originally from eastern North Dakota, Jessica Christy has a BS in art from Valley City State University (2007) and an MFA in printmaking and

Figure 6. Sarah Christianson's photograph *The Skogens' bedroom window, Cartwright, ND* (2013, printed 2014, C-print), from her series *When the Landscape is Quiet Again*. Photo courtesy of the artist.

mixed media from the University of North Dakota (2011). She moved to Minot in 2013 to become an Instructor in the Department of Art at Minot State University. After relocating, Christy felt the impact of the Bakken boom on her quality of life: "I live in a 250-square-foot apartment, certain groceries are a luxury, I carry mace with me, I don't go out after dark, and I'm living a different life as a single woman in North Dakota than I would in the eastern part of the state (where I was born and raised). I can't help but take this subject on in my work."

5.

Lucinda Cobley, Houston, Texas
The Last Tree, 2014, Acrylic and resin colored with paint and pigments on synthetic black tulle and plastic film
Surface Tension, 2014, Acrylic and graphite on cast acrylic with monofilament

Lucinda Cobley's *The Last Tree* is a monumental floor installation exploring the dichotomy between the preservation of the environment and the prosperity of oil companies drilling at the Bakken Shale Formation (Figure 9). It forms the silhouette of a hackberry tree, a tree native to North Dakota, and is made of painted plastic film and synthetic black tulle, out of which flows an oil spill composed of cast resin. Cobley produced the piece in response to a Cree prophesy, "Only after the last tree has been cut down. Only after the last river has been poisoned. Only after the last fish has been caught. Only then will you find that money cannot be eaten."

In the dazzling ceiling installation *Surface Tension*, Cobley raises awareness to the potential for flowback—recovered fluids from hydraulic fracturing—to contaminate the water table (Figure 10). To make this intriguing piece, the artist used 80 cast acrylic discs measuring 7 inches in diameter—the same as some oil drilling equipment—and painted them in shades ranging from blue to black, the former representing clean water and the latter being water polluted with flowback. Simulating the water table, the discs hang from the ceiling in an amorphous cluster at varying heights. Both of Cobley's installations explore our everyday relationship with the oil and gas industry; all of Cobley's materials are forms of plastic, which are derived from petrochemicals.

Originally from the UK, Lucinda Cobley relocated to Houston, Texas in 1998. Since then, she has focused exclusively on her painting and printmaking practices and recently embraced site-specific installations, such as the two works included in this exhibition. Cobley holds a DATEC Diploma in Art and Design from Bournville College of Art (1982), a BA

Figure 7. Visitors look at Jessica Christy's installation *Through the Window* (2014-15, Mixed media) in the Fred J. Donath Gallery during the opening reception of *Bakken Boom!*. Photo courtesy of Amy Richardson.

Figure 8. 1 of the 150 shadow boxes in Jessica Christy's *Through the Window*. Photo courtesy of the artist.

in glass design from North Staffordshire Polytechnic (1985), a PG Dip in illustration from Central Saint Martins College of Art and Design (1993), and a FETC from the Institute of Education, University of London (1998). Color, mark-making, and the refraction of light are key elements in her art, which she makes on multiple layers of glass, vellum, or plastic.

6.
Michael Conlan, Grand Forks, North Dakota
Bounty, 2013, Backlit photograph, wheat, wood, and gold leaf
The Truth or Something Beautiful-3 and *The Truth or Something Beautiful-5*, 2013, Inkjet prints, screenprints, and 22k gold leaf
Rush, 2014, Wood, vinyl, and gold leaf

For *Bakken Boom!*, Michael Conlan presents artworks from an ongoing series he created in response to the current oil boom, all of which are united by the material of gold leaf. In the enticing mixed media installation *Bounty*, the artist dramatically interweaves photographic images and sculptural objects (Figure 11). The large piece features three backlit photographs of bountiful wheat fields mirrored in three gold-covered floor boxes, out of which grow wheat. Here, Conlan advocates the exploitation of the prairie for the more profitable oil and gas industry.

The two intriguing works on paper are from the artist's ongoing series *The Truth or Something Beautiful* (Figure 12). A combination of inkjet prints and screenprints, their stark monochromatic imagery depicts portraits of vernacular farm structures in idyllic fields. In these works, Conlan memorializes the buildings through the application of gold leaf, forcing us to ponder North Dakota's agricultural heritage and the future of the industry.

While Conlan produced *Bounty* and *The Truth or Something Beautiful Rush* several years ago, *Rush* is a new piece he premiered in *Bakken Boom!* It is a large wall-mounted sculpture in the shape of the Bakken Shale Formation, which underlies not only western North Dakota but also parts of Montana, Saskatchewan, and Manitoba (Figure 13). Conlan built this piece from wood and vinyl and covered it with a thin layer of gold leaf symbolizing the immense economic prosperity of the current oil boom. The gallery's lighting produces a glowing halo around the work, which is also reflected on the floor in a ghost image, perhaps alluding to eventual bust of the Bakken oil boom.

North Dakota native Michael Conlan has explored the current oil boom in his conceptually-driven mixed media practice for several years now. His art practice focuses on the idea of place, and he uses the landscape as a visual motif to confront current social and environmental

Figure 9. Artist Lucinda Cobley (left in the group of 3 on the right) puts the final touches on *The Last Tree* (Mixed media, 2014), which took the artist, Curator Rebecca A. Dunham (far right), and Curatorial Intern Aliza Rux (middle in the group of 3 on the right) 4 days to install. Also pictured is Ryan Stander (far left), another artist in the exhibition. Photo courtesy of Amy Richardson.

Figure 10. At the top left is Lucinda Cobley's *Surface Tension* (2014, Acrylic and graphite on cast acrylic with monofilament), which is in the William and Anna Jane Schlossman Gallery. Photo courtesy of Amy Richardson.

issues. After earning a BFA in art practices from Portland State University (2011), he completed his MFA at the University of North Dakota in 2014. For his MFA exhibition, *Extracted Landscapes*, he presented an entire body of work about the Bakken boom, a selection of which are presented here.

7.
Michael Crowder, Houston, Texas
Selections from *Refined Crude*:
Refined Crude 46.80, 2005, Cast lead crystal, slate, mahogany, and felt
Refined Crude 58.65, 2005, Cast lead crystal, slate, mahogany, and flocking
Refined Crude 60.57, 2005, Cast lead crystal, photograph, mahogany, and flocking
Refined Crude 147.27, 2008, Cast lead crystal, lead, gold, mahogany, and felt
Refined Crude 106.90, 2013, Cast lead crystal, cast glass, mahogany, and black plexiglas
Refined Crude 83.25, 2013, Cast lead crystal, cast glass, mahogany, and black plexiglas

Michael Crowder examines oil as a commodity to be bought and sold in the international marketplace in his ongoing series *Refined Crude* (Figure 14). Each wall-mounted sculpture contains a diminutive cast spiral imitating oil drilling equipment, and the artist placed real drops of crude oil inside each spiral during the casting process. Crowder inserted these against various backgrounds, and once finished, he titled the pieces according to the closing price of a barrel of oil on the day of completion. For this exhibition, the artist presents already made pieces and new works inspired by the volatile market within the last year, which has experienced drastic dips and spikes in the price of oil.

Originally from New Orleans, Louisiana, Michael Crowder is a conceptually-driven mixed media artist based in Houston, Texas. Exploring ideas of fragility and impermanence, Crowder makes "art/ifacts" with the *pâte de verre* glass casting technique, which is an intricate and challenging form of kiln casting. He often incorporates ephemeral materials in his mixtures such as sugar, chocolate, marble, cigarette ashes, and, in this case, oil. The artist was recently honored with a nomination for the Louis Comfort Tiffany Biennial Award and was awarded an Artist-in-Residence Fellowship at the Dora Maar House in Ménerbes, France.

Figure 11. Michael Conlan's *Bounty* (2013, Backlit photograph, wheat, wood, and gold leaf). Photo courtesy of the artist.

Figure 12. Michael Conlan's *The Truth or Something Beautiful-3* (2013, Inkjet prints, screenprints, and 22k gold leaf). Photo courtesy of the artist.

8.

Empire Builder
Carol Inderieden, Pepin, Wisconsin and Chandler O'Leary, Tacoma, Washington
Manifest Destiny, 2013–14, Inkjet print
Empire Builder, 2013–14, Digital prints on Hahnemuhle paper with binder's board

Displayed in accordion fashion, *Empire Builder* is an artist's book about the famous Great Northern passenger train "Empire Builder" that runs through the Upper Midwest, northern Great Plains, and Pacific Northwest (Figure 15). Working collaboratively, Carol Inderieden and Chandler O'Leary created the book's enchanting maps, charts, and landscapes to illustrate how the railroad travels through the Bakken region and connects areas relevant to the current oil boom, such as western Wisconsin, where sand is mined for hydraulic fracturing, and the Port of Tacoma, an important export center. Their book also examines the energy industry's exploitation of the people and places in these regions. A related print, *Manifest Destiny*, is above the book.

A native of Minneapolis-St. Paul, Carol Inderieden currently lives and works in rural western Wisconsin. She is a printmaker and photographer and also co-publishes *Midwest Art Fairs*, an annual directory of festivals and events in the Upper Midwest. In 2013, Inderieden penned a series of articles about a proposed sand mine in western Wisconsin for the *Twin Cities Daily Planet*, an online newspaper covering local and regional issues in Minneapolis-St. Paul.

Formerly of Fargo, Chandler O'Leary was born near Wall Drug, South Dakota, grew up in Cape Cod, Massachusetts, and currently lives and works in Tacoma, Washington. She attended the Rhode Island School of Design and has owned and operated Anagram Press since 2004. O'Leary is also the author and artist of the illustrated travel blog *Drawn the Road Again*, and one half of the collaborative team behind the *Dead Feminists* poster series. A recipient of numerous awards, she is represented in over thirty-five museum and corporate collections, has been in over eighty solo and group exhibitions, and has participated in prominent artist residency programs.

Figure 13. Michael Conlan's *Rush* (2014, Wood, vinyl, and gold leaf), which is displayed in the Fred J. Donath Gallery. Photo courtesy of Rebecca A. Dunham.

Figure 14. Michael Crowder's *Refined Crude* 58.65 (2013, Cast crystal, slate, mahogany, and felt). Photo courtesy of the artist.

9.
Elise Forer, Chicago, Illinois
All We Have, All For Nothing, Up In Smoke, 2014, Mixed media installation:
Relief print with watercolor on newsprint mounted to wood

Emerging artist Elise Forer created the print-based installation *All We Have, All for Nothing, Up in Smoke* exclusively for *Bakken Boom!* (Figure 16). It brings to light how hydraulic fracturing may contaminate the residential water supply in the Bakken region. Above a series of freestanding houses are shelves stacked with jars and vessels containing water that is discolored, cloudy, and filled with debris from fracking. Homeowners often track their water supply in monthly samples like these, a process Forer accounts for in the empty jars yet to be filled. Also, Forer fears the health of those residing in the region may be negatively affected due to their contact with contaminated water.

A Minnesota native, Elise Forer developed an intimate relationship with the natural world as a child and staunchly believes the drilling technology utilized in the Bakken region will irreversibly damage the landscape of the Upper Midwest. She creates large-scale installations such as *All We Have, All for Nothing, Up in Smoke* with ephemeral materials (the deinstallation of the work destroys it) to parallel the ephemeral nature of the environment. After graduating with a BFA from Minnesota State University Moorhead (2013), Forer attended the Penland School of Craft. She is currently based near Chicago, Illinois, where she is a studio fellow at Spudnik Press Cooperative and also works at Paper Source in Oakbrook and Bottle and Bottega in La Grange.

10.
Danielle Frankenthal, Hoboken, New Jersey
Selections from *Crossroads*, 2014 and *Turbulence #4*, 2013, Acrylic on acrylite

The vivid hues and rhythmic marks of Danielle Frankenthal's paintings are hypnotic. While her three paintings displayed in the exhibition feature an abstract gestural language, their titles—*Crossroads* and *Turbulence*—speak directly to the condition of the people and places in North Dakota that results from the Bakken oil boom (Figure 17). All of the works are also united in the gold and silver backing, which represents the financial opportunities of the oil boom. Additionally, Frankenthal works exclusively with plastic art materials, which are derived from petrochemicals, thus exploring the relationship between the visual arts and the oil and gas

Figure 15. Installation of *Empire Builder* and *Manifest Destiny*, an artist's book (2013–14, Digital prints on Hahnemuhle paper with binder's board) and print (2013–14, Inkjet print), respectively, about the famous Great Northern passenger train "Empire Builder" by Carol Inderieden and Chandler O'Leary in the Fred J. Donath Gallery. Photo courtesy of Rebecca A. Dunham.

Figure 16. The site-specific installation *All We Have, All For Nothing, Up in Smoke* (2014, Mixed media: Relief print with watercolor on newsprint mounted to wood) by Elise Forer in the Fred J. Donath Gallery. Photo courtesy of Rebecca A. Dunham.

industry. Lucinda Cobley also explores these issues in her installations, resulting in the artists' works being displayed side-by-side (Figure 18).

Born in New York City, painter Danielle Frankenthal lives and works in Hoboken, New Jersey. She earned a BA in philosophy from Brandeis University and attended the Art Students League of New York. Frankenthal's art practice emphasizes light, specifically how light interfaces with her formalist concerns of color and mark-making. She paints exclusively with acrylic on pieces of transparent acrylate, which she layers to create the effect of simultaneity. The phenomenon of light shining on, through, and behind her surfaces serves as a metaphor for how we see and interpret visual data, especially as a result of cultural programming and life experiences.

11.
Isaac Gale, Minneapolis, Minnesota
Sweet Crude Man Camp, 2012, Film, 10:34 minutes

When visitors enter the Fred J. Donath Gallery, their attention is immediately piqued by the sound coming from a screening of Isaac Gale's *Sweet Crude Man Camp*, which activates the gallery. Gale's gritty black-and-white film tracks the day-to-day lives of Bakken "roughnecks," the nickname for laborers in the oil and gas industry (Figure 3). Shot in December 2012, the film captures the workers with surprising yet haunting intimacy. On this project, Gale worked in the role of director, camera man, and editor, while photographer Alec Soth, whose photographs are also featured in this exhibition, co-produced the film with Ryan Debolski, and B. J. Burton and Adam Burlburt provided the original score. Since Gale shot his film while accompanying Soth on travels for his project, both artists' works feature some of the same individuals.

Isaac Gale is a Minneapolis-based filmmaker, video artist, and musician. His music video work has been shown on MTV, Pitchfork, Interview Magazine, and at the SXSW Film Festival, and his experimental video work for the band Bon Iver was featured in *Time Magazine*. Gale is new to the genre of short documentary films; *Sweet Crude Man Camp* is his first venture. It has been screened at the Palm Springs International Shortfest and Rooftop Films, and won "Best Documentary" at both the Dakota Digital Film Festival and Edindoc.

Figure 17. Danielle Frankenthal's, *Turbulence #4* (2013, Acrylic on acrylite). Photo courtesy of the artist and Wade Wilson Art, Santa Fe, New Mexico.

12.
Wayne Gudmundson, Moorhead, Minnesota
Selections from *Faces of the Oil Patch*: *City*, *Faces of the Oil Patch*, *Help Wanted*, *Realtors*, *Rural*, *Wives*, 2012, C-prints
Wayne Gudmundson and Prairie Public Broadcasting, *Faces of the Oil Patch*, 2012, Film, 57 minutes

Originally produced as film stills for Prairie Public's 2012 documentary *Faces of the Oil Patch*, Wayne Gudmundson's large color photographs document the social landscape of the Bakken oil boom. The artist approached the series from an unbiased, photojournalistic perspective and organized his images into categories based on their content. Figure 19 portrays a law enforcement officer and is from the category *Faces of the Oil Patch*, which features head portraits of various people living in the Bakken region. Rather than displaying the photographs as fine art in frames, they are hung directly on the walls with magnets (Figure 20). The documentary is screened side-by-side with Gudmundson's photographs.

Acclaimed for his brooding monochromatic landscapes of the Upper Midwest and Iceland captured with a large format camera, Wayne Gudmundson shot *Faces of the Oil Patch* with a digital camera, printing the raw yet vivid portraits of the people, places, and phenomena of the oil boom as chromogenic color prints. The artist first became interested in photography while in the Navy and later pursued a BA and BS from Minnesota State University Moorhead (MSUM), an MS from the Tri-College University, and an MFA from the University of Minnesota. Over the past forty years, his photographs have appeared in over thirty-five exhibitions, nine books, and four television documentaries. Gudmundson also recently retired from teaching at MSUM's Department of Communications after twenty-five years.

13.
John Holmgren, Lancaster, Pennsylvania and Ellensburg, Washington
Man Camp #1–#16, 2014, Inkjet prints, screenprints, transfers, and graphite on paper

Along with fellow *Bakken Boom!* artist Kyle Cassidy, John Holmgren is a member of the North Dakota Man Camp Project, (NDMCP) an interdisciplinary team of researchers investigating "man camps," or living accommodations for itinerant workers in the oil and gas industry and related services. In his series *Man Camp*, Holmgren layers a variety of art mediums, a process that parallels our mind's way of layering information based on our experiences. Photography serves as the foundation

Figure 18. View with Danielle Frankenthal's paintings displayed on the walls next to Lucinda Cobley's floor piece *The Last Tree* in the William and Anna Jane Schlossman Gallery. To the far left is TV screening *Running on Fumes in North Dakota* (2014, Film, 7 minutes)by The Cheddar Factory. Photo courtesy of Rebecca A. Dunham.

for these works, which Holmgren cultivated further by adding screen-printed imagery, applying transfers, and inserting drawings and text in graphite (Figure 21). Hung in a single horizontal row, the installation of Holmgren's sixteen works on paper reinforces the traditional reading of text and the landscape.

Originally from Lakewood, Washington, John Holmgren holds a BA in studio art from Central Washington University (2004) and an MFA in photography from the University of Minnesota (U of M) (2007). His artistic practice explores connections between time and place, the landscape and the environment, and their connections to personal memory. Since 2010, the artist has taught at Franklin and Marshall College. Previously, he worked at U of M, the University of Oregon, Prescott College, and Wright State University. Holmgren has exhibited his work nationally and internationally and has been awarded numerous grants and awards. He is also an active member of the Society for Photographic Education and the College Art Association. Please see number two of the checklist, Kyle Cassidy, for information about NDMCP.

14.
Joel Jonientz, Grand Forks, North Dakota
Chérie, tu vois quelque chose de nouveau ici? (My dear, do you see something new here?), 2014, Hand-colored lithograph

Joel Jonientz's hand-colored lithograph portrays an elderly couple peering over their shoulders at oil drilling equipment, railroad cars, oil barrels, and "roughnecks," or laborers in the oil and gas industry (Figure 22). The husband asks his wife, "Chérie, tu vois quelque chose de nouveau ici?" (My dear, do you see something new here?). Jonientz created this print in homage to Honoré Daumier (1808–79), who created over 5,000 prints commenting on social and political life in nineteenth-century France, and it incorporates Daumier's signature style of strong visual imagery supplemented by a humorous caption. It also illustrates the historical role of printmaking as a democratic means of disseminating information about politically-charged topics.

Joel Jonientz passed away in 2014 and previously was an associate professor in the Department of Art and Design at University of North Dakota (UND). Born in Seattle, Washington, Jonientz earned his BA in experimental animation from the Evergreen State College (2000) and his MFA in painting from the Savannah College of Art and Design (2006). His primary focus was technology-based arts and new media. Jonientz created this print at the invitation of Dr. Arthur Jones, professor and chair of UND's Department of Art and Design, to serve as a contemporary

Figure 19. A selection from Wayne Gudmundson's series *Faces of the Oil Patch* (2012, C-print). This photograph depicts a young man, who at the time was the most senior law enforcement officer in his town, attesting to the lure of high-salaried oil industry jobs. Photo courtesy of the artist.

Figure 20. Installation of Wayne Gudmundson's series Faces of the Oil Patch in the William and Anna Jane Schlossman Gallery. Photo courtesy of Rebecca A. Dunham.

complement to Honoré Daumier's work in the exhibition *Honoré Daumier (1808–1879)* (UND Art Collections Gallery, April 24–July 14, 2014). Jonientz received assistance from Kim Fink, professor of art at UND and director and master printer of the university's printmaking studio Sundog Multiples, who printed Jonientz's lithograph on a restored nineteenth century French Brisset press—the same type of press Daumier used.

15.
Kent Kapplinger, Fargo, North Dakota
Rude I, 2013, Screenprint, AP X and *Rude II*, 2013, Screenprint, AP I
Hell of a Mess, 2013, Screenprint in acrylic with hand-lettering in enamel on vinyl
Blood Drive, 2011, Screenprint, AP VII
OMG, 2013, Screenprint in acrylic with hand-lettering in enamel on vinyl

Kent Kapplinger makes prints in response to concerns raised by authors, reporters, and researchers, and a majority of his work addresses environmental issues. He began incorporating the Bakken boom into his output when the boom started in 2006. The artist is particularly interested in the oil and gas industry's policies regarding land ownership and capital development, which he believes negatively impact the land and the daily lives of North Dakotans. *Rude I* and *Rude II* are some of Kapplinger's best known prints about these topics (Figure 23).

OMG and *Hell of a Mess* are one-of-a-kind monumental prints Kapplinger executed on vinyl banner material (Figure 24). While prints are traditionally made on sheets of paper, these experimental works underscore Kapplinger's graphic style. Both pieces also contain a clever play with words: *OMG* is the acronym for the phrase "oh my god" and *Hell of a Mess* is a twist on the Hess Corporation, an oil company drilling in the Bakken. Kapplinger often incorporates articles into his work, as seen in the prints' green background texts, and a binder with this source material is on the pedestal below a small print in between the two large banners.

Printmaker Kent Kapplinger is known for his graphic style incorporating elements of Pop Art, humor, and text. He earned a BA from Augustana College and both an MA and MFA in printmaking from the University of Iowa. The artist has been a professor of art at North Dakota State University since 1992, and he founded the department's Printmaking, Education, and Research Studio (PEARS) program in 1998. Throughout his career, Kapplinger has exhibited his work in more than 230 solo and group exhibitions and is represented in more than forty public and corporate art collections.

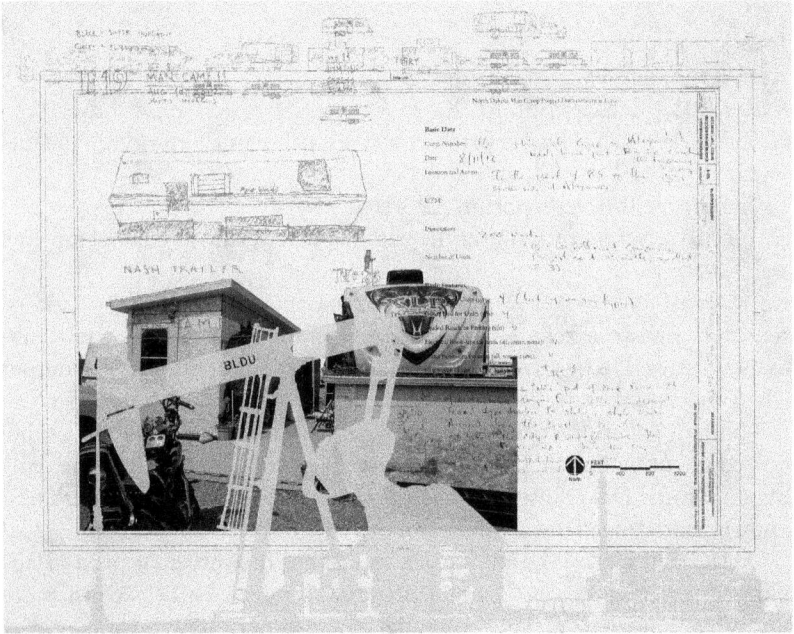

Figure 21. John Holmgren's *Man Camp* #7 (2014, Inkjet print, screen-print, transfer, and graphite on paper). Photo courtesy of the artist.

16.
Meredith Lynn, Moorhead, Minnesota
West Fargo, Minnesota, 2014, Digital media

Meredith Lynn conceived of *West Fargo, Minnesota* in response to a digital mishap: faulty connections between the GPS systems in smart phones and FaceBook's location software created the nonexistent town of "West Fargo, Minnesota." Lynn embraced this blunder as an opportunity to explore the impact of the Bakken oil boom on the Fargo-Moorhead community. She fabricated the fictitious town of West Fargo, Minnesota as an oil boom town via a website and invites you to learn more about the town and become a participant on the website through an iPad (Figure 25). By participating in the project, you have an opportunity to stimulate conversations about events unfolding out west. Lynn created this unique piece with funding provided by Northern Lights and the Jerome Foundation.

Meredith Lynn earned a BFA in painting and drawing from Cornell University (2006), and then earned both an MA in painting and drawing (2010) and an MFA in painting, drawing, and printmaking (2011) from the University of Iowa. She is the founder and artistic director of Rust Belt Bindery, a book bindery committed to producing and distributing new work as well as repairing and rebinding existing objects, and an adjunct faculty member in the Department of Art and Design at Minnesota State University Moorhead. Lynn is also the director of the Nemeth Art Center and is the director of the Rourke Art Museum.

17.
Molly McLain, Bismarck, North Dakota
Impede and *Gold Boom/Critical Habitat*, 2014, Mixed media on canvas

In *Bakken Boom!*, Molly McLain presents two new mixed media works on canvas, *Impede* and *Gold Boom/Critical Habitat* (Figure 26). She was inspired to make these intimately scaled pieces in response to reports indicating that two pollinators, the Dakota Skipper and Poweshiek Skipperling, are being threatened by continuous land development for the oil and gas industry. In spite of the loss of their habitat, these pollinators are waiting to be listed as endangered. McLain is enraged that political leaders refuse to acknowledge these reports for fear of inhibiting the industry. Both works feature heavily built surfaces of oil paint, acrylic transfers, collages of newspaper clippings, and the application of gold leaf.

Artist Molly McLain graduated with a BA from Valley City State University and recently moved to Bismarck. The heart of McLain's art is her passionate engagement with environmental issues. She sees dichotomies

Figure 22. Joel Jonientz's print *Chérie, tu vois quelque chose de nouveau ici?* *(My dear, do you see something new here?)* (2014, Hand-colored lithograph 2014). Photo courtesy of Rebecca A. Dunham.

between the natural wisdom of agriculture and advancements in modern technology, the latter of which she believes has a negative long-term impact on the health of the planet. McLain expresses these beliefs in her practice, which embraces numerous mediums such as oil painting, collage, photography, mosaic, and mural painting.

18.
J. Earl Miller, Fargo, North Dakota
What Lies Beneath, 2014, Digital inkjet print

J. Earl Miller's intriguing photograph depicts the Theodore Roosevelt National Park, which consists of three separate areas of badlands in western North Dakota (Figure 27). It also shows the encroachment of oil and gas companies on the park as they attempt to access the crude oil near and underneath its beautiful and rugged terrain. Hydraulic fracturing is now used in 90 percent of domestic oil and gas wells, and Miller's photograph reveals the fine line between balancing the nation's energy needs and preserving America's national heritage. Here, the photographer implores us to ponder, "This is what we see above the ground, but what is happening underground?" Also, take a closer look to see Miller's personal touch—the artwork is actually two photographs of the same scene, the top of which is laser cut to reveal a layer of oil between the imagery.

J. Earl Miller has garnered a regional reputation for his quasi-documentary style photographs capturing humorous scenes and the open roads of North Dakota. He utilizes both analog and digital technology to shoot straight photographs or create complex manipulations and montages. Miller began taking photographs at the age of ten and later attended Central Lakes College and Minnesota State University Moorhead. After his studies, he apprenticed with photographer David Wolfe. Today, he lives and works in Fargo as a freelance photographer, with a majority of his editorial work appearing in *High Plains Reader* and in ad campaigns throughout the area.

19.
Max Patzner, Minot, North Dakota
When Will They Feed Us Again?, 2014, Artist's book

Composed of vintage, grainy photographs, Max Patzner's artist's book *When Will They Feed Us Again?* explores the negative impact of the oil boom on small towns, the once untouched prairies, and Native American sacred grounds (Figure 28). For the latter, he focused especially on New Town, North Dakota, the largest city and administrative center of

Figure 23. Kent Kapplinger's *Rude I* (2013, Screenprint, AP X). Photo courtesy of the artist.

Figure 24. A selection of Kent Kapplinger's prints in the William and Anna Jane Schlossman Gallery, from left to right: *Hell of a Mess* (2013, Screenprint in acrylic with hand-lettering in enamel on vinyl), *Blood Drive* (2011, Screenprint, AP VII) and Kapplinger's binder with article clippings, and *OMG* (2013, Screenprint in acrylic with hand-lettering in enamel on vinyl). Photo courtesy of Rebecca A. Dunham.

the Fort Berthold Reservation and home to the Three Affiliated Tribes of the Mandan, Hidatsa, and Arikara Nation. The title and content of *When Are They Going to Feed Us?* was inspired by a story Patzner heard while visiting New Town. According to legend, a female ghost—perhaps a figure of Mother Nature—appears to oil workers and asks them when they are going to give the land back to the people. In his book, Patzner asks us to consider, "The money is rushing in but at what cost?"

A native of Minot, which is on the eastern edge of the Bakken oil boom, Max Patzner is a photographer, printmaker, designer, and musician. His artistic sensibility is informed by the terrain and the lifestyle of western North Dakota. In his photography practice, he utilizes old-fashioned analog cameras to create imagery conveying a sense of timelessness and longing for the past.

20.

Ryan Stander, Minot, North Dakota
Missing Information, 2014, Digital inkjet prints on paper mounted on plywood with plexiglas
Nothing To See Here ..., 2015, Digital inkjet prints on paper mounted to plywood with plexiglas

Ryan Stander combines elements of his own photographs with found materials, vernacular photos, or appropriated imagery, which he frequently manipulates with computer software. In *Missing Information*, a monumental wall installation about the Casselton train derailment, he altered a film still from a video shot by Darrin Rademacher (Figure 29). The deconstructed image is both a literal and metaphorical commentary on the relationship, or lack thereof, between the oil and gas industry and the population of western North Dakota. It also expresses Stander's belief that the industry purposefully hides information from the public.

Nothing to See Here ... is a group of four photographic prints, each representing a facet of the Bakken oil boom's impact on western North Dakota (clockwise from top left): the presence of oil equipment, dangerous driving conditions, flaring—the burning of natural gas associated with oil extraction processes, and temporary housing structures (Figure 30). Stander pulled information from various websites related to these topics and layered the texts over the imagery. To make this piece and *Missing Information*, the artist mounted inkjet prints to plywood, which he covered with found pieces of plexiglas. As evidenced by the person's reflection at the intersection of the four photographs in Figure 30, Stander's use of Plexiglas forces viewers to insert themselves in his artworks and contemplate the artist's message.

Figure 25. Meredith Lynn's hand-built kiosk with her piece *West Fargo, Minnesota* (2014, Digital media) in the Fred J. Donath Gallery. Photo courtesy of Rebecca A. Dunham

Figure 26. Molly McLain's *Gold Boom/Critical Habitat* (2014, Mixed media on canvas). Photo courtesy of the artist.

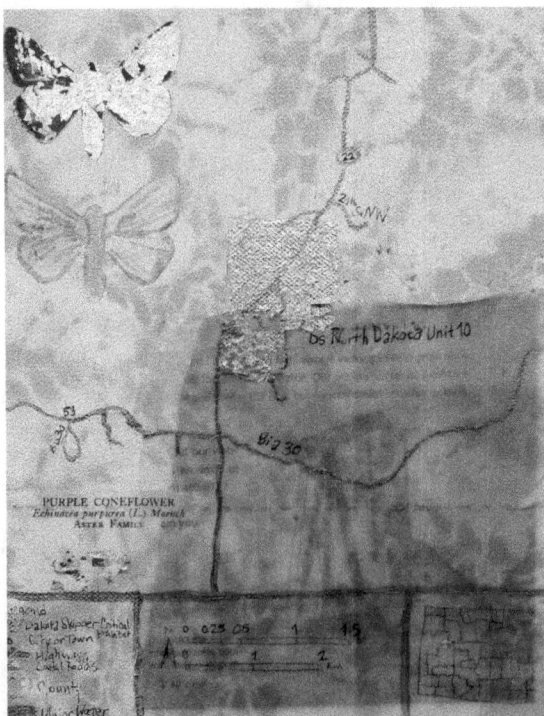

Originally from northwest Iowa, Ryan Stander pursued a BA in art at Northwestern College (1998), after which he earned an MA in theology from Sioux Falls Seminary (2003) and an MFA in mixed media from the University of North Dakota (2011). He moved to Minot in 2012 to become an assistant professor of art at Minot State University. Stander's interdisciplinary interests amalgamate the arts and theology into a dynamic visual language. He investigates the reciprocal relationship between humanity and the physical world, particularly within cultural frameworks such as belief systems, biases, and assumptions that guide people's interactions with places and objects.

21.
Eric Syvertson, Fargo, North Dakota
House Party, 2014, Oil on canvas

Eric Syvertson's ongoing series *House Party* portrays ordinary house parties—an easily recognizable subject—as a means to explore the over-indulgence and lure of instant gratification transpiring with the Bakken oil boom (Figure 31). Syvertson's source material is real house parties; he makes his paintings after screenshots of YouTube videos. Depicted in a photorealistic style, the partygoers' insolent behavior foreshadows the negative side of an oil boom going bust: oil companies abandoning drilling equipment, deserted and dilapidated man camps, and six-lane highways cutting across the prairie. While Syvertson painted earlier *House Party* paintings in color, he executed this triptych in black-and-white with iridescent glazes imitating an oil slick.

A native of North Dakota, Eric Syvertson is an emerging artist, educator, and arts advocate based in Fargo. He earned a BA in art education from Minnesota State University Moorhead (2008), after which he taught art at West Fargo High School. He recently completed his MFA at the Minneapolis College of Art and Design (2014). In the last year, the artist has garnered regional acclaim for his series *House Party*, and he created the three works on display in *Bakken Boom!* exclusively for the exhibition. Syvertson has been an active member in several professional arts organizations and has served as president of the Fargo-Moorhead Visual Artists.

22.
The Cheddar Factory, Minneapolis, Minnesota
Running on Fumes in North Dakota, 2014, Film, 7 minutes

The Cheddar Factory analyzes the benefits and shortcomings of the Bakken oil boom in the short documentary *Running on Fumes in North*

Figure 27. J. Earl Miller's *What Lies Beneath* (2014, Digital inkjet print). Photo courtesy of Rebecca A. Dunham

Dakota (Figure 18). The film profiles Jonnie Cassens, a young woman who left California for the Bakken region to be a contract "hotshot" truck driver—a round-the-clock special-delivery person. Expecting lucrative opportunities, instead she faced a meager paycheck and an isolated life-style in the male-dominated industry. Here, she shares her agonizing existence and how she finds refuge in her Chihuahua, TV, and M&M's candy. Cassens's story also challenges the assumption that hard work and courage bring a decent living in contemporary America—a longstanding promise this nation makes to its citizens.

Based in both Minneapolis, Minnesota and Williston, North Dakota, The Cheddar Factory is a film and video production company founded by James Christenson, Eliot Popko, Jonah Sargent, and Lewis Wilcox. The company specializes in character-driven documentaries. It received international exposure when their short piece *Running on Fumes in North Dakota* appeared on the *New York Times*'s website "Op-Docs" page in January 2014. Embedded on the front lines of the Bakken boom, the company has chronicled a wide range of people and stories to document the transformation of the oil-rich prairie landscape of western North Dakota into thriving and sustainable communities. It is currently editing additional pieces, which will appear on the *New York Times*'s website "Op-Docs" page at a future date.

23.
Road to Williston, Duluth, Minnesota
2014, Mixed media installation: film, digital projects, and textile

Native service organizations Gimaajii Mino-Bimaadiziyaan and Mending the Sacred Hoop have partnered with Kathy McTavish, Erika Mock, Tina Olson, Shiela Packa, and Jessica Tillman to create *Road to Williston*, a dynamic art installation featuring sounds, texts, and images (Figures 32–33).[5] Its title refers to US Highway 2, which connects Duluth, Minnesota, and Williston, North Dakota. This route has become synonymous with human trafficking and sexual violence against Native American girls and women, especially within the Bakken region. Many believe the oil boom has spurred this depraved treatment of women, and this project seeks to both raise awareness to the issue and combat it. *Road to Williston* was conceived as part of the Creative Community Leadership Institute (CCLI) run by Intermedia Arts and funded by the Bush Foundation. McTavish oversaw the installation of *Road to Williston*, which is in a room-like space

---

[5] For more information about *Road to Williston*, please visit roadtowilliston.org.

Figure 28. The display of Max A. Patzner's *When Will They Feed Us Again?* (2014, Artist's book) in the Fred J. Donath Gallery. Visitors are invited to put on the gloves and flip through the book, which includes Patzner's stunning photographs and original text he wrote to accompany his imagery. Photo courtesy of Rebecca A. Dunham.

that is best understood when visitors enter the room and physically experience the piece.

Developed by the American Indian Community Housing Organization (AICHO), Gimaajii Mino-Bimaadiziyaan (an Ojibwe phrase meaning "Together we are beginning a good life") is a service organization for Native Americans based in Duluth, Minnesota. It is the first project of its kind in the nation to combine permanent supportive housing for families, single individuals, and elders with a center providing cultural and recreational opportunities for Native people. Based on a multigenerational family structure, Gimaajii has twenty-nine housing units that provide a safe place in which residents can interact with others who share similar traditions and histories. The Gimaajii Gathering Place includes thirteen office and community meeting spaces, an art gallery, a gymnasium, and the HOPE clinic staffed by the students from the University of Minnesota, Duluth School of Medicine.

Based in Duluth, Minnesota, Mending the Sacred Hoop is a nonprofit organization that seeks to end violence against Native women and children as well as restore the safety, sovereignty, and sacredness of Native women in their tribal communities. Originally founded in the 1980s as an advocacy and support group for survivors of domestic violence, it later operated within the Domestic Abuse Intervention Programs (DAIP). It separated from DAIP in 2006 and today provides training and technical assistance on responding to violence against Native women to tribes and Native communities nationally. Further, the organization works at local and state levels to address domestic violence against Native women through the Sacred Hoop Tribal Domestic Violence Coalition. The organization recently moved their offices into the Gimaajii Gathering Place.

Sarah Curtiss has worked for Mending the Sacred Hoop since 2009. Curtiss trains tribal and urban audiences on the unique issues Native women face concerning domestic violence and trains programs on how to work with survivors from a holistic cultural perspective. She is a member of the Circle Keepers (Board of Directors) for the Minnesota Indian Women's Sexual Assault Coalition and sits on various committees across the state that address violence against women. As a member of the *Oshkii Giizhik Singers*, a women's traditional hand drum group, Curtiss incorporates Ojibwe traditions and encourages Native women to use their voices in their communities to end violence against Native women and children. She feels that her most fulfilling role is that of being a mother to her beautifully energetic three-year-old son, Allan.

Elizabeth "Lyz" Jaakola is a musician and educator and an enrolled member of the Fond du Lac band of Lake Superior Ojibwe in Cloquet, Minnesota. She teaches music education and American Indian studies at

Figure 29. Ryan Stander's response to the Casselton train derailment, *Missing Information* (2014, Digital inkjet prints on paper mounted on plywood with Plexiglas) in the William and Anna Jane Schlossman Gallery. Photo courtesy of Rebecca A. Dunham.

Fond du Lac Tribal and Community College. Jaakola performs and composes in many styles and genres including traditional Anishinaabe music, jazz, blues and opera. She has performed as close to home as Duluth, Minnesota and as far as Rome, Italy for the Rome Opera Festival. Her Native-based compositions have also been heard on radio and television. The artist has arranged many Native pieces for solo and choral performances and also directs the *Oshkii Giizhik Singers*.

Kathy McTavish is a cellist, composer, and multimedia artist based in Duluth, Minnesota. Her diverse background in mathematics, ecology, music theory, and software development deeply informs her artistic practice. She blends these research areas to create dynamic systems and structures based on chance, myth, improvisatory forms, polyphony, interactive webs, harmonic relationships, and the orchestration of sound, light, and color. Her recent work has focused on creating generative methods for building multichannel video and sound environments. McTavish earned a BS in mathematics from the University of Minnesota in Duluth and an MS in applied mathematics from the University of Minnesota (U of M). She has also completed her PhD coursework in theoretical ecology and scientific visualization at U of M.

Erika Mock is a Swiss-born, award-winning textile artist, boundary seeker, maker, and owner of Textiles for Body and Soul. Mock's studio is housed in Superior's Artspace, the Trade and Commerce Marketplace, and she lives in a renovated caboose in the Woodlands of northwest Wisconsin. Suspended offerings to places and people, her installation weavings express interconnectedness. Mock constructs them with filaments, cords, yarns, and torn discarded clothing to explore identity, boundaries, embodiment (absence and presence), and the invisible stories still present in the cloth. According to the artist, "I see fiber as the basic element that connects us organically and symbolically to each other and our precious planet. The patterns, cycles, and emotional patinas are a vital plexus of threads that tatter, fray, knit, weave a community. From plant and animal fibers to our very bodies of hair, skin, sinew, bone and heart; we are all raw material immersed in the mystery of life."

Tina Olson has worked on issues surrounding domestic violence for over 25 years. As director for Mending the Sacred Hoop, Olson has organized numerous domestic violence training sessions, including Law Enforcement, Building A Coordinated Response, and Creating a Process of Change for Men Who Batter. In addition, she has also worked as a women's advocate, men's group facilitator, and group facilitator for women who are arrested, and is one of the original founders of Mending the Sacred Hoop's coordinated response efforts in Carlton and St. Louis Counties. Olson is the proud mother of four daughters, who, like herself,

Figure 30. Ryan Stander's *Nothing To See Here...*(2015, Digital inkjet prints on paper mounted to plywood with Plexiglas). Photo courtesy of Rebecca A. Dunham.

Figure 31. Eric Syvertson's triptych *House Party* (2014, Oil on canvas). Photo courtesy of the artist.

work in service-based industries such as the law, social work, nursing, and teaching. A grandmother of nine grandchildren, she lives with her partner in Duluth, Minnesota.

Jessica Tillman grew up in the small rural town of Barnum, Minnesota. Moving to Duluth, Minnesota after high school, she attended Lake Superior College and the University of Wisconsin Superior. Tillman worked in the hospitality industry and college radio at KUWS before becoming Duluth Mayor Don Ness's administrative assistant in 2010. She currently serves as a board member of the Program for Aid to Victims of Sexual Assault (PAVSA) and facilitates the Duluth Public Arts Commission.

Sheila Packa lives in northern Minnesota near Lake Superior and writes poetry and prose. She also spent several years as a social worker, specializing in women's issues. Her work explores migration, immigration, change, and metamorphosis in northern wilderness and industrial landscapes. She has penned four books of poems, *The Mother Tongue*, *Echo & Lightning*, *Cloud Birds*, and *Night Train Red Dust: Poems of the Iron Range*, and edited the collection of poems *Migrations: Poetry and Prose for Life's Transitions*, which received recognition at the North East Minnesota Book Awards. Her poems have also been featured in several anthologies, including *The Heart of All That Is*, *When We Were Weavers*, *Good Poems American Places*, *Finnish-North American Literature in English*, *Beloved on the Earth: 150 Poems of Grief and Gratitude*, and *To Sing Along the Way: Minnesota Women Poets from Pre-Territorial Days to the Present*. Duluth's Poet Laureate 2010–12, Packa also does narrative performances, frequently collaborating with visual artists, musicians, and composers. In collaboration with the Women's Coalition, Domestic Abuse Intervention Program, and the Family Justice Center, she facilitated several writing workshops. The recipient of numerous grants and fellowships, she currently teaches English at Lake Superior College in Duluth, Minnesota.

24.
Patrick Vincent, Moorhead, Minnesota
Howling Winds, 2014, Charcoal drawing, screenprint on vellum, and digital print on mylar
Bluster and *Well of Bones*, 2014, Lithographs

Printmaker Patrick Vincent's *Howling Winds* is a spellbinding installation featuring a man dressed in a crumpled suit (Figure 34). A cluster of ghost-like foxes escape from his head as stock tickers with data related the oil and gas industry fall from his hands. Vincent created this piece, and the related lithograph *Bluster*, in response to media pundits who use the Bakken oil boom to push political agendas. The color palette, which at

Figure 32-33. *The installation of Road to Williston* (2014, Mixed media) in the William and Anna Jane Schlossman Gallery. Photo courtesy of Rebecca A. Dunham.

first glance belies Vincent's intense scrutiny of the media, is a reaction to the landscape of the Great Plains. Displayed alongside *Bluster* is Vincent's print *Well of Bones*, which is a meditation on crude oil as a product of decayed bodies of plants and animals (Figure 35).

Originally from Minneapolis, Patrick Vincent is the owner and operator of Twin Bee Press. Vincent earned both a BFA and a BA in cultural studies and comparative literature from the University of Minnesota and an MFA in printmaking from Arizona State University (ASU). He currently serves as the assistant professor of printmaking at Minnesota State University Moorhead. Previously, he was an artist-in-residence and instructor at the Lawrence Arts Center, an instructor at ASU, and a youth education associate at the Minnesota Center for Book Arts. He has also worked at Studio on Fire and Pyracantha Press. With this foundation in books, printmaking, and design, Patrick creates original works of art as well as collaborates with individuals through print media.

25.
Susanne Williams, Fargo, North Dakota
Bakken Bride, 2014, Heat manipulated white plastic garbage bags

Bakken Bride is an elegant, form-fitting gown Susanne Williams made by manipulating white plastic garbage bags with heat (Figures 36). The inventive piece is from the artist's series *Up/Recycled*, in which she repurposes nontraditional materials such as garbage bags and bicycle tubes to make garments. Created exclusively for the Museum's exhibition, this fragile, pristine white garment contradicts its material form—plastic—which is derived from petrochemicals. Like other artists in *Bakken Boom!*, Williams challenges us to ponder our relationship with material objects stemming from the oil and gas industry.

Susanne Williams spent twelve years in the academic world, teaching communication courses at Minnesota State University Moorhead, before retiring to pursue her dream of being a full-time artist. Williams owns and operates an art business, Willi Nilli, which is based in downtown Fargo. While she has worked with various artistic mediums throughout her life, today she is known as a self-taught textile artist. In her practice, she explores new ways to manipulate materials to create three-dimensional pieces by hand without the aid of mechanical presses, molds, or water. Her tactile experiments emerge as sculptural creations that are both aesthetically pleasing and utilitarian in function.

26.
Selections from the Museum's portfolio *Oil and Water*:
Katelyn Bladel, *Reframed Landscape*, 2013, Etching
Michael Conlan, *Bakken #1*, 2013, Screenprint with digital images and gold leaf
Kim Fink, *(State of Affairs) Oliophilic*, 2013, Woodcut
Elise Forer, *It's Bad Stuff*, 2013, Hand-colored screenprint
Renae Hansen, *Black Gold Boom*, 2013, Screenprint
Dani Pauley, *Happy Little Oil Rigs*, 2013, Screenprint
Kelly Pontius, *Too Much Too Fast*, 2013, Lithograph
Lydia Rusch, *Soiled*, from 2013, Etching
Ryan Stander, *Untitled*, 2013, Lithograph with digital images
Jeremiah Valle, *Forewarn*, 2013, Screenprint
John Volk, *It's hard to let go of a familiar land*, 2013, Lithograph
Linda Whitney, *Ooh Mr Howdy you're so strong*, 2013, Mezzotint
Gift of NDSU, MSUM, Concordia College, University of Manitoba, MSU, UND, and VCSU
Plains Art Museum, 2013.007.0001.g, 2013.007.0001.h, 2013.007.0001.i, 2013.007.0001.k, 2013.007.0001.l, 2013.007.0001.o, 2013.007.0001.p, 2013.007.0001.q, 2013.007.0001.w, 2013.007.0001.z, 2013.007.0001.ff, 2013.007.0001.ii,

On several pedestals in both galleries are selections from the portfolio *Oil and Water*, which is in the Museum's permanent collection (Figure 37). This engaging portfolio is comprised of thirty prints in which artists responded to how the natural resources of oil and water have shaped the lives of those living in the Upper Midwest. Here, the Museum showcases twelve of the prints about the Bakken oil boom.

Oil and Water is a 2013 print exchange portfolio organized by Kent Kapplinger, associate professor of printmaking and drawing at North Dakota State University (NDSU), Heidi Goldberg, associate professor of printmaking at Concordia College, and John Volk, former professor of printmaking at Minnesota State University Moorhead (MSUM). The organizers invited printmaking faculty and students from seven regional colleges and universities (NDSU, University of Manitoba, Concordia, MSUM, Minot State University, Valley City State University, and the University of North Dakota), to create and submit an edition of thirty prints, and in exchange, receive twenty prints from other artists. The Museum hosted the exchange event in the spring of 2013 and was given the first impression of the portfolio for its permanent collection.

Community Conversations

The program series "Community Conversations" has and continues to provide the framework to harvest—make meaning and build upon—*Bakken Boom!*, ensuring it fulfills its purpose of stimulating public discussions about the current oil boom. The Museum launched the series with Final Friday Art Break, a series of informal gallery talks on the final Friday of each month during the noon lunch hour. Designed for a small audience, the Art Breaks feature artists, art educators, or Museum staff members who lead conversations in response to the artworks and resources in the galleries. For the first Art Break (January 30, 2015), Dunham led a gallery discussion between artists Jessica Christy, Michael Conlan, Sarah Christianson, Lucinda Cobley, Kathy McTavish, J. Earl Miller, Susanne Williams, and Patrick Vincent with an audience of twenty-five people.

One of the most effective aspects of the series thus far is the Gallery Activity. In this activity, Dunham and Bergquist created a series of prompts—questions or thoughts—and invited visitors to write their responses with the pencils and paper provided, place their responses on a platter, and pick up and read others' responses. These prompts have and continued to serve as conversation starters. Dunham and Bergquist changed the prompt each month. Listed below are the responses visitors wrote in the William and Anna Jane Schlossman Gallery for the February prompt: *As I look at the works of art in this exhibition, I feel...*

Amazed.
Stop destroying nature!
Bad, because it ruins the land and water. Also oil is a non-renewable resource.
At what cost?
So sad for North Dakota!
Bad, because it's killing a lot of things, pretty things.
Very concerned
Very shocked and worried for these people's health.
Weird, this is how it really is even though they are enjoying money.
Suffer of love
Dragging North Dakota backwards. We've sold our community and reap no reward. We're not sipping champagne—we're drinking crude.
Grateful to artists
Art is a medium that captures the complexity of oil well. Will those who most need to see this exhibit come?

Figure 34. Curator Rebecca A. Dunham assisting artist Patrick Vincent with the installation of *Howling Winds* (2014, Screenprint with charcoal on vellum and digital print on mylar) in the Fred J. Donath Gallery. Photo courtesy of Amy Richardson.

Figure 35. Patrick Vincent's *Well of Bones* (2014, Lithograph). Photo courtesy of the artist.

Waste

I feel … inspired by the ideas the artists have shared … heart-broken for our land, environment.

Happy

Sad. Who's on first? Someone needs to oversee this.

This is very eye opening.

New faces, new norms, need to keep inspiring to find good in all.

Jubilant

Connected

Sense of loss, of things and times that can never be reclaimed and a question of "what's next?"

Drill baby drill.

The complexity of the success and issues that the oil industry can bring to society, an economic boom that will have long-term negative environmental and social consequences

A sense of home—a sense of excitement—a sense of loss.

Inspired, stop destroying the environment, you can take trash and make it into art.

If they keep drilling, there'll be no one left.

Let my people go.

As if the place I knew and loved is being destroyed by greed and self-interest, short term desires causing long-term loss.

Overwhelmed.

Overwhelmed the topic of oil in North Dakota is so heavily charged—it's worth reflection.

The artists only focused on the bad! The western part of North Dakota is awesome to live in!

What happens when the gasses of Earth are gone?

Awesome.

Walk-a-thon for hybrid technology.

Before this, I was unaware of the issues and damage. Very eye opening.

There is good talent in everyone.

I am interested

Living costs are too expensive, especially for native North Dakotans.

Yearning for the golden fields of wheat, not such a common sight as they once were in the Dakota's.

Why can't we stop? We know what we're doing, all of us. So why can't we stop?

Oil is necessary for our survival. Thank God he has blessed us so richly. Many people are discovering the beauty of North Dakota.

The fracking—what does it do to the ground water? Is it safe?

Hopeless …

Figure 36. Susanne Williams's *Bakken Bride*, (2014, Heat manipulated white plastic garbage bags). Photo by Dan Francis Photography.

Like we need more in the world than we think we need.

It's bad

Bad for the homeless and poor, I feel obligated to help but these people are going through so much.

Abundance, hope, salvation, opportunity.

Boom=Box Store

… Powerless, powerless against greed, corruption, desperation.

Sad. In 50 years our grandchildren will ask. "What were they thinking?

Despair. It feels like the boom has provoked layers of misery that hadn't occurred to me before.

I feel as good as the artists are feeling.

Opportunity lost, opportunity wasted.

Sad

Artistic, happy, sad, impressed.

… like I'm looking at home … like I'm looking for home (I grew up out there)

Reduce consumption! Think about it: How much oil was used to produce this exhibit?

"Bakken Boom or bust.com"

I feel shocked by the display of art which surrounds drinking.

I am happy

Happy today

Amazed, what if I ended up like that …

Feel lost in the art

Money

Dead and brainwashed

I like the work here

I'd like to see more artwork forcing us to reflect on how much each of us is responsible for the demand for crude …

I feel amazed

I pray that we preserve our environment. It cannot be replaced.

To call my father

North Dakota is defeated by money and greed.

And so the boy cut down her trunk and made a boat and sailed away. And the tree was happy … but not really.

Greed, why was this allowed without caution and concern?

A cultural shift both physically and mentally. The loss of the spiritual constructs [that] made us resilient is lost to greed. Loss, land, integrity, and common sense. The positive effects of oil in North Dakota will outweigh and outlast the negative ones in the lifetimes of millions.

Figure 37. A selection of prints from the portfolio *Oil and Water*, which is in the Museum's permanent collection, in pedestals in William and Anna Jane Schlossman Gallery. From left to right, the prints are: Michael Conlan's *Bakken #1* (2013, Screenprint with digital images and gold leaf), Renae Hansen's *Black Gold Boom* (2013, Screenprint) and Dani Pauley's *Happy Little Oil Rigs* (2013, Screenprint). Photo croutesy of Rebecca A. Dunham.

Some of these pieces are very thoughtful and I can appreciate the
worry about social degradation.
Only believe the truth, not only the lies.
Sad, a lot of people are living in cars and trailers!
Lonely
We are ruining the planet, it poisons our water.
Depressed, hollow, heartbroken, hopeless, confused.
Sadness, rage.

Here are the responses visitors wrote in the Fred J. Donath Gallery for
the February prompt: *As I look at the works of art in this exhibition, I feel ...*

Jarring images, sounds and motion, depth.
Heartsick. The "Road to Williston" installation next to "Faces of the
Oil Patch" are stark contrasts to me. Where are the native women's
faces in the documentary?
We don't have the "god given right" to manipulate and destroy the
land for our own needs. I'm terrified—don't want it to be like Wil-
liston everywhere.
Ominous
Just the beginning
Very sad—tears came to my eyes—I was born in North Dakota and
still live in North Dakota and it breaks my heart to see what money
and crude oil has done to my home.
In a way I am sort of scared for the future and what will happen when
it's gone and there are more people on earth.
Start using the train
You are fearfully and wonderfully made.
Getting late to rein in corporate America.
I feel exhilarated
I've feared for our world as this boom has become reality. Now I fear
greatly for a friend who will birth a girl in such a lack of environ-
ment and earth-ruining society.
There is a lot of positives about the oil boom!
Very sad and sick to my stomach. I have lost several family members
to the impact of oil in the Bakken area.
The same raw emotions I felt at the holocaust museum in Wash-
ington, DC.
Stricken by the muses.
It's my family's home. Thank you to the artists who have captured the
rope of the land, the hellish aftermath, the opportunities for local

economies, and prosperity for families. The Bakken is our heaven and hell collided.

Thank who came before—those who came after.

My senses buzz … art, nature, audio, visual blending together is intellectually challenging.

Empowered to act, to learn to stay abreast of this topic.

Between the diversion in the valley and the boom out west North Dakota seems nice like a thick of yesterdays. Best of luck to us all, it's not just a North Dakota issue.

Sad, overwhelmed

As someone who grew up in western North Dakota, I want to weep. Our state politicians care more about power and money than the future of our land.

What are we willing to give up to put a stop to this?

The Frustration is expressed that many of us feel, I feel the problem of pollution, (illegible) of our beautiful state is gone not to be retrieved.

CO_2, CO_2, CO_2, …

I feel mad and wow at the same time.

Like, I want to move away and not come back.

Weird

Overwhelmed.

Like I'm a small part of a big universe—and to quote *Beasts of the Southern Wild*, "That's ok."

YIKES

STOP the Greed

I do respect the art there

This is a thought-provoking exhibit.

This exhibit would not be possible without oil "*HESS of a MESS*, Stop driving your *car*!!

Disturbed by the destruction and what we have done. What happens when the water is toxic, women who are raped and killed, what is the true lost? It can't be measured in dollars.

When you reach the end of your rope. Tie a knot and *Hang On*. —T. Roosevelt

Change is expected and a part of life! It's now a part of North Dakota and I'm proud to be from here!"

Inspired to create.

Under-educated about my home state and the occurrences around me.

That the viewers need to adequately realize how their lifestyle and culture provides the demand for oil extraction.

Afraid, interested to know more.

North Dakota Finally *Sold Out*

HEADACHE-Y.

On the surface—jobs, money, opportunity. The Bakken is much less and poorer, scarier than we could've imagined, I'm afraid for my future children."

Degradation of this country's morals have lost, and nothing to do with oil but with the heart even of these liberal artists.

Should have let the Native Americans be in charge—they have respect for the land. Look what we paid to them and what we're doing to the earth. No respect. So sad …

Opinion with NO action.

Very deep

We should just blow up the place.

Exploitation

Drill baby drill

Love is power

I feel disgusted that we are so short-sighted. Short-term money for abusing land and people, in particular Native peoples.

Something needs to be done. Stop the destruction of the land.

Save our planet.

Enlightened

I want to know more.

Slimey

A finite world with an infinite plan.

Like I'm looking at a different planet … aliens.

When will we learn how truly detrimental greed like this is to our environment and human existence? The violence and destruction is not worth any money.

Follow the money.

Yes—It's a Mell of a Hess. I'm conflicted. It's still home (but I don't live there anymore).

The word "Boom" insinuates an event that happens quickly. Just as quickly as an event begins in a boom, it disappears in a poof.

You fund your state with oil taxes, the oil lobby, and new resident employees own you. Sad but true.

The fire makes me feel scared.

I feel in awe, small compared to the events going on around me—and so helpless.

I am frustrated that artists use material from oil.

It is nice where artists bring the face of something to us all so we can see and understand.

Sad, helpless, disgusted
Overwhelmed by what I don't know so many perspectives so much
  info to learn so little time.
Like the place is just haunted. Eerie. Haunted.
At what cost have we allowed this to happen in North Dakota?
It is nice for artists to show us current crisis so we can help the people.

At the conclusion of each month, the responses are recorded in a Word document, which is laminated and placed in the gallery to give visitors the option to read previous prompts and responses. Also, the pieces of paper on which visitors' wrote their responses are bound as a book and placed in the gallery. The book allows visitors to form personal, albeit anonymous, relationships with other visitors by touching the paper and seeing the handwritten responses.

While the Gallery Activity is an introspective program relying on individual participation, IdeaExchange—the most complex program in "Community Conversations"—is a collective program modeled on the World Café method, a flexible format of hosting group discussions. At this event, a series of prompts inform small group discussions in rounds that are recorded, after which the conversations are shared with the larger group.

The first exchange (February 12, 2015) centered on the lives, land, and labor of the Bakken oil boom, and the Museum invited the following artists and scholars to create the event's prompts: Dr. Carol Archbold, associate professor, Department of Criminal Justice and Political Science, North Dakota State University (NDSU); Dr. William (Bill) Caraher, associate professor, Department of History, University of North Dakota, co-director of the North Dakota Man Camp Project; Dr. Carol Davis, senior associate of the Tribal Nations Research Group, member of the Turtle Mountain Band of Chippewa; Dominic Fischer, assistant professor, landscape architecture, NDSU; Dr. Roy Hammerling, professor, Department of Religion, Concordia College, executive producer and consultant on *My Country, No Country* documentary about the oil boom in western North Dakota; participating artists Kent Kapplinger and Molly McLain.

Below is a list of discussion points from the event's first round. The prompts were: *As you explore, consider what work of art you are drawn to, and why you find it compelling. What voices/themes are present? What voices/themes are absent? What questions are coming up for you?*

Empire Builder—Book of trucks, story of empire
Lucinda Cobley, *The Last Tree*—scale, poignant, strong visual, only
  after the last tree has been cut down, made an impact

Bakken Bride—unique, inventive

Michael Conlan's wonderful use of the nature's gold, *Bounty*, use of wheat

Danielle Frankenthal—love abstract color, 3-D, that are made of oil

Variety and quality of photography, different display

Road to Williston—human trafficking, impacts on indigenous communities, gritty, light/video installation, sex traffic

Jeremiah Valle

Molly McLain, Dakota

Lucinda Cobley—*Surface Tension*

Kent Kapplinger, *Hell of a Mess*, Hess Corp

Isaac Gale—*Sweet Crude Man Camp*—day to day life of roughnecks

Running on Fumes

Everything's for sale

House Party

Boxes of detritus

Ryan Stander

Elise Forer

Mug shots

Classical images—Alec Soth photos

Kim Fink

Jessica Christy—objects in all the boxes—what are the stories behind them?

In the second round, attendees discussed the following when prompted with: *If there was one thing that hasn't been said in order to reach a deeper level of understanding/clarity, what would that be?*

What's missing—women's viewpoint, vulnerable

Go with the flow

Realtors—the only happy ones, jazz hands

There are no photos of elected officials— they're the ones that put these laws in place

Son is out in Belfield—worry about her granddaughter

Tough in challenging circumstances

Dick Cheney and Halliburton got a law passed in 2005 that exempted fracking from the clean water act

Money—easy come, easy go

Money in the boxes—casual about money

Is it worth it? Not sure the pay, housing, quality of life is worth it?

A lot of information needs to get out more—feels like it's missing

It's exhausting to talk and think about this—it's sad. The trash tells a
  devastating story
Why don't businesses feel more responsibility as stewards?
Parallels to *Grapes of Wrath*—came from nothing
The laws are absent. Where is the legislature responsibility?
Peaceful backdrop for the man in front that's covered with oil
See the beauty, the glowing beauty
A lot of my friends have gone out to western ND and I've experienced
  it through them
Things need to slow down to create a long-term viability plan
We're wasting, not being efficient, thinking of the future—flaring, I
  hate the waste.
We need to think about all the products made with oil. Why not con-
  serve it? What right do we have to use all of it?
Landfill tubes—generating gas to be used
There have been mini booms and busts over the years, agriculture has
  kept it going
We need to see it, feel it—we need a Dorothea Lange
Who is the keeper of the secrets?
Where are the farmers' and ranching voices?
Uncertainty—where will it go now?
The roughnecks always chase the jobs
Devil's Lake? Refinery
What about an E&W split? A 51st state: Bakken to control their own
  resources
3 oil booms—1. 1950s, 2. 1980s, 3. 2010s. Boom and Bust
Sense of loss and excitement
Locals see the beauty in it all
All areas of growth make mistakes—even Fargo. The same is true of
  the west
The media—shapes the story for us. E tends to negative. W tends to
  positive
I know a lot of those people who are being bowled over
The conversations will give people a sense of what is happening in
  the west
1981, I saw Art Link's legacy to see how they had to reformulate the
  landscape
Losing?
Invasion
Unsettled
The big allure: make money but what is the ratio of cost of living?
Bakken oil as gold and wheat is color gold—monoculture

People who come sans plan
Children in hotels while adults at Bakken jobs
Gold rush—wheat monoculture
It really is a mess, sloppy dirty work, squeegee-ing oil off platform,
   etc. ...
Art Link's legacy—re-capping over developed coal mine
What are we losing, at what expense
Intrigued by subjects of land, lives, and labor
Cousin works construction in Watford city
Excited to hear artist's perspective/ability to document and respond
   to oil boom
Worked as organizer with Dakota Resource Council, concerned about
   environment—glad this exhibit brought awareness in the east
Wealth of the state has now come from the west
How can we tolerate the flaring?
"oil works"
What was missing? More mechanical/how processes of machinery
   works
Money is so important in this one time harvest
We look at things as progress ...
If there was one thing that hasn't been said—"consequences"—"future"
Law makers are absent. There should be pictures of the legislature
   who passed laws to allow fracking
Gold No Bison
Money = they spend it loosely
Worry about family living there, especially young women
Female camp needed
Female = sex traffic
Workers like mules, health issues in future for workers covered with
   oil
70s and 80s open wheat fields, today = had to drop out oil field things
How do you carry on normal life?
Missing hope
Missing Native American voices, female voices, rancher/farm
Historically women talked about the seedy side—still do
Where are the faces of oil companies
No positive vibes
Power to reverse is absent
Money talks and people mumble
What's the long term effect?
Losing water
Comfort is missing

Absent theme—reverse damage or how to fix damage

Halliburton evil character

What was missing from show—hope

Native American voices missing

What are we gaining—finance and money

We could lose a lot of *water*—even more than before

5 billion gallons of water/day to run one anhydrous ammonia plant in Bismarck

Fossil fuel industry has the power to do anything they want

Oil—coal is a "one time harvest"

Gov. Art Link go to Hwy 83 from Bismarck to Minot—see the land reclamation from 1980s

Dakota skipper is a moth

Dakota Resource Council—"going so much faster than other booms"

This exhibit brings it over to the east (Fargo)

Most people here go to the MN lakes, not to western ND

We may lose things that never come back

Wealth

Immersive

Plastics

No time to rest

Oil boom is the opposite of an artist colony

Oil companies don't care if they pollute the drinking water

Nestle CEO—"water should not be free. You should buy it like groceries."

Epitome of extractive colonialism—everything's for sale

How do people raise children in hotels in the Bakken

What do you do after work?

You can work hard and financially not make it

Where are the voices from reservation communities—the epicenter of the boom?

Where's the money going?

I liked the exhibit a lot. It really is a mess. Not just to the earth but just to work in the oil industry

I enjoyed the exhibit. I would like to see more engineering structures

Colored photos vs. black and white

Awareness of crime?

Live. Love.

Anxiety, money, embrace, absurdity

Trains and oil/rail cars

Humanity

Despair in contrast to the beauty of Bakken Bride

Minot pre-Bakken and today: community disrupted and trust has
   changed
Ft. Berthold heavily impacted. Help!
Native American view?
Insider perspective
Growing up a farmer near Wishek—imagining oil there?
Impact on natural landscape?
Transient population
Like the impact of black and white
Flaring intruding on areas

In round three attendees conversed about the following in response to: *If
you could imagine what you want life to be like in North Dakota 30 years from
now, what would it be?*

In 30 years ... safety regulations
30 years ... 2015 was a turning point and the Bakken Boom exhibition
   stimulated people to take back their state
In 30 years ... start with Gov. Art Link's tradition of making industry
   accountable—there *is* a North Dakota tradition
In 30 years ... make our state government accountable
In 30 years ... everyone is educated about the impact of fracking on
   lives, land, water
In 30 years ... the entire state will be an art project
In 30 years ... art and education will flourish, investment in the public
   good
The hidden things that we can't see are going to impact us in 30 years
Chuck Suchy farmers singing in their fields ... in 30 years
In 30 years, more thoughtful and more measured in development
In 30 years, forecast: Buffalo Commons Not Anymore

Conclusion

As previously stated, the need for projects like *Bakken Boom!* is immediate.
The data culled from the program series "Community Conversations"
attests to the exhibition's success in stimulating public dialogue and
debate about the current oil boom. While North Dakota had previous
short-lived oil booms, the Bakken oil boom is unprecedented in size and
duration, and some believe it may carry on for another twenty-five to
forty years. However, due to recent events, others think it may go bust
soon. Regardless, North Dakota has achieved celebrity status in the global
energy industry, and the people and places have and continue to adapt to

this newfound role and the shifting dynamics associated with and caused by the boom.

While galleries and museums around the nation have mounted minor exhibitions about this historical oil boom, none have explored the topic to the extent of Dunham's *Bakken Boom!* exhibition. The exhibition has proven to serve several important purposes for the community: the artists provide specific themes and topics about which to ponder and converse, the galleries offer a safe, neutral forum in which to conduct these conversations, and the program series provides a framework for further discussion in the galleries and beyond. Therefore, Plains Art Museum will display the groundbreaking exhibition three times the normal length of such a project, from January 29 to August 5 of 2015. During this time, "Community Conversations" will continue with additional Final Friday Art Breaks, Gallery Activities, and IdeaExchanges along with additional popup programs with collaborative partners, including upcoming events with the Red River Valley Writing Project and Theatre B. Please visit www.plainsart.org to learn more and become part of the conversation.

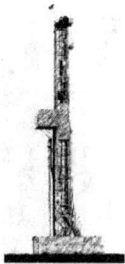

CHAPTER 16

MAN CAMP #1, #2, #3, #5, #8, #9, #10, #12, #16, AND #17

John Holmgren

I have been collaborating with the research team of the North Dakota Man Camp Project headquartered at the University of North Dakota in Grand Forks, North Dakota since they began their exploration and documentation of the workforce housing on the Bakken oil field in 2012. The team is examining whether the temporary housing in the Bakken exhibits historical strategies that are common to short-termed settlement in other areas of the world, and what social and architectural strategies are being used to live in recreational vehicles and other substandard housing. The artwork that I am producing in conjunction with this project looks at human presence in the landscape, and the social and material conditions of the oil boom workforce housing on the Bakken. I start with my own images of the man camps and then start to layer the data collected by the research team using screening printing and transfers. This work would not be possible without the generosity of Bret Weber, Bill Caraher, Aaron Barth, Kostis Kourelis and Richard Rothaus

Man Camp #1

Man Camp #2

Man Camp #3

Man Camp #5

Man Camp #8

Man Camp #9

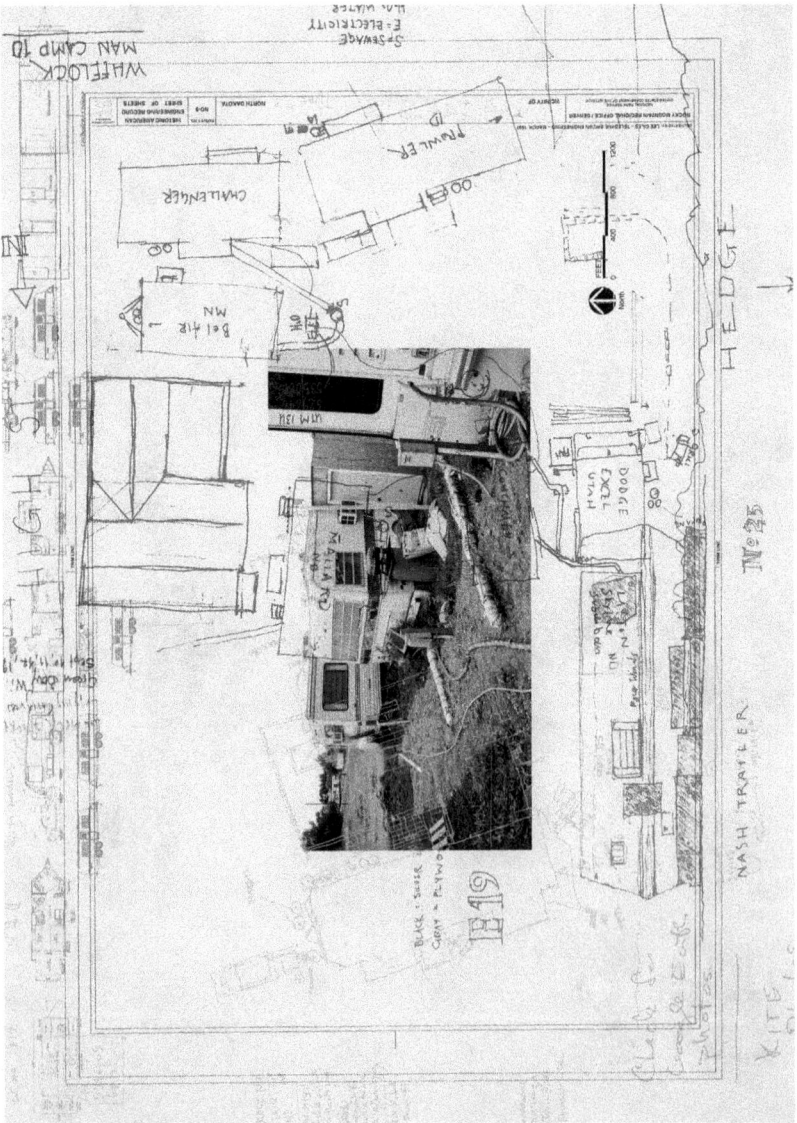

Man Camp #10

Man Camp #12

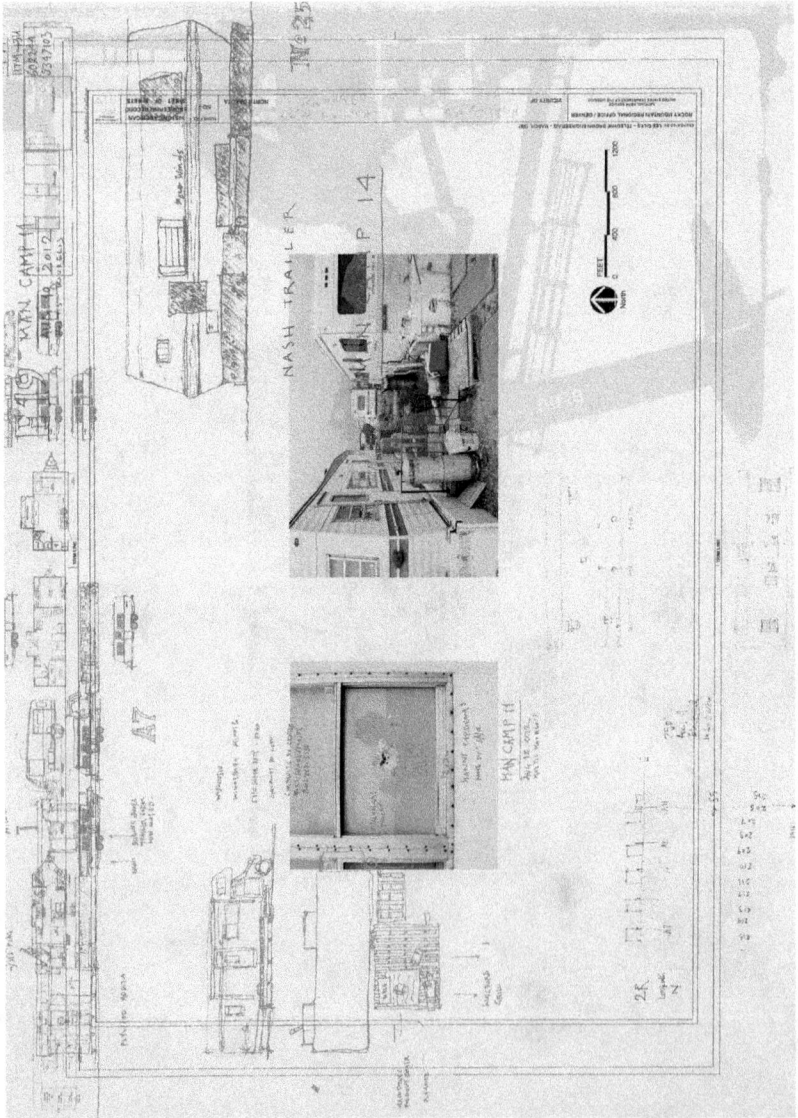

Man Camp #16

Man Camp #17

CHAPTER 17

PHOTOGRAPHING THE BAKKEN

Kyle Cassidy

The first thing which I recommend is to burn the wagons we have got, so that we may be free to march wherever the army needs, and not, practically, make our baggage train our general. And, next, we should throw our tents into the bonfire also: for these again are only a trouble to carry, and do not contribute one grain of good either for fighting or getting provisions. Further, let us get rid of all superfluous baggage, save only what we require for the sake of war, or meat and drink, so that as many of us as possible may be under arms, and as few as possible doing porterage. I need not remind you that, in case of defeat, the owners' goods are not their own; but if we master our foes, we will make them our baggage bearers.

Xenophon, Anabasis

The fog froze on the trees last night.

As it crept slowly through Tioga, crystal by crystal fog collided with trees, with the occasional building, with blades of grass, with fences and came to rest, and other crystals nestled next to them, and in the morning the world looked like a faerie palace, everything was white, encased in half an inch of frozen fog (Figure 1).

It's cold here in the western part of North Dakota. The coldest temperature ever recorded in the Bakken was in February of 1936 where, in the sleepy town of Parshall, population 1,929, part of the Fort Berthold Indian Reservation, just a few miles from where we are right now, the mercury fell to sixty-degrees below zero.

And there are winds here too. After these winds caused the great dust-bowl of 1934 by blasting the topsoil into the air, killing everything and driving vast numbers of people west form the planes into California, New Mexico, and Washington looking for work in the greatest migration this country has ever known, the federal government planted shelter belts of trees to keep it from happening again – they grow in inexplicable rows

Figure 1. Capital Lodge near Tioga, ND. Photo by Kyle Cassidy.

across the landscape. But in the 1970s and 80s as family farms began to become consolidated by large agro business, the shelter belts began to be cut down because they were obstacles for farm equipment that had to spend precious time navigating around them, so the winds are returning. These winds take the cold air and hurl it across the prairie. And it's not just the extreme cold, but the persistence. Once the temperature falls, it stays that way. On average, January temperatures move only between -2 and 15 with an average temperature of 7. In January of 2014 the temperature in Williston dipped into the negative double digits nine out of thirty-one days. The number of days with below freezing temperatures vacillates between 180 and 201 days out of the year.

On top of the persistence is the isolation; Toronto and Winnipeg all have climates similar to the Bakken, but they were designed and built as cities. There are things to do. In western North Dakota, in the winter, there's one thing to do: get oil out of the ground. The infrastructure exists for this and precious little else.

Apart from a constant drone of trucks which come, even in the early morning, at a rate of four or five a minute, and a slowly flapping American flag, the only thing moving in this Tioga Type II man camp is Clint Breeze, a 37-year-old over-land truck driver from Southern Idaho who moved here a year and a half ago to take a job hauling water and fracking fluid (Figure 2).

> "I moved my family out here 8 months ago," he says, "and it just wasn't working so I'm moving them back home today. It's nice to have the family together, but not a good place for them, nothing for them to really do." Clint's wife and three children spent days in a trailer provided by his employer while Clint worked regular shifts of 12 hours on, 12 hours off, 28 days in a row. The cold and the isolation got to them. Eight months was all they could take. Clint, like many workers in the oil patch is making money hand over fist, it's just a question of how long he can hold out.

So much of surviving here is in the preparation. Lewis and Clark arrived in North Dakota in October of 1804 and stayed for an entire miserable winter, erecting a high walled fort, meeting Sacagawea, and preparing for their demise by copying down all of the notes they'd made so far to send back to Saint Louis as soon as the thaw came.

Towards the end of April, Lewis climbed a bluff in present day Williston and observed "a most delightful view of the country, the whole of which except the valley formed by the Missouri is void of timber or underbrush, exposing the first glance of the spectacular, immense herds

Figure 2. Clint Breeze in his trailer near Tioga, ND. Photo by Kyle Cassidy.

of buffalo, elk, deer, & antelopes feeding in one common and boundless pasture."

There are still elk and deer, though the buffalo seem to all be behind fences, raised as cattle ("too dry" remarks one local) there are still lots of other animals around. Pheasants, for one thing, seem to exist like pests, dotting nearly every field and continually darting in front of cars. As I'm dragging my suitcase into the SUV outside of the Roosevelt Inn in Watford City a truck blasts its horn three times and a mule deer bounds up into the parking lot, rushing past me before I can get my camera to my eye and loping off, looking for some place to call its own in what has become a residential patch on a hilltop.

Settled a hundred years after Lewis and Clark left, the town of Tioga occupies less than one and a half square miles. Its population quadrupled in the 1950s when oil was first discovered in Williston and at its largest, in the 1960s, slightly more than 2000 people lived there. It's big enough now to maintain a high school and a newspaper. Tioga means "peaceful valley" though there's not really one to be seen. It looks like a pool table.

Twenty two miles southwest of Tioga is the smaller town of Wheelock. Wheelock's population was at its height in the 1930s when there were more than a hundred people living there—by the 1990s that had dwindled to twenty-three. Now on its third wave of occupation, a smattering of houses and permanent structures are augmented by a series of RV's and trailers (Figure 3).

It's like the Salton Sea in its remoteness and the people who populate it; it sports a self-proclaimed mayor and a motorcycle club and every year hosts a legendary fourth of July party. Wheelock busted but it never boomed, from its founding in 1892 the number of inhabitants has hovered around 100, dipping to 23 or so at its low point in the 1990's but now mobile homes are springing up adding somewhat to the population. The town disincorporated in 1994. "The dogs outnumber the people here," says Samantha who lives in a small green house by the eastern edge of the town with her two daughters (Figure 4).

* * *

When scientists go to a place it is to find truth. When artists go to a place, I think, it is to find beauty. When artists and scientists work together they have the potential to produce that, rarest of all things: something which is both useful and beautiful.

North Dakota is a beautiful place—and a place filled with beauty—these are two different things. Everything that you see is abut the poetry of the intersection of people and landscape—from that mule deer in the motel parking lot to the very act of oil coming out of the ground which is

Figure 3. Truck, house and trailers. Wheelock, ND.
Photo by Kyle Cassidy.

Figure 4. Samantha and her two daughters outside their home. Wheelock, ND. Photo by Kyle Cassidy.

an amazing feat of chemistry, engineering, management and desperation
—to the questions of providing for the people who do these things. These
are thoughts on a grand scale: What makes a *town*? What's the difference
between a *house* and a *home*? What do *people* need to stay *human*? What is
work? And what can an employer expect from an employee?

This is a place filled with beautiful and terrible stories, with people
who are happy and people who are living at the very edges of what a
person will do to care for their family. Here, often, are the ends of stories
that begin "I had no other choice...." and they're complicated—it can be a
difficult place to raise a family, the working hours are long, but the money
can be extremely good. People with engineering skills, the people who
find the oil and drive the drill bits to their destination through miles of
rock can make money at astounding rates, but for unskilled laborers the
stories are often grim.

These are all the stories you have to work with; all influenced by the
grand and empty landscape, by the cold, and by the isolation and by a
nation hungry for oil.

Working with scientists also ties all your art to a very specific set of
data points. You can't make a photograph and wonder five years later
"whatever became of that group of houses?" because the scientists have
tagged the GPS coordinates of every corner of each house in your photo
and you can go back forty-five years later and find the sewage lines in
the same place. Your art, you realize, is itself just a data point in a greater
collection of *truth*. But if you're doing your job right, your data points are
fuzzy, you tell the stories that are happy and sad at the same time, your
work is hard to quantify, but it makes people pause while looking at the
data, that in the truth of science, they might, for a moment, glimpse a
greater, but impossible to grasp, truth about humanity.

About the Contributors

Carenlee Barkdull, PhD, LCSW, is associate professor and chair of the Department of Social Work at the University of North Dakota. Dr. Barkdull has numerous years of experience in the public and nonprofit sectors encompassing policy advocacy, administration, and community practice. Her involvement with the North Dakota Man Camp Project has led to a keen interest in the effects of extractive industries on vulnerable populations and the human service sector, especially child welfare and child and family wellbeing.

Karin L. Becker received her PhD in communication from the University of North Dakota. With a focus in health communication, her research explores provider-patient communication preferences among individuals with chronic pain and addresses the utility of computer-mediated communication as a mechanism to provide support for marginalized populations. While working as a researcher at the Center for Rural Health at the University of North Dakota School of Medicine and Health Sciences, she conducted community health needs assessments on critical access hospitals and facilitated strategic implementation planning sessions with hospitals located in the oil patch. She has over fifteen years of teaching experience and currently teaches in the School of Entrepreneurship at UND. Originally from Durango, CO, she is an avid hiker and landscape photographer but currently, her lens is focused on her son and daughter.

Nikki Berg Burin is an assistant professor of history and women and gender studies at the University of North Dakota. She received her PhD in history from the University of Minnesota in 2007. Nikki is working on a book project that puts the history of prostitution and sex trafficking in North Dakota in conversation with the commercial sexual exploitation of women and children in the state today. Nikki also serves on the Advisory Committee for FUSE (North Dakota's anti-sex trafficking coalition).

Sebastian Braun is associate professor of anthropology and director of American Indian Studies at Iowa State University. He earned a lic. phil.I in ethnology, history, and philosophy from University of Basel and a PhD in anthropology from Indiana University. He is the author of *Buffalo Inc. American Indians and Economic Development* and editor of *Transforming Ethnohistories. Narrative, Meaning, and Community*. Among other publications, Braun has written the chapter on the United States for *The Indigenous World*, the yearbook of the International Work Group for Indigenous Affairs (IWGIA) since 2005. His interests lie in the intersections of ecology, economics, and politics.

William Caraher is an associate professor in history at the University of North Dakota. His took his PhD at Ohio State University in ancient history. He has directed archaeological project in Cyprus and worked extensively in Greece. He is the co-director of the North Dakota Man Camp Project with Bret Weber and the co-author of *Pyla*-Koutsopetria *I: Archaeological Survey of An Ancient Coastal Town* with R. Scott Moore and David K. Pettegrew.

Angela Cary is a proud North Dakotan and third-year graduate student at the University of North Dakota in Grand Forks. She will complete her master of arts degree in communication in 2016. This is Cary's second degree from UND—she also earned her BA in advertising and visual arts from the university in 1990. Cary's professional background is in television production. She spent seventeen years writing and producing commercials and promotional videos before making the decision to return to graduate school. She hopes to continue working as a communication instructor following her graduation from UND.

Kyle Cassidy is the author of the #1 bestselling art book *Armed America: Portraits of Gun Owners in Their Homes*, as well as 2012's *War Paint: Tattoo Culture & the Armed Forces*. He has published viral photo essays of Librarians, Occupy Wall Street protesters, Science Fiction authors and, in 2015, the scientists behind the New Horizons mission to Pluto. Find him online at kylecassidy.com as @kylecassidy on Twitter.

Kyle Conway taught at the University of North Dakota for six and a half years before joining the Department of Communication at the University of Ottawa in January 2015. He studies the ways people talk across cultural or linguistic borders, and he asks whether and how they negotiate a common vocabulary. His books include *Everyone Says No: Public Service Broadcasting and the Failure of Translation* (2011), *Beyond the Border: Tensions Across the Forty-ninth Parallel in the Great Plains and Prairies* (coedited with Timothy Pasch, 2013) and Little Mosque on the Prairie *and the Paradoxes of Cultural Translation* (forthcoming).

Dr. **Simon Donato** is best known as the host of the Esquire Network's adventure sports television show *Boundless*. He is the founder of Adventure Science, a volunteer-based organization formed in 2008, which pairs scientists with adventure athletes and has since conducted over fifteen global projects exploring everything from archaeological ruins in Oman, to searching for missing people in New Mexico, to conducting exercise physiology projects on ultra-distance runners in the Canadian Rocky Mountains. When he's not racing or exploring, he spends his days running Stoked Oats, his gluten-free oatmeal company. He holds a PhD in Geology and lives in Canmore, Alberta.

Rebecca A. Dunham is the curator of collections and exhibitions at the Nora Eccles Harrison Museum of Art at Utah State University in Logan. Dunham specializes in modern and contemporary art, particularly works on paper and ceramic arts. Previously, she worked at Plains Art Museum, the Museum of Fine Arts in Houston, and two university-affiliated museums. She earned a BA in art history from the University of North Carolina at Chapel Hill, an MA in art history from the University of Florida, and completed PhD studies in art history and classical archaeology at the University of Missouri.

Julia C. Geigle, MSW, LGSW, has practiced in the areas of school social work and crisis stabilization, assessment, and counseling services for individuals with chemical and mental health issues. She obtained both her master's and bachelor of social work degrees from the University of North Dakota. Her thesis addressed the social impacts of western North Dakota's early twenty-first century oil boom.

John Holmgren received his Bachelor of Arts from Central Washington University in 2004, and in 2007 received his Master of Fine Arts in photography from the University of Minnesota in Minneapolis, Minnesota. In 2010 he accepted a position at Franklin & Marshall College in Lancaster, Pennsylvania. He has exhibited his work nationally and internationally and has been awarded many grants and awards.

Heather Jackson (MA, MPH) is from North Dakota. Now she resides in New England and works as a birth doula, case manager of pregnant and parenting teens, and early childhood education data collector. She is co-editor of *Feminist Parenting*, an anthology published by Demeter Press (demeterpress.org). Her writing has also been published on thepushback. org, hipmama.com, girl-mom.com, muthamgazine.com, and in many books and zines. She is also the single mother of a teenager, and she rides bike, goes to the beach, and plays guitar.

Ann Reed is a cultural anthropologist and adjunct assistant professor in the Department of World Languages and Cultures at Iowa State University. Her research interests have focused on the interface of political economy and culture, both in North Dakota and in Ghana. Since the 1990s, she has carried out long-term field research in Ghana on the construction of diaspora African identity, heritage tourism, globalization, and political economy. Her most notable publication to date is *Pilgrimage Tourism of Diaspora Africans to Ghana* (2014), but she has also published in *Museum Anthropology* and contributed book chapters for edited volumes on tourism, heritage, and diaspora from Palgrave MacMillan, Ashgate, Blackwell, and Routledge. She teaches courses in African and African American studies, anthropology, and international studies.

Andrew Reinhard publishes the work of the American Numismatic Society and previously served as publisher for the American School of Classical Studies at Athens. Educated at the University of Missouri-Columbia and the University of Evansville, he has excavated in Greece, Italy, Kansas, New Mexico, and Illinois. Andrew most recently led a team of "Punk Archaeologists" as they dug the now infamous "Atari Burial Ground" in Alamogordo, New Mexico, uncovering thousands of games while being filmed for a documentary. Reinhard now studies the intersection of archaeology and video games.

Dr. **Richard Rothaus** holds a BA from The Florida State University, an MA from Vanderbilt University and a PhD from The Ohio State University. Rothaus has pursued historical and archaeological research in North America, the Mediterranean, the Middle East, Asia, and Central America. Rothaus has been involved with Adventure Science since the beginning, and has traveled the world with some of his colleagues on the Badlands adventure. Rothaus is currently the Interim Vice Chancellor of Academic and Student Affairs for the North Dakota University System and a research assistant at the Center for Heritage Renewal at North Dakota

State University. Rothaus lives in Bismarck with his wife and youngest son; his older sons live in Minnesota and Washington.

Jessica Sobolik is director of alumni and community relations for the University of North Dakota School of Medicine and Health Sciences, which aims to educate physicians and other health professionals and to enhance the quality of life in North Dakota. She earned a Bachelor of Arts degree in Communication from UND and is currently pursuing a Master of Arts degree in the same field. She lives in Minto, ND, with her husband Ryan and two children, Josie and Luke.

Melissa Rae Stewart is a public relations professional and savvy entrepreneur, working in the endurance sport and outdoor industries. Founder of Sufferfest Media and Digitainment Group, as well as sports agent and publicist to various professional athletes, Melissa is a recognized and respected expert in the field of public relations. She has provided communications programming and support for various scientific expeditions throughout the globe.

Laura Tally is a 2014 graduate of Saint Catherine University with a B.S. in communication studies. Through the capstone class Global Search for Justice: Women and Work with economist Dr. Shika, she examined the intersection of domestic violence and the Bakken oil boom. The opportunity to educate her classmates and professors on this topic evolved into a commitment to share the stories of domestic violence survivors and service providers with dignity, relevance, and in a language both scholars and policy makers can use to effect change. She currently lives in rural Stevensville, Montana, and volunteers with SAFE in the Bitterroot.

Ryan Taylor is a fourth generation cattle rancher from Towner, ND. A graduate of North Dakota State University, Taylor wrote his "Cowboy Logic" column for twenty-one years for multiple agricultural newspapers and had them published in three separate books. Taylor was elected to the North Dakota Senate three times, serving from 2002 to 2012; was elected by his peers to be senate minority leader; and was the Democratic NPL candidate for governor in 2012. In 2013, he was named a leadership fellow of the Bush Foundation, St. Paul, MN. In August, 2015, he was appointed by the President to serve as state director for USDA Rural Development, making critical investments in the infrastructure of the state's rural communities. With his wife, Nikki, they are raising their three young children.

Bret A. Weber, PhD, LCSW, is an associate professor in the Department of Social Work at the University of North Dakota. His terminal degree is in U.S. History with emphases on twentieth century social policy and environmental history. As a member of the Grand Forks City Council, and as codirector of the North Dakota Man Camp Project (including service on the boards of the local Housing Authority and Community Land Trust), he focuses on social justice issues related to housing, and the social, physical, and economic environment.

Dr. Joshua E. Young is an assistant professor of communication studies at St. Gregory's University and a recent PhD graduate of the communication and public discourse program at the University of North Dakota. Young's research focuses on the way that rhetoric and public discourse create the relationships between and within communities. For instance, he has published work on budget struggles between university administration and other education stakeholders and presented work at the Smithsonian Institute on the contemporary relationship between non-Natives and American Indians in the context of powwow.

www.ingramcontent.com/pod-product-compliance
Lightning Source LLC
Chambersburg PA
CBHW071220290326
41931CB00037B/1476